Marcus Crassus and the Late Roman Republic

MARCUS CRASSUS
AND THE LATE
ROMAN REPUBLIC

Allen Mason Ward

University of Missouri Press
Columbia & London

Copyright © 1977 by

The Curators of the University of Missouri

University of Missouri Press, Columbia, Missouri 65201

Library of Congress Catalog Card Number 76–56794

Printed and bound in the United States of America

ISBN 0–8262–0216–0

Library of Congress Cataloging in Publication Data

Ward, Allen M   1942–
Marcus Crassus and the late Roman Republic.

Bibliography: p.
Includes index.
1. Crassus, Marcus Licinius.   2. Statesmen—
Rome—Biography.   3. Businessmen—Rome—Biography.
I. Title.
DG260.C73W37   937'.05'0924 [B]   76–56794
ISBN 0–8262–0216–0

D. M.
MILITI WARD
AVO BENE MERENTI

Preface

Marcus Licinius Crassus was one of the central figures in the century that saw Marius, Sulla, Pompey, Cicero, Caesar, Cato the Younger, and the Fall of the Roman Republic. I have tried to give a detailed and coherent analysis of Crassus's role that will lead to a better understanding of both him and his time. He was a much more important and capable figure than he is usually depicted. Many of the problems that are often discussed from others' points of view can be understood better when they are placed in the context of Crassus's goals, aspirations, and political activities. By the same token, his individual actions can be analyzed more effectively when they are treated as a whole in the light of his historical context.

My first step, therefore, has been to set forth in Chapter I a general account of the social, economic, and political milieu of the late Roman Republic. The last element is particularly important since the nature of politics in the late Roman Republic is now a matter of considerable debate among contemporary historians. In the body of the chapter, I have tried to give the less specialized reader a clear and concise picture of the general political groupings in Crassus's time, without obscuring the fact that the individuals who made up these groups constantly changed, or at least shifted around a central core, as they interacted with each other. Specialists will find much more detailed and complex treatments of important points in the chapter's three appendixes.

Throughout the rest of the book, one of the major difficulties in dealing with Crassus specifically is the highly fragmentary nature of the evidence in the ancient sources. Therefore, it has been necessary to resort to conjecture and hypothesis more often than one would prefer in order to explain isolated facts or even determine if something is a fact at all. Again, because direct evidence is often lacking, I have had to rely greatly on prosopography (i.e., the study of personal relationships, and data that might reveal such relationships, to infer the political position of an individual). I am well aware of the limitations of the prosopographical approach, especially when any other type of evidence is unavailable. In all instances, moreover, where the evidence, whatever its nature, can suggest no more than probability, or only mere possibility, I have tried to make that fact clear.

In the end, however, I hope that a consistent and coherent picture will have been developed from the available information to provide the reader with a better understanding of both Crassus and the late Roman Republic, in which he played an important role.

Whatever success I have achieved in this task is owed to the work of many, especially those who have helped in numerous personal ways. Despite any disagreement expressed on particular points, I am very grateful to Professors E. S. Gruen and B. A. Marshall, who have kept me up to date with timely offprints of their numerous pertinent articles. I regret that my work was virtually complete when Professor Gruen's important study, *The Last Generation of the Roman Republic,* became available. I have tried to incorporate as many references to it as practicable, but it was impossible to be as systematic as I could have wished.

Professor W. C. McDermott has been a constant source of advice and encouragement. He has followed the project from its inception and saved me from numerous pitfalls. I should also like to thank Professor E. Badian for reading the penultimate draft in its entirety and making several valuable suggestions for improvement. Where I have rejected the advice of friends and colleagues, I have done so at my own peril, and the responsibility for all faults must rest with me.

Thanks for financial assistance are also cheerfully given. The University of Connecticut Research Foundation provided two crucial grants, one that helped me to collect the books and articles necessary for researching the modern scholarship, and one that permitted me to travel extensively in southern Italy and test my conclusions about various details of the war with Spartacus against the actual topography. To the latter end, Professor S. L. Dyson also made available to me his technical

Preface

expertise and much pertinent information. On the more general level, a summer stipend from the National Endowment for the Humanities provided the opportunity for wide reading and uninterrupted thought that contributed to many of the ideas eventually developed in this book.

Extra kudos is due the copy editor, Pamela Long, who undertook her task on short notice and brought order out of my chaos.

Finally, and most importantly, I should like to express my deep gratitude to my wife, Ellen Evans Whiting, who gave me the love, security, and peace of mind necessary for finishing what I had started.

A. M. W.

Note on Citations and Abbreviations

All citations of ancient authors and works are abbreviated in accordance with the usual practices of classicists and ancient historians. For anyone not familiar with the field, the meaning of the abbreviations used herein will, despite minor differences, be readily apparent from consultation of the lists in standard reference works. A convenient list for all ancient authors and works can be found in the front of either the first or second edition of the *Oxford Classical Dictionary* (*OCD*). One for Latin authorities is available in either Lewis and Short, *A Latin Dictionary*, or the *Oxford Latin Dictionary* (*OLD*), edited by A. Souter et al., and one for Greek authorities is given in Liddell and Scott, *A Greek-English Lexicon*, ninth edition by H. Stuart Jones and R. McKenzie (*LSJ*).

Books by modern authors are given full bibliographical references when they are first cited in each chapter. Thereafter, they are cited by shortened titles or letter abbreviations that have become fairly standard in the field. All should be readily recognizable either from the initial reference in the chapter or the full entry in the Bibliography.

Similarly, each journal article receives a full bibliographical reference in the first citation in each chapter. Included in that will be the full title of the relevant journal. Subsequent citations in each chapter will contain a title, shortened where appropriate, and, where one is commonly employed, a standard letter abbreviation for the journal's title. Such abbreviations should be clear from the initial citations or from the full entries in the Bibliography.

Articles in A. F. von Pauly's *Real-Encyclopädie der classischen Altertumswissenschaft* (abbreviated as *RE*), edited by G. Wissowa and his successors, have not been listed in the Bibliography. Similarly omitted are the volumes of the *Cambridge Ancient History* (abbreviated as *CAH*), edited by F. E. Adcock et al., as well as those of the *Corpus Inscriptionum Latinarum* (abbreviated as *CIL*), edited by Th. Mommsen et al.

Contents

Introduction

Scholars and historians, both ancient and modern, have often failed to give an adequate treatment of Crassus in their works. There are two primary reasons for this failure. First, he violated the aristocratic code of antiquity by unashamedly amassing a fortune through personally conducted business operations rather than primarily through agriculture or warfare. Since ancient writers either were from the upper class or held upper class values, they were prejudiced against Crassus, and most quickly passed over him as being beneath their dignity and as being an unworthy subject for their attention. Plutarch very clearly reflects the prevailing attitude of antiquity in the following anecdote: When Crassus told Cicero that he liked the Stoics because they depicted the good man as rich, Cicero replied, "No! Consider rather that they say all things belong to the wise" (Plut. *Cic.* 24.3). Crassus was viewed only as a paradigm of avarice, an *exemplum* of what not to be (Cic. *off.* 3.85; Plut. *Crass.* 6.5, *Comp. Nic. et Crass.* 1. 1–4; cf. Cic. *Parad. Stoic.*, 42–52).

This aristocratic bias against a man who dirtied his hands with filthy lucre has been accepted and perpetuated by modern writers. Drumann disparagingly wrote:

> So much more powerful was this love of money for which
> he found fault in others. He wished to possess much, not in
> order to enjoy as Lucullus, nor even to rule as Caesar, but
> in order to possess. This was his pride, his highest good; in
> this should no one be comparable to him.[1]

Gelzer declared:

1. W. Drumann, *Geschichte Roms*, 4, ed. 2 by P. Groebe (Berlin and Leipzig, 1908), p. 123.

> Despite his origin from the old nobility, the attributes of
> the true Grandseigneur escaped him, and he always remained
> the calculating bourgeois, who constantly treated even poli-
> tics as an economic undertaking.[2]

Heitland remarked:

> . . . Crassus, though an adept in the tricks of Roman
> finance, was no match for the subtleties of oriental guile.[3]

Cary perpetuated the view in one of the most widely read his-
tories of Rome:

> A resolute speculator in the field of finance, in which he
> had acquired unprecendented wealth, he lacked the nerve
> to throw in his life after his purse.[4]

Even Ferrero, who gave Crassus more credit than many have
given, could not extinguish all bias against Crassus the business-
man:

> Unfortunately Crassus was by nature a rather careful and
> hard-headed man of business, than a prodigal and high-
> spirited politician capable of dominating and inspiring a
> city crowd.[5]

Grant has continued to popularize the prejudice:

> Crassus was a courteous, affable, crafty man, whose political
> ambitions were hampered by defective qualities of leader-
> ship, which he sought to make up for by money. His financial
> flair was enormous.[6]

Recently the picture has been reproduced in the scholarly
literature by Meier:

> In the face of all decisive situations he was at a loss and
> sought to extricate himself from affairs by half measures.
> He served anyone, never gave offence if possible—Cicero
> once characterized him with the words: verbum nullum

2. M. Gelzer, RE 13.1 (1926), 296.7–14, s.v. "Licinius" (68).
3. W. E. Heitland, *The Roman Republic*, 3 (Cambridge, 1909), p.
238.
4. M. Cary, *A History of Rome down to the Reign of Constantine*,
ed. 2 (London, 1954), p. 366 and ed. 3, revised by H. H. Scullard
(London, 1975), p. 243.
5. G. Ferrero, *The Life of Caesar*, trans. A. E. Zimmern (New York,
1962), p. 91.
6. M. Grant, *Julius Caesar* (London, 1969), pp. 44–45.

contra gratiam—*and he believed that, by piling up favors
and money, he could finally reach a height great enough to
found a principate.*[7]

The second reason why Crassus has been overlooked or ill-
remembered is that he suffered a disastrous military defeat at
the end of his life. Historians are not kind to "losers" and are
not quick to forgive such a man unless he has left behind a
body of great writings like Cicero's or great conquests like
Pompey's and Caesar's. In the end, however, the real difference
between Crassus and the latter two men is that they lost on a
grander scale than he did.

The scorn and neglect with which Crassus has been treated
is illustrated by the lack of any extant likeness of him among
the remains of ancient portraiture. Marius, Sulla, Cicero, Pompey, and Caesar, the other great heroes, or devils, of the late
Roman Republic, all have their famous busts or portraits to
grace the frontispieces of their biographies. Crassus has none.

The lack of modern biographers of Crassus is acute. Drumann dutifully recorded his life and career in his biographical
account of Roman history.[8] Deknatel produced a little-read
dissertation on Crassus in 1901.[9] Groebe's slight revision of
Drumann appeared in 1908, and Gelzer's encyclopedia article
was published in 1926.[10] Garzetti produced a series of long
articles in the early 1940s that added little to what had already
been said and are wrongheaded or uncritical in many crucial
places.[11] The two most recent and sympathetic treatments of
Crassus, by Cadoux and Adcock, are simply too limited in scope
and conception to make up for the faults of others.[12] It is time
to redress the balance.

7. Chr. Meier, *Res Publica Amissa* (Wiesbaden, 1966), pp. 274–75.
Erich Gruen now has made the most serious challenge to the picture
presented above, but, given the nature of his topic, he did not present
a complete analysis of Crassus's career: E. S. Gruen, *The Last Generation of the Roman Republic* (Berkeley and Los Angeles, 1974), p. 67
and passim.
8. Drumann, *Geschichte* 4, pp. 84–127.
9. Chr. Deknatel, *De Vita M. Licinii Crassi* (Leiden, 1901).
10. Gelzer, *RE* 13.1 (1926), 295–331, s.v. "Licinius" (68).
11. A. Garzetti, "M. Licinio Crasso," *Athenaeum* 19 (1941): 3–37;
20 (1942): 12–40; 22 (1944): 1–62.
12. T. J. Cadoux, "Marcus Crassus: A Revaluation," *Greece and
Rome* 2nd. ser. 3 (1956): 153–61; F. E. Adcock, *Marcus Crassus, Millionaire* (Cambridge, 1966).

I do not propose to press down too far on the opposite arm and make Crassus a hero. Far from it. I do hope to show, however, that the third member of the so-called First Triumvirate was a potent force to be reckoned with right up to his premature end. The kind of man he was, his power, and his role in the period from Sulla to Caesar will be the subject of this book.

I

The Historical Situation

Marcus Licinius Crassus, son of P. Licinius Crassus (consul in 97 B.C.), was born into the age of turmoil and civil strife that produced Marius and Sulla. His life, his values, and his political career, just as those of his more intensively discussed contemporaries, Cicero, Pompey, and Caesar, were radically shaped by this age. In order to understand him, therefore, one must understand the situation with which he was confronted through most of his active life.

Traditionally, Rome had been governed by an informal oligarchy of leading senators drawn from a fairly small number of patrician and plebeian families, who counted among their members or immediate ancestors men who had held the office of consul. Their power was based not only on the prestige gained from high office, but also on landed wealth, patronage of significant numbers of voters, and a rather tangled array of friendships, alliances, and intermarriages.[1] By the late second century B.C., however, the vast economic and social changes that had resulted from the Punic Wars and from Rome's rise to the position of the dominant power in the Mediterranean world posed great threats to the old regime of these established noble families.

Discouraged by the increased competition from slave labor in agriculture, and attracted by the booty-fed economy of the cities, many small landowners migrated to urban centers, especially to Rome.[2] This influx from the countryside swelled the number of voters available in Rome and made it more difficult for the nobility to control the electoral and legislative assemblies by traditional means. The citizens of allied com-

1. Cf. M. Gelzer, *The Roman Nobility*, trans. R. Seager (Oxford, 1969), pp. 54–155.
2. H. C. Boren, "The Urban Side of the Gracchan Economic Crisis," *American Historical Review* 63 (1957–58): 890–902.

munities throughout Italy had posed a further threat by demanding equality with the Romans, whose wealth and power their faithful military service had helped to win. At the same time, increased trade and commerce had produced a significant class of prosperous businessmen with equestrian census status, whose interests were often different from those of the landed nobility. Similarly, when the economic resources of Rome had proven inadequate for the large number of poor, rural immigrants, the urban plebs developed interests of their own that were not congenial to those of the ruling elite.[3]

In 133 B.C., Tiberius Sempronius Gracchus and, ten years later, his brother, Gaius, had tried to institute reforms to satisfy these new interests and remedy some of the socioeconomic problems confronting Rome.[4] Their efforts were, unfortunately, tied to the internal rivalries of the nobility, and their political enemies united against them with many others who thought that changes made in the interest of the urban plebs, the equestrian class, or the Italian allies would destroy their own powers and privileges.[5]

According to one's particular bias, the conservative-minded nobles and their supporters, who often opposed significant change in the face of new conditions, came to be known in political rhetoric as *optimates* (the best men) or *pauci* (the few).[6] For convenience, *optimates* is the term that will be used in this study. This usage, however, is not to imply that the men who can be classed as *optimates* functioned as a modern political party or maintained the same stand on all issues. Political parties, with their institutionalized structures and stable loyalties, were non-existent in ancient Rome. In many cases where their common interests were not clearly at stake,

3. Ibid.
4. Cf. such standard accounts of their proposals as T. Rice Holmes, *The Roman Republic* 1 (Oxford, 1923), pp. 15–31, and H. Last, *CAH* 9 (1932): 1–101. For corrections and specialized treatments, see E. Badian, "From the Gracchi to Sulla (1940–1959)," *Historia* 11 (1962): 197–214, and "Tiberius Gracchus and the Roman Revolution," *Aufstieg und Niedergang der Römischen Welt* 1 (Berlin and New York, 1972), pp. 668–731.
5. D. C. Earl, *Tiberius Gracchus: A Study in Politics* (*Collection Latomus* 66, Brussels, 1963); E. S. Gruen, *Roman Politics and the Criminal Courts, 149–78 B.C.* (Cambridge, Mass., 1968), pp. 45–78.
6. For these terms, see, e.g., Cic. *Sest.* 38, 98, 100, and *Corn.* fr. 2.11, 424 Schoell/64 Puccioni; Sall. *Cat.* 21.4, *Jug.* 31.19.

those men broadly classed as *optimates* pursued vigorous and often bitter rivalries in the contest for the power and glory that were highly prized in the ancient aristocratic value system.

Men who sought to redress the grievances of the social, economic, and political groups outside of the senatorial aristocracy, or at least to play up to their interests for political support in the struggle for offices and honors at Rome, came to be known in political propaganda by the general term *populares* (favoring the populace).[7] In many cases, such as those of the Gracchi or of Livius Drusus the Younger, they were members of the nobility. In some cases, such as that of C. Marius, they were from families who had no senatorial or consular ancestors. As a whole, they were often motivated as much by considerations of political expediency in the aristocratic competition for power and high office as by concern for those whose welfare they claimed to champion.[8] Again, however, as with the *optimates*, it must be emphasized that those men classed as *populares* did not function as a cohesive political party. Rather, they were individuals who often competed against each other for the same goals but used similar means.

One of the main weapons of the *populares* was the office of tribune.[9] Before the dictatorship of Sulla in 82, the *tribuni plebis* had several privileges and powers that made them potentially dangerous to the *optimates*. Unlike the consuls, they were not legally barred from consecutive terms of office, and they had the power of veto over the actions of consuls and other magistrates as well as over proposals placed before the Senate or the several public assemblies. They themselves, on the other hand, without interference from the consuls, could initiate actions in the *Concilium Plebis*, which was less easily manipulated by the nobility than was the *Comitia Centuriata* with its inequitable distribution of votes between rich and

7. For this term, see Cic. *Sest.* 96; J. Hellogouarc'h, *Le vocabulaire latin des relations et des partis politiques sous la république romaine* (Paris, 1963), pp. 518–25; and Chr. Meier *RE* Supp. 10 (1965), 549–615, s.v. "Populares."

8. Cf. D. Stockton, *Cicero, a Political Biography* (London, 1971), p. 33.

9. Of course, the *optimates* could utilize this office, too, as they did in 122, through Livius Drusus the Elder (Cic. *Brut.* 109, *Fin.* 4.66).

poor.[10] Accordingly, Ti. Gracchus, C. Gracchus, and Livius Drusus the Younger had all held the office of tribune when they introduced their reforms, and C. Marius had relied on tribunes friendly to him for obtaining desired legislation.

Of course, the ambitious *popularis* sought a major military command, as did most aspirants to high positions at Rome. Marius had used it in the war with Jugurtha and then against the bands of Cimbri and Teutoni who had threatened to sweep into Italy from Gaul. To meet these military emergencies, from 108 to 100 he held six consulships, five of them consecutively from 104.[11]

After Marius's sixth consulship and the lack of further military emergencies, the *optimates* had succeeded for a while in reestablishing their dominance at Rome. In 91, however, the tribunate of Livius Drusus the Younger and the outbreak of the Social War with Rome's allies gave Marius a chance to restore his fortunes.[12] The result was a vicious Civil War between Marius and his supporters, who followed a *popularis* program, and L. Cornelius Sulla, many of whose supporters revealed an optimate bias. Eventually, after a war in the eastern provinces against Mithridates VI intervened, Sulla's side prevailed. In 82, Sulla was elected dictator for writing the laws and reconstituting the state.[13] While he conducted bloody proscriptions to exterminate his political enemies and acquire needed money, he reorganized the Roman state to place it firmly in the control of his friends and optimate backers.[14] Then he retired in the hope that he had made a *popularis* career such as that of Marius impossible for the future and that the optimate-controlled aristocracy would be able to engage in the traditional competition for power and prestige in peace and security.

In the period after Sulla's reforms, the leading *optimates*

10. For the *Comitia Centuriata*, see L. R. Taylor, *Party Politics in the Age of Caesar* (Berkeley and Los Angeles, 1949), pp. 63, 154, and *Roman Voting Assemblies* (Ann Arbor, 1966), pp. 85–106.

11. T. R. S. Broughton, *The Magistrates of the Roman Republic* 1 (New York, 1951), pp. 550, 554, 558, 562, 567, 570, 574.

12. T. F. Carney, *A Biography of C. Marius* (*Proceedings of the African Classical Association*, Supplement 1, 1962), pp. 54–70.

13. Broughton, *MRR* 2, p. 66.

14. For a discussion of Sulla's reforms, see E. Badian, "Lucius Sulla, the Deadly Reformer," *Seventh Todd Memorial Lecture* (Sydney, 1970).

were those men of consular families and their political allies who had supported Sulla in the Civil War and who sought to preserve his constitution, which helped to perpetuate their domination of the Roman political scene. Compromise was employed when necessary to avoid a repetition of the recent war, but in general they maintained a conservative stance. They also sought to prevent the acquisition of too much power by one individual, who might become another Marius and overwhelm them for his own political advantage.

Many of the *optimates* were linked together by traditional ties of birth, marriage, friendship, and shared political views. Sometimes overlapping relationships created conflicting loyalties and confusing shifts of political alliances in the dynamic competition for power, position, and prestige among them. For the most part, however, the leading *optimates* appear as a recognizable group, with a common set of general political goals and numerous personal bonds setting them apart as a powerful oligarchy within the Roman state.[15]

15. Again, it must be emphasized that *optimates* does not refer to a formal organization, but to a number of individuals sharing a common viewpoint on certain key issues, social ties, and often family relationships. Most of the important political figures at Rome, however, were often aligned in personal or family factions. For example, both Pompey and Caesar built up great followings based on marriage, friendship, and reciprocal political service—followings that can legitimately be called factions. Another faction can also be seen focused on important members of the great plebeian house of the Caecilii Metelli: among the leading *optimates* to be discussed below, several share the name or are members of the family on their mothers' sides, and they, along with a number of other figures sharing Metellan connections, followed the same course on significant occasions.

The problem in applying the factional analysis to Roman politics is is that factions were dynamic, with shifting membership outside of a key individual or individuals, that under severe stress a faction could break up altogether, and that our records are often too fragmentary for adequate interpretation (cf. T. F. Carney, "Prosopography: Payoffs and Pitfalls," *Phoenix* 27 [1973]: 156–79). As a result, the view that factions pursuing concerted goals dominated the political scene in the late Roman Republic has lately come under increasing attack. Many historians have seen P. A. Brunt's article " 'Amicitia' in the Late Roman Republic," *Proceedings of the Cambridge Philological Society* n.s. 11 (1965): 1–20 (reprinted in R. Seager, *The Crisis of the Roman Republic* [Cambridge, 1969], pp. 199–218) as a severe blow against the factional interpretation. What it does refute is any idea that the words *amicitia* and *amicus* can automatically be used when found in reference to a person to establish his membership in a particular *factio*.

The most comprehensive argument to date against the factional interpretation is Christian Meier's *Res Publica Amissa* (Wiesbaden, 1966).

Men such as Q. Caecilius Metellus Pius, Q. Caecilius Metellus Creticus, L. Licinius Lucullus, Q. Lutatius Catulus, and the three Aurelii Cottae stand out as representatives of this group.[16] They, the other optimate heirs of Sulla, and candidates supported by them held a majority of the consulships from 80 to 60, and were a dominant force in post-Sullan Roman politics.[17] Despite their power and prestige, however, they were not able to rule Rome unchallenged and preserve the system that Sulla had established. Sulla condemned his system to failure by his inability to quench the flames of personal ambition, which his own example merely helped to fuel, and by his failure to solve the basic social, economic, and political problems that ambitious men could exploit, often by *popularis* methods, to their own advantage against that of the optimate oligarchy.[18] To be sure, many of these ambitious men had no plan or desire to destroy the constitution and basic system that Sulla had created, but that was the ultimate effect of what

He has performed a valuable service in demonstrating conclusively that a relationship between two men through birth or marriage cannot by itself, without any other hard data, be an adequate basis for declaring them factional allies. Other obligations, personal considerations, or even accidental circumstances could lead two members of the same family on conflicting courses of action (cf. D. R. Shackleton Bailey, "The Roman Nobility in the Second Civil War," *Classical Quarterly* 10 [1960]: 253–67).

Meier has gone too far, however, in denying the validity of the factional view altogether. Although the word *factio* had several different meanings, one of them clearly denoted a group of individuals working together for mutual political goals (cf. R. Seager, "*Factio*: Some Observations," *Journal of Roman Studies* 62 (1972): 53–58. For the purposes of analysis, therefore, when adequate data are available, it is legitimate for the modern scholar to use this term to designate any group of people allied by family or other ties for common political purposes at Rome. Thus, the so-called First Triumvirate legitimately can be called the *factio* of Pompey, Crassus, and Caesar (Gelzer, *Roman Nobility*, p. 124).

16. For a detailed exposition of their position as optimate leaders, see Appendix A of this chapter. Others could also be mentioned, but these seven provide a good sample.

17. For a complete analysis of the consuls from 80 to 60, see Appendix B of this chapter.

18. It is not that Sulla did not try to solve some of them. Rather, his solutions were inadequate. For example, he may have hoped to satisfy the interests of the *Equites* by admitting 300 of them to membership in the Senate. In a short time, however, these new senators were bound to assimilate the ideals, values, and prejudices of the consular nobility, who were the senatorial leaders. Hence, the vast majority of *Equites* were left in the same inferior status that had been the cause of their discontent.

they did in their struggles with their fellow aristocrats for power and prestige.

The most successful of these ambitious individuals from 80 to 60 was Cn. Pompeius Magnus, Pompey the Great. Originally, he had opportunistically joined Sulla in 83 (Plut. *Pomp.* 5–6). Sulla sought to secure the loyalty of Pompey by arranging a marriage between his stepdaughter Aemilia and this valuable young ally (ibid., 9.2). As daughter of his wife Caecilia Metella, Aemilia also came from the family of Sulla's most important optimate supporters, the Caecilii Metelli. This marriage tie was soon broken, however, when Aemilia died. Note long afterwards, Pompey forced Sulla to grant him a triumph for his successful operations against remnants of Sulla's Marian opponents, a triumph that was unwarranted by Sulla's own regulations (ibid., 14.1–6). Nevertheless, Pompey obtained another connection with the Caecilii Metelli, through his marriage to Mucia. This marriage took place probably in 80, and there can be no doubt that at this time it signalled close cooperation between Pompey and the optimate Metelli and others allied with them.[19]

The date is very significant, because it was before the death of Sulla in 78 (Liv. *Per.* 90; Plut. *Sull.* 37; App. *BC* 1.12.105). Pompey naturally sought the support of Sulla's powerful allies, and they, despite the young man's recent actions, were anxious to secure his military talents for the future.[20] After Sulla's death, the situation was completely different. There existed a much wider scope for Pompey's ambitions, which led him to set his own interests above those of the *optimates.*[21] Some

19. I have argued for this date in *Phoenix* 24 (1970): 126, n. 37. Mucia was the uterine sister of Q. Metellus Celer and Q. Metellus Nepos. For the latest discussion of the parentage of these people, see T. P. Wiseman, "Celer and Nepos," *Classical Quarterly* 21 (1971): 180–82.

20. Badian, *Foreign Clientelae* (264–70 B.C.) (Oxford, 1958), p. 249.

21. Pompey was seldom one to place personal loyalty above personal ambition if the two came into conflict. His demand for a triumph from Sulla, despite Sulla's own regulations, has already been noted. He also refused to obey Sulla when he told him to stop supporting Lepidus for the consulship in 79 (Plut. *Sull.* 34.4–5, *Pomp.* 15.1–3). This self-serving double-dealing did, of course, gain Pompey the chance to carry the banner of the Sullan oligarchy in yet another war and enhance his prestige (Plut. *Sull.* 34.5, *Pomp.* 16.1–2). In 58, Pompey sacrificed Cicero to Clodius's wrath despite previous assurances to Cicero that he would not (Cic. *Att.* 2.24.5). In 52, he abandoned his anti-Clodian ally, Milo (Cic. *Mil.* 68–69).

nobles who had been loyal to Sulla and might otherwise have remained in the camp of men such as Metellus Pius, Catulus, and Lucullus, supported Pompey for various reasons.[22] Most of the *optimates*, however, were not willing to satisfy his ambitions.[23]

Despite their hostility, Pompey's star rose steadily from 77 to 61. In that initial year, he received a major military command against Sertorius in Spain, where he earned another triumph. Upon his return to Italy in 71, he added to his laurels by annihilating a fleeing band of men who had fought in the revolt of Spartacus. Then, secure in his prestige and the loyalty of his troops, he demanded and received from the Senate permission to seek the consulship, for which he was not yet qualified under the laws of Sulla. In 67 and 66, his supporters obtained two more great commands for him: first, against the Mediterranean pirates; then against Mithridates, who again was threatening Rome's control of the eastern Mediterranean. In both instances, he won great successes. He returned to Rome in 61 with immense prestige and hopes for holding an unchallengeable position among the Roman nobility.

By the 70s, and throughout the 60s, therefore, two of the great power-centers in post-Sullan Roman politics are clear. One contained the loyal optimate heirs of Sulla, especially prominent consulars like Metellus Pius, Metellus Creticus, Q. Catulus, L. Lucullus, and the Aurelii Cottae. The other was focused on the personality of Pompey the Great in his ambitious rise to power and prestige within the Roman aristoc-

22. For example, Mucia's half-brothers, Metellus Celer and Metellus Nepos, remained loyal to Pompey until he divorced her in 61. In 77, L. Marcius Philippus overrode the wishes of Catulus and argued successfully for Pompey's commission against Sertorius in Spain (Cic. *Phil.* 11.18, *Leg. Man.* 62, *Dom.* 123). In 66, P. Servilius Vatia Isauricus, who had been another loyal supporter of Sulla and who was a son-in-law of Metellus Macedonicus, opposed Catulus and Lucullus, and supported the appointment of Pompey to the command against Mithridates (Cic. *Leg. Man.* 68; cf. Appendix B, under the year 79). Similarly, C. Scribonius Curio supported Pompey in 66 (cf. Appendix B, under the year 76).

23. His support of Lepidus in 79 already must have disturbed many of them (cf. Appendix B, under the year 78). Indeed, Sulla pointedly cut Pompey out of his will (Plut. *Pomp.* 15.2–3). For a detailed argument to support this view, see Appendix C of this chapter.

racy. There were other power-centers,[24] but it is primarily in the context of these two that Marcus Licinius Crassus sought to advance his own claim to high honors and create a base of power in competition with his peers.[25]

24. For example, P. Cornelius Cethegus, a successful opportunist who had profited through Sulla, controlled enough power among senators of lower rank that L. Lucullus and M. Antonius had to enlist his support to gain their commands in 74 (Cic. *Parad. Stoic.* 5.40, *Brut.* 178; Plut. *Luc.* 6.1–3; Pseud. Ascon *ad Verr.* 2.2.8, 259 St).

25. It should also be emphasized that, although a person may be identified primarily with one or another leading group or person, he could have overlapping and even conflicting connections with others. Often, in the scramble for position and high office, people would seek support from many sources, and it would be extended by many in the hope of establishing useful claims for the future. Which competing hopes and expectations would be fulfilled depended on many factors. Therefore, although for the sake of analysis it is necessary to make sharp distinctions, these distinctions should not be viewed as more than convenient categories that are subject to numerous reservations and qualifications, which, if constantly stated, would make any discussion of events too cumbersome to handle.

Appendix I-A

Seven Leading Optimates

One of the most prestigious *optimates*, until his death in 63 or 62, was Q. Caecilius Metellus Pius.[1] Significantly, he and the rest of his family were connected with Sulla through the woman whom Sulla had married in 89, Caecilia Metella, daughter of L. Caecilius Metellus Delmaticus, who had been Pontifex Maximus (Plut. *Sull.* 6.10).[2] In 83, Pius threw his support behind Sulla and became one of the chief political beneficiaries of Sulla's program of restoring power to the hands of an optimate oligarchy. It is no surprise that he became Pontifex Maximus in 81 (Ascon. *Corn.* 79 C/62 St; Plut. *Iul.* 7.1; Macrob. *Sat.* 3.13.10–11; Dio 37.37.1), and he served as Sulla's colleague in the consulship of 80.[3] In 79, he went to Spain as proconsul to prosecute the war against Q. Sertorius, who had refused to recognize Sulla's authority and was carrying on a serious rebellion against the central government.[4]

A second important optimate from the family of the Caecilii Metelli was Q. Caecilius Metellus Creticus. He was commissioned to conduct a war against Mediterranean pirates in 68 after he had reached the coveted consulship for 69.[5] While waiting outside Rome for his triumph, he dutifully supported the optimate establishment by protecting Apulia during the Catilinarian disturbance, and in 62, he celebrated his triumph over the Cretan pirates.[6]

1. He was alive in 65 (Ascon. *Corn.* 60, 63, 79 C/49, 51, 62 St). No other Pontifex Maximus is known until Julius Caesar, who was elected in 63: G. J. Szemler, *The Priests of the Roman Republic* (*Collection Latomus* 127 [1972]), pp. 129–32. Hence, Pius probably died in late 64 or early 63.

2. She was the widow of M. Aemilius Scaurus, who had been *Princeps Senatus*: F. Münzer, RE 3.1 (1897), 1234–35, s.v. "Caecilius" (134); Badian, FC, p. 231.

3. Broughton, MRR 2, p. 79.

4. Ibid., p. 83.

5. Ibid., pp. 131, 139.

6. Ibid., pp. 168–69, 176. In 68, he was succeeded in the consulship by L. Caecilius Metellus, apparently his brother: Münzer, RE 3.1 (1897), 1204–5, 1210–12, s.v. "Caecilius" (74 and 87). In 60, a fourth Metellus, Q. Caecilius Metellus Celer, reached the consulship: Broughton, MRR 2, p. 182. Although Celer and his brother, Nepos, had not followed the

L. Licinius Lucullus was another loyal lieutenant of Sulla who maintained an optimate stance throughout the 70s and 60s.[7] He reached the consulship in 74 and was related by birth and marriage to other important *optimates*. His mother was a sister of Q. Metellus Numidicus (Plut. *Luc.* 1.1), and his wife, Clodia, was a granddaughter of Metellus Balearicus.[8] Moreover, Clodia was the daughter of Ap. Claudius Pulcher, another conservative supporter of Sulla and consul in 79.[9] During his consulship, Lucullus won command of the critical war against Mithridates in Asia Minor (Plut. *Luc.* 6.1–5).[10] His brilliant generalship almost defeated Mithridates, but his refusal to cater to the wishes of his troops at a crucial point ultimately caused him to lose his command (ibid., 33.1–5).[11]

One of the most famous optimate leaders was Q. Lutatius Catulus, whom Licinius Macer is reported to have called a tyrant crueler than Sulla (Sall. *Hist.* 3.48.9 M). In 79, he was one of the candidates backed by Sulla (Plut. *Pomp.* 15.1–2). His connections with other *optimates* are clear. His homonymous father had close connections with the family of Metellus Pius, and his mother may have been the daughter of a Caecilia Metella.[12] In 87, both he and his father went to Metellus Pius's camp and besought him to defend Rome against Sulla's enemies, Marius and Cinna (Gran. Licin. 25 Bonn./19–20 Fl.; cf. App. *BC* 1.8.68). During his consulship in 78, he loyally defended the Sullan constitution against his rebellious colleague,

lead of the other Metelli and their optimate allies for most of the period from 80 to 60, they became closely identified with this group after Pompey had divorced their half sister, Mucia (Dio 37.49.3–50.6; cf. Cic. *Att.* 1.12.3; Plut. *Pomp.* 42.7). Had Celer not died prematurely, he might have gone on to become the leading member of the Metellan faction and the *optimates* in general (cf. Cic. *Att.* 1.18.5, 20.5; *Cael.* 59–60).

7. For Lucullus's role in the late Republic, see J. Van Ooteghem, *Lucius Licinius Lucullus* (Namur, 1959).

8. For L. Lucullus's career as a supporter of Sulla, see E. Badian, "Waiting for Sulla," *Journal of Roman Studies* 52 (1962): 54–55/*Studies in Greek and Roman History* (Oxford, 1964), pp. 220–21. For his marriage, see F. Münzer, *RE* 4.1 (1900), 107, s.v. "Clodius" (67).

9. For Appius Claudius Pulcher, see Appendix B, under the year 79.

10. Of course, optimate support alone was not enough. He had to gain the cooperation of the powerful faction of Sulla's old lieutenant, Cethegus.

11. His problems were exacerbated by his disloyally ambitious brother-in-law, P. Clodius, who was serving on his staff at the time (Plut. *Luc.* 34.1–5).

12. E. Badian, "Caepio and Norbanus," *Historia* 6 (1957): 322–24, 330, n. 100/*Studies in Greek and Roman History* (Oxford, 1964), pp. 37–40, 66, n. 100.

Lepidus (Cic. *Cat.* 3.24; Sall. *Hist.* 1.54–73 M; Liv. *Per.* 90). In 67, he opposed Pompey's command against the pirates, a command that undercut Q. Caecilius Metellus Creticus (Cic. *Leg. Man.* 52–56; Vell. Pat. 2.31.1; Val. Max. 8.15.9; Plut. *Pomp.* 25.5). In the following year, he sought to help Lucullus retain his command against Mithridates, which was coveted by Pompey (Cic. *Leg. Man.* 51, 59–63, 66; Plut. *Pomp.* 30.4). In 65, he appeared with Metellus Pius and several other leading *optimates* as a witness against the ex-tribune C. Cornelius (Ascon. *Corn.* 60, 79 C/49, 62 St), who had proposed a number of laws dangerous to optimate power.[13]

Throughout his life, therefore, Catulus was a stout defender of the optimate cause. His loss was keenly felt when he died in 61 or 60. Cicero was particularly disheartened and mourned the demise of this conservative champion (*Att.* 1.20.3).

C. Aurelius Cotta and his two brothers, Marcus and Lucius, were all important figures. Gaius had thrown in his lot with Sulla during the Civil War (Cic. *Brut.* 311), and according to Sallust's version of the speech of Licinius Macer that was recorded for 73, they were viewed as staunch members of the optimate oligarchy fostered by Sulla (Sall. *Hist.* 3.48.8 M).[14] Nevertheless, it has been argued that at least by the early sixties the Cottae had fallen out of favor with the other leading *optimates*.[15] The evidence cited is the successful prosecution of M. Cotta by C. Papirius Carbo in about 67 (Memnon 59 *FGrH* 3 B, 366–67; Val. Max. 5.4.4; Dio 36.40.3–4) and the difficulty that L. Cotta had in obtaining the consulship, which he finally secured by a circuitous route in 66 (Ascon. *Corn.* 75 C/59 St), although he was eligible to stand for election as early as 68.

The reasons adduced to explain how the Cottae fell from grace are C. Cotta's bill that restored the right of tribunes to seek higher magistracies in 75 and L. Cotta's jury-reform bill of 70 that broke the senatorial monopoly of jury seats (ibid., 67, 78 C/54, 61 St).[16] At first glance, these two acts would

13. For the significance of this trial, see A. M. Ward, "Politics in the Trials of Manilius and Cornelius," *TAPA* 101 (1970): 951–54.

14. Sallust's words in reference to C. Cotta are *ex factione media consul* and signify his intimate association with the optimate oligarchy: M. I. Henderson, "Review of Scullard, *Roman Politics, 200–150 B.C.*," *Journal of Roman Studies* 42 (1952): 115.

15. R. Seager, "The Tribunate of Cornelius: Some Ramifications," *Hommages à Marcel Renard* 2 (*Collection Latomus* 101), ed. J. Bibauw (Brussels, 1969), 680–86.

16. Ibid., 682–84.

appear to provide sufficient reason for a break between the Cottae and conservative *optimates* such as those mentioned above. In fact, Cicero, during his defense of Cornelius, said that the *nobiles* had become *inimicissimi* to C. Cotta as a result of his law (ibid., 78 C/61 St). Cicero was pleading a case, however, and purposeful misrepresentation or exaggeration must not be discounted (cf. Cic. *Cluent.* 139). When viewed in its actual context, C. Cotta's law allowing tribunes to stand for higher magistracies seems to be a necessary move to salvage as much as possible from a bad situation for the *optimates*.[17]

In 76, the tribune Sicinius had stirred up serious agitation for full restoration of the pre-Sullan tribunate (Sall. *Hist.* 2.23–26, 3.48.8.10 M; Plut. *Crass.* 7.9; Pseud. Ascon. *ad. Div.* 8, 189 St). By 75, the situation had become chaotic. The tribune Opimius continued to agitate on this issue, and a serious shortage of grain made the plebs so much more discontented with optimate domination of the political scene that a mob physically attacked C. Cotta and his colleague, Octavius, as they escorted Q. Caecilius Metellus (Creticus) along the *Via Sacra* during his campaign for the praetorship (Sall. *Hist.* 2.23–26, 45, 48–50 M). The situation was desperate, and some significant step had to be taken. Indeed, Sallust had Licinius Macer declare in his speech of 73 that fear of popular unrest was the major factor in Cotta's bill to restore to tribunes the right to stand for higher magistracies (ibid., 3.48.8 M).

There is little real reason, therefore, to see C. Cotta as breaking with his fellow *optimates* on the issue of tribunician rights. Meaningful measures to alleviate popular grievances had to be taken by men who wished to remain in control. For example as aedile, Q. Hortensius Hortalus, Catulus's brother-in-law and staunch backer of the optimate cause, distributed grain to the Roman populace at a price well below that on the open market (Cic. *Verr.* 2.3.215). Hortensius certainly lost no favor with his fellows as a result of this move, one that was often associated with *popularis* figures.

Similarly, Cotta should not have lost favor for his action. Just prior to his tribunician law, he was loyally supporting the candidacy of Q. Caecilius Metellus (Creticus) for the praetorship (Sall. *Hist.* 2.23.26, 45, 48–50 M). Afterwards, Cotta was granted a triumph for some insignificant military actions dur-

17. Cf. F. B. Marsh, A *History of the Roman World from 146 to 30 B.C.*, ed. 3, H. H. Scullard (London, 1963), p. 144. For the weakened state of the *optimates* in 75, see Meier, RPA, pp. 268–69.

ing his governorship of Cisalpine Gaul in 74 (Cic. *Pis.* 62; Ascon. *ad. Pis.* 62, 14 C/19–20 St). If Cotta really had become hated by the powerful optimate leaders, it is doubtful that he would have received a triumph for his obvious military opportunism.[18]

M. Cotta's prosecution at the hands of the tribune C. Papirius Carbo, sometime around 67 (Memnon 52, 59, 60 *FGrH* 3 B, 363–64, 366–68; Val. Max. 5.4.4; Dio 36.40.3–4), does not necessarily mean that he had fallen from the favor of the leading *optimates* either. He had been honored by the Senate upon his return from Pontus (Memnon 52 *FGrH* 3 B, 363–64). Carbo reveals no connection with the *optimates*. He was probably a young man out to advance himself through the newly restored tribunate and make his mark against one of those *optimates* whom Licinius Macer had previously excoriated. M. Cotta was hardly a popular figure. He was a rival of Pompey (Sall. *Hist.* 2. 98 *fin.* M), the popular hero, while he may have been open to further popular animosity because of his military difficulties in the war against Mithridates (App. *Mith.* 10.71; Sall. *Hist.* 4.69.13 M; Cic. *Mur.* 33; Eutrop. 6.6.2) and his rather imperious attack on Oppius by letter (Quint. *Inst.* 5.13.20–21).

L. Cotta's reform of the juries in 70 would not have placed him at odds with other optimate leaders any more than C. Cotta's tribunician reform in 75 had hurt that older member of the family. The situation in 70 was like that of 75—agitation for the removal of senators from the juries was strong (Cic. *Verr.* 1.36–49, 2.2.174, 3.223–24).[19] Clearly, the *optimates* needed to compromise if they were to maintain influence on the juries and still mollify public opinion. As Catulus agreed, there was no use in antagonizing the public unduly (ibid., 1.44). L. Cotta's bill was the required compromise.[20]

18. L. Licinius Crassus (cos. 95) was denied a triumph under similar circumstances (Cic. *Pis.* 62, *Inv.* 2.111).

19. Although Cicero may have exaggerated the situation with respect to the juries at the time of Verres' trial, there should be no doubt that in 70 there had been some who had been calling for the complete removal of the senators from the juries, as had been the case under C. Gracchus.

20. E. S. Gruen, *The Last Generation of the Roman Republic* (Berkeley and Los Angeles, 1974), pp. 34–35. That also explains why Hortensius likewise favored Cotta's jury bill and answers the question recently raised by B. A. Marshall concerning political alignments at this time: "Q. Cicero, Hortensius and Lex Aurelia," *Rheinisches Museum für Philologie* 118 (1975): 136–52.

Any difficulty that L. Cotta faced in obtaining the consulship can be attributed to the volatile electoral conditions created by the restoration of the censorship and the full powers
of the tribunes in 70 (Sall. *Cat.* 38.1; Dio 36.38.1–2). Also,
the unpopularity of the *optimates* was increasing as the war
against Mithridates continued to drag on. If L. Cotta did run
for the consulship in 68 and 67, he lost, not because he was
not supported by the optimate leaders, but because conditions
were unfavorable to optimate candidates. That L. Cotta still
enjoyed the support of the leading *optimates* in the 60s is
confirmed by his censorship after the resignation of Catulus
and Crassus (Cic. *Dom.* 84; Plut. *Cic.* 27.2; Dio 37.9.4). He
carried on the optimate opposition to the tribunes, even
though it had been impossible to block the restitution of full
tribunician powers. The tribunes, therefore, felt it necessary to
use their vetoes to prevent Cotta and his censorial colleague
from revising the roll of the Senate, for they feared that they
would be the first to be struck off (Dio 37.9.4). L. Cotta was
rightly viewed as an important member of that conservative
circle of optimate oligarchs.

Appendix I-B

The Political Alignments of Roman Consuls
From 80 to 60 B.C.

The following year-by-year analysis of the consuls from 80 to 60 attempts to determine the political orientation, alliances, and backers of each man. The evidence for identifying the consuls of each year may conveniently be found in T.R.S. Broughton's *Magistrates of the Roman Republic*, vol. 2 (New York, 1952). Within each year, the order in which each consul is discussed is not necessarily the one that Broughton gives.

80   Q. Caecilius Metellus Pius, the leading representative of the Caecilii Metelli, has already been discussed in Appendix A of this chapter. Sulla, of course, put his own personal stamp on the 80s, but his debt to the *optimates* cannot be overlooked. That he held the consulship in 80, with Metellus Pius as his colleague, is certainly significant. More importantly, his rise to power was aided through a mutually opportunistic marriage to Metella (Plut. *Sull.* 6.10–12).[1]

79   Ap. Claudius Pulcher had prosecuted the siege of Nola for Sulla in 87 (Liv. *Per.* 79) and suffered exile under Cinna for his loyalty to Sulla (Cic. *Dom.* 83). He also was closely linked with the powerful Metelli. His wife was another Caecilia Metella, daughter of Metellus Balearicus. There is good reason, therefore, to count him with the *optimates* in 79.[2]

The same is true of P. Servilius Vatia Isauricus. He was not only a loyal follower of Sulla, but also the son of still another Caecilia Metella, daughter of Metellus Macedonicus (Cic. *Verr.* 2.3.211, *Dom.* 123). Earlier, Servilius, and perhaps also Ap. Claudius, had supported optimate resistance to Pompey's first triumph. Then, no doubt after Pompey had married into the Metelli through Mucia, Servilius reversed himself in Pompey's favor (Frontin. *Strat.* 4.5.1; Plut. *Pomp.* 14.5).[3]

---

1. She was the daughter of L. Caecilius Metellus Delmaticus, who had been Pontifex Maximus, and she was the widow of M. Aemilius Scaurus, who had been *Princeps Senatus.* Cf. F. Münzer, *RE* 3.1 (1897), 1234–35, s.v. "Caecilius" (134); and Badian, *FC,* p. 231.
2. Münzer, ibid., s.v. "Caecilius" (135).
3. The text of Frontinus reads *Servilio et Glaucia,* but is often emended to *Servilio et Claudio.* This emendation makes much sense,

78 Q. Lutatius Catulus has been extensively discussed in
Appendix A of this chapter. His optimate stance is clear. His
colleague, M. Aemilius Lepidus, is a different sort, however.
He had at one time sided with Sulla's enemies, but had
switched his loyalties in time for subsequent rewards of financial profit and a praetorship under Sulla's dictatorship.[4] After
81, Lepidus seems to have fallen out of favor. In 80, Metellus
Celer and Metellus Nepos were going to prosecute him for
his misdeeds in Sicily but then dropped the charges because
of his popularity.[5] When Pompey came out in support of
Lepidus's candidacy, Sulla is said to have warned Pompey of
dire consequences (Plut. *Sull.* 34.4–5, *Pomp.* 15.1–2).[6] After
Sulla's death, he did indeed prove to be a revolutionary and
had to be put down by Catulus and by Pompey, who made up
for his previous support.[7]

77 The consuls D. Junius Brutus and Mam. Aemilius Lepidus Livianus had favored and been favored by Sulla (Sall. *Hist.*
1.55.3 M).[8] The election of both appears to have been promoted by the Metelli and the other loyal supporters of the
Sullan regime.[9] Further association between Brutus and the

---

but it has been challenged by E. Badian, "The Date of Pompey's First
Triumph," *Hermes* 83 (1955): 108. Later, Servilius and C. Scribonius
Curio (see the year 76, below) broke with the majority of *optimates* and
supported the appointment of Pompey, now L. Lucullus's bitter rival, to
the command against Mithridates in 66 (Cic. *Leg. Man.* 68). Apparently
the chance to even an old feud with the Luculli helped to determine
Servilius's action (Plut. *Luc.* 1.1; Cic. *Acad. Pr.* 2.1, *Prov. Cons.* 22). Cf.
F. Münzer, *RE* 2A.2 (1923), 1815.43–53, s.v. "Servilius" (93).

4. Cf. Gruen, *LGRR*, p. 7.

5. No doubt, their brother-in-law, Pompey, also influenced them, since
he supported Lepidus in the consular elections of 79 (Plut. *Pomp.*
15.1–2).

6. Gruen argues that Sulla's perspicacity in this case may be owed to
the excellent hindsight of the ancient sources: *LGRR*, pp. 122–23. On
the other hand, Sulla cannot have been completely confident in all those
who had shifted to his side out of sheer opportunism and may well have
had reservations about the advisability of a consulship for Lepidus, particularly after his record as governor of Sicily (Cic. *Verr.* 2.3.212).

7. See Broughton, *MRR* 2, p. 85 and references.

8. F. Münzer, *RE* 10.1 (1918), 968.13–26, s.v. "Iunius" (46). The
strength of Lepidus's relationship with Sulla can be seen in his successful
intercession with Sulla on behalf of his kinsman, Julius Caesar (Suet.
Iul. 1.2–3).

9. G V. Sumner, "Manius or Mamercus?" *Journal of Roman Studies*
54 (1964), 45–46. Indeed, Sulla may already have supported Mam.
Lepidus in an unsuccessful contest against M. Aemilius Lepidus in 79:
E. Badian, "Waiting for Sulla," *Studies in Greek and Roman History*
(Oxford, 1964), p. 234, n. 17/*Journal of Roman Studies* 52 (1962):
61, n. 17. Gruen questions this hypothesis (*LGRR* p. 123, n. 4), but it
remains entirely possible (see n. 6, above).

optimates cannot be found.[10] Mam. Aemilius Lepidus Livianus can, however, be seen in close connection with the Metelli. He appears to have been a legate of Q. Metellus Pius in 88, and captured Norba for the Sullan cause.[11] His son may have been a legate of L. Lucullus in 73,[12] and in 65 he appeared with four other staunch *optimates* as a witness against the Pompeian ex-tribune, C. Cornelius.[13]

76   Connections between Cn. Octavius and other members of the nobility cannot be determined firmly with the available evidence.[14] There are some clues, however. Most of the important Octavii with the *praenomina* Gnaeus, Marcus, and Lucius seem to be closely related.[15] All of those who are known in any detail appear to have been very conservative. For example, the M. Octavius who gained an important niche in history as the tribune who opposed Ti. Gracchus was a member of this family.[16] These Octavii probably would have been favorable to the Sullan regime. As consul, an earlier Cn. Octavius had helped Metellus Pius defend Rome against Marius and Cinna in 87 (Cic. *Cat.* 3.24; Gran. Licin. 25–29 Bonn./19–23 Fl.; App. *BC* 1.8.68). That the present Cn. Octavius enjoyed the support of leading *optimates* for the consulship may be indicated by the action of his cousin, L. Octavius, who was a more important figure and as consul in 75 openly supported the candidacy of Q. Caecilius Metellus Creticus for the praetorship (Sall. *Hist.* 2.45 M).[17]

C. Scribonius Curio was another longtime supporter of Sulla.[18] Although prior to Sulla's ascendancy he had prosecuted

10. That he may not have wished to take an active role in suppressing the attempt of M. Aemilius Lepidus to overthrow the Sullan system is understandable from familial considerations: F. Münzer, *RE* 10.1 (1918), 968.30–34, s.v. "Iunius" (46). Mam. Aemilius Lepidus, however, was given command of an army, although when he took command of it is not clear (Cic. *Cluent.* 99; cf. Sumner, "Manius," *JRS* 54 (1964): 46 and n. 57).

11. Broughton, *MRR* 2, pp. 43, 45, n. 10; Supplement, pp. 11 (Metellus Pius), 27 (P. Gabinius); Badian, "Waiting for Sulla," *Studies*, p. 217/ *JRS* 52 (1962): 53.

12. Sumner, "Manius," *JRS* 54 (1964): 47. See also the discussion of L. Lucullus under the year 74, below.

13. See Sumner, ibid., pp. 41–48, for a correction of Asconius, *Corn.* 60, 79 C/49, 62 St, and consult the discussions of Q. Catulus, M. Lucullus, and Q. Hortensius under the years 78, 73, and 69, respectively.

14. F. Münzer, *RE* 17.2 (1937), 1818 s.v. "Octavius" (22).

15. Ibid., 1802, 1819–20, s.v. "Octavius" (25–29).

16. Ibid., 1820, s.v. "Octavius" (31).

17. Cf. ibid., 1819, s.v. "Octavius" (26).

18. Ibid., *RE* 2A.1 (1921), 862.56–863.18, s.v. "Scribonius" (10).

Q. Metellus Nepos, consul in 98 (Ascon. *Corn.* 63 C/51 St; Apul. *Apol.* 66), he appears to have cooperated with the *optimates* until he supported Pompey's Mithridatic command in 66 (Cic. *Leg. Man.* 68).[19] In 78, he withdrew from the consular campaign in favor of Mam. Aemilius Lepidus Livianus (Sall. *Hist.* 1.86.M). He was opposed to the restoration of the tribunate (ibid., 3.48.10 M; Pseud. Ascon. *ad Div.* 8, 189 St), and, along with several Metelli, he supported Verres (Cic. *Verr.* 1.18–21).[20] In order to postpone Verres' trial to a more favorable time, he may have cooperated in setting up a rival extortion trial under the pretext that he was being prosecuted in the fulfillment of a vow by the younger Metellus Nepos to avenge his father.[21] At any rate, an accommodation with Nepos was reached, and the charges were dropped (Ascon. *Corn.* 63 C/51 St).

75 For the possible association of L. Octavius with the *optimates*, see the discussion of Cn. Octavius under the previous year. The case for cooperation between C. Aurelius Cotta and the other leading *optimates* is argued in Appendix A of this chapter.[22]

74 M. Aurelius Cotta is discussed in the same place as his brother Gaius and also seems to have enjoyed optimate support.[23] Indeed, Gaius's support of Metellus Creticus's praetorian candidacy in 75 (Sall. *Hist.* 2.45 M) may well reflect Metellan support of Marcus's own consular campaign as part of an electoral bargain.[24] L. Licinius Lucullus's role as an optimate is also discussed in Appendix A of this chapter.[25]

73 M. Terentius Varro Lucullus, the brother of L. Lucullus, was also closely linked with the *optimates* (Cic. *Acad. Pr.* 2.1, cf. *Att.* 13.6.4; Plut. *Luc.* 1.6, 37.1, *Sull.* 27.8; Gran. Licin. 39 Bonn./32 Fl.). He had been a legate of Sulla (Plut. *Luc.* 27.7, 37.1). In 65, he appeared as a witness with Q. Metellus Pius and three other friends of the Metelli against the Pompeian ex-tribune C. Cornelius (Ascon. *Corn.* 60 C/49 St).

19. He was, however, not so closely linked with them as were others and always had a rather independent cast of mind: W. C. McDermott, "Curio *Pater* and Cicero," *American Journal of Philology* 93 (1972): 381–411.

20. For the significance of this trial, see Appendix C, pp. 42–45.

21. F. Münzer, *RE* 2A.1 (1921), 864.60–865.12, s.v. "Scribonius" (10).

22. Above, pp. 16–18.

23. Above, pp. 16, 18.

24. For the electoral significance of the appearance of a man like C. Cotta with a candidate, see Meier, *RPA*, pp. 177–78.

25. Above, p. 15.

C. Cassius Longinus shows no links with the *optimates* or their associates. He may have been friendly towards Pompey. He appeared as a witness against Verres in 70 (Cic. *Verr.* 2.3.97) and urged Pompey's commission in 66 (Cic. *Leg. Man.* 68).

72 The consuls Cn. Cornelius Lentulus Clodianus and L. Gellius Publicola appear to have been friends of Pompey. Gellius had been a youthful associate of C. Papirius Carbo, a friend of the Gracchi (Cic. *Brut.* 105). This association would hardly recommend Gellius to Sulla or his allies. In fact, his political career had been severely retarded since his praetorship of 94.[26] As consul, Lentulus, backed by a decree of the Senate, introduced a bill for the collection of payments for the goods of the proscribed, which Sulla had remitted to friendly buyers (Cic. *Verr.* 2.3.81–82; Sall. *Hist.* 4.1 M). The political meaning of this move is difficult to interpret. Several motives may be intertwined. Some senators, perhaps, felt it just; others may have lined up on the basis of struggles between powerful men such as Pompey and Crassus; still others may have had uppermost in mind the practical need for revenue in the face of the continuing war in Spain and the growing threat to Italy posed by Spartacus.[27]

There are other indications, however, that Lentulus and his colleague were friendly toward Pompey. Both of them brought in a law to confirm Pompey's grants of citizenship (Cic. *Balb.* 19, 32, 33).[28] In 70, despite their poor showing against Spartacus and subsequent recall by the Senate in 72, they were elected to the censorship, which had been abandoned since Sulla's time, but which Pompey helped to restore (Cic. *Div. Caec.* 8, *Verr.* 2.5.15, *Cluent.* 117–34, *Flac.* 45, *Dom.* 124; Plut. *Pomp.* 22.5).[29]

It seems clear, despite Meier's recent denial, that the revival of this office was part of Pompey's plan to undercut the power

26. For his praetorship, see Broughton, *MRR* 2, p. 12. That Pompey had been closely tied to Sulla in the 80s should not have stood in the way of a political alliance between Pompey and Lentulus, since Pompey was now in conflict with the most ardent optimate supporters of the Sullan regime.

27. The first two motives are suggested by Gruen, *LGRR*, pp. 36, 39, 41. Crassus, of course, would have been one of those to suffer.

28. That Metellus Pius also enjoyed the right of granting citizenship at that time (Cic. *Arch.* 26, *Balb.* 50) is no obstacle to viewing the consuls' move as pro-Pompeian: see Appendix C, p. 40.

29. Cf. Broughton, *MRR* 2, p. 116 for the last previous election of censors.

of his optimate foes.[30] The holding of a new census was part of growing popular demands (Cic. *Div. Caec.* 8), and the successful completion of this first census since 86 resulted in just what the *optimates* feared, the enrollment of large numbers of new voters owing debts of gratitude to Pompey and his supporters.[31] Moreover, the censors struck from the rolls of the Senate sixty-four members (Liv. *Per.* 98), many of whom must have been Sullan appointees. Many of them had also been involved in the notorious *iudicium Iunianum* of 74 that had added to popular anger at the senatorial juries (Cic. *Cluent.* 72–79, 119–34), whose reform Pompey had supported.[32]

Further evidence also reveals connections between Pompey and both Gellius and Lentulus. Lentulus was prepared to give evidence against the Metelli's friend, Verres, in 70 (Cic. *Verr.* 2.5.15).[33] Both of them were legates of Pompey in 67 (App. *Mith.* 14.95; Flor. 1.41.9).

71 Nothing significant can be deduced about Cn. Aufidius Orestes. He was an Aurelius Orestes by birth (Cic. *Dom.* 35) and, therefore, came from an established consular family. One could postulate support from his optimate *gentiles*, the Aurelii Cottae, but there is no evidence. P. Cornelius Lentulus Sura is also difficult to classify at this time. Through malfeasance as *quaestor urbanus* in 81, he had found disfavor with Sulla (Cic. *Verr.* 2.1.37; Plut. *Cic.* 17.1–2).[34] He was probably no friend of Pompey either, since in the following year he was expelled from the Senate by Gellius and Lentulus (Cic. *Cluent.* 117–34). Perhaps the *optimates* had supported him for the moment in the elections of 72, but by 63 he had joined Catiline's conspiratorial plot (Sall. *Cat.* 17.3). This move would indicate that he saw no political future with either Pompey or any of the *optimates*.

70 That Pompey was a rival of the senior Metelli and the other *optimates* in 70 is argued in Appendix C of this chapter. Crassus, who was Pompey's colleague, also cannot be viewed as enjoying the support of the *optimates* at this time. Despite the fact that he could count on the favor of many senators, his

---

30. Meier *RPA*, p. 269, n. 22.
31. L. R. Taylor, *The Voting Districts of the Roman Republic* (Rome, 1960), p. 120; T. P. Wiseman, "The Census in the First Century B.C.," *Journal of Roman Studies* 59 (1969): 65.
32. For the significance of jury reform, see n. 67, below.
33. For the significance of Verres' trial, see Appendix C, pp. 42–45.
34. Cf. F. Münzer, *RE* 4.1 (1901), 1399.49–61, s.v. "Cornelius" (240).

advocacy of restoring tribunician powers (Liv. *Per.* 97; Pseud. Ascon. *ad Div.* 8, 189 St) would have made him highly suspect in the eyes of loyal *optimates* and their friends, who had yielded reluctantly and only partially on the tribunician issue through C. Aurelius Cotta in 75. Both Crassus and Pompey were eagerly embracing an action that the *optimates* were strenuously resisting.

69 For 69, the *optimates* dominated the consular elections in 70. One consul was the optimate Q. Caecilius Metellus Creticus.[35] The other was Q. Hortensius Hortalus. He was married to Lutatia, sister of Q. Catulus and, perhaps, grand-daughter of a Caecilia Metella.[36] In 77, he and C. Cotta had helped defend Dolabella against Julius Caesar's judicial attack (Cic. *Brut.* 317). He had close ties with L. Lucullus, consul of 74 and firm ally of the Metelli (Plut. *Luc.* 1.5; Cic. *Arch.* 6, cf. *Acad. Pr.* 2.9–10, 148, *Hortensius* frr. 2, 3, 11 Grilli). In 74, with Catulus and Curio, he helped prosecute the troublesome tribune Opimius (Pseud. Ascon. 255 St. *ad Verr.* 2.1.155). In 70, of course, he was Verres' chief counsel (Cic. *Verr.* 1.33–34), and in 67 and 66, he staunchly opposed the *lex Gabinia* and *lex Manilia* for Pompey's commands against the pirates and Mithridates (Cic. *Leg. Man.* 51–52, 56, 64, 66).

68 L. Caecilius Metellus apparently was the brother of Quintus, consul in the previous year, and should be placed in the optimate camp.[37] Q. Marcius Rex was very closely linked with the Claudii Pulchri and the Caecilii Metelli. Although the evidence is not conclusive, he, too, probably should be considered an optimate. His wife was Clodia Tertia, daughter of Ap. Claudius Pulcher (consul in 79) and Caecilia Metella (Plut. *Cic.* 29.4; Dio 36.17.2).[38] His mother-in-law, therefore, was a cousin of his colleague, L. Metellus and his predecessor, Q. Metellus.[39] In the following year, Rex's loyalties under-standably may have been torn between his wife's brother, P. Clodius, and her brother-in-law, L. Lucullus (Sall. *Hist.* 5.14 M; Dio 36.15.1, 17.2), but in the end he remained true to the conservative spirit of the majority of the Metelli and Claudii

35. Broughton, *MRR* 2, p. 131. For the position of this man as a leading optimate, see Appendix A, above, p. 14.
36. See the discussion of Catulus in Appendix A above, pp. 15–16.
37. F. Münzer, *RE* 3.1 (1897), 1204–5, 1210–12, s.v. "Caecilius" (74 and 87).
38. F. Münzer, *RE* 4.1 (1901), 108, s.v. "Clodius" (72); W. C. Dermott, "The Sisters of P. Clodius," *Phoenix* 24 (1970): 39–47.
39. F. Münzer, *RE* 14.2 (1930), 1584.28–40, s.v. "Marcius" (92).

Pulchri and cut P. Clodius out of his will (Cic. *Att.* 1.16.10).[40]

67 C. Calpurnius Piso appears among the optimate opponents of Pompey.[41] He fought vehemently against Gabinius's proposal aimed at giving Pompey command of the pirate war (Dio 36.23.4–24.3; Plut. *Pomp.* 25.4). He tried to block Pompey's recruitment efforts in Gaul (Dio 36.37.2–3; Plut. *Pomp.* 27.1), and he opposed the actions of the Pompeian tribune C. Cornelius (Ascon. *Corn.* 58 C/48 St; Dio 36.38–39). He also thwarted the attempt of Pompey's friend M. Lollius Palicanus to gain a consulship for 66 (Val. Max. 3.8.3; cf. Cic. *Att.* 1.1.1). Finally, in 61, P. Clodius linked him closely with two staunch optimate leaders, L. Lucullus (consul in 74) and Q. Hortensius (consul in 69) (Cic. *Att.* 1.14.5).

Although the consul Acilius Glabrio was once married to Sulla's stepdaughter, Aemilia, daughter of M. Aemilius Scaurus and a Caecilia Metella (Plut. *Sull.* 33.3, *Pomp.* 9.2), he may have been a friend of Pompey by this time. Sulla, at the prompting of the young woman's mother (now his wife), had made Glabrio divorce Aemilia, despite her pregnancy, so that she could marry Pompey (ibid.). This act may have aroused in Glabrio more enmity towards Sulla and his optimate supporters than towards Pompey. Moreover, after Aemilia's unfortunate death, Pompey had married Mucia, who not only remained loyal to Pompey after his break with the majority of the Metellan family, but was related to Glabrio on his mother's side.[42] If, as Klebs assumes, this Acilius Glabrio is the Acilius who had L. Lucullus's curule chair smashed in a fit of pique (Dio 36.41.2),[43] then it would be very reasonable to see Glabrio as a friend of the man who became Lucullus's bitter rival.

Cicero also indicates that, as praetor in charge of Verres' trial, Glabrio was unable to be influenced on behalf of this man closely linked with the Metelli (*Verr.* 1.4, 29, 41, 51–52, 2.130, 2.5.76, 163). That Pompey's friend Gabinius obtained passage of a law to replace Lucullus with Glabrio in command of the Mithridatic War (Cic. *Leg. Man.* 5, 26; Dio 36.14.4,

40. Clodia Tertia, unlike her two sisters, Quarta and Quinta, seems to have been more the example of a sober Roman *matrona* (McDermott, "Sisters," *Phoenix* 24 (1970): 39–47).

41. Cf. E. S. Gruen, "Pompey and the Pisones," *California Studies in Classical Antiquity* 1 (1968): 156–59; R. Syme, "Imperator Caesar: A Study in Nomenclature," *Historia* 7 (1958): 172–73, and "Piso Frugi and Crassus Frugi," *JRS* 50 (1960): 14–20.

42. F. Münzer, *RE* 16.1 (1933), 448–49, s.v. "Mucius" (26 and 28).

43. Klebs, *RE* 1.1 (1894), 257.28–30, s.v. "Acilius" (38).

17.1) is another indication that Glabrio was friendly toward Pompey and hostile to the senior Metelli and other leading *optimates*.[44]

66 M'. Aemilius Lepidus and L. Volcacius Tullus are virtual unknowns before their year of office. This fact makes any connection between them and the *optimates* unlikely. Recent remarks not withstanding,[45] as Sumner has said concerning Lepidus, "Elected in a year dominated by Cn. Pompeius Magnus, it is a fair presumption that he (and his colleague L. Volcacius) benefitted by not being identified with the optimate opposition to Pompeius." [46] Actually, there is good reason to believe that these consuls were both friendly toward Pompey, since they both appeared in support of the Pompeian ex-tribune Cornelius at his first trial for *maiestas* (Ascon. *Corn.* 60 C/49 St).[47]

65 This year is a complicated one because two sets of consuls were elected for it: originally, P. Cornelius Sulla and P. Autronius Paetus; then, after these two were convicted of electoral bribery, L. Aurelius Cotta and L. Manlius Torquatus.[48] Their political allegiances require considerable analysis.

Of the first pair, Syme has tantalizingly suggested that P. Sulla was connected with Pompey through marriage to Pompey's sister, the widow of Pompey's quaestor C. Memmius, who died in 75.[49] This idea rests on two identifications made by Münzer, namely, that C. Memmius L. f. of the tribe Galeria was Pompey's quaestor in 76,[50] and that C. Memmius, the tribune of 54, and the stepson of P. Sulla (Cic. *Q. Fr.* 3.3.2), was this man's son.[51] Wiseman has now constructed a new stemma for the Memmii based on the distinction between the more important branch, belonging to the tribe Menenia, and the lesser branch, belonging to the tribe Galeria.[52] Although he points to the possibility that the tribune

44. Cf. L. Hayne, "The Politics of M'. Glabrio, Cos. 67," CP 69 (1974): 280–82.
45. Seager, "The Tribunate of Cornelius," *Hommages à Marcel Renard* 2 (*Coll. Latomus* 102), p. 685.
46. Sumner, "Manius," *JRS* 54 (1964): 42.
47. Ibid., pp. 41–48.
48. Broughton, MRR 2, p. 157; cf. Chapter Six, p. 148, n. 60.
49. R. Syme, *Sallust* (Berkeley and Los Angeles, 1964), p. 102, n. 88.
50. F. Münzer, RE 15.1 (1931), 607–9, s.v. "Memmius" (6, 7).
51. Ibid., 616, s.v. "Memmius" (9).
52. T. P. Wiseman, "Prosopographical Notes." Appendix Two of M. H. Crawford, "The Coinage of the Age of Sulla," *Numismatic Chronicle* 4 (1964): 156–57.

of 54 was the son of Pompey's quaestor, this identification is not necessary. Within the basic structure of Wiseman's stemma, it is possible that Pompey's quaestor was the son of an unrecorded son of L. Memmius C.f. Men., the *praetorius* of 129,[53] while the tribune of 54 may have been the son of an unrecorded son of C. Memmius, the tribune of 111. This solution is less economical than Wiseman's, but, for lack of any other evidence, it cannot be excluded.

On purely prosopographical grounds, therefore, we are at an impasse. The political associations of P. Sulla and his stepson may be revealed through their actions. Memmius had long been known as a supporter of the *optimates* (Cic. *Rab. Post.* 7). In 54, both he and his stepfather laid a charge of *ambitus* against A. Gabinius (Cic. *Q. Fr.* 3.1.15, 2.1, 3.2), who had been Pompey's protegé as consul (Plut. *Pomp.* 48.3, *Cat. Min.* 33.4; Dio 38.9.1) and whom Pompey vigorously protected with all of his resources (Cic. *Att.* 4.18.1, *Q. Fr.* 3.4.1; Dio 39.62.3–63.5). Pompey's relatives or not, their actions do not seem compatible with the view that P. Sulla and his stepson were supporters of Pompey. Still, the possibility of some favorable connection with Pompey in 66 cannot be ruled out.

Any possible connection with Pompey notwithstanding, however, in the elections of 66, P. Sulla was probably a principal choice of the *optimates*. He was a *propinquus* of Sulla the dictator (Cic. *Off.* 2.29), who had benefited the *optimates*.[54] At his trial in 62, he was defended not only by Cicero (who had fallen from Pompey's favor after his much-vaunted consulship), but also by Hortensius, whose loyalty to the optimate cause is clear.[55] He was also supported at his trial by many other *ornamenta ac lumina rei publicae* (Cic. *Sull.* 5).

Again, it must be remembered that Sulla was a man of many connections. It is quite possible that Crassus aided him, too. That Sulla enjoyed aid from many sides may be indicated by his plurality among all the centuries (Cic. *Sull.* 91).

As for P. Autronius Paetus, although he probably was a

53. Taylor suggests that the praetor or pro-praetor honored in Egypt in 112 may have been the son of the *praetorius* of 129: VDRR pp. 233–34.

54. Dio (36.44.3) calls him a nephew (ἀδελφιδοῦς), but the exact relationship is not clear: cf. F. Münzer, RE 4.1 (1901), 1518.56–1519.5, s.v. "Cornelius" (385–86).

55. See the discussion of Hortensius under the year 69, above.

legate of M. Antonius Creticus in 73,[56] there is no good reason to believe that many *optimates* would have supported him for the consulship. In view of the elections of Glabrio, M? Lepidus, and Volcacius Tullus, it seems better to link this relative light-weight in Roman politics primarily to Pompey or some others outside the main optimate circles. Indeed, Crassus should not be ruled out as one who supported his election.[57]

Of the second pair, it is argued in Appendix A of this chapter that L. Cotta probably enjoyed strong optimate support for the consulship.[58] Torquatus, on the other hand, can definitely be linked with Pompey. His wife came from Pompey's bailiwick of Picenum (Cic. *Sull.* 25), and he had been a legate with Pompey in 67.[59] Pompey, therefore, might not have been displeased to see Torquatus's son prosecute Sulla and pave the way for the election of a man more closely identified with himself.

64   L. Julius Caesar must have had powerful backing, for his election was a foregone conclusion to Cicero in 65 (*Att.* 1.1.2). It is quite possible that the leading *optimates* and their friends were prominent among these backers. His father joined Marius's enemies by 90 [60] and was killed by the Marians in 87 (Cic. *de Or.* 3.10, *Tusc.* 5.55; Liv. *Per.* 80; Val. Max. 9.2.2). Moreover, he was a first cousin of Q. Lutatius Catulus, already shown to be a leading optimate.[61]

Perhaps the *optimates* made a concerted effort to get two men elected for 64. C. Marcius Figulus's family was closely connected with his colleague's.[62] Certainly the actions of both men showed an optimate bias. Under these consuls, the Senate passed decrees limiting the number of attendants upon electoral candidates and outlawing the political clubs, *collegia*, that were then making it difficult for the *optimates* to get favored candidates elected (Cic. *Mur.* 71, *Pis.* 8; Ascon. *ad Pis.* 8, 7 C/15 St).

63   Sallust (*Cat.* 23.5–6) and many modern writers claim

56. Broughton, MRR 2, p. 112.
57. Syme, *Sallust*, p. 103, n. 2.
58. See above, pp. 18–19.
59. Syme, *Sallust*, pp. 149, 151, n. 16.
60. Badian, "Caepio and Norbanus," *Studies*, pp. 337–38/*Historia* 6 (1957): 52–53.
61. See the discussion of Catulus in Appendix A of this chapter, pp. 15–16. L. Caesar's father was L. Caesar, consul in 90 (F. Münzer, *RE* 10.1 [1918], 468, s.v. "Julius" [143]) and half-brother of Catulus's father (Cic. *de Or.* 2.12, 44, 3.9–10, *Off.* 1.133, *Dom.* 114).
62. F. Münzer, *RE* 14.2 (1930), 1559–60, s.v. "Marcius" (63).

that the optimate nobility united behind Cicero's candidacy out of fear of Catiline and Antonius.[63] Cicero, however, was strongly identified with Pompey in this campaign (Cic. *Att.* 1.1.2, *Leg. Agr.* 2.49; Q. Cic. *Comm. Pet.* 5, 14–15, 51). He was hard put to convince most optimate nobles to support him (Q. Cic. *Comm. Pet.* 13–14; cf. Cic. *Att.* 1.1.2). It is highly doubtful that he could ever have convinced Pompey's inveterate foes among the *optimates* to support him. Indeed, Cicero even passed up an opportunity to take on a case in the interest of L. Lucullus, P. Scipio Nasica (soon to be Q. Caecilius Metellus Scipio), and Lucullus's *familiaris*, Q. Caecilius (Cic. *Att.* 1.1.3; Nep. *Att.* 5.1). He felt that the people on the other side were more valuable, especially L. Domitius Ahenobarbus, who appears to have been one of the few men from the high nobility really to support his candidacy (Cic. *Att.* 1.1.3–4).

If, after Cicero's speech *In Toga Candida*, most of the *optimates* supported any one of the candidates, that man probably would not have been C. Antonius or Cicero. The latter achieved his goal mainly through a combination of Pompey's supporters and his own *clientela* won in the law courts or courted in the Italian towns. Antonius, to be sure, does have some links with the *optimates*. His father had supported the Metelli against Marius in the previous generation,[64] and Asconius says that it was his father's reputation that made the difference between him and Catiline (*Tog. Cand.* 94 C/72 St). Antonius had followed Sulla and been removed from the Senate by the Pompeian censors of 70 (ibid., 84 C/65 St). Nevertheless, his major support seems to have come from Crassus and Crassus's ally, Caesar (see Chapter Six, pp. 145–51). Therefore, it is difficult to see many *optimates* promoting his election in 64. Despite the weaknesses seen by Cicero, the patrician P. Sulpicius Galba or the noble plebeian L. Cassius Longinus may well have attracted the favor of leading *optimates* (cf. Cic. *Att.* 1.1.1; Ascon. *Tog. Cand.* 82 C/64 St). Or, perhaps they supported C. Licinius Sacerdos, who, although not a man of the first rank, had recently been a legate of Metellus Creticus (cf. Ascon., ibid.; Cic. *Planc.* 27).

63. Cf., e.g., L. A. Thompson, "Cicero the Politician," *Studies in Cicero*, ed. J. Ferguson et al. (Rome, 1962), p. 58. Plutarch (*Cic.* 10.1) also seems to follow Sallust.

64. Badian, "Caepio and Norbanus," *Studies*, pp. 341–44/*Historia* 6 (1957): 56–57.

62 D. Junius Silanus must have counted Crassus and
Caesar among his supporters. His failure in his canvass of 64
(cf. Cic. *Att.* 1.1.2) indicates a lack of optimate backing, despite
his connection with Cato. He was able to reach his goal in 63
only by extensive bribery, prosecution for which he escaped
solely because he was Cato's brother-in-law (Cic. *Mur.* 82;
Plut. *Cic.* 14.6, *Cat. Min.* 21.2). That he had backing from
Crassus and Caesar is indicated by both his heavy use of
bribery and his switch to Caesar's side in the debate on the
fate of the Catilinarian conspirators in 63 (Suet. *Iul.* 14.1; Plut.
Cic. 21.3, *Cat. Min.* 22.3–5).

L. Licinius Murena probably was strongly backed by the
optimates, despite evidence that might suggest a link with
Crassus. Although his branch of the Licinii had never before
produced a consul (Cic. *Mur.* 15, 55, 83), he was closely connected with L. Lucullus and had served with him in Asia
(ibid., 20). Both Murena and his father had served under
Sulla (App. *Mith.* 5.32, 9.64–66; Plut. *Sull.* 17.3–7, 18.2, 19.2–
4; Cic. *Mur.* 11–12). At his trial in 63, the *optimates'* chief
advocate, Hortensius, was one of his defenders (Cic. *Mur.* 10).
On the other hand, one of Murena's prosecutors and his
closest competitor in the consular elections, Ser. Sulpicius
Rufus, was supported by Cicero and the younger Cato, who
was aspiring to the optimate leadership.[65]

61 M. Valerius Messalla Niger, although the first of his
family to reach the consulship in a hundred years, was clearly
an optimate consul (Cic. *Att.* 1.13.3, 14.6). Sulla, perhaps
because of the connection through his fifth wife, Valeria, had
rejuvenated the fortunes of this decayed patrician family.[66]
A connection with the Metelli can be seen in Messalla's cooperation during the defense of Roscius of Ameria in 80 (Cic.
Rosc. Am. 149).[67] He had been expelled from the Senate by
the Pompeian censors of 70 (Val. Max. 2.9.9). Finally, in 62,

65. B. Kübler, *RE* 4A.1 (1931), 852–53, s.v. "Sulpicius" (95). Servius
Sulpicius Rufus's political career was successfully resumed with Pompey's
support only after Pompey had gained influence with the *optimates*
against Caesar. Therefore, no connection should be made between him
and Pompey in 62. For further discussion of Silenus and Murena, however, see Chapter Seven, pp. 170–72.
66. R. Syme, "Missing Senators," *Historia* 4 (1955): 70–71; "Review
of A. E. Gordon, *Potitius Valerius Messalla Consul Suffect 29 B.C.*,"
Journal of Roman Studies 45 (1955): 156–57.
67. For the role of the Metelli in this trial, see A. M. Ward, "The
Early Relationships Between Cicero and Pompey until 80 B.C.," *Phoenix*
24 (1970): 127–28.

he was one of those who obtained Cicero's services for P.
Sulla (Cic. *Sull.* 20).[68]

M. Pupius Piso Frugi, on the other hand, was clearly Pompey's man.[69] He had been a *legatus pro praetore* under Pompey
in 67.[70] Five years later, he was avidly promoted for the
consulship by Pompey (Plut. *Pomp.* 44.1–3, *Cat. Min.* 30.1–4).
After being elected, Pupius Piso proposed the settlement of Asia
according to Pompey's wishes and rendered service to Pompey
throughout his year in office.[71]

60 The consuls of 60 were clearly split between a Pompeian and one of Pompey's optimate opponents. Q. Caecilius
Metellus Celer was no longer closely bound to Pompey after
the latter divorced Mucia. He became completely identified
with the other Metelli and their friends in their bitter opposition to his former brother-in-law (Dio 37.49.3–50.6; cf.
Cic. *Att.* 1.12.3; Plut. *Pomp.* 42.7).[72] In contrast, L. Afranius
was a faithful follower of Pompey for his whole active life
(Plut. *Sert.* 19, *Caes.* 53.2–3; Cic. *Fam.* 9.18.2; [Caes.] *BAfr.*
95; Suet. *Iul.* 75). In 61, Pompey scandalously lobbied for his
election to the consulship (Cic. *Att.* 1.16.12; Plut. *Pomp.* 44.3–
4, *Cat. Min.* 30.5).

From this study of the forty-four men elected consul for the
years 80 to 60,[73] it is clear that a fairly well-defined optimate

68. Apparently, he switched his allegiance sometime in 60, for in 59,
he appears as one of Caesar's land-commissioners. He was also an interrex
and censor in 55 (Broughton, MRR 2, pp. 192, 215, 217).

69. He is often assigned a second cognomen, Calpurnianus, (cf.
Broughton, MRR 2, 178), but D. R. Shackleton Bailey sees no basis for
it (*Cicero's Letters to Atticus* 1 [Cambridge, 1965], p. 303, comments
ad ep. 1.13). For further light on this man, see E. Badian, "M. Calpurnius M. F. Piso Frugi," *Acta of the Fifth Epigraphic Congress* (1967):
209–14.

70. Broughton, MRR 2, p. 149.

71. H. Gundel, RE 23.2 (1959), 1989.55–1990.60, s.v. "Pupius,"
(10); R. Syme, *The Roman Revolution* (Oxford, 1939), p. 33. Meier,
RPA, p. 19, says that Piso evidently received valuable support from his
cousin C. Calpurnius Piso (consul 67), Pompey's enemy, because C.
Piso was given first place in senatorial debate for after 61 (cf. Cic. *Att.*
1.13.2 and the comments by Shackleton Bailey, *Letters to Atticus*, p.
303.) There is no need to see Calpurnius Piso supporting Pupius Piso
Frugi's election. It could be that Pompey and Pupius Piso Frugi were
trying to neutralize Calpurnius Piso's opposition to Pompey in the
Senate by honoring him with the position of primacy in senatorial debate
and were trying to undermine the standing of Cicero, who had expected
the position himself.

72. For the relationship of Metellus Celer to Pompey and his estrangement from the senior Metelli and their associates, between 78 and 61,
see the main text of this chapter, p. 12, n. 22.

73. Exclusive of the poorly attested suffect consul of 68.

group, linked together by birth, marriage, friendship, and loyalty to the Sullan constitution, maintained a strong grip on the consulship that could be broken only by an occasional turn of fortune or by the tenacious efforts of ambitious and resourceful individuals, such as Crassus, Cicero, Pompey, or, as in the elections of 60, Caesar.[74]

74. Of course, one must bear in mind the qualification raised at the end of the main text of this chapter, p. 13, n. 25.

Appendix I-C

Pompey and the Optimates

Despite the continuing loyalty of Metellus Celer and
Metellus Nepos after 77, the senior members of the Caecilii
Metelli and other leading *optimates* opposed Pompey.[1] The
bulk of the evidence points to a break between Pompey and
the leading *optimates* in 77 over the question of Pompey's
command against Sertorius.[2] Pompey's deference to Metellus
Pius during the Civil War in 82 (Plut. *Pomp.* 8.4–5) has no
bearing on their relationship in 77, after Sulla's death. Fresh
from his suppression of Lepidus's supporters, Pompey, despite
the opposition of the proconsul, Q. Catulus, kept his men
under arms near Rome and agitated for a command against
Sertorius in Spain (ibid., 17.3–4). To be sure, Metellus Pius
had been having a difficult time against Sertorius since 79
(ibid., 17.1–2, *Sert.* 12.4–13.6; Sall. *Hist.* 1.110–21 M; App. *BC*
1.13.108, *Ib.* 16.101). There is, however, no indication that he
was calling for reinforcements from home in 77.[3] Yet, even
if it is granted that Metellus was looking for reinforcements

1. Pompey's marriage to Cornelia, the daughter of Q. Caecilius Metellus Scipio Nasica, in 52 cannot be used to infer continued good relations
between Pompey and the majority of the Metelli and other staunchly
conservative *optimates* during the 70s and 60s. The situation by 52 had
changed completely again with the dramatic growth of Caesar's power.
Therefore, his former opponents among the *optimates* found it mutually
advantageous to join forces once more.

2. Recently, two strong positions have been taken against this view:
E. S. Gruen, "Pompey, Metellus Pius, and the Trials of 70–69 B.C.:
The Perils of Schematism," *American Journal of Philology* 92 (1971):
1–9, and B. L. Twyman, "The Metelli, Pompeius and Prosopography,"
Aufstieg und Niedergang der Römischen Welt 1.1 (Berlin and New York,
1972), pp. 839–62.

3. Sallust (*Hist.* 2.32 M) does not refer to any need for aid on
Metellus's part in 77, but does to Pompey's need for assistance at the
battle of Lauron in 76 (B. Maurenbrecher, *C. Sallusti Crispi Historiarum
Reliquiae* [Leipzig, 1891], 71). Actually, until 75, Metellus seems to
have relied on resources nearer to hand than Rome and the Senate. In
79, he called on the proconsul of Nearer Spain, Domitius, for assistance
(Sall. *Hist.* 1.111 M; Plut. *Sert.* 12.4). In 78, L. Manlius, the proconsul
of Gallia Transalpina, lent his aid (Plut. ibid.). In 77, Metellus captured
Dipo in Lusitania without aid and found winter quarters at Corduba
(Sall. *Hist.* 1.113, 2.28 M). In 76, the province of Gallia Transalpina
supplied him with what he needed (ibid., 2.98.9 M).

from Rome in 77, it is not to say that he would have welcomed a proconsular colleague, who would have received equal credit for ending the war.

The order of the proconsul Catulus that Pompey disband his army is best interpreted as a move in favor of Metellus Pius's desire not to have Pompey as a colleague against Sertorius. It cannot be explained by arguing that Catulus may have opposed the *imperium*, but the consuls, in effect, made it possible by resigning their posts.[4] If Metellus had wanted Pompey as a colleague, Pompey would not have had to agitate for the command, and Catulus, who was always a loyal supporter of the other leading *optimates*, would not have opposed him.[5] Sumner's analysis that the consuls refused commands against Sertorius in deference to Metellus still appears correct.[6]

If Metellus had wanted a colleague, Catulus, who was already a proconsul and had equally distinguished himself in battle against Lepidus, was readily available (Sall. *Hist.* 1.77.22 M; Liv. *Per.* 90; Val. Max. 2.8.7; Plut. *Pomp.* 17.3; App. *BC* 1.107). Yet there is no indication anywhere that Catulus was even suggested. On the other hand, there is clear evidence of stiff opposition to Pompey from others in the Senate besides Catulus (Plut. *Pomp.* 17.4; Cic. *Leg. Man.* 62, *Phil.* 11.18). Granted, there is no need to conjure up a vision of a Sullan coalition seeking to deny Pompey the Spanish command.[7] Rather, this opposition is a perfectly good example of rivalry among different groups of Sulla's old optimate supporters. Marcius Philippus, who gained fame as one of Pompey's backers in senatorial debate (Cic. *Leg. Man.* 62, *Phil.* 11.18;

4. Gruen, "Pompey, Metellus Pius," *AJP* 92 (1971): 5.
5. Twyman's argument that Pompey was backed by a Claudio-Metellan faction and opposed by a faction of Catulus fails to take into account the evidence linking Catulus with the leading Metelli: see above, n. 1 and Appendix A, pp. 15–16.
6. Sumner, "Manius," *JRS* 54 (1964): 46. The possibility that Metellus's critics could have persuaded the Senate to bestow an independent, proconsular command on a private citizen who was not even a senator must have seemed remote to his supporters (cf. Last, *CAH* 9 [1932], pp. 317–18). Such a move would seem extreme, whatever measures Sulla had provided for defense in critical situations. In earlier times, *privati* who were granted proconsular *imperium* had previously held a magistracy, even Scipio Africanus in 210, who had been curule aedile in 213 (cf. W. F. Jashemski, *The Origins and History of the Proconsular and the Propraetorian Imperium to 27 B.C.* [Chicago, 1950], 91–92; Broughton, *MRR* 1, 263). Moreover, no *privatus*, except Marius, seems to have been granted proconsular *imperium* since 198 (Jashemski, ibid., pp. 39 and 92).
7. Gruen, "Pompey, Metellus Pius," *AJP* 92 (1971): 5; cf. 5–7.

Plut. *Pomp.* 17.4), had been a trusted legate of Sulla in 82 (Liv. *Per.* 86). In this debate, he and a majority of the other senators (many of whom owed their positions to Sulla) were able to override the wishes of more conservative *optimates*.

Now that the revolt of Lepidus had been crushed in Italy, more and more of the senators must have become impatient with Metellus's lack of progress in Spain. Pompey was a proven general, popular with many senators,[8] and eager to fight Sertorius. Despite Metellus and his friends, Philippus's proposal to give Pompey a proconsular command against Sertorius met with the approval of a majority of the Sullan Senate. Naturally, Pompey went as a loyal supporter of this Senate.[9]

The argument that once Pompey received the command, there were no clandestine maneuvers at home to sabotage him is plausible.[10] When he wrote his famous letter of 75 (Sall. *Hist.* 2.98 M), there were grave financial exigencies and even famine at Rome because of war, the necessity of maintaining armies in Asia and Cilicia, and the inability to safeguard supplies by sea (ibid., 2.45, 47 M). Both commanders in Spain were now requesting money, men, arms, and food (ibid., 2.47.6 M). The generally straitened circumstances, therefore, could help to account for the Senate's failure to heed Pompey's repeated requests for aid.

Nevertheless, supporters of Metellus, like Lucullus and the Cottae, may well have turned Rome's misfortunes to their advantage by persuading the Senate, with its resources severely limited, to grant only the requests of Metellus, who had been in the field longer, rather than to send aid to the more recently commissioned Pompey. C. Cotta, in his apologetic speech to the people, said that the commanders in Spain had requested aid but gave no indication as to actions taken or not taken (ibid.). Actually, Metellus seems to have acquired money in 76 (ibid., 2.34 M), while Pompey did not.[11] If Mauren-

8. Ibid., p. 6.

9. His desire was to become the leader of the Senate, not to destroy it. Cf. W. E. Caldwell, "An Estimate of Pompey," *Studies Presented to David Moore Robinson* (St. Louis, 1953), 954–61.

10. Gruen, "Pompey, Metellus Pius," *AJP* 92 (1971): 7–8.

11. An issue of silver denarii bearing the legend Q. C[aecilius] M[etellus] P[ius] I[mperator] may be identical with this money mentioned by Sallust. Unfortunately, the date of issuance cannot be firmly fixed. E. A. Sydenham dates it to 79 or 78: *The Roman Republican Coinage*, rev. ed. (London, 1952), p. 122, no. 750. Th. Mommsen places it in 75: *Geschichte des römischen Münzwesens* (Berlin, 1860), p. 612, no. 244 and n. 425. It could also be dated to any time from the

brecher's chronology is correct, Pompey continued in difficulties during the winter of 74/3, while Metellus was well-off (cf. ibid., 2.70, 3.46 M).[12]

Certainly Sallust's version of Licinius Macer's speech in 73 makes it clear that Pompey was being sabotaged at home (ibid., 3.48.21 M). His rendering of Pompey's letter of 75 also indicates that Pompey was a victim of more than simple neglect:

> *Si adversus vos patriamque at deos penatis tot labores et
> pericula suscepissem, quotiens a prima adulescentia ductu
> meo scelestissimi hostes fusi et vobis salus quaesita est, nihil
> amplius in absentem me statuissetis, quam adhuc agitis,
> patres conscripti, quem contra aetatem proiectum ad bellum
> saevissumum cum exercitu optime merito, quantum est in
> vobis, fame, miserrima omnium morte, confecistis. Hacine
> spe populus Romanus liberos suos ad bellum misit? Haec
> sunt praemia pro volneribus et totiens ob rem publicam fuso
> sanguine? Fessus scribendo mittendoque legatos omnis opes
> et spes privatas meas consumpsi, cum interim a vobis per
> triennium vix annuus sumptus datus est! Per deos immortalis,
> utrum censetis vicem me aerari praestare an exercitum sine
> frumento et stipendio habere posse? (Sall. Hist. 2.98.1–3 M)*

With proper allowance for rhetorical license on Sallust's part, Pompey had apprised the Senate of his desperation several times before, and, contrary to assertion,[13] the response was not swift when news of his plight reached Rome. Indeed, C. Cotta's speech earlier in 75, before the receipt of this letter, indicates awareness of Pompey's previous requests (ibid., 2.47.6 M).[14] It was only after repeated pleas and the thinly veiled threat at the end of the letter to let the war spill over into Italy (ibid., 2.98.8–10 M) that senators like L. Lucullus and M. Cotta took meaningful action. Although Sallust does

---

winter of 74/3 to the end of 71, when Metellus had access to the famous gold and silver mines that were located in the southwestern corner of his own province of Farther Spain. For the location of the mines, see S. G. Checkland, *The Mines of Tharsis* (London, 1967), pp. 35–40.

12. Maurenbrecher, *C. Sallusti Crispi*, p. 126, commentary on fr. 3.46. The reports of Metellus's luxurious living during the winter of 74/3 (Sall. *Hist.* 2.70 M; Plut. *Sert.* 22.2–3) were, no doubt, exaggerated by his enemies, but they must have been based on some disparity between his situation and Pompey's.

13. Gruen, "Pompey, Metellus Pius," *AJP* 92 (1971): 7–8.

14. It seems reasonable to include Pompey among the unnamed *imperatores* to whom Cotta referred.

not exactly parallel Plutarch and say that Lucullus was anxious to keep Pompey in Spain in order to have a free hand in obtaining a command against Mithridates (ibid., 2.98. *fin.* M; Plut. *Pomp.* 20.1, *Luc.* 5.2–3), he does make it clear that it was not only the state's welfare but also private ambitions that prompted the consuls to help him (*Hist.* 2.98. *fin.* M). Furthermore, he implies that many of the nobles who now supported their efforts had not been sincere in any verbal support of Pompey prior to his last letter.[15] Therefore, there is good reason to believe that many *optimates* had been working to Pompey's disadvantage at Rome.

The admitted rivalry between Pompey and Metellus in Spain (Plut. *Pomp.* 19.1) hardly inspires confidence in the view that Pompey's appointment did not rankle with Metellus.[16] Metellus and Pompey did make a public show of solidarity, however (Plut. *Pomp.* 19.5). That kind of a display is good for the morale of troops and is prudent policy in the midst of hostile territory. It is not necessarily a true indication of private feelings. There are several reasons for Metellus's decision to leave the final operations in Spain to Pompey in 72 (App. *BC* 1.13.115). Metellus had already earned a triumph, and Sertorius, the great adversary, was now dead, having been treacherously assassinated (ibid., 1.13.113).[17] Pompey's exploits, too, had already guaranteed him a triumph. No great glory would be attached to defeating Sertorius's less accomplished assassin, Perperna (Plut. *Sert.* 27.1; App. *BC* 1.13.115).[18] Metellus's presence in his own province may well have been required by pressing administrative problems subsequent to the surrender of rebellious tribes there.[19] Lastly, an

15. It is interesting that in 75, the populace took out its frustrations on the consuls, C. Cotta and L. Octavius, as they were escorting Q. Caecilius Metellus (Creticus), who was a candidate for the praetorship, and almost lynched them (Sall. *Hist.* 2.45 M).

16. Cf. Gruen, "Pompey, Metellus Pius," *AJP* 92 (1971): 7.

17. Sertorius's assassination has usually been placed in 72 on the basis of Appian (*BC* 1.13.113), but W. H. Bennett has argued that it occurred sometime in the first half of 73: "The Death of Sertorius and the Coin," *Historia* 10 (1961): 459–72.

18. Though clearly not so inspiring a leader as Sertorius, Perperna may not have been so inferior a general as our hostile tradition has presented him. Cf. Bennett, ibid.

19. Metellus's province was Hispania Ulterior and Pompey's was Hispania Citerior (T. Rice Holmes, *The Roman Republic* 1 [Oxford, 1923], 380). After Sertorius was assassinated at Osca (Huesca), a town in Hispania Citerior (Strabo 3.4.10; Vell. Pat. 2.30.1), many places throughout Spain surrendered (Plut. *Sert.* 27.1).

experienced and cautious politician like Metellus Pius may have wished to avoid the difficult problem of dealing with captured Roman citizens and possible documents embarrassing to powerful figures at home. He might have hoped that his younger rival would undo himself here, although the actual event proved otherwise (Plut. *Sert.* 27.2–3).

Nor can it be argued that because Metellus Pius also enjoyed the right of granting citizenship, the proposal of the consuls Lentulus and Gellius in 72 to give Pompey this right is no indication of rivalry (cf. Cic. *Balb.* 19, 32, 33, 50, *Arch.* 26). There is no evidence for assuming that Metellus received the privilege at the same time as Pompey. On the contrary, Cicero plainly states that in granting Balbus citizenship, Pompey was simply following the precedent set by others, including Metellus (*Balb.* 50–51). Cicero's references to the *lex Gellia et Cornelia* in the *Pro Balbo* (19, 32, 33) clearly indicate that it was passed for Pompey's sole benefit. Gellius and Lentulus, therefore, seem to have helped Pompey in the Senate by obtaining an explicit decree confirming him in the same right of granting citizenship that Metellus had previously exercised. Similarly, the equal treatment of both men as regards triumphs and land grants to their veterans need not indicate lack of contention, but rather the relative equality of their support in the Senate.[20]

On balance, therefore, the argument that Pompey's command against Sertorius in 77 signalled a break with Metellus Pius and other leading *optimates* is much stronger than the argument that there was no friction over Pompey's command. By 71 at the latest, a break must have been evident. Surely, no one can doubt that in 71, Pompey's brazen demand for a consulship frightened and angered most of the conservative optimate nobility and their followers. Admittedly, extraordinary military commands were not uncharacteristic of the Sullan regime;[21] elections to the consulship without prior fulfillment of the strict requirements of the *cursus honorum* laid

20. Cf. Gruen, "Pompey, Metellus Pius," *AJP* 92 (1971): 9. That the Senate voted land grants for the veterans of both Pompey and Metellus is also no indication of good will between the two, since funds were not provided to make the grants (Dio 38.5.1). Indeed, since Pompey, as a challenger to the entrenched *optimates*, was dependent on the loyal veterans for political support much more than Metellus was, the Senate's failure to provide money for operation of the land law was detrimental to Pompey, but not to Metellus.

21. Gruen, "Pompey, Metellus Pius," *AJP* 92 (1971): 6.

down by Sulla were.[22] These requirements were made to protect the power of the Sullan oligarchy from overly ambitious men.[23] The optimate leaders and their close friends had been among the chief beneficiaries of the Sullan dispensation and had provided a large majority of the consuls up to this point.[24] Indeed, Q. Caecilius Metellus (Creticus) probably would have been elected one of the consuls for 70 if it had not been for Pompey. He had already met the legal requirements for the office and was duly elected for 69.[25] Since he was the older man and from a much more distinguished family, he is not likely to have stepped aside willingly in favor of Pompey's candidacy in 71.[26]

In 70, therefore, Pompey assumed his unprecedented consulship. The first thing that he did was to guarantee his military and political future by bringing in successful legislation to restore the full powers of the tribunate.[27] In this way, he could count on using friendly tribunes to obtain for him what the optimate-dominated magistrates and Senate would not grant.

Despite recent denials, this move was a great blow to the Sullan constitution and the optimate oligarchy.[28] From this point on, men like Pompey, Clodius, and Caesar were able to use the tribunate to thwart much of the opposition to their personal ambitions. Catulus was definitely opposed to the idea of a fully restored tribunate but admitted that the pressure for restoration was too great (Cic. *Verr.* 1.44).[29] However much Catulus and the other *optimates* objected, there was no way to stop Pompey. He was a very popular military hero who

22. Cf. Cic. *Leg. Man.* 62. Sulla had made this point very clear with his summary execution of Lucretius Ofella, who had insisted upon a consular canvass, despite Sulla's objections (Plut. *Sull.* 33.4). Although Plutarch does not state the grounds for Sulla's objections, lack of prerequisite offices seems certain, since the only record of Ofella's earlier career is a prefecture in 82 (Broughton, *MRR* 2, p. 72).

23. Last, *CAH* 9 (1932), pp. 288–91.

24. See Appendix B for the years 80 to 71.

25. Broughton, *MRR* 2, p. 108, n. 3; 131.

26. Badian, *FC*, p. 282.

27. Although Crassus cooperated in passing this measure, the law went under Pompey's name alone: W. C. McDermott, "LEX POMPEIA DE TRIBUNICIA POTESTATE (70 B.C.)," *Classical Philology* 72 (1977): 49–52. See also Chapter Five, p. 104.

28. Gruen, *LGRR*, p. 28; U. Laffi, "Il Mito di Silla," *Athenaeum* 55 (1967): 203–5.

29. He may have hoped that the promise of jury reform would have undercut support for the restoration of the full tribunician powers: *quodsi in rebus iudicandis populi Romani existimationi satis facere voluissent, non tanto opere homines fuisse tribuniciam potestatem desideraturos* (Cic. *Verr.* 1.44).

counted many veterans from the Sertorian war among his supporters. The common people greatly favored the restoration of
the full powers to an office that they deeply cherished.[30] As
consul, Pompey had the legal authority to lay the matter before a legislative assembly. Only civil war could have blocked
him in his desire to allow expression of the popular will. His
optimate opponents were not prepared to take such a course
only a little more than ten years after the destructive Civil
War that they had experienced. They were willing to accept
the lesser of two evils, but they would not have disliked Pompey any less for forcing them to make such a choice.[31]

Despite recent vigorous denials, evidence of the rift between
Pompey and his former optimate allies in the 70s is also found
in the famous trial of Verres in 70.[32] Of course, the senior
Metelli and other *optimates* involved would have come to the
aid of their relative and friend Verres whether or not Pompey's interests were involved. The point is that Pompey's interests *were* involved. This fact gave the case its political
dimension. No one claims that Verres' depredations were
politically motivated or guided. Badian has already pointed out
that Verres was not particular about whose clients he injured
in Sicily.[33] As Cicero demonstrates (*Div. Caec.* 4–33), the
Metelli and other *optimates* were willing to sacrifice their
clients in order to protect Verres, who was much more important to them.[34] Pompey, however, could not afford to ignore
the plight of his Sicilian clients if he were to maintain his

30. For the history of popular agitation concerning the office of tribune
after Sulla, see Gruen, LGRR, pp. 23–28.

31. A similar situation existed in relation to Pompey's support for
reform of the Sullan juries, another move inimical to the interests of the
optimates (Cic. *Verr.* 1.45). Gruen has sought to play down the importance of this move (ibid., 34–35). He fails to take into account,
however, that in 74, when Quinctius used the outrageous case of Op-
pianicus to create such a furor that the Senate voted to look into the
matter, it was the optimate consuls, L. Lucullus and M. Cotta, who
conveniently delayed action on the decree (Cic. *Cluent.* 136–37). Although the fragmentary evidence for the intervening years preserves no
further instances of popular discontent with senatorial juries, we have
the authority of Catulus that it was a live issue with the public in 71
(Cic. *Verr.* 1.44). When Pompey declared his intention to do something
about it (ibid., 45), the *optimates* were forced to produce L. Cotta's
compromise, which kept one-third of the jury seats for senators.

32. Gruen, "Pompey, Metellus Pius," *AJP* 92 (1971): 9–12; LGRR,
p. 45, n. 137.

33. Badian, FC, p. 282.

34. M. Lucullus is the only one who is elsewhere associated with
Verres' optimate supporters (see Appendix B, under the year 73) and
supported one of his clients against Verres (Cic. *Verr.* 2.2.23–24).

standing as an important political as well as military figure in his struggle for prominence against the entrenched optimate nobles.

The case for Pompey's involvement in the prosecution of Verres rests on more than the involvement of Sthenius.[35] Numerous Sicilians had sought help from Pompey against Verres (Cic. *Verr.* 2.3.45, 204). Cicero made prominent mention of a number of Pompey's clie.its who bore witness against Verres and helped gather the n(cessary evidence against him despite the obstacles thrown up by his friends: Sextus Pompeius Chlorus (*Verr.* 2.2.23, 102), Cn. Pompeius Theodorus (ibid., 102), Cn. Pompeius Basiliscus (ibid., 4.25), the Pompeii Percennii (ibid.), and Cn. Pompeius Philo (ibid., 48). These clients show that Pompey's interests were involved. He could not afford to sacrifice them, and, as an added benefit, he would have earned the gratitude of the clients of Verres' optimate defenders, who had not been able to get the support of their patrons against Verres.[36]

Sthenius, of course, is prominent. Late in 72, while Pompey was still in Spain, he went to Rome to ask his friends for protection against Verres. The consuls, Lentulus and Gellius, who had been favorable to Pompey earlier in the year, made an immediate proposal to aid him (Cic. *Verr.* 2.2.95).[37] They may have made their proposal simply because they were the consuls,[38] but it is also possible that they chose to act because they were favorable to Pompey and his clients. Likewise, that Sthenius also sought the help of Pompey's friend, the tribune Lollius Palicanus, in 71 is significant despite the fact that Palicanus's motion on his behalf was unanimously approved by all ten tribunes (Cic. *Verr.* 2.2.100).[39] Sthenius's choice of

35. Contra Gruen, "Pompey, Metellus Pius," *AJP* 92 (1971): 11.

36. The Claudii Marcelli, another family with close Sicilian ties, did support their clients against Verres (Cic. *Div. Caec.* 13–14, *Verr.* 2.1.35; cf. Thompson, "Cicero the Politician," *Studies in Cicero*, p. 53). At this time, however, the Claudii Marcelli were not very important. They had not produced a consul since the third consulship of M. Claudius Marcellus in 152. They did not regain prominence until after Pompey had become champion of the *optimates* against Caesar, when they produced three consuls in a row (in 51, 50, and 49). By 70, the Marcelli may well have decided to attach their fallen fortunes to Pompey's rising star. This connection would not, of course, have prevented them from taking independent positions at times, especially when they had regained their stature (cf. Gruen, *LGRR*, p. 102).

37. For Lentulus and Gellius, see Appendix B above, under the year 72.

38. Contra Gruen, "Pompey, Metellus Pius," *AJP* 92 (1971): 11.

39. For Palicanus and Pompey, see Badian, *FC*, pp. 282–83.

Pompey's friend to aid his cause indicates whence his chief support came.

The clash of Pompey's interests with those of the senior Metelli and other leading *optimates* also rests on more than the connection between Verres and one branch of the Caecilii Metelli.[40] Metellus Pius may not have been directly involved. Indeed, he may not have returned to Rome before the preparations for the case had been made.[41] Nevertheless, one of Verres' defenders was P. Scipio Nasica (Cic. *Verr.* 2.4.79), a man with strong optimate connections and later adopted by Metellus Pius himself (Cic. *Brut.* 212, *Dom.* 123, *Att.* 6.1.17; Dio 40.51.3). The chief counsel for the defense was, of course, Hortensius (Cic. *Verr.* 1.33–34), who consistently appears associated with other leading *optimates* against Pompey (Cic. *Leg. Man.* 52; Ascon. *Corn.* 60, 78 C/49, 62 St).[42]

The earlier interpretation of Verres' trial still stands. It was not a minor event. The monumental length of the published Verrine orations could have been justified only by a case of paramount importance to the men of Cicero's day. Despite the

40. Contra Gruen, "Pompey, Metellus Pius," *AJP* 92 (1971): 9.

41. If Appian, *BC* 1.14.121, is correct that Pompey and Crassus did not disband their armies until sometime after they had entered office in 70 because Pompey was awaiting Metellus's arrival, then Metellus clearly did not return to Rome until after much work had been done on Verres' case. But, assuming, as many do, that Pompey and Crassus did not retain their troops after 29 December 71, one can still conclude on the evidence of Appian, Dio, and Velleius Paterculus that Metellus did not return to Rome until at least January 70. Although Velleius states that both Pompey and Metellus earned triumphs for their Spanish campaigns (2.30.1), in the following sentence he says simply that Pompey triumphed on 29 December 71 (2.30.2). If they had both triumphed on that day, it is odd that Velleius did not simply carry on the compound subject of the previous sentence. Appian is right that Pompey did not want to disband his army until after Metellus had returned. Dio reports that the people of Rome feared that Metellus would return with his army to Rome, as Sulla had, to destroy his political enemies (52.13.2, 56.39.2). Pompey would not have wished to be without his army under these circumstances. Metellus disarmed everyone's fears, however, by disbanding his troops as soon as he crossed the Pyrenees (ibid. cf. Sall. *Hist.* 4.49 M; Vall. Max. 5.2.7). When word of this action reached Rome, there was great relief (ibid.). Pompey no longer would have felt the need to retain his army (there was no threat from Crassus, who was now his colleague as consul-elect). He could have immediately held his triumph on 29 December, whereas Metellus would have arrived sometime later, after the first of January. For the relevance of Dio 52.13.2 and 56.39.2 to Metellus Pius, see J. A. Crook, "A Metellus in Two Passages of Dio," *Classical Review* 62 (1948): 59–61, and A. R. Burn, "A Metellus in Two Passages of Dio (CR lxii, p. 59)," *Classical Review* 63 (1949): 52–53.

42. For Hortensius and his association with other leading *optimates*, see Appendix B above, under the year 69.

contest for oratorical supremacy in the Forum, few would have been interested in seven speeches (including five undelivered ones) on a minor or commonplace trial that had already been decided. A number of important *optimates* exerted all of their influence to save Verres. Pompey was eager to protect his clients. Cicero, not yet a noble, needed a powerful political ally in advancing his drive for the consulship past the obstacles that the Metelli and their friends would put in his way (cf. Cic. *Verr.* 1.15, 2.4.81, 2.5.180–81). He saw an opportunity to acquire Pompey's political support, and undertook Verres' prosecution. Far from being at odds with Pompey over the question of jury reform, as is claimed,[43] Cicero's position complemented Pompey's on this issue.[44] Cicero and Pompey were both desirous of breaking the senatorial monopoly of the courts and helping the *Equites,* but had no wish to see the whole senatorial order humiliated. Neither Cicero nor Pompey was a bridgeburner. The successful prosecution of Verres not only enhanced Cicero's oratorial reputation, but also made possible the acceptance of L. Cotta's compromise bill that saved one-third of the jury seats for the Senate.[45]

Hostility between Pompey and the leading *optimates* continued unabated in the 60s. Pompey had already clashed with Q. Caecilius Metellus Creticus through the trial of the latter's brother-in-law, Verres. After gaining command of the war against the pirates in 67, he came into even greater conflict with Creticus over the conduct of operations on Crete, where Metellus had been in charge since 68.[46] In 66, Q. Catulus and Q. Hortensius were among the foremost opponents of the effort to transfer command of the Mithridatic war to him (Cic. *Leg. Man.* 51–52, 56, 61–66), and he earned the undying enmity of L. Lucullus, who had preceded him in this highly prized post (Plut. *Pomp.* 46.1–3, *Luc.* 42.5–6, *Cat. Min.* 31.1). When he returned to Rome in 61, the combined fury of many *optimates* shattered his hopes of holding a position of unchallenged dignity and prestige at Rome (Dio 37.49.1–51.6).

43. Gruen, "Pompey, Metellus Pius," *AJP,* 92 (1971): 9–10.
44. A. M. Ward, "Cicero and Pompey in 75 and 70 B.C.," *Latomus* 29 (1970): 68–70.
45. For further discussion of L. Cotta and his role in the jury reform compromise, see the discussion in Appendix A above, pp. 18–19.
46. Cf. Broughton, MRR 2, pp. 144–45 and references. For a discussion of questions concerning the nature of Pompey's *imperium,* see S. Jameson, "Pompey's *Imperium* in 67: Some Constitutional Fictions," *Historia* 19 (1970): 539–60.

II

Crassus and His Family

The primary evidence concerning Crassus's life is often poor. This situation may be illustrated by the problem of dating his birth. The birthdates of Cicero, Pompey, and Caesar, with whose careers his is interwoven, can be calculated precisely.[1] For Crassus, the sources do not permit exactitude. Only Plutarch gives a clue. He says that Crassus was just beyond his sixtieth year at the time he twitted the aged King Degotarus of Galatia for founding a new city very late in life.[2] Since Crassus set out from Brundisium late in 55, before the beginning of good sailing weather, and passed through Galatia on his way to Syria (Plut. *Crass.* 17.1), this incident must have occurred in the first half of 54. Accordingly, Crassus's birth can be dated to some time in 115 or early 114, at the latest.[3] Many writers have not even named Crassus correctly. They assign him the cognomen Dives (Rich) and place him in the wrong branch of the Licinii Crassi.[4] Since Crassus's wealth is proverbial, this error is natural and easy to accept, but the evi-

---

1. Cicero and Pompey were both born in 106 B.C., Cicero on 3 January (Gell. *NA* 15.28.3) and Pompey on 29 September (Vell. Pat. 2.53.4; Plin. *HN* 37.13). Caesar was born on 13 July 100. For the ancient evidence and modern scholarship that confirms 100 as the date of Caesar's birth against Mommsen's arguments for 102, see M. Gelzer, *Caesar, Politician and Statesman,* trans, P. Needham (Cambridge, Mass., 1968), p. 1, n. 1.

2. Ἦν δ' ὁ Κράσσος ἑξήκοντα μὲν ἔτη παραλλάττων, . . . (*Crass.* 17.2). For a parallel usage of the participle παραλλάττων by Plutarch, see *Alc.* 17.1.

3. Cf. Groebe arguing against Drumann's dating of before 115; W. Drumann, *Geschichte Roms* 4, ed. 2 by P. Groebe (Berlin and Leipzig, 1908), p. 84, n. 6. See also G. V. Sumner, *The Orators in Cicero's Brutus: Prosopography and Chronology,* Phoenix suppl. 11 (1973), pp. 123–24.

4. E.g. Drumann, *Geschichte* 4, pp. 61, 84; M. Gelzer, *RE* 13.1 (1926), 295, s.v. "Licinius" (68); A. Garzetti, "M. Licinio Crasso," *Athenaeum* 19 (1941): 7; J. M. Cobben, *OCD* ed. 1 (London, 1949), s.v. "Crassus" (4); T. R. S. Broughton, *The Magistrates of the Roman Republic* 2 (New York, 1952), p. 214; E. Badian, *OCD* ed. 2 (Oxford, 1970) s.v. "Crassus" (4).

dence does not support it. Münzer pointed out the problem some time ago, and Cadoux restated it.[5] Plutarch nowhere uses the cognomen Dives in his life of Crassus. Surely he would not have passed up a chance to comment upon it in the biography of a man who was supposed to illustrate the vice of avarice.

The passages used to support the name Crassus Dives are misinterpreted. Macrobius refers to Crassus's father as P. Licinius Crassus Dives (*Sat.* 3.17.7). Probably Macrobius's knowledge of Cicero's writings misled him. In *de Officiis* 2.57, Cicero refers to a "P. Crassus cum cognomine Dives tum copiis" who presented magnificent games as aedile. This man, however, was P. Licinius Crassus Dives Mucianus, consul in 131.[6] In a letter of April 59, Cicero also refers to a Crassus Dives, who was losing the basis for his cognomen as rapidly as Pompey was losing it for Magnus (*Att.* 2.13.2). Sanders proved that this man was not our Crassus but the Crassus Dives whom Cicero mentioned again a short time later (*Att.* 2.24.4).[7] His full name was P. Licinius Crassus Dives, and he was *iudex quaestionis*, presiding over the *quaestio de vi* in the trial of Vettius. In the latter passage, Cicero naturally referred to him as Crassus Dives to distinguish him from his more famous contemporary. He was praetor in 57 (Cic. *Orat. Post. Red.* 22–23). Since ex-aediles regularly presided over courts that were not in the charge of a praetor, he was doubtless an aedile in 60.[8] The diminishing of his fortune by the well known financial burdens of aedilician games accounts for Cicero's punning references in the earlier letter to his and Pompey's *cognomina*.

Crassus's own family was not very wealthy by the standards of the Roman nobility. Plutarch says that Marcus and his two married brothers lived together and shared a modest house with their parents (*Crass.* 1.1). Their avoidance of extravagance, in comparison with other nobles, was probably dictated

5. F. Münzer, *RE* 13.1 (1926), 246, s.v. "Licinii Crassi"; T. J. Cadoux, "Marcus Crassus: A Revaluation," *Greece and Rome* 2nd. series 3 (1956): 160–61. See now also B. A. Marshall, "Crassus and the Cognomen Dives," *Historia* 22 (1973): 459–67.

6. Münzer, ibid., 288, s.v. "Licinius" (61).

7. H A. Sanders, "The So-Called First Triumvirate," *Memoirs of the American Academy in Rome* 10 (1932): 63.

8. Cf. Broughton, *MRR* 2, p. 184.

by economic necessity as much as by basic values. Crassus's
father apparently had resorted to a fairly common expedient
for easing the financial burdens of the less wealthy nobility
by marrying outside noble circles into a well-to-do family from
one of the Italian towns.[9] The family of his wife, Vinuleia,
which seems to come from Etruria, is scarcely known during
the Republic.[10] Similarly, one of Crassus's brothers was married to Tertulla, a woman from another unknown family,
whom Crassus himself married upon his brother's death (Plut.
Crass. 1.1). No doubt, his father's desire to retain her dowry
was as important as any natural sentiments arising from close
acquaintanceship in Crassus's decision to marry her.

After the death of the rest of his family in the Civil War
between Marius and Sulla, Crassus started out with only 300
talents or 7,200,000 sesterces (Plut. *Crass.* 2.2; 4.1). How
much of this money represents his inheritance is not clear,
but it was probably a considerable proportion.[11] That such
resources were of little account among the nobility of the Late
Republic can be seen from the fact that in 62, Cicero paid
Crassus 3,500,000 sesterces for one house (Cic. *Fam.* 5.6.2).
A little later, the consul Messalla bought a house for
13,400,000 (not 3,300,000).[12] Clodius is said to have paid

9. Cf. T. P. Wiseman, *New Men in the Roman Senate* 139 B.C.–
A.D. 14 (Oxford, 1971), pp. 53–64.

10. The text of Cicero, *Att.* 12.24.2 gives her name as Venuleia, but
Vinuleia seems correct; W. Schulze, *Zur Geschichte lateinischer Eigennamen*, reprint of 1904 ed. (Berlin, Zurich, Dublin, 1966), pp. 380,
459.

11. Drumann argued that since his father had been persecuted and
robbed by the Marians, Crassus's inherited wealth could not have
amounted to much: Drumann, *Geschichte* 4, p. 123. Cf. also Garzetti,
"Crasso," *Athenaeum* 19 (1941): 8. There is, however, no evidence
that the property of Crassus's father was confiscated and Crassus denied
his rightful inheritance. Perhaps his father may have already deposited
a large share of his assets in Spain; cf. F. E. Adcock, *Marcus Crassus,
Millionaire* (Cambridge, 1966), p. 1. Or he might have benefited from
the policy of moderation and reconciliation that Cinna initially tried to
pursue. For this policy of Cinna, see E. Badian, *Foreign Clientelae*,
(264–70 B.C.) (Oxford, 1958), pp. 240–42. Nor is there any reason
to think that Crassus lost property in Italy as a result of his self-imposed
exile. His wife and overseers could have continued to manage his
property while he was absent. Moreover, if he did lose any property in
Italy, he would have recovered it when he returned with the victorious
Sulla in 82.

12. Cic. *Att.* 1.13.6. For the discrepancy in the figures, see D. R.
Shackleton Bailey, *Cicero's Letters to Atticus* 1 (Cambridge, 1965), p.
306 and p. 202, n. 32, below.

14,800,000 for one of his (Plin. *HN* 36.103). It is clear that Crassus, therefore, was not born into the branch of the Licinii Crassi known for its wealth, and despite his later immense wealth (reckoned at 7,100 talents in 55), he continued the modest traditions of his upbringing (Plut. *Crass.* 2.2–7).

As a young man, Marcus Crassus had the usual education of a senator's son. He received a good grounding in rhetoric (Cic. *Brut.* 233, 308), and he acquired a polite interest in history and philosophy (Plut. *Crass.* 3.7). He also received military training under his father, who fought as a proconsul from 96 to 93 against the Lusitanians in Spain (*CIL* 1², 661; Plut. *Crass.* 4.1). Doubtless, this training was furthered while his father fought as a legate in the social war during 90 (Cic. *Font.* 43; App. *BC* 1.40–41; *Diod.* 37.23; Frontin. *Strat.* 2.4.16, 4.7.41).

Crassus's father, of course, was no small influence on him. This statement is even more true for him in his time than for a person in the modern era. In the Roman household, the father's position was one of overwhelming authority, as exemplified by the rights of the *pater familias*. The traditions of one's ancestors were religiously passed down from father to sons. Sons, instilled with the *mos maiorum*, were expected to model themselves on their fathers and grandfathers, and, among the upper class, to increase, or at least preserve, the standing of the family in competition with the other leading houses.[13]

Crassus's family had a strong tradition to be upheld. Their origin may be found among the Etruscans.[14] If so, Crassus would have been able to look back on a heritage older than that of many other Roman nobles. Be that as it may, his immediate forebears were an important part of the plebeian nobility. In 171, his great-grandfather, P. Licinius Crassus, and C. Cassius Longinus had made up the second plebeian col-

13. For the Roman family and the powerful influence of the father, see Adolf Berger, *OCD* ed. 1, 653–54, s.v. "Patria Postestas," and H. I. Marrou, *A History of Education in Antiquity*, trans. G. Lamb (New York, 1964), pp. 312–19.
14. The *nomen* Licinius is apparently derived from the Etruscan word *lecne* and is found on inscriptions from Etruria: Schulze, *Geschichte*, p. 108, n. 3.

lege of consuls in Roman history.[15] His grandfather, also named Marcus, seems to have been a stern and sober Roman in the mold of Cato the Elder. He earned the nickname *Agelastus*—the one who never laughed. Perhaps Crassus resembled him somewhat when he revived the practice of decimation as punishment for cowardice in battle (Sall. *Hist.* 4.22 M; Plut. *Crass.* 10.3). This use of calculated brutality was a trademark of traditional Roman discipline. Agelastus's failure to advance beyond the praetorship was the result of an early death rather than of any lack of ability or important backers.[16]

Crassus's father, Publius, was the embodiment of a successful noble. Although there is no clear record of his earlier offices, he was consul in 97, had a triumph in 93, and was elected censor for 89.[17] No young Roman noble could have had a better example to emulate.

Publius Crassus had also been a firm *optimate*, allied with the highest circles of the Roman oligarchy during the time when Marius was leading a strong *popularis* challange to their power.[18] For example, at some time prior to the death of the satirist Lucilius, which occurred in about 102, he, probably as a tribune, sponsored the sumptuary law that bears his name, the *lex Licinia sumptuaria* (Fest. s.v. *centenariae*; Gell. *NA* 2.24.7–10, 15.8; Macrob. *Sat.* 3.17.7–9).[19] This law would have been useful to the *optimates*, because Marius and his support-

15. F. Münzer, *RE* 13.1 (1926), 286, s.v. "Licinius" (60); Broughton, *MRR* 1, p. 416.

16. One of his advisors as praetor was P. Mucius Scaevola (consul 133): Münzer, *RE* 13.1 (1926), 269–70, s.v. "Licinius" (57.)

17. Broughton, *MRR* 2, pp. 6, 15, 32.

18. On the basis of parallels between the death of P. Crassus and those of Q. Lutatius Catulus and the two Julii Caesares in 87, E. Badian has sought to link P. Crassus with Marius in his earlier career: "Caepio and Norbanus," *Historia* 6 (1957): 332, 336–37, and *Studies in Greek and Roman History* (Oxford, 1964), pp. 46, 51–52. There is no other evidence to support this idea, however. It is not necessary to explain Marius's treatment of P. Crassus as a result of his having switched his allegiance from Marius to the *optimates*. P. Crassus's close association with L. Julius Caesar from 90 on, after the Caesares had broken with Marius, would have been sufficient reason for Marius's hatred.

19. G. Rotondi suggests 103 as the year of Lucilius's death: *Leges Publicae Populi Romani* (Milan, 1912), pp. 327–28. A. Kapplemacher gives the year as 202/1: *RE* 13.2 (1927), 1617, s.v. "Lucilius" (4). Some have seen a reference to an aedileship in Cicero (*Off.* 2.57), but this passage refers to Crassus Dives Mucianus: F. Münzer, *RE* 13.1 (1926), 288, 334–35, s.v. "Licinius" (61, 72).

ers had greater access to cash than anyone else in Rome at that time.[20] By limiting personal expenditures, therefore, the *lex Licinia* would have helped the *optimates* to prevent their opponents from using ready money to offset their traditional advantages of high status, patronage, and voter recognition. Later, in 100, Crassus's father was undoubtedly one of those Crassi who supported the conservative cause by taking up arms against Marius's supporters Saturninus and Glaucia (Cic. *Phil.* 8.15). Finally, L. Julius Caesar, the optimate consul of 90, chose him as a legate in the Social War (Cic. *Font.* 43; App. *BC* 1.5.40).[21]

Previously, P. Crassus had been rewarded for his status and political reliability by being elected consul for 97. The most eventful act of his consulship perhaps was the forbidding of human sacrifice (Plin. *HN* 30.12). Later, as governor of Farther Spain from 96 to 93, he had to enforce this ban (Plut. *Quaest. Rom.* 83).[22] At the same time, he conducted military operations against the Lusitanians and received a triumph in 93 (Ascon. *Pis.* 58, 14 C/19 St; Schol. Bob. *ad Sest.* 48, 131 St; Plut. *Crass.* 1.1).

The elder Crassus also put the time in Spain to good use for the future. He firmly established wide connections and interests there. The town of Castra Licinia, sixty-four kilometers northeast of Merida, near Toledo, commemorates his name (Ptolem. 2.56).[23] Perhaps he even acquired valuable sources of revenue.[24]

His military reputation was so well established as a result of his Spanish campaigns that even the crushing defeat he received as L. Caesar's legate in 90 (Frontin. *Strat.* 2.4.15–16; Diod. 37.23; App. *BC* 1.5.41) seems not to have had an adverse effect. Cicero recalls him as a "man of great courage"

20. Carney, *Marius*, 100 and n. 192.
21. For the anti-Marian position of L. Julius Caesar, see Badian, "Caepio and Norbanus," *Historia* 6 (1957): 336–38, and *Studies*, pp. 52–53.
22. Cf. C. Cichorius, *Römische Studien* (Leipzig and Berlin, 1922), pp. 9–10.
23. A. Schulten, "Éin römisches lager aus dem sertorianischen Kriege," *Jahrbuch des kaiserlich deutschen archäologischen Instituts* 33 (1918): 781.
24. There is a question whether Strabo is referring to Crassus's father or son when he mentions a P. Crassus who owns a "Tin Island" (3.176): cf. F. Haverfield, *RE* 10.2 (1919), 2331.24–54, s.v. "Κασσιτερίδες."

(*de Or.* 3.10) and "very brave" (*Sest.* 48, cf. *Tusc. Disp.* 5.55), while the year 89 saw him reach the pinnacle of a senatorial career, the censorship.[25]

That his colleague was his previous commander, L. Julius Caesar, again shows the closeness of Crassus's father to the most important optimate circles.[26] As censors, their primary duty was to enroll the Italian allies as citizens under the terms of several laws designed to halt the spread of the Social War and hastened the end of hostilities.[27] They did not succeed in carrying out their census, however (Cic. *Arch.* 11; Festus, 366 L). L. Caesar himself had sponsored a law that provided for the new citizens to be enrolled in such a way that their vote would be virtually meaningless according to the Roman system of voting (App. *BC* 1.6.49).[28] This provision was designed to benefit the *optimates* by preventing the undermining of the control that they had established over the other tribes through *amicitia, clientelae,* or less savory means. Marius and others sought political advantage by offering the Italians a fairer arrangement, and discontent prevented the censors from completing their task (Liv. *Per.* 77; App. *BC* 1.7.55–56; *Vell. Pat.* 2.88; Plut. *Mar.* 34, *Sull.* 8).

The only other act recorded for the censorship of Publius Crassus and Lucius Caesar is one that prohibited the sale of foreign perfumes (whose prices probably had been driven up because of shortages resulting from troubles in Asia) and controlled the prices of Greek and Aminian wines (Plin. *HN* 13.24, 14.95). Münzer attributes these actions to the sober character of Publius, who had previously sponsored sumptuary

25. Broughton, *MRR* 2, pp. 32–33

26. For the censors of 89, see Broughton, ibid.

27. The first of these laws was the *lex Iulia,* carried by L. Caesar himself at the end of 90 (App. *BC* 1.6.49; Gell. *NA* 4.4.3; Cic. *Balb.* 21; *Vell. Pat.* 2.16; and Dessau, *ILS,* 8888). The others were the *lex Calpurnia* (Sisenna, fr. 17, 119–20 Peter), which is dated also to 90 by R. Syme ("Missing Senators," *Historia* 4 [1955]: 58); the *lex Plautia-Papiria* (Cic. *Arch.* 7, Schol. Bob. *ad Arch. argumentum,* 175 St.; App. *BC* 1.6.53; *Vell. Pat.* 2.17); and the *lex Pompeia* of 89 (Ascon. *Pis.* 3 C/12 St; Pliny, *HN* 3.20.138). For discussions of these laws, see Rotondi, *Leges Publicae,* pp. 338–42; R. Gardner, *CAH* 9 (1932), pp. 194–96; H. H. Scullard, *From the Gracchi to Nero* ed. 2 (London, 1959), pp. 69–70; and L. R. Taylor, *The Voting Districts of the Roman Republic* (Rome, 1960), pp. 101–3.

28. For a discussion of the way in which the enrollment was carried out, see R. G. Lewis, "Appian B.C. I, 49, 214 δεκατεύοντες Rome's New Tribes 90–87 B. C.," *Athenaeum* 46 (1968): 272–91.

legislation.[29] It seems more likely, however, that the basic motivation was not moral reform but the desire to channel money into more basic imports, such as grain, and alleviate some of the economic distress caused by the Social War.

Nothing further is heard about the elder Crassus until 87, when he, along with Cn. Octavius and Q. Metellus Pius, was one of the leaders of the optimate defense against Marius and Cinna (Gran. Licin. 25, 29 Bonn./19, 23 Fl.; App. BC 1.8.69). Their failure to keep Marius and Cinna from gaining possession of the city resulted in the deaths of Crassus's father and brother.[30] P. Crassus's head was severed and hung with those of Marius's other optimate foes on the Rostra (Cic. *Tusc. Disp.* 5.55).

Thus Marcus Crassus was left to face the Roman political arena alone, without the help of close kin, who were often essential for success in electoral and legal battles. Nevertheless, when Plutarch says that Crassus himself, being very young, escaped immediate danger after his father and brother perished in the Marian proscriptions of 87, we must not think of him as a mere stripling. He was twenty-seven or twenty-eight years old.[31] In the eyes of the Romans, however, despite the acquisition of the *toga virilis* at about the age of fifteen, one was a youth for a long period of time. A man could be called an *adulescens* or an *iuvenis* up to the age of forty, and even beyond (Cic. *Fam.* 2.1, *Att.* 2.12, *Phil.* 2.46; cf. *adulescentulus* in Sall. *Cat.* 49 and Cic. *Or.* 30).

It was not Crassus's youthfulness (in the modern sense of the word) that helped him escape proscription, but his lack

29. F. Münzer, *RE* 13.1 (1926), 259, s.v. "Licinius" (61).

30. How they died is confused in the sources. Plutarch says that they were both caught and killed (*Crass.* 4.1). Livy says that Fimbria's horsemen killed Crassus's brother, but that his father committed suicide (*Per.* 80). Appian reports that the father first killed his son and then himself (*BC* 1.8.72). A. Garzetti favors Appian's account: "M. Licinio Crasso," *Athenaeum* 19 (1941): 13, n. 3. If the epitomator of Livy is accurate his account may be trustworthy, since Livy was nearer to the event in time than the others. Regardless of whether one prefers Appian or Livy, it is clear that Crassus's father committed suicide. Cicero asserts that twice (*de Or.* 3.10, *Sest.* 48). In the case of the *pro Sestio*, Crassus was present in the court. Surely Cicero could not have been in error then. The praenomen of the brother in question is unknown.

31. B. Perrin is clearly wrong when he says that in 87 Crassus was "not quite twenty years of age": *Plutarch's Lives* 3, LCL (London and Cambridge, Mass., 1916), p. 323, n. 1.

of importance. Before Sulla's revision of the *cursus honorum*, the quaestorship might be held as early as twenty-five, as Astin has demonstrated.[32] Even then, however, it was usually not held before thirty, and Sulla's laws seem to have set thirty as the minimum age for this office, the first that brought membership in the Senate. Marcus Crassus, therefore, was probably still a year or two away from that office when his father and brother perished in 87. Even if he had held the quaestorship, he probably would not have entered the Senate, since the quaestorship did not secure automatic admission to that august body until after Sulla's reorganization of the state in 81 (Cic. *Leg.* 3.12.27; Tac. *Ann.* 11.22).

Crassus did not immediately go into exile upon the deaths of his father and brother—another indication that he had not yet held an important office. He did not flee until almost two years later in 85.[33] The question is why Crassus decided upon exile at that time. No one has yet attempted to give an answer. Garzetti thought it especially puzzling, because Cicero records that the years 86 to 84 under Cinna were peaceful and that oratory revived modestly (*Brut.* 308).[34] Nevertheless, significant developments did occur in 85. Sulla took over the army of C. Flavius Fimbria, who then committed suicide.[35] Thus, no army loyal to Cinna stood between Sulla and Italy. Fearing Sulla's imminent return, Cinna and his followers made preparations to oppose him. No doubt, anyone who might have been suspected of sympathy with Sulla's side would have received closer scrutiny than before. Because of his background, Crassus must have been viewed with renewed or greater suspicion. Not wishing to press his luck too far, he sought the safety of exile.

One of the reasons Crassus remained in Italy after the tragic

32. A. E. Astin, "The Lex Annalis before Sulla," *Latomus* 17 (1958): 52–64/*Collection Latomus* 32 (Brussels, 1958), pp. 34–46.

33. Drumann, *Geschichte*, 4, p. 85, n. 1. Marius and Cinna did not take control of Rome until well into the second half of 87. Plutarch records that Crassus was in exile only eight months before Cinna died (*Crass.* 6.1). Cinna died sometime in the early part of 84 (App. *BC* 1.9.78).

34. "Crasso," *Athenaeum* 19 (1941): 14. Of course, those orators mentioned in *Brutus* 308 would seem to be men against whom Cinna had little complaint. His enemies shunned the courts.

35. Broughton, *MRR* 2, p. 59.

events of 87 may have been concern for his family. His eldest
brother, Publius, had died sometime before 87, the year their
father and other brother perished amidst civil strife. Crassus,
in biblical fashion, had married this brother's widow, Tertulla
(Plut. *Crass.* 1.1; Cic. *Att.* 12.24.2; Suet. *Iul.* 50.1).[36] Also, it
appears from the following discussion that the elder son of
Marcus and Tertulla had been born no later than 89. Therefore, he would have been about two years old in 87. No doubt,
Crassus had hesitated to subject his wife and young child to
the rigors of exile or leave them behind to an uncertain fate.

Contrary to universal opinion, Crassus's first son was Publius,
not Marcus.[37] The usual assumption is that Marcus was the
elder son because it was a common Roman practice to name
first-born sons after their fathers. None of our sources refers
to Publius as the younger son, however. Plutarch simply calls
him "the young man Crassus" to distinguish him from his
father on the Parthian expedition (*Crass.* 18.1).

A good indication that Publius was older than Marcus is
that Publius accompanied Caesar in Gaul from 58 to 56 and
was given important assignments there. He was in command
of cavalry units the first year and legions thereafter (Caes.
BGall. 1.52.7, 2.34, 3.20–27). Marcus was sent there only in 54,
during his quaestorship (ibid., 5.24.3 and 47.1, 6.6.1). It is
strange that Publius would have been sent to Gaul in 58 before
an elder brother. Likewise, it is strange that Crassus would
have taken his younger son, instead of the elder, to Syria in
55/4.[38] By analogy with the career of his brother Marcus, therefore, it would seem that Publius Crassus had gone to Gaul
as a quaestor in 58.

One might object, however, by pointing out that Caesar
twice uses the title quaestor in connection with Marcus, but

36. P. Groebe in Drumann, *Geschichte*, 4, p. 83, n. 3. Adcock erroneously identifies Tertulla as the widow of the son who died with his father
in 87: *Crassus*, p. 2.

37. For the majority opinion, see e.g., Drumann, *Geschichte*, 4, p.
129; F. Münzer, *RE* 13.1 (1926), 291, s.v. "Licinius" (62); M. Gelzer,
Caesar (trans. Needham), p. 132; and R. Syme, *The Roman Revolution*
(Oxford, 1939), p. 36, n. 3.

38. One might argue that Crassus took Publius, although he was the
younger, because he had more experience than Marcus. But, Publius
may have been the more experienced precisely because he was the
elder son and therefore had started his career before Marcus.

never with Publius (*BGall.* 1.52.7, 2.34, 3.20, 5.24.3, 6.6.1).
The reason is that both times he refers to Marcus as quaestor,
legates were also mentioned in the same sentence, and Caesar
was careful to maintain the distinction between the two types
of officers. Thus, there is no obstacle to viewing P. Crassus
as being Caesar's quaestor in 58 and older than his brother
Marcus.[39]

There is a very good reason why Crassus should have named
his firstborn son Publius instead of Marcus. Apparently, his
eldest brother, Publius, whose widow Crassus married, had
died without issue. It would have been fitting for Crassus to
have named his first son Publius in memory of his dead
brother, whose firstborn son probably would have been named
Publius if he had lived to father one. Also, Publius may have
been the favored *praenomen* of the family, as witnessed by
Crassus's father and great-grandfather. Accordingly, Crassus
would have desired to name his first son Publius in order to
ensure that the principal *praenomen* of the family was carried
on as it should have been by the first son of his eldest brother,
Publius.

The young Marcus Crassus probably was born in 85, since
it is likely that a son of the elder Marcus Crassus elected
quaestor for 54 would have been elected *suo anno* at the age
of 30.[40] Therefore, Crassus may have had to leave his wife in

39. On the basis of a coin issued by Publius and depicting the
goddess Venus, scholars have identified Publius Crassus as a moneyer
in years ranging from 59 to 54: cf. Broughton, *MRR* 2, p. 443. E.
Babelon has argued that he issued the coin as quaestor in 58: *Monnaies
de la République romaine* 2 (Paris, 1886), pp. 133–34. More recently,
H. Mattingly has argued that Publius's quaestorship was in 55: "The
Denarius of Sufenas and the *Ludi Victoriae*," *Numismatic Chronicle*
16 (1956): 189–203. This date would also support the argument that
Publius was the elder son, because it would still place his quaestorship
before his brother's. Nevertheless, the argument for choosing 55 is not
strong. The representation of Venus on the coin need not refer to any
celebration of the *Ludi Victoriae Sullanae*. All of those who tried to
gain the leading position at Rome after Sulla sought to identify themselves as favorites of Venus, especially Caesar, whose quaestor Publius
would have been in 58. Finally, Publius could have been a moneyer in
55, after having been quaestor in 58: cf. the parallels with C. Claudius
Pulcher (*CIL* 12, 200) and P. Plautius Hypsaeus (C. D. Hamilton,
"The Tresviri Monetales and the Republican 'Cursus Honorum,'" *Transactions and Proceedings of the American Philological Association* 100
[1969]: 198).

40. If there is no other evidence for the date of birth, it is usually
very dangerous to speculate about a person's birthdate by assuming that

an even worse situation than he would have if he had fled Italy in 87. In 85, she would not only have had young Publius to care for, but would also have been carrying Marcus, if he had not already been born in that same year.[41]

Certainly, the future of Crassus and his family did not seem very bright as he, the only surviving adult, fled into exile and left behind his wife and two young sons. Nevertheless, he still had much in his favor. Though not a wealthy family by the standards of the Roman nobility, his branch of the Licinii Crassi was resourceful. Crassus had learned from his father to exploit what he had and acquire more when the time was right. Moreover, he had two potent goads to spur achievement in the Roman political arena: the *imagines* of his father, grandfather, and great-grandfather would call him to emulate their accomplishments;[42] and filial piety demanded that he seek to restore the prestige of his family lost through the brutal deaths of his father and brother in civil war.

---

he was elected to some office *suo anno* when any concrete evidence for his being so elected is also lacking. In this case, however, given Crassus's power at Rome from 60 to 55 (see chapters Eight to Ten, below), it seems highly probable that his son, elected to the first office of the *cursus honorum* in 55, would have been elected *suo anno*.

41. If Cicero's famous pun ἄξιος Κράσσου was occasioned by a well-known likeness between Crassus's son Marcus and a certain Axius (Plut. *Cic.* 25.4), then it would have had even more point and thrust if Marcus had been born after his father had gone to Spain in exile. See Chapter Eleven, n. 11.

42. I use the term *imagines* metaphorically, of course, since it is not known whether or not Crassus actually had any of these ancestral wax portraits that Cicero so scorned and envied (*Pis.* 1), but it is likely that he did.

III

Exile and Bid for Prominence

According to Plutarch, Crassus left Italy with three friends and ten slaves (*Crass.* 4.1). He sought refuge in Spain, appropriately enough, because there he had ties of friendship and clientage, which had been established during his father's lengthy term as governor of Farther Spain (ibid.). The extent of his family's patronage cannot be determined exactly, but an idea of its magnitude can be gained from the following facts: of the Republican *gentes* that produced consuls from 100 to 49 B.C. (with the exception of houses that later supplied emperors—the Aurelii, Claudii, and Julii—and with the addition of five others outside of this time span), the Licinii are represented by the third highest number of Roman citizens of known Spanish origin who took the *nomina* of their Roman patrons. There are only three other Licinii, representing two other *stirpes* of the *gens*, known to have been governors or generals in Spain, and all more than fifty years earlier: L. Licinius Lucullus, C. Licinius Nerva, and A. Licinius Nerva. Of these, Lucullus served in Spain two years, the others only one each, while Crassus's father served four.[1] Therefore, it is likely that the largest number of Spaniards bearing the *nomen* Licinius were the clients of Crassus's family. Indeed, at the end of his exile, Crassus was able to recruit a private army of 2,500 picked men in Spain (Plut. *Crass.* 6.1). To acquire these troops, he no doubt relied heavily on numerous friends and clients whom his father had acquired during his long governorship.[2]

During the eight months that Crassus remained in hiding, he stayed concealed in a cave on the property of one Vibius

---

1. E. Badian, *Foreign Clientelae* (264–70 B.C.) (Oxford, 1958), Appendix B (ii) (a) and (ii) (b), pp. 309–10, 316.
2. Cf. ibid., pp. 266–67.

Paciaecus, who acted as his protector (ibid. 4.2). Unfortunately there is little concrete information about Paciaecus.[3] He seems to have no connections with other Vibii, but he may have been descended from an Italian family of Roman citizenship that had been lured to Spain in the second century by its rich business prospects.[4] That he aided Crassus in hiding from the Cinnan regime is an indication that he favored Sulla's cause. Indeed, it may well be that his name should be read for that of the Paccianus whom Sulla sent as an envoy in 81 to aid Ascalis against Sertorius in Mauretania (Plut. *Sert.* 9.3).[5] Likewise, the Paccianus who was captured when Crassus fell at Carrhae may have been the son of Crassus's protector (Plut. *Crass.* 32.2).[6] If so, the friendship that Paciaecus demonstrated by aiding Crassus in Spain was long and lasting.[7]

Probably Paciaecus and his property were known to Crassus from the days of his father's governorship. Plutarch would have us believe that Crassus dared not trust him at first and revealed himself only after forced by necessity to do so (ibid. 4.2–3). That aspect of the story may be a fabrication to heighten its dramatic effect. The remainder of the story of Crassus's stay in Paciaecus's cave as related by Plutarch clearly seems to be more romantic fiction than historical fact (ibid., 4.3, 5.4). First of all, the three friends and ten slaves are conveniently forgotten, as Paciaecus's slave brings just one meal a day to the cave (ibid., 4.3). The very wealth of detail supplied about the cave itself makes this part suspect as a piece of imaginative reconstruction on the part of Fenestella, or his source, who apparently supplied the basis of the story concerning Crassus's concealment (ibid., 5.4).[8] Even more suspect is the episode of the two attractive slave girls with whom Paciaecus supplied Crassus to ease the loneliness of his con-

3. For the variant spellings of this name, see F. Münzer, *RE* 18.2 (1942), 2061–62, s.v. "Pac(c)iaecus."
4. T. P. Wiseman, *New Men in the Roman Senate 139 B.C.—A.D. 14* (Oxford, 1971), p. 21.
5. E. Gabba, "Le origini delle guerra sociale e la vita politica romana dopo l' 89 a.C." *Athenaeum* 32 (1954): 307, n. 4.
6. Wiseman, *New Men*, p. 248, no. 300.
7. Plutarch reports that the younger Paciaecus (Paccianus) most resembled Crassus among those captured at Carrhae (*Crass.* 32.2).
8. Adcock prudently omits the whole story of Crassus's concealment: *Marcus Crassus, Millionaire* (Cambridge, 1966), p. 3.

finement and act as messengers (Plut. *Crass.* 5.2.4). If Fenestella actually did get the story from an old woman who claimed to have been one of the slave girls (ibid., 5.4), it is more a mark of his credulity than his scholarship that he believed her. It sounds like wishful thinking on the part of an old woman who hoped to give significance to her life by association with one of the important figures of her day.

Upon hearing the news of Cinna's death, Crassus immediately started to raise a private army from friends and clients to support the cause championed by Sulla (ibid., 6.1). Probably he was inspired by a similar action taken by Q. Metellus Pius in the province of Africa (ibid., 6.2).[9] Metellus, however, was still a proconsul and had some legal pretext for his action (App. *BC* 1.9.80; Liv. *Per.* 84).[10] Crassus, as a purely private citizen, without even membership in the Senate, was engaging in an act of outright usurpation.[11]

First, Crassus made the rounds of various cities in Spain (Plut. *Crass.* 6.1). Doubtless he was seeking supplies and the loyalty of the local governments. It seems incredible that Crassus would not have met with some organized resistance from one of the governors in Spain, but there is no record of any action on their part. The *fasti* for Spain are completely blank after 94 in Nearer Spain and after 93 in Farther Spain until Sertorius assumed the governorship of Nearer Spain for 83.[12] If they are reliable, the reports that Crassus plundered the city of Malaca may reflect some local opposition raised against him (ibid.). Malaca was the chief port serving communications between Farther Spain and Africa. It must have been there that Crassus obtained the ships with which he and his followers crossed over to join Metellus in Africa (ibid., 6.2).

Crassus himself, however, vehemently denied that he had plundered Malaca (ibid., 6.1). If the Malacans did not willingly provide Crassus with ships, any method that he would have had to use in obtaining them could have easily given his

9. Cf. Badian, *FC*, pp. 266–67.
10. Ibid., p. 266.
11. Ibid., p. 267.
12. Cf. App. *Hisp.* 16.100–101, and W. F. Jashemski, *The Origins and History of the Proconsular and Propraetorian Imperium* (Chicago, 1950), p. 126.

detractors the basis for the accusations against him. Perhaps, however, the mere fact that he had obtained ships there was the only basis for the hostile tradition.[13] There was little reason for the Malacans not to have provided Crassus with transportation willingly. Not only would they have rid themselves of Crassus's army, but they may well have been sympathetic towards his undertaking. Throughout the Sertorian War in Spain a few years later, the south coastal area, of which Malaca was a part, favored the Sullan regime.[14] Moreover, the success of Crassus's concealment and his recruitment of troops in 84 indicate that there was previously much sympathy in the area with those who opposed the Cinnan regime.

Once in Africa, Crassus soon quarrelled with that testy aristocrat, Metellus Pius (Plut. *Crass.* 6.2). Possibly they disagreed about the mechanics of supporting Sulla, but more likely than not, their clash was personal. After raising his own army and leading it safely to Africa, Crassus probably expected to be granted a high position with Metellus. Metellus, however, was never one to share power and position with his juniors. Frustrated in gaining any significant recognition from Metellus, Crassus reembarked and sailed directly to join Sulla in Greece (ibid.).[15]

Sulla, who needed all the support he could get in preparing to invade Italy, granted him the honor that Metellus had refused (ibid.).[16] After arriving in Italy, Sulla sent Crassus on an important and dangerous mission to recruit troops among the

13. That Crassus used Malacan ships for the short voyage across to Africa does not necessarily mean that the Malacans lost possession of their vessels, but merely that they provided ferry service on the occasion of his crossing.

14. Gabba, "Le origini," *Athenaeum* 32 (1954): 309–10. Cf. A. Garzetti, M. Licinio Crasso," *Athenaeum* 19 (1941): 5 for the view that the story about Crassus was a piece of propaganda later fabricated by Crassus's enemies

15. Adcock has Crassus join Sulla only after Sulla had returned to Italy: *Crassus*, pp. 3–4. Plutarch's narrative, however, makes it clear that he joined Sulla before the latter crossed over to Italy (*Crass.* 6.2). Cf. Badian, *FC*, p. 267, n. 6. It is questionable whether Crassus brought with him all of the 2,500 men recruited in Spain. Badian thinks not: ibid., n. 5. Sulla's request that he recruit soldiers in Italy does indicate that Crassus was not at the head of any significant force once he arrived in Italy (Plut. *Crass.* 6.2–3).

16. Significantly, Metellus did not join Sulla until after Sulla had landed safely at Brundisium and appeared to have a good chance of success (App. *BC* 1.9.80).

Marsi (ibid.). To his credit, despite his initial fears, Crassus performed his task successfully and earned a place as one of Sulla's valuable lieutenants in the Civil War (ibid., 6.3).[17]

The main historical tradition, which is represented by authors who were prejudiced against Crassus for one reason or another, has patently obscured the role that he played as one of Sulla's commanders.[18] In the spring of 82, Sulla sent Metellus, Pompey, and Crassus with detachments of troops to defeat his enemies in Umbria and Cispadane Gaul. Using Picenum as a base, they were all successful (App. *BC* 1.10.87–90). Crassus himself besieged the Marian forces in the Umbrian town of Tuder and captured it (Plut. *Crass.* 6.5). In a joint operation on the plain of Spoletium, he and Pompey defeated a force under Carrinas, a lieutenant of the consul Carbo, and penned him up in the town of Spoletium itself (App. *BC* 1.10.90).[19] Nevertheless, Carrinas managed to slip out of

17. Gelzer is quite unfair to Crassus concerning his recruitment of troops among the Marsi: *RE* 13.1 (1926), 330.52–53, s.v. "Licinius" (68).

18. Cadoux has not emphasized this point strongly enough: "Marcus Crassus: A Revaluation," *Greece and Rome* 2nd ser. 3 (1956): 154. Of the extant ancient writers, only Plutarch gives us an indication that Crassus was equal to men like Pompey, Lucullus, and Q. Caecilius Metellus Pius. Plutarch seems to have relied on a biographical source more favorable to Crassus at this point, perhaps the memoirs of Sulla, rather than the tradition represented by Livy and his derivatives. Cf. Plut. *Sull.* 14.2 and 17.1 for references to Sulla's memoirs, and see also Adcock, *Crassus*, pp. 8, 55–57. Crassus's capture of Tuder and his important feat of saving Sulla's right wing at the battle of the Colline Gate are nowhere evident in the extant Livian tradition represented by the *Periochae* (88), Velleius Paterculus (2.27.1), Appian (*BC* 1.10.93), Eutropius (5.8.1), Florus (2.9.23), and Orosius (5.20.9). Only Appian mentions the role of Crassus in the discomfiture of Carrinas at Spoletium (*BC* 1.10.90).

19. Cf. Flor. 2.9.27. Plutarch reports that charges were made against Crassus on the ground that he misappropriated the booty from Tuder (*Crass.* 6.5). There is, however, no way to confirm this accusation, and it may well be a fabrication created for propaganda purposes by Crassus's political enemies. Deknatel accepts it. He argues that after the defeat of Carrinas, Crassus was assigned to hold the territory between the Via Flaminia and Clusium to protect Sulla's flank at Clusium and that then Crassus sacked Tuder and misappropriated the booty, so that Sulla no longer permitted him an independent command: Chr. Deknatel, *De Vita M. Licinii Crassi* (Diss. Leyden, 1901), p. 5. E. Gabba believes that Crassus had taken Tuder before joining forces with Pompey against Carrinas: *Appiani Bellorum Civilium Lib. I* (Florence, 1962), p. 238. It appears as if Crassus had been sent southward to prevent the Marian forces in Etruria from coming up from Etruria while Metellus and Pompey engaged Carrinas and Carbo in the north, on the

Spoletium on a dark and stormy night (ibid.). At this point, Pompey and Crassus split their forces again. Crassus may have marched to Clusium in Etruria, where Sulla was engaged with another force under Carbo, who seems to have made his way safely southward after the fall of Ariminum (ibid., 1.10.89).

Since the contest at Clusium had been equal, Sulla would have welcomed reinforcements. After Pompey had beaten back a relieving force that Carbo had sent under Marcius to aid Marius at Praeneste, Sulla had then fallen back to hold off a reported 70,000 Samnites and Lucanians under the generals Marcus Lampronius, Pontius Telesinus, and Gutta of Capua. They were attempting to join Carbo's lieutenants Damasippus, Carrinas, and Marcius to relieve Marius, who was still shut up in Praeneste (ibid., 1.10.90–92).[20] Having failed to penetrate Sulla's blockade, this force wheeled around and made a desperate dash towards Rome, which was not protected by any significant forces, in the hope of seizing it from Sulla's partisans (ibid., 1.10.92). Sending his cavalry ahead to harass them, Sulla made a forced march and intercepted the enemy forces at the Colline Gate after they had proceeded to lay siege to the city. He arrived at about noon on 1 November 82 (ibid., 1.10.93; Vell. Pat. 2.27.1).[21] At about 3 or 4 o'clock in the afternoon, despite the lateness of the hour, Sulla decided to fight.

Crassus was given the task of commanding the right wing, while Sulla commanded the center (Plut. *Crass.* 6.6, *Sull.*

---

border between Umbria and Picenum. Cf. App. *BC* 1.10.87. Tuder is on the border between Etruria and Umbria and sits athwart the road paralleling the Via Flaminia. This road leaves the Via Cassia just above Veii and joins the Via Flaminia just above Iguvium. After his defeat at the hands of Metellus on the Aesis river and the subsequent retreat of Carbo to Ariminum (App. ibid.), Carrinas probably marched southwards by the Via Flaminia and the road that branches off at Forum Flaminii in order to clear the way for the forces in Etruria to move north and relieve Carbo. Pompey, however, having defeated Marcius and sacked Sena Gallica (Ibid., 1.10.88), must have headed south in pursuit of Carrinas and caught up with him on the road near Spoletium, where Crassus joined the fray from the west after taking Tuder.

20. Carbo and his main force had moved northwards to attack Metellus, Pompey was placed in charge of defeating the remaining forces at Clusium, and Lucretius Ofella was left to invest Praeneste (App. *BC* 1.10.88, 91–92).

21. Cf. Groebe in W. Drumann, *Geschichte Roms* 4, 2nd ed., P. Groebe (Berlin and Leipzig, 1908), p. 85, n. 10.

29.5).[22] On the left and center, Sulla's forces were driven back against the wall of the city and were probably saved from destruction only by the advent of darkness. Crassus, however, not only held the right, but actually broke up the enemy's left wing and drove it in a rout as far as Antemnae, a little to the north of Rome (Plut. *Crass.* 6.6, *Sull.* 30.1).[23] With his flank turned, the enemy was in an impossible position, and the victory went to Sulla.[24]

Crassus showed himself to be a competent and valuable lieutenant of Sulla in the Civil War, and, as we shall see, acquitted himself well as a general against Spartacus. His reputation has been unduly maligned by a basically hostile tradition and the unforgivable sin of losing at Carrhae.[25] Had he continued from the start, as Pompey did, to seek military laurels, it might not have been so easy to denigrate his martial skills. Crassus, however, felt that he had no need to continue his career in the military sphere. Unlike Pompey, who was too young, Crassus was old enough now to take up the real business of the Roman nobility—a career in the Senate and the senatorial magistracies.

When Sulla took up the reorganization of the Roman constitution in 81, Crassus was able to make up for time lost during the political turmoil of the 80s and enter the Senate. The numbers of the Senate had been drastically reduced as the result of the Civil War, proscriptions and natural attrition (Oros. 5.22.4; Eutrop. 5.9.2; App. *BC* 1.11.100, 12.103).[26] As

22. Perhaps Dolabella or Torquatus, who expressed reluctance to fight at this late hour, was in command of the ill-fated left wing (Plut. *Sull.* 29.4). It is clear that Sulla did not start out in command of the left, because Plutarch says that when Sulla saw the left wing in trouble, he personally rode over to aid it (ibid. 29.5): cf. Deknatel, *Vita*, p. 6.

23. Adcock's reconstruction, which has Crassus march to Antemnae by a separate road from the direction of Praeneste in a preplanned flanking movement, has no basis whatsoever in the sources; Sulla could have sufficiently emphasized his *felicitas* in his memoirs without going to the elaborate lengths that Adcock has read into the account: *Crassus*, pp. 6–8.

24. Deknatel believes that Sulla waited until the next morning to slaughter the Samnites, who had retreated: *Vita*, p. 6. That may well be, but there is no proof.

25. Cf. Garzetti, "Crasso," *Athenaeum* 22 (1944): 35–58 and Cadoux, "Marcus Crassus," *Greece and Rome* 2nd ser., 3 (1956): 154–55.

26. E. Gabba estimates that in 81 there were only 150 senators left alive: "Il ceto equestre e il senato di Sulla," *Athenaeum* 34 (1956): 124.

dictator in 81, Sulla made good these losses and also increased the membership of the Senate to 600 by raising to senatorial rank those who were sympathetic to this regime or who had served him faithfully.[27] One of these new senators was Crassus.[28] He was probably not required to stand for the quaestorship, since he was several years beyond the minimum age for that office.[29]

After having entered the Senate, Crassus does not appear to have held an aedileship. The ancient sources contain no mention of Crassus in this office. If he had held it, with the wealth acquired in Sulla's service or later, he would hardly have escaped unnoticed.[30] Whether Crassus chose not to seek the aedileship and save his money for other purposes or whether he was unable to obtain that office cannot be said. The aedileship was not a mandatory step in the offices leading to the

---

This calculation is based upon the assumption of 300 as the normal membership of the Senate, coupled with the figure of 200 senatorial deaths from 91 to 81 supplied by Orosius (5.22.4) and Eutropius (5.9.2). That 300 was the normal membership of the Senate down to Sulla is clear (Liv. 21.10; Dionys. 5.13); cf. Th. Mommsen, *Römische staatsrecht* 3 (Leipzig, 1887), pp. 846–47.

27. Gabba argues that Sulla bestowed membership in the Senate first on those who had served with him. These men would have included men like the *primipilaris* Fufidius (Oros. 5.21.3) and the sons of former senators. Then he says that 300 men were chosen from the men of the equestrian census in order to double the normal size of the Senate to 600 (Liv. *Per.* 89; App. *BC* 1.11.100). He points out that there is no need to maintain, as H. Hill does (below, n. 28), that the 300 men were chosen from only the eighteen centuries of *Equites equo publico* ("Il ceto equestre," pp. 127–28, 131–32); cf. R. Syme, "Review of Gelzer," *JRS* 34 (1944): 102.

28. H. Hill, "Sulla's Military Oligarchy," *Proceedings of the Classical Association* (1931): 64; "Sulla's New Senators in 81 B.C.," *Classical Quarterly* 26 (1932): 170–77.

29. Deknatel claims that Crassus actually held the quaestorship: *Vita*, p. 10. He is followed by M. Gelzer: *RE* 13.1 (1926), 302, s.v. "Licinius" (68). There is no evidence for this office. Rather, it is much more likely that since Crassus's career had been retarded under Cinna, Sulla allowed Crassus and the other new appointees to skip this office.

30. Gelzer says that he must have held an aedileship but gives no evidence to support his view: ibid. Cadoux suggests that Sicinius's statement that he did not attack Crassus because Crassus had "hay on his horns" (Plut. *Crass.* 7.9) indicates a magistracy in 76, which would be an aedileship: "Marcus Crassus, G&R 2nd ser., 3 (1956): 154, n. 5. Broughton duly cites Cadoux: *Supplement to the Magistrates of the Roman Republic* (New York, 1960), p. 34. Within the context of Sicinius's remark as reported by Plutarch, one might include Crassus among the popular leaders. Nevertheless, there is no reference here to any official power, but rather to Crassus's influence as a creditor. See below, p. 78).

consulship, and he could have forgone it. On the other hand, if he sought the aedileship not long after 80, he may have been unsuccessful in the face of powerful opposition.

According to one story, Crassus lost Sulla's favor soon after the Civil War. It seems that Sulla had placed Crassus in charge of carrying out part of the proscriptions instituted at the beginning of his rule.[31] Plutarch says that in Bruttium, Crassus inserted a man's name into the list of the proscribed without Sulla's knowledge, in order to obtain the man's estate; when Sulla found out about this incident, he refused to have anything further to do with Crassus (*Crass.* 6.7). This story of Crassus's abuse of his position cannot be independently confirmed or denied. Nevertheless, if it were publicized at this time, opposition from Sulla or, more likely, from Sulla's noble supporters could have blocked any attempt by Crassus to obtain election to the aedileship. The nobles who supported Sulla were well aware how the position of the regime that they were establishing in conjunction with Sulla would be undermined if his subordinates were allowed to take outrageous personal liberties in carrying out the proscriptions. The case of Roscius Amerinus provides an apt illustration.[32]

In 80, not long after Crassus is said to have manipulated the proscription lists to obtain the estate in Bruttium, Cicero (then a virtual unknown) defended Sextus Roscius of Ameria from an attack by two of his relatives, Capito and Magnus, and Sulla's personal henchman, Chrysogonus (Cic. *Ros. Am.* 6; 17).[33] After Roscius's father had been murdered (apparently through their agency), they had conspired to insert the father's name in the proscription lists. In this way, they had hoped to buy up his confiscated estate, worth 6,000,000 sesterces, for a mere 2,000. At the same time, they sought to foil the claims of

---

31. Gelzer, *RE* 13.1 (1926), 298.17–22, s.v. "Licinius" (68).

32. I use this case only as an illustration of the type of activity in which Crassus was alleged to have engaged. T. A. Dorey has argued that Cicero's *pro Roscio Amerino* was an indirect attack upon Crassus: "A Note on the Pro Roscio Amerino," *Ciceroniana* 2 (1960): 147–48. W. V. Harris has effectively refuted this idea, however: *Rome in Etruria and Umbria* (Oxford, 1971), p. 274, n. 2.

33. J. Carcopino argued for the date 79: *Sylla ou la monarchie manquée* ed. 3 (Paris, 1931), p. 156. Nevertheless, Gellius confirms the date 80 (*NA* 15.28.3); cf. M. Gelzer's review of Carcopino in *Gnomon* 8 (1932), 607; *Kleine Schriften* 2 (Wiesbaden, 1962), p. 105 and Badian, *FC*, p. 297, n. u.

the son, rightful heir to the property, by accusing him of his own father's murder (ibid., 18–29). Chrysogonus's actions produced a public outcry in Ameria (ibid., 25), but apparently he was so close to Sulla that he was able to get his way, as Crassus supposedly had not. Nevertheless, Roscius enjoyed *hospitium* with three of the most powerful families among Sulla's supporters, the Caecilii Metelli, the Servilii, and the Cornelii Scipiones (ibid., 15). In order to perserve the semblance of a just regime and their credibility as patrons, the Metellii arranged for Roscius's defense (ibid., 149).[34] Accordingly, with their help, Cicero pled Roscius's case, and Chrysogonus was discredited.

Although it cannot be supposed that the Bruttian whom Crassus may have wronged had had any connection with the Metelli, they would not have been sorry to see him lose Sulla's favor or fail to advance in political office. After all, Metellus Pius had quarrelled with Crassus in Africa and probably would not have been well disposed toward him. Moreover, there are reports of other irregularities that cast shadows on Crassus's early career—for example, the story that he had plundered Malaca and the charge that he had kept for himself the booty captured at Tuder in the Civil War (Plut. *Crass.* 6.1.5).

Given the state of the evidence, it is difficult to say whether or not these accounts of Crassus's improprieties in his early years are true or even were in circulation at that time. Nevertheless, it is clear that Crassus was not favored by those who dominated Roman politics after Sulla. As will be seen below, his known connections in the 70s were with men from families of the second and third ranks. Regardless of the circumstances surrounding his omission of the aedileship, Crassus's career in

34. A certain Caecilia Metella was the one who gave Roscius protection and arranged for his defense. She was the daughter of Metellus Balearicus and sister of the elder Metellus Nepos: F. Münzer, *RE* 3.1 (1897), 1207–1208, s.v. "Caecilius" (82) and 1216, s.v. "Caecilius" (95). She was also a cousin of Metellus Pius, Sulla's colleague in the consulship for 80 and wife of Appius Claudius Pulcher, consul in 79: ibid., 1229–30, s.v. "Stammtafel" and 1235, s.v. "Caecilia" (135). Cicero's words, *Patronos huic defuturos putaverunt; desunt* (*Rosc. Am.* 30), in no way mean that Roscius's patrons had abandoned him. They refer, rather, to the difficulty that Rocius's patrons had in finding an advocate who would defend Roscius in court without, at the same time, being so identifiable with them as to cause a break with Sulla, whose power and good favors they needed.

this period was retarded. He was not able to reach the praetorship until 73, two or three years after he was first eligible.[35] If he had enjoyed the support of the leading *optimates,* a man of Crassus's background should have attained that office *suo anno.*

Although Crassus might appear to have had a bleak political future in 80,[36] he was not deterred by opposition to his ambitions among powerful political leaders. He understood the uses of a very great weapon—wealth. Carefully and skillfully he set about to amass a large fortune in order to build up a powerful, independent political position.[37] Crassus, of course, is chiefly remembered for his wealth, which was proverbial, even among his contemporaries (Cic. *Att.* 1.4.3, *Tusc. Disp.* 1.12; Sall. *Cat.* 48.5; Plin. *HN.* 33.134; Plut. *Crass.* 11.1; Tertul. *Apol.* 11). From the days of Cicero and Plutarch, it has been the fashion to hold him up reproachfully as an example of the greedy man. Cicero once remarked that Crassus would dance in the Forum if he should suddenly find himself with the power to have himself named as an heir in a will by simply snapping his fingers (*Off.* 3.75). Plutarch said at the beginning of his biography that Crassus's virtues were obscured and all other vices weakened by the one vice of avarice (*Crass* 2.1).[38]

At another time, however, Cicero correctly pointed out that the real motivating force behind Crassus's acquisition of wealth was ambition for the political power it could bring (*Off.* 1.25):

In quibus autem maior est animus, in iis pecuniae cupiditas spectat ad opes et ad gratificandi facultatem, ut nuper. M. Crassus negabat ullam satis magnam pecuniam esse ei, qui in re publica princeps vellet esse, cuius fructibus exercitum alere non posset.[39]

35. See below, n. 84.
36. Cf. Garzetti, "Crasso," *Athenaeum* 19 (1941): 17.
37. Garzetti ignores this factor in his general assessment of Crassus's situation: ibid., pp. 18–20.
38. The first part of this statement recalls Velleius Paterculus's judgment of Crassus: *Vir cetera sanctissimus immunisque voluptatibus, neque in pecunia neque in gloria concupiscenda aut modum norat aut capiebat terminum* (2.46.2).
39. Modern scholars have not entirely ignored this fact: e.g. Drumann, *Geschichte* 4, p. 85, n. 6; Gelzer, *RE* 13.1 (1926), 299, s.v. "Licinius" (68); and M. Grant, *Julius Caesar* (London, 1969), pp. 44–45. Having acknowledged it, however, they still present an overall view of him as a

The dictum quoted at the end of this passage, that no one wishing to be a first-rate power at Rome could count his fortune great enough unless he could support an army with his own income, makes Crassus's motive in amassing wealth very clear (cf. Cic. *Parad. Stoic.* 6.45; Plut. *Crass.* 2.7; Dio 40.27.3).[40] Marius and Sulla had both demonstrated that, in the turbulent world of the Late Republic, no one who aspired to be one of the great political forces in the state, a *princeps civitatis*, could afford to be without a loyal army to back him.

Crassus is no more or less an example of the avaricious man than Marius, Sulla, Pompey, or Caesar. In fact, Pompey and Caesar became much wealthier than Crassus.[41] All of these men understood that great political power in the Roman Republic of their day could not be secured without great per-

man corrupted by the love of money: Drumann wrote, "Die Natur hatte ihm nicht den Stempel der Grösse aufgedrückt. Nur mit fremden Flügeln vermochte er sich zu erheben, und auch dann ruchte sein Blick auf dem Staube, Gold zu erspähnen (*Geschichte* 4, p. 126); Gelzer called him "ein gemeinschädliche Ausbeuter" (*RE* 13.1, 330). In support of the view expressed in the text, see now E. Gruen, *The Last Generation of the Roman Republic* (Berkeley and Los Angeles, 1974), pp. 67–69.

40. Pliny the Elder substitutes "legion" for "army" in his version of this remark (*HN* 33.134). E. Badian has speculated that Pliny's version is more accurate, especially if it is taken as a reference to Crassus's payment of troops during the war against Spartacus in 72 and 71: "Additional Notes on Roman Magistrates," *Athenaeum* 48 (1970): 7, and *Roman Imperialism in the Late Republic* (Ithaca, 1968), p. 109, n. 20. Recently, B. A. Marshall has argued for the larger force: "Crassus and the Command against Spartacus," *Athenaeum* 51 (1973): 117–18. Some rough calculations will support him and show that Crassus easily could have supported Cicero's figure of six legions for a year's service in 72/71 (Cic. *Parad. Stoic.* 45). At this time, the ordinary Roman legionnaire received 112½ denarii a year, and the average legion had about 4,000 men. These and the following figures are based on G. R. Watson, *The Roman Soldier* (London, 1969), pp. 21–25, 89–101). At 100 denarii to the mina and sixty minae to the talent, that would add up to 450 talents in annual pay for six legions. In addition, each legion had 1,000 auxiliaries, who received one-third of the legionary pay, so that the auxiliaries for six legions would have cost 37½ talents. Finally, the 500 cavalrymen attached to each legion received two-thirds of the legionary pay, so that for six legions, they would have cost another 37½ talents. The total for these amounts is 525 talents. With allowances for the higher pay given to men of higher ranks, 550 to 600 talents would be a reasonable figure for the annual pay of six legions in 72/71. Even if Crassus had not acquired quite half of the 7,100 talents he was worth in 55 (Plut. *Crass.* 2.2), he could have supported six legions for a year without seriously diminishing his wealth. What he could not have handled from income could have been met with loans.

41. Badian has made their extraordinary wealth abundantly clear: *Roman Imperialism*, pp. 81–83, 89–90.

sonal wealth. Large amounts of cash were needed to hold splendid games, give largess to the populace, hire thugs to intimidate the opposition, pay armies, reward veterans, bribe the voters in the *comitia*, buy off the jurors in trials instigated by one's political rivals, and win the support of others by loans of money to pay off the debts that they had incurred in doing the same things.[42] The reason that men like Pompey and Caesar were not and are not criticized for greed is that they acquired their huge fortunes, in large part, directly or indirectly from military conquests.

The aristocratic values of the Roman ruling class countenanced profits derived from booty, because military glory was one of the aristocrats' greatest goals. Otherwise, the opportunities for profit open to members of the ruling elite were severely limited. Only investments in agricultural land were viewed as really honorable. According to Livy (21.63.4), the profits of trade were thought improper for Roman Senators, and the *lex Claudia* of 218 sought formally to debar them from commercial activity. Although this law was commonly circumvented in Cicero's day (*Verr.* 2.5.45), obvious or large-scale participation in business was still frowned upon by the Roman aristocracy (Cic. *Off.* 1.151, *Phil.* 5.26).[43]

Both of the approved activities were not really practical for Crassus, however, if he wished to pursue a great political career. Investment in agricultural land produced a relatively low rate of return, especially in the short run, so that those senators who did invest primarily in landed estates were chronically short of cash.[44] On the other hand, since official advancement was hampered, and since Pompey was surpassing him in the military sphere (Plut. *Pomp.* 8–12), Crassus's prospects for obtaining a lucrative provincial assignment or military command were nil. Crassus had to take advantage of every possible way to acquire wealth in order to achieve the power he desired (Plut. *Crass.* 7.1–2). As a result, his money became the subject of a hostile literary tradition that was set by his political

42. M. Gelzer has given a detailed account of the activities and the financial obligations of Roman politicians in the late Republic: *The Roman Nobility*, trans. R. Seager (Oxford, 1969), pp. 110–23.
43 Cf. Wiseman, *New Men*, p. 79 and E. Badian, *Publicans and Sinners* (Ithaca, 1972), pp. 101–7.
44. Gelzer, *Roman Nobility*, pp. 23–24.

enemies, who scorned the methods Crassus adopted or who sought to play upon this attitude in others for their own political advantage.[45]

That is not to say that Crassus shared none of the Roman nobility's traditional interest in landed estates. His own statement that his worth at the beginning of his career was 300 talents indicates that he must have inherited much of his family's property after his father and remaining brother had perished (Plut. *Crass.* 2.2).[46] At the rate of 24,000 sesterces (*HS*) to the talent, he was, therefore, worth 7,200,000 *HS*, a large amount of which would have been represented by landed estates.[47] Regardless of any direct manipulation of proscription lists, Crassus hardly could have failed to take legal advantage of the low prices resulting from Sulla's proscriptions to acquire more estates (ibid., 2.3, 6.6–7).[48]

Crassus acquired so many estates that Adcock saw him soon running short of ready cash and unloading them at a profit to Sulla's new senators.[49] Some, perhaps, he did sell, but many others he must have kept. Besides respectability, large, well-run estates still could provide significant revenue from rents and the sale of their products for use in more speculative investment ventures.[50] Furthermore, Plutarch specifically mentions the value of Crassus's land holdings and their laborers in outlining his wealth (ibid., 2.5).

At the beginning of his career, a more lucrative source of ready profits probably was selling Sulla's new senators houses

45. Although his name is not mentioned, the full opprobrium heaped upon Crassus may be seen in Cicero, *Paradoxa Stoicorum*, 6. H. Rackham's argument that Crassus is not being alluded to is based upon the incorrect belief that Crassus was a member of the equestrian order, for which business enterprises were considered appropriate: Cicero, *De Oratore Book III LCL* (Cambridge, Mass., and London, 1942), 253.

46. See Chapter Two, note 11.

47. Although this was not a great fortune among the nobility, it was comfortable. Wiseman argues persuasively that 1,000,000 *HS* stood as the minimum property qualification for a senator in the late Republic: *New Men*, pp. 66–67.

48. Cf. Gelzer, *RE* 13.1 (1926), 298.8–17, s.v. "Licinius" (68). To keep Crassus's action in perspective, however, there were few who did not do the same as he when they had the chance, even M. Aemilius Lepidus, who later followed a *popularis* course (Sall. *Hist.* 1.55.18 M).

49. Adcock, *Crassus*, p. 16.

50. Wiseman, *New Men*, p. 78. Cato the Elder had given much attention to money-making in many of the same ways as Crassus—through buying up profitable lands and loaning money (Plut. *Cat. Mai.* 21.5–8).

in Rome rather than country estates, of which many new sena-
tors were sufficiently possessed, since they were already wealthy
and important men in other areas of Italy.[51] After becoming
Roman senators, however, they would have needed homes at
Rome in keeping with their newly bestowed status and for
use when the Senate was in session.[52] Crassus dealt extensively
in real estate at Rome. Plutarch tells a famous story of how
Crassus was able to buy up a great deal of property in the city.
Since there were no zoning regulations or building code at
Rome, buildings were often crowded together and poorly
constructed or designed. As a result, fires were endemic. Crassus assembled a corps of more than 500 slaves trained in archi-
tecture and building trades. When fires broke out in Rome,
he or his agents would offer to buy for a low price burning
buildings, or ones nearby. Not wishing to face the risk of
losing everything or to bear the expenses of rebuilding, many
owners took Crassus's offers (Plut. *Crass.* 2.4). If some of
these properties subsequently escaped the flames, so much the
better for Crassus, who had acquired prime real estate at prices
well below market value. Those buildings that were burned
were repaired or replaced by Crassus's skilled slaves on land
that could not otherwise have been bought so reasonably in
the crowded metropolis. Indeed, he became proverbial for
his building activity (Plut. *Cat. Min.* 19.5).

It is often assumed that Crassus had organized fire brigades
to put out the fires once he had purchased burning or threatened buildings from their owners. None of the ancient sources
gives information to this effect, but it does seem reasonable
that Crassus would have taken steps to put out or halt the
spread of the fires once he had made a purchase. The less rebuilding necessary, the greater his margin of profit. Moreover,
Crassus went to great lengths to win popular favor by his
services (Plut. *Crass.* 3.1–3), and, as the case of M. Egnatius

51. E.g., the sons of the wealthy Munatius Mazius of Aeclanum (Vell.
Pat. 2.16.2) and Statius, the rich Samnite (App. *BC* 4.25). Cf. R. Syme,
"Caesar, the Senate, and Italy," *Papers of the British School at Rome*
14 (1938): 22–24, and Hill, "Sulla's Military Oligarchy," *PCA* (1931):
65. An interesting parallel from almost twenty years later is Crassus's
sale of a house on the Palatine to the *novus homo* Cicero for 3,500,000
HS (Cic. *Fam.* 5.6.2).

52. Adcock, *Crassus*, p. 16.

Rufus illustrates sixty years later under Augustus, great popularity could be gained from putting out fires with private troops of slaves (Vell. Pat. 2.91.3; Dio 53.24.4).

Plutarch actually claimed that Crassus gained possession of the largest part of Rome (*Crass.* 2.4). This exaggeration has led some scholars to view Crassus as a great slumlord, milking rents from countless tenements in the teeming *insulae* where Rome's lower classes dwelt.[53] Tying up capital in vast amounts of rental property is not the way to make a great fortune quickly. The quickest and largest profit would have been made from selling many of the new or refurbished buildings to others. No doubt, Crassus was familiar with the example of C. Sergius Orata, whom his famous relative, the orator L. Licinius Crassus, had represented in a suit against M. Marius Gratidianus in 91 (Cic. *de Or.* 1.178, *Off.* 3.67). Orata had made a fortune in Campania by furnishing old villas with central heating and selling them at handsome profits to wealthy Romans (Val. Max. 9.1.1; Pliny *HN* 9.79, 168–169; Collum. 8.16.5).[54] Had Crassus held on to the property that he acquired in Rome, he, too, would have faced heavy losses from fires, and perhaps unpopularity as a landlord. New owners could be left to worry about upkeep and the collection of rents.

Crassus used skilled slaves not only in his real estate activities but probably in other areas as well. According to Plutarch, trained slaves, such as readers, copyists, silversmiths, stewards, and table servants were the basis of a large portion of his wealth. Since Crassus did not waste money in the possession of numerous houses and villas, as did men of much more modest means (Plut. *Crass.* 2.5), it is difficult to see why he would have needed these slaves entirely for his personal use. It would seem that he had discovered the principle behind modern manpower rental services. If someone needed the temporary services of a reader or copyist, Crassus, for a fee, could

53. E.g., Drumann, *Geschichte* 4, p. 123; Gelzer, *RE* 13.1 (1926), 299.33-35, s.v. "Licinius" (68); Adcock, *Crassus*, pp. 16–17.
54. For a full account of Orata's activities, see J. H. D'Arms, *Romans on the Bay of Naples* (Cambridge, Mass., 1970), pp. 18–23. Pliny's account (*HN* 9.168) does not necessarily indicate that Orata invented the use of *pensiles balneae* to heat villas, yet the use of the perfect instead of the pluperfect tense may mean that he did.

fill the need from the ranks of his trained slaves. If someone were giving an unusually large banquet, Crassus was right there with the necessary extra personnel.

Mines provided Crassus with another source of income. Plutarch reports that he owned silver mines (*Crass.* 2.5). These mines probably were in Spain, where most of the silver was being produced at the time, where Crassus's father had been a governor, and where Crassus himself had fled a few months before Cinna's death.[55] Perhaps he also had an interest in tin mining, or at least the tin trade. Again the connection goes back to his father, who had opened for the Romans the sea route from Spain to Cornwall and the Scilly Isles (Strabo 3.5.11).

Although Plutarch does not mention it, Crassus is not likely to have overlooked the profit to be gained from investing in the farming of taxes. Such an interest in the activities of the *publicani* would help to explain why he took up their cause in 61, when they discovered that they had overbid for the taxes of Asia. They were threatened with bankruptcy, and Crassus led their efforts in petitioning the Senate for a revision of the contracts (Cic. *Att.* 1.17.9).[56]

Other ways of acquiring money were also ascribed to Crassus. They are less honorable, hence more favored by the gossipers and political enemies that have influenced the biographical tradition. For example, a certain Vestal Virgin named Licinia, perhaps a relative, is said to have had a suburban villa that Crassus coveted. Because he allegedly spent much time with her in trying to persuade her to sell the property at a low price, he was charged with corrupting a Vestal. According to Plutarch, however, the jury, believing that the driving force in Crassus's life was avarice, had no doubt that Licinia's property was his only interest, and he was cleared of any sexual impropriety (Plut. *Crass.* 1.2, *Inimic. Util.* 6).

Perhaps there is some foundation to the story that Crassus cultivated the Vestal's friendship for her property. Neverthe-

---

55. For a history of silver mining in Spain, see S. G. Checkland, *The Mines of Tharsis* (London, 1967).

56. Badian, *Roman Imperialism*, p. 75, and *Publicans and Sinners*, pp. 100–104. For a full discussion of this incident see Chapter Eight.

less, the only solid fact is that Crassus did acquire Licinia's villa (ibid.). He might not have paid her undue attention at all, and the whole story may have been created after it had become known that he had purchased this property from Licinia at a very favorable price. If she was related to Crassus, the low price comes into better perspective, and the story of excessive attention need not be believed uncritically.

Regardless of that question, however, the name of Licinia's accuser immediately raises suspicion about the validity of the charge that Crassus had behaved improperly toward the Vestal. Plutarch identifies the man as a certain Plotius. There are only two known Plotii of real significance in the 70s and 60s, the period during which this prosecution could have been made.[57] One is an otherwise unnamed Plotius (Plautius), who is thought to have been a tribune in 70 and to have proposed the *lex Plotia agraria* dealing with land allotments for Pompey's veterans from the Sertorian war.[58] The other is one A. Plautius (Plotius), who served as one of Pompey's legates in the pirate war and the war against Mithridates.[59] In 56, as a tribune of the *plebs*, he supported Pompey's desire to restore Ptolemy Auletes to the throne of Egypt (Dio 39.16.2). As praetor in 51, he was favorable to the Pompeians (Cic. *Att.* 5.15.1, *Planc.* 17) and in 49–48 he probably held the governorship of Pontus and Bithynia as part of Pompey's eastern bulwark (Cic. *Fam.* 13.29.4).[60] If either of these men is the Plotius who laid the charge of *incestum* against Licinia, one can rightly suspect political propaganda behind the whole story of Crassus's dealings with Licinia.[61]

Valerius Maximus recalls a story that Crassus, along with

57. The date of Crassus's trial was probably ca. 73. Cf. Broughton, *Magistrates*, 2, p. 114.
58. R. E. Smith, "The Lex Plotia Agraria and Pompey's Spanish Veterans," *Classical Quarterly* 7 (1957): 82–85. Cf. Gruen, LGRR, p. 41.
59. Broughton, MRR 2, pp. 149, 156, 160, 164, 171.
60. Ibid., pp. 263, 267.
61. Another possibility is that the otherwise unidentified Plotius, tribune of 70, was P. Plautius Hypsaeus, who was Pompey's proquaestor from 64 to 61: see Broughton, MRR 2, pp. 163, 169, 176, 181 for Hypsaeus's service with Pompey. It does not seem probable, however, that he would have been a tribune before being a quaestor. Smith, "*Lex Plotia Agraria,*" CQ (1957): 85, n. 67, suggests that the tribune of 70 and A. Plautius are one and the same. In this case, however, a second tribunate would have to be accepted for 56: Broughton, MRR 2, p. 209.

that pillar of the optimate establishment, Q. Hortensius, had shared in a false inheritance from the estate of one L. Minucius Basilus (9.4.1). This story is the basis of Cicero's claim that Crassus would have danced in the Forum if he were offered the power of getting himself named as an heir when he was not one (*Off.* 3.75). It is significant that Crassus is singled out by Cicero, who knew full well that his own friend Hortensius attempted to share in the false inheritance from Minucius (*Off.* 3.73–74). The practice of gaining inheritances by questionable means was not uncommon in the Late Republic and in the Empire. Crassus was probably no more or no less guilty of this type of practice than many of his contemporaries.[62]

Similarly, although advocates at court were not supposed to receive fees from their clients,[63] all successful pleaders found ways to circumvent this prohibition. No doubt, Crassus also received ample considerations from those innocent and not-so-innocent men whom he was always willing to defend (Plut. *Crass.* 7.2; Sall. *Cat.* 48.8; Cic. *Parad. Stoic.* 6.46).[64] The noble Hortensius once again provides a parallel in the valuable ivory sphinx that he received from Verres (Pliny *HN* 34.48; Plut. *Cic.* 7.6). Even Cicero, despite his moralizing, was not able

62. In the case of Minucius, Crassus's motives may have been more political than monetary. Minucius's rightful heir was M. Satrius, one of Sulla's former lieutenants and a powerful man in Pompey's home district of Picenum (Cic. *Off.* 3.73–74). Although this evidence does not guarantee any connection between Satrius and Pompey, it is possible that there was some tie and that Crassus (and the *optimates*, through Hortensius) may very well have been hoping to weaken one of Pompey's important friends in this crucial source of support and manpower, as Julius Caesar succeeded in undermining Pompey there later: cf. R. Syme, *The Roman Revolution* (Oxford, 1939), p. 92, n. 5. F. Münzer dates this incident to 70 or 69, when either Crassus or Hortensius had been consul, or even to 74, when Verres was praetor and sought to assign the estate of a certain Minucius to an unlawful heir (Cic. *Verr.* 2.1.115–16): *RE* 15.2 (1932), 1947, s.v. "Minucius" (37). The former dates are possible, but 74 seems very probable. The name Minucius makes it highly likely that the references in Valerius Maximus and Cicero are all to the same event. Moreover, 74 would fit in well with the political maneuvering between Pompey and Crassus described above in connection with the accusation laid against Crassus concerning his relationship with the Vestal Licinia. Likewise, Hortensius and Verres were closely connected with Pompey's optimate opponents: cf. Appendix C to Chapter One.

63. According to the *lex Cincia de donis et muneribus:* cf. G. Rotondi, *Leges Publicae Populi Romani* (Milan, 1912), pp. 261–63.

64. Cf. Drumann, *Geschichte* 4, p. 124.

to resist profiting from cases. While he was defending P. Sulla from charges of involvement in the Catilinarian conspiracy of 63, Sulla loaned him 2,000,000 sesterces toward the purchase of an expensive house (*Gell.* 12.12).

More significant to Crassus, however, than any money gained from his services as advocate was the political capital that he built up among grateful clients (Plut. *Crass.* 3.2). Crassus fits the picture of a great political boss, passing out a benevolent smile here, fixing a troublesome legal matter there, bailing out a friend with a loan—all repayable in the currency of respect and support in contests with his rivals. Always attentive to the little details that make a large personal empire work efficiently, Crassus knew the value of the favors and kindnesses that bind the smaller man to the greater. Men of lower rank were graciously invited to be guests at his pleasant table. On the streets, he greeted passers-by, no matter how obscure, by name and with a warm clasp of the hand (ibid., 3.1–3).

Friends knew that they would always find a sympathetic ear with Crassus if they were in financial trouble, and Crassus often extended them interest-free loans (ibid., 3.1).[65] One such friend was Julius Caesar, the future dictator. After the expenses of his magnificent aedileship in 65 and those leading up to his election as praetor for 62, Caesar was so far in debt that his creditors attached his baggage when he was about to take up a provincial governorship in Spain (Caes. *BC* 3.16.3; Sall. *Cat.* 49.3; Vell. Pat. 2.3.4; Suet. *Iul.* 9.2–11; Plut. *Caes.* 6.1–4). Crassus guaranteed the creditors 830 talents and saved Caesar serious embarrassment (Plut. *Crass.* 7.6).

Naturally, Crassus's generosity was calculated.[66] Men potentially or previously unfriendly might be disposed to profess friendship in return for a loan. A man in one's debt on especially favorable terms is a loyal friend indeed, and can be very useful when the occasion demands. The power over others that Crassus gained from his generosity is aptly illustrated on two occasions: one fairly early in his career; the other thirteen years later. In 76, the tribune Sicinius railed against many

---

65. Conventional business loans were made at interest, of course: Adcock, *Crassus*, p. 18.
66. Garzetti, "Crasso," *Athenaeum* 19 (1941): 11–12.

powerful men in his campaign to have the pre-Sullan powers
of the tribunate restored (Cic. *Brut.* 216–17; Quintil. *Inst.*
11.3.129; Sall. *Hist.* 2.23–26, 3.48.8 M). When asked why Crassus was the only one whom he did not attack, he replied that
Crassus had hay on his horn (Plut. *Crass.* 7.9). Plutarch interprets this remark as a reference to Crassus's power, because
the Romans used to wrap hay around the horn of an ox prone
to gore, so that someone noticing the hay would take steps
to avoid the horn (ibid.).[67] Plutarch missed a significant pun
here, however. In Latin, the word for hay, *faenum,* and the
word *faenerator,* money lender, share the same root.[68] Those
in debt to Crassus (Sicinius or some of his supporters among
them?) certainly would have been afraid to gore his ox.[69]

The breadth of Crassus's power through financial obligations is clear from the second incident. During a meeting of
the Senate in 63, at the height of the turmoil over Catiline's
conspiracy, the informer Lucius Tarquinius named Crassus as
one of the conspirators. Sallust reports several reactions: some
of the senators thought the charge was incredible; others believed it, but thought that such a powerful man ought to be
mollified, not angered; and many men, obligated to him
through private dealings, alleged perjury and demanded that
the question be opened to debate. Accordingly, the full Senate
voted that Tarquinius's testimony seemed false (Sall. *Cat.*
48.5–6). As Gelzer succinctly put it, "The richest man thus
became the most powerful, because by lending money he could
put most politicians under an obligation." [70]

Of course, Crassus's personal supporters were not made up
merely of those who were in debt to him. His many kindnesses
netted him a large number of friends and clients at Rome, in
the Italian municipalities, and throughout the provinces.
M. Caelius Rufus, the subject of Cicero's famous speech, *pro*

67. Cf. Hor. *Sat.* 1.4.34.
68. *Oxford Latin Dictionary,* s.v. "faenerator" and "faenum."
69. In terms of age, Q. Sicinius, the moneyer of 49, could have been
the son of Cn. Sicinius. If he were, one might speculate that Sicinius's
family was involved in banking, since moneyers were often chosen from
families experienced in financial affairs: Wiseman, *New Men,* pp. 85–86.
Hence, the likelihood of Cn. Sicinius's having dealings with Crassus would
be increased. No relationship can be shown, however: Münzer, RE 2A2
(1923), 2198, s.v. "Sincinius" (9, 12).
70. Gelzer, *Roman Nobility,* p. 114.

Caelio, who was accused of trying to poison the infamous sister of the equally infamous P. Clodius, had received part of his early training in Crassus's own house—a fact often ignored in discussing the circumstances of his celebrated trial (Cic. *Cael.* 9). It is natural, therefore, that Crassus appeared as one of the speakers in his defense (ibid., 18, 23).

Another famous person whom he defended with Cicero was L. Licinius Murena, the consul of 62 (Cic. *Mur.* 10, 48). Murena was the first of his family to have reached the coveted consulship. There were immediate political reasons for Crassus to join in his defense,[71] but he would not have been unmindful of future dividends from this service.

In 56, there were two other men whom Crassus defended in partnership with Cicero. The first was the tribune of 57. Q. Sestius, who had aided Cicero's return from exile and was being prosecuted at the instigation of P. Clodius (Schol. Bob. *ad Sest. argumentum,* 125 St; Cic. *Sest.* 15, 26, and passim). The second man was L. Cornelius Balbus, the influential friend of Pompey and Caesar (Cic. *Balb.* 17). It is fortunate that Crassus had Cicero for a partner in these cases, otherwise his role would be unknown. If Crassus had left an independent record of his oratorical career, there would be many more names to be added to the list of men who owed him a debt of gratitude.

Some of Crassus's friends can be revealed by the names of those who served on his military staffs in 72/1 and 54/3. The M. Mummius who was *praetor urbanus* in 70 may have been his legate in 72 (Plut. *Crass.* 10.1–3).[72] Q. Marcius Rufus, who is recorded as Crassus's legate in 71 (Frontin. *Strat.* 2.4.7), may have become tribune in 68.[73] Another legate, C. Pomptinus (ibid.), was the first of his family to enter the Senate, and became a praetor in 63.[74] In that year, he, as did Crassus, played a prominent role in the exposure of Catiline's conspiracy (Cic. *Cat.* 3.5, 14, *Flac.* 102, *Prov. Cons.* 32; Sall. *Cat.* 45). Similarly, the Quintus Arrius who was an associate of

71. Cf. Chapter Seven, p. 188.
72. Broughton, *MRR* 2, p. 119.
73. Ibid., p. 138.
74. The text of Frontinus gives the erroneous spelling "Pomptinius." T. R. S. Broughton, *Supplement to the Magistrates of the Roman Republic* (New York, 1960), p. 48.

Crassus in the courts and who also helped in the exposure of the Catilinarian conspiracy, probably served with Crassus during the war with Spartacus and may have served in Crassus's Parthian campaign in 54/3 as well.[75] L. Quinctius, who served against Spartacus during 71 (Frontin. *Strat.* 2.5.25; Plut. *Crass.* 11.4), had been a tribune in 74, had agitated for the restoration of tribunician powers, and had helped to reveal the corruption of the senatorial law courts in the case of the infamous *iudicium Iunianum*.[76] Finally, Cn. Tremellius Scrofa, Crassus's quaestor, could boast of only praetors in his family and did not rise beyond that rank himself.[77]

Less is known about the men who served with Crassus in 54/3. Arrius has already been mentioned in the previous paragraph. The most well known individual was Crassus's proquaestor, C. Cassius Longinus. His father had been consul in 73 and was proconsul of Cisalpine Gaul in 72, when Crassus prosecuted the war against Spartacus. Politically, Cassius's father may have favored Pompey, so that it would make sense to see Crassus attach the younger Cassius to his staff, possibly at the request of his triumviral partner.[78] It was this man who escaped from Carrhae to gain immortal fame as the instigator of Caesar's assassination and as co-commander of the Republican forces at Philippi.[79]

Other members of Crassus's staff in Parthia are scarcely more than names, but they may have had some interesting connections. That Paccianus may have been the son of Vibius Paciaecus, who gave Crassus refuge in Spain, has been mentioned earlier.[80] The two Roscii brothers mentioned by Plutarch (*Crass.* 31.2) are otherwise unknown, but there may be

75. He, or perhaps his son: see Chapter Seven, pp. 185–86 and nn. 43 and 46 for a full discussion.
76. Broughton, *MRR* 2, p. 103.
77. Apparently, his ambitions did not reach higher. He seems not to have taken a governorship after his praetorship (Cic. *Att.* 6.1.13). He appeared on only the fringes of politics thereafter (ibid. 7.1.8) and devoted much of his time to agriculture (Varro, *RUST.* 2.4.2).
78. For the elder Cassius see Chapter One, Appendix B, under the year 73. J. Linderski has shown conclusively that the son could not have been a quaestor in 53 and must have been a proquaestor: "Two Quaestorships," *Classical Philology* 70 (1975): 35–37.
79. Broughton, *MRR* 2, pp. 320, 360.
80. See above, p. 159.

a connection with Roscius Otho, who may have acted in Crassus's favor as tribune in 67.[81]

Concerning the two known legates, Octavius and Vargunteius (ibid., 27–31; Polyaen. 7.41; Oros. 6.13.3), speculation about Octavius would be idle, since that name is fairly common in the *fasti* and there is no other information given than his nomen and manner of death. Vargunteius, however, is not at all a common name, and immediately brings to mind L. Vargunteius, a bankrupt senator, who lost his life participating in the Catilinarian Conspiracy of 63 (Sall. *Cat.* 17.3, 47.3; Cic. *Sull.* 6, 67).

Little at all can be said of Petronius, Crassus's military tribune in Syria (Plut. *Crass.* 30–31; Polyaen. 7.41), or of his two prefects, Coponius and Egnatius (Plut. *Crass.* 27.6–8), but that in itself is significant.[82] Plutarch's brief remark to the contrary notwithstanding (ibid., 10.1), with the exception of Cassius, who came from the consular nobility, the men who served with Crassus in 72/1 and 54/3 were from second- and third-rank families, among whom Crassus had assiduously cultivated a large following to counterbalance the more prominent followings of the *optimates* and Pompey.

Outside Rome, Crassus probably was on a more nearly equal footing with them. His mother, Vinuleia, and his wife, Tertulla, illustrate his connections with the municipal aristocracy.[83] He also had inherited connections in the important Lucanian city of Heraclea through his father's grant of citizenship to one Alexas of that city (Cic. *Balb.* 50). In the provinces, Crassus inherited influence in Spain, as revealed during his exile, and, perhaps, in Istria (Tac. *Hist.* 2.72). He himself

81. Cf. the discussion of Roscius's actions in Chapter Five, p. 114 and nn. 55, 56.

82. The only other known Petronius of the late first century is the senator L. Petronius Rufus, who signed a decree of the Senate on 23 May, 17 B.C. (*CIL* 6, 32323). Coponius and his brother were praised as upstanding young men by Cicero (*Cael.* 24, *Balb.* 53). In these two cases, it may be significant that Crassus was co-counsel with Cicero. The younger Coponius brother, Gaius, barely escaped proscription at the hands of Marc Antony (App. *BC* 4.40). Egnatius could be related to the Egnatius who was a juror in the infamous *iudicium Iunianum* of 74 (Cic. *Cluent.* 135) and to the father and son who perished together in the proscriptions of 43, since he escaped death at Carrhae (Plut. *Crass.* 27.7–8).

83. Cf. Chapter Eleven, p. 292, n. 11 for the Axii of Reate.

naturally sought to further his provincial *clientela*. For example, he granted citizenship to a resident of Avennio in southern Gaul (Cic. *Balb.* 50), and he actively sought enfranchisement of Cisalpine Gaul when he was censor in 65 (Dio 37.9.3).

Thus Crassus's early actions, despite occasional setbacks, showed the tenacity, skill, and flexibility with which he pursued his later career. In exile, he prudently bode his time until it was possible to join a successful attack on his family's political enemies. He raised his own private force in Spain, and when rebuffed by Metellus Pius in Africa, he boldly joined Sulla to perform valuable military services in the civil war of 82. Then, when he lost the support of Sulla or Sulla's backers, Crassus vigorously exploited other sources of political strength. His detractors sought to discredit him with malicious gossip and falsehoods, but they have not shown that his success in acquiring financial resources and loyal followers was undeserved.

The power that Crassus amassed through his acquisition of wealth, clients, and friends enabled him to overcome his lack of favor among powerful nobles. Probably without ever having held an elective office, even the expensive but almost essential aedileship (an office that not even Caesar omitted), Crassus was elected praetor for 73.[84] The next step on the *cursus honorum* would be the coveted consulship and the complete restoration of his family's position within the Roman nobility. In the meantime, however, Rome was severely shaken by the fearsome revolt of the slaves under Spartacus, and Crassus seized the chance to be a military hero for the state.

84. For the political fate of a man who omitted the aedileship, see Cic. *Off.* 2.58. For Crassus's praetorship, see I. Shatzman, "Four Notes on Roman Magistrates," *Athenaeum* 46 (1968): 349; E. Badian, "Additional Notes on Roman Magistrates," *Athenaeum* 48 (1970): 6–7; and B. A. Marshall, "Crassus and the Command Against Spartacus,"*Athenaeum* 51 (1973): 109–21. For arguments to support the contention that Crassus never held the quaestorship, see above, pp. 65–66. Moreover, by 74, the aedileship was not important for Crassus, because he had already gained through other means the popularity that this office often brought.

IV

The War with Spartacus

The rebellion of Spartacus had broken out in 73,[1] and Crassus received his chance for a command in late 72, after a long series of Roman reverses. The last and most disastrous were the defeats of the consuls of 72, Cn. Cornelius Lentulus and L. Gellius Publicola, and of the governor of Cisalpine Gaul, C. Cassius Longinus, at Mutina (Liv. *Per.* 96; Flor. 2.8.10; Oros. 5.24.4; App. *BC* 1.14.117; Plut. *Crass.* 9.7). After Mutina, fear and desperation gripped the Romans (Plut. *Crass.* 10.1; App. *BC* 1.14.118; Oros. 5.24.5). Crassus became the man of the hour. At the request of the Senate, he took over command of the war from the consuls, Lentulus and Gellius (ibid.; Liv. *Per.* 96; Flor. 2.8.12).[2] Others were understandably

1. Some have placed the event in 74: e.g., C. O. Ward, *The Ancient Lowly* 1 (Washington, 1889), p. 283, and F. E. Adcock, *Marcus Crassus, Millionaire* (Cambridge, 1966), p. 21. They seem to have relied on Eutropius's date, A.U.C. 678 (6.7), which, with the Polybian foundation date of 751 (Dion. Hal. *Ant. Rom.* 1.74), would mean 74. Nevertheless, the majority of the evidence makes it certain that the year was 73: the epitomator of Livy places the event between 74 and 72 (Per. 95); and Orosius, in dating the outbreak of the war, names the consuls of 73, Lucullus and Cassius, and adds the A.U.C. date of 679 (5.24.1), which, with the Polybian foundation date of 751, also yields 73. G. Rathke accepts this date but argues that the month was October, probably about the 15th, on the grounds that the appearance of Claudius Glaber in the Senate the day before the Ides of October 73, occurred before he took command of the forces sent out against Spartacus: *De Romanis Bellis Servilibus* (Diss., Berlin, 1904), pp. 79–81. F. Münzer, however, thinks that this appearance of Glaber in the Senate occurred after he had returned from his engagement with Spartacus: F. Münzer, "Der erste Gegner des Spartacus," *Philologus* 55 (1896): 387. This arrangement of events seems better because it permits a more reasonable amount of time for the events that transpired between the end of his command and the winter of 73/2. It may well be that the gladiators in Lentulus's school were being readied for the *Ludi Romani*, that began on 4 September every year.

2. The People may also have taken a hand in the creation of the special command held by Crassus: E. Badian, "Additional Notes on Roman Magistrates," *Athenaeum* 48 (1970): 7–8. Z. Rubinsohn has rightly pointed out that the Senate did not abrogate the counsuls'

reluctant to risk taking such a command (App. *BC* 1.14.118), and from a practical point of view, Crassus was a good choice. He had proven his ability while fighting for Sulla, he was a good organizer, he had many friends, and he possessed great wealth to supplement a strained treasury.[3] Under these circumstances, even the leading *optimates*, who were basically distrustful of him, probably supported his command.

Crassus looked upon this command as a great opportunity. It would be easy, of course, to condemn him as a villainous, capitalistic exploiter who was anxious to take command of the war because he was one of Rome's great slave owners. No doubt, his personal financial interests were involved to some extent, but he cannot be condemned for not being a man from beyond his time. Unfortunately, slavery was viewed as a natural state in antiquity. It was unquestioned by most of the great philosophers and moralists of the time.[4] So much was slavery accepted in antiquity that not even the New Testament, the

---

imperium or dismiss them from office: "A Note on Plutarch *Crassus* X.1," *Historia* 19 (1970): 625–26. These actions were not in the Senate's power. As Rubinsohn argues, Plutarch's word ἐκέλευσεν must mean that the Senate "advised" or "recommended" that the consuls cease their military operations. The distinction here is a legal one; in practice, there was little difference: a recommendation from the Senate to the consuls was not lightly ignored. The Senate would, if necessary, have made it clear that it would not prorogue their commands beyond the end of the year if they protested, but they were probably quite happy to give up the prospect of having to face Spartacus again.

Rubinsohn also suggests that the consuls were further induced to return to Rome by a deal with Crassus in return for his support of their joint censorship that followed in 70. B. A. Marshall accepts this idea with the added speculation that since Lentulus and Gellius were adherents of Pompey, Crassus was now beginning to cooperate with Pompey: "Crassus and the Command against Spartacus," *Athenaeum* 51 (1973): 115–21. Both of these interpretations seem doubtful. Lentulus and Gellius were clearly in an untenable position, and there was no need for Crassus to make a deal with them. Moreover, Crassus may not yet have had in mind the revival of the censorship; that seems to have been Pompey's idea in 70 (see Chapter Five, p. 104). Finally, there is no reason to look for the beginning of cooperation between Crassus and Pompey at this time. Crassus had no need of it. With Pompey away in Spain, Crassus had the advantage at Rome and, if his present plans should work out, would continue to have it.

3. Adcock, *Crassus*, pp. 21–23. J.-P. Brisson unfairly treats Crassus as the best of a bad bargain in view of the lack of willing commanders: *Spartacus* (Paris, 1959), p. 223. A. Garzetti underestimates Crassus's influence with the Senate in obtaining this command: "M. Licinio Crasso," *Athenaeum* 19 (1941): 27–28.

4. Athenaeus (6.272) presents a few interesting exceptions.

foundation of a religion whose adherents now condemn slavery, was able to break out of a pattern of thought that viewed the relationship between master and slave as naturally ordained (cf. *Matt.* 10:24–25, 25:14–30, *Luke* 12:47, 1 *Pet.* 2:18). Crassus's primary reason for welcoming the command against Spartacus was not to perpetuate an unjust economic system, but to further his own political career.

After his praetorship, Crassus had not taken a provincial governorship. He did not need the money that Roman governors usually extorted from their provinces, and he doubtless preferred to remain in Rome to preside over his own personal empire.[5] A military command in Italy in late 72 had real advantages, however. With Sertorius dead and the war coming to a close in Spain, Pompey was expected to return soon. Speculation as to what he would do was rife (Plut. *Pomp.* 21.3). At worst, he would bring civil war, at best, he would demand a consulship out of turn. In either case, a military command was desirable for Crassus. Indeed, at Rome, the successful military commander was almost guaranteed entrance to the highest offices. Crassus's year for the consulship was 70, according to the interval between praetorship and consulship set by Sulla. But Pompey was the military hero who had captured the popular imagination. If Pompey should be allowed to run for one of the consulships of 70, his election would be assured. Crassus wanted to make certain that he would fill the other post. With the command against Spartacus in Italy, Crassus could keep track of his personal affairs while acquiring the needed military power and reputation in rivalry with Pompey, whose success in manipulating the Sullan oligarchy for his own personal glorification must have rankled considerably, especially in the light of Crassus's own loss of favor.[6]

Crassus was made propraetor with proconsular *imperium*, and he quickly set to work.[7] Many ambitious young men were

5. Hortensius in 68 and Cicero in 62 perferred to remain in Rome rather than take provincial commands.

6. Cf. Chr. Deknatel, *De Vita M. Licinii Crassi* (Diss., Leyden, 1901), p. 13 and Brisson, *Spartacus*, pp. 228–29.

7. Confusion over Crassus's position and the nature of his *imperium* has been great. Many have identified him as a praetor in 72: e.g., W. Drumann, *Geschichte Roms* 4, ed. 2, P. Groebe (Berlin and Leipzig,

induced by his reputation and friendship to join his staff (Plut. *Crass.* 10.1), and he recruited six new legions, probably at his own expense (App. *BC* 1.14.118; Cic. *Parad. Stoic.* 6.45).[8] Unlike his predecessors, he did not rely on raw recruits, but enrolled battle-tested veterans who had finished serving with Sulla ten years before.[9] The farms that Sulla had given them were threatened by the servile war. To protect them or seek adventure by serving under Sulla's old lieutenant probably was attractive.[10] These legions were added to the remnants of those already in the field, for a total of about 40,000 to 45,000 men (App. *BC* 1.14.118; Oros. 5.24.5).

Crassus showed himself a prudent and determined general. His first move was to secure the territory around Picentia in order to protect the approach to Rome should Spartacus mount the long-feared attack.[11] Next, he sent out a detachment of two legions under Mummius with explicit orders to observe Spartacus's movements but not to engage him under any circumstances (Plut. *Crass.* 10.1).[12] Mummius, however, could not resist the temptation of independent glory. He offered battle at the first chance. Of course, he was decisively defeated. Many men were killed, and many others threw away their weapons in cowardly retreat (ibid., 2.10.2).

1908), p. 91; Last, *CAH* 9 (1932), p. 333; Adcock, *Crassus*, p. 24. Some have said that he was a praetor in 71: e.g., Rathke, *RBS*, pp. 86–87, and Groebe, in Drumann, *Geschichte* 4, p. 91, n. 6. There should be no doubt, however, that he was a praetor in 73 and a *privatus* before receiving the command against Spratacus in 72: see above, Chapter Three, n. 84. Given the size and importance of his command, his *imperium* must have been proconsular: see Eutropius 6.7; M. Gelzer, *RE* 13.1 (1926), 302.62–63, s.v. "Licinius" (68); Garzetti, "Crasso," *Athenaeum* 19 (1941): 21–22; and R. E. Smith, *Service in the Post-Marian Roman Army* (Manchester, 1958), p. 1. Rubinsohn has correctly argued that his full title was *propraetor pro consule*: "A Note on Plutarch," *Historia* 19 (1970): 624–27.

8. Cf. Chapter Three, pp. 79–80, for his staff, and n. 40 for his legions.

9. So Adcock has argued: *Crassus*, pp. 22–23. And he receives some support from Sallust: *Omnis, quibus senecto corpore animus militaris erat* (*Hist.* 4.21 M).

10. Adcock, ibid.

11. Rathke accepted Plutarch's location, Picenum (*Crass.* 10.1): *RBS*, p. 57. Clearly, however, Plutarch confused Picenum with Picentia: Cf. Drumann, *Geschichte* 4, p. 91, n. 10; Gelzer, *RE* 13.1 (1926), 303.59–62, s.v. "Licinius" (68); T. Rice Holmes, *The Roman Republic* 1 (Oxford, 1923), pp. 388–89; F. Münzer, *RE* 3A2 (1929), 1533.56–62, s.v. "Spartacus"; and Garzetti, "Crasso," *Athenaeum* 19 (1941): 28, n. 4.

12. No praenomen or rank is given. Broughton lists him among the legates for 72: *MRR* 2, p. 118.

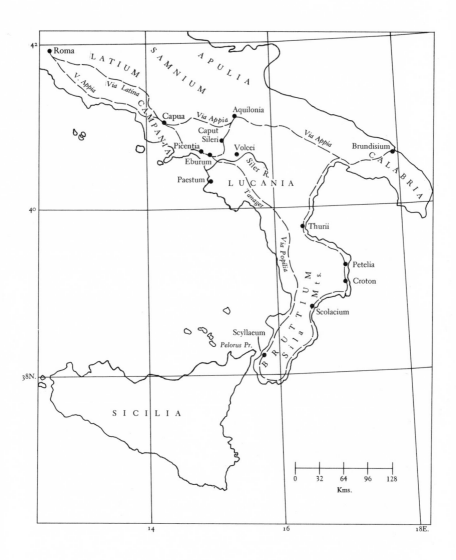

The two legions assigned to Mummius were probably from those who had served under Lentulus and Gellius.[13] Their actions support the charges of lax discipline on the part of the consuls (Plut. *Cat. Min.* 8.1). Accordingly, Crassus made use of decimation, a disciplinary measure that had not seen recent use in the Roman army. He chose fifty men by lot from the cohort that had most distinguished itself for cowardice and executed them in the traditional manner by having them beaten to death with clubs (Sall. *Hist.* 4.22 M; Plut. *Crass.* 10.3).[14] This punishment was a brutal object lesson, and Crassus has been roundly condemned for his action.[15] Yet times were desperate, and desperate measures were needed. The Romans were never famed for compassion. Many of them, like Cato the Younger, who had complained of the laxity under Gellius (Plut. *Cat. Min.* 8.1), would have heartily approved of this return to the *mos maiorum*. In this context, therefore, it would not be fair to criticize Crassus's behavior as unnaturally vicious.

Having disciplined the troops, Crassus led them out against Spartacus. The lesson of decimation had not gone unlearned. The Romans actually inflicted a defeat upon Spartacus's forces.[16] Accordingly, Spartacus realized that he had a real ad-

13. Cf. Appian, *BC* 1.14.118.

14. Appian (ibid.) says that Crassus decimated the legions of the consuls and also reports that he found another version of the story in which Crassus reportedly decimated the whole army to the sum of 4,000 men. This latter story is an incredible (perhaps even malicious) exaggeration. The former version is probably a slight corruption of the one Plutarch reported, which involves one cohort out of the legions that had been assigned to Mummius, and probably one that had formerly served under one of the consuls.

15. Cf. Garzetti, "Crasso," *Athenaeum* 19 (1941): 28.

16. Holmes rejects the story that Crassus defeated Spartacus's forces before Spartacus retreated south: *RR* 1, pp. 389–90; cf. Garzetti, "Crasso," *Athenaeum* 19 (1941): 29. First, Holmes argues that when he reported that Crassus defeated a force of 10,000 slaves and killed two-thirds of them, Appian was thinking of the victory that, according to Plutarch (*Crass.* 11.1–2), Crassus gained over a detachment of slaves near a Lucanian lake. Second, Holmes thinks that Appian had in mind the later defeat of Castus and Cannicus when he said that Crassus defeated Spartacus himself. Plutarch's account, however, does not rule out a victory for the Romans in battle at this time, and, contrary to Holmes's assertion, the passages cited from Florus (2.8.12) and Orosius (5.24.5) clearly refer to at least one Roman victory shortly after Crassus took command. Orosius even gives the enemy's losses as 6,000 dead and 900 captured, figures that correspond fairly well with Appian's report of two-thirds slain out of 10,000.

versary now and deemed it prudent to retreat to the south of Bruttium, where the terrain was difficult for legionary warfare and where he might find escape across the strait of Messina to Sicily (Flor. 2.8.12; App. *BC* 1.14.118; Plut. *Crass*. 10.3–4; Oros. 5.24.5). There he met with some of the numerous Cilician pirates who infested the Mediterranean at this time.[17] He made a bargain with them to transport at least part of his men to Sicily and stir up a new servile war there (Sall. *Hist*. 23.29 M; Flor. 2.8.13; App. *BC* 1.14.118; Plut. *Crass*. 10.3).[18] The pirates, however, insisted upon payment in advance and then sailed off to leave Spartacus stranded (Plut. *Crass*. 10.4).[19]

Spartacus's forces were concentrated on the promontory of Scyllaeum while he was attempting to find a way over to Sicily. Crassus took advantage of this situation by digging a trench and throwing up a wall and paling that completely cut off the rebel forces from the rest of the mainland (App. *BC* 1.14.118; Plut. *Crass*. 10.4–5).[20] After being disappointed by the faithless

17. The pirate menace had become so great that the Romans had commissioned M. Antonius (Creticus) in 74 to rid them from the entire Mediterranean. The task was so great, however, that it was not accomplished until Pompey took over in 67: Broughton, *MRR* 2, pp. 101–2, 146.

18. Plutarch says that Spartacus planned to ship over only 2,000 men. He had many times this number. Probably the initial 2,000 were expected to raise the standard of rebellion once they had landed on Sicily and make provision for bringing over the rest.

19. Brisson has conjectured that the pirates did not want to tarry on a coast that was in the vicinity of a force the size of Crassus's and that they may also have been fearful of landing on the opposite shore in the light of preparations made by the Roman governor, C. Verres, despite Cicero's attempt to discredit him (Cic. *Verr*. 2.5.5; Sall. *Hist*. 4.32 M): *Spartacus*, p. 232. The first point is reasonable. On the other hand, in the light of Verres' general administration of military affairs in Sicily and his refusal to aid Tempsa in Bruttium as he was passing by, when it was besieged by remnants of Spartacus's forces (Cic. *Verr*. 2.5.40–41), it is difficult to take Verres' preparations seriously. In fact, Verres seems to have been on rather good terms with the pirates in his area (ibid., 6.5.64–76). He may well have been party to their betrayal of Spartacus. For Verres' military administration, see F. H. Cowles, *Gaius Verres, an Historical Study* (Ithaca, N.Y., 1917), pp. 136–53.

20. Plutarch says that Crassus cut a ditch fifteen feet wide and fifteen feet deep across the whole peninsula of Bruttium, for a distance of 300 stades. That equals about thirty-five miles, or fifty-five kilometers. All scholars seem to have accepted this story at face value. Cf. Th. Mommsen, *The History of Rome* 4, trans. W. P. Dickson (New York, 1895), p. 362; Drumann, *Geschichte* 4, p. 92; Holmes, *RR* 1, p. 159; Gelzer, *RE* 13.1 (1926), 304, s.v. "Licinius" (68); Münzer, *RE* 3A.2 (1929), 1534, s.v. "Spartacus"; Last, *CAH* 9 (1932), p. 331; Garzetti, "Crasso," *Athenaeum* 19 (1941): 30–31; Gabba, *Appiani* B.C., p. 318; Brisson,

pirates, Spartacus had tried to construct makeshift rafts and cross over to Sicily (Sall. *Hist.* 4.30–31 M; Flor. 2.8.13). Unfortunately, winter weather and the tricky currents of Scylla and Charybdis completely wrecked this venture (Sall. ibid., 31 M). Now, with provisions getting low, he found himself shut in by Crassus's barricades, whose construction he had at first ignored (Plut. *Crass.* 10.6).

Spartacus's first attempt to break out met with serious re-

Spartacus, p. 233; Adcock, *Crassus*, p. 25. Two routes have been suggested: Mommsen, *History* 4, p. 362, preferred a line at the latitude of Thurii, which in air distance is roughly equal to the figure given by Plutarch; Münzer, *RE* 3A.2, 1534, and Gabba *Appiani B.C.*, p. 318, think a southern line at the latitude of Squillace (Scolacium) is more likely, where the distance would be about twenty-five miles (air distance) or forty kilometers.

Either route is ridiculous. First of all, even at the southern line, such a siege work would have served no purpose. Spartacus would have been left as the virtual king of about 1,600 square miles of territory, or one-third as much again as the state of Rhode Island, with a major port at Rhegium; while the northern line would have left him in control of about 5,000 square miles, a territory roughly equal to that of Connecticut. In either case, Spartacus could not have been starved out.

Second, at either line, such a ditch and wall as Plutarch describes would have been the eighth wonder of the Ancient World. It would have involved the displacement of hundreds of thousands of cubic feet of earth and stone in each case: at least 1,540,000 cubic feet in the north and 1,100,000 cubic feet in the south. Moreover, all of the foregoing figures assume level terrain. In actuality, it is hilly, rising to mountainous all over this area, so that the true distances covered would have been much more than appears on a map. Even with today's technology and machinery, it would have been a challenging task for a modern army.

Third, either of these two lines is impossible because Crassus's forces would have been strung out so thinly along so many miles that they would have been useless for conducting a meaningful blockade.

Finally, Sallust (*Hist.* 4.23–32 M) makes it fairly certain that Crassus shut up Spartacus in the area of Scyllaeum (modern Scilla), a much more feasible operation, since Scyllaeum is a modest promontory north of Rhegium and just across the strait from Pelorus on Sicily. As the modern town of Scilla illustrates, this promontory is large enough to have accommodated a body of men such as Spartacus's army. Moreover, it is easily cut off by an opposing force because the landward part is already separated from the surrounding territory on the east and the west by the deep ravines of the Torrente Livorno and the Vallone d'Angelo, while the short line between them on the south could reasonably have been fortified in the manner described by Plutarch.

Support for Scyllaeum as the site of Crassus's siege is also found in the alternate reading of Sallust, *Hist.* 4.33 M: *In silvam Silam fugerunt.* Sila is a large mountain to the east and north of Rhegium. It would have been the nearest and most appropriate place to which Spartacus and his men could have escaped once they had broken through Crassus's siege.

pulse (App. *BC* 1.14.119).[21] He then tried harassing tactics—frequent sallies against various points to test the line, bundles of burning branches tossed into the ditch to frighten and annoy the Romans. According to Appian, he even crucified a Roman prisoner in the space between the lines. He wanted to show his men the fate that awaited them if they were beaten, and hoped to spur them on to greater effort (*BC* 1.14.119).[22]

The news that the war had become bogged down in a siege did not please the populace at Rome. With the war against Sertorius in Spain just recently completed, Pompey's partisans saw a fine opportunity for advancing their hero's cause: a vote was obtained for Pompey to reinforce Crassus as he returned from Spain (App. *BC* 1.14.119).[23] Therefore, the *optimates*, who did not want the popular hero Pompey to gain any greater success and reputation than he already had, may have persuaded the Senate to vote a similar measure of the optimate general M. Terentius Varro Lucullus, brother of Pompey's rival L. Lucullus, who was about to return from Macedonia. With luck, it would be possible to end the war before Pompey arrived from Spain.[24]

21. When Appian says that Spartacus was trying to make an incursion into Samnium, he must have had in mind the ultimate goal of Spartacus. Lucania intervened between that territory and Bruttium. His assessment of Spartacus's losses as 12,000 dead, compared with only three men dead and seven wounded for the Romans, is ridiculous for both sides, as Gabba rightly comments: *Appiani B.C.*, p. 329.

22. This story sounds apocryphal, but it is not impossible. It does illustrate the desperation that Spartacus must have felt. In the same section, Appian also reports that Spartacus was waiting for a detachment of cavalry before making another major effort to break through Crassus's lines. Later (*BC* 1.14.120), he says that Spartacus used this cavalry finally to break the siege. It is impossible to see whence this cavalry could have come, and it seems likely that Appian has, at best, confused accounts of different battles. Plutarch (*Crass.* 10.6) gives an entirely different account of the final breakout, without any mention of cavalry at all.

23. Cf. Last, *CAH* 9 (1932), p. 331 and Holmes, *RR* 1, p. 159. This act gave Pompey a legal excuse for not disbanding his army when he crossed the Alps, as Gabba points out: *Appiani B.C.*, p. 330.

24. Plutarch says that Crassus had requested the Senate to call in both Pompey and M. Lucullus (*Crass.* 11.2). Appian reports only that the People summoned Pompey (*BC* 1.14.119). Rathke argued that Appian's version was a condensation of that given by Plutarch: *RBS*, p. 87. On the contrary, it seems that Plutarch is the one who confused and conflated events here. Crassus may well have asked for some additional troops, but it is difficult to believe that he would have asked for assistance from either Pompey or M. Lucullus. Such assistance would have lessened the prestige that he could have hoped to gain in under-

Under the lengthening shadow of Pompey, Crassus redoubled his efforts to obtain a decisive engagement with Spartacus, who, in turn, hoped to use Crassus's fear of Pompey to
bargain for a negotiated settlement. Crassus, of course, rejected
the proposal summarily (App. *BC* 1.14.120). Any negotiated
end to a servile war would not have been tolerated at Rome.
Crassus would have been disgraced, and he would have been
totally frustrated in all he had hoped to achieve by taking
command of the war in the first place. Finally, therefore,
Spartacus seized the opportunity to escape on a cold, snowy
night (Plut. *Crass.* 10.6; Sall. *Hist.* 4.35 M). Rushing a poorly
guarded section of the line, Spartacus's men hurled into the
trench whatever they could find—dirt, stones, wood, even the
dead bodies of men and animals—and rushed across to freedom (Sall. *Hist.* 4.36 M; Plut. ibid.; Frontin. *Strat.* 1.5.20).[25]

After the breakout from the siege in Bruttium, Spartacus's
forces split in two once more and headed north along the route
of the Via Popilia. The Celts and Germans were headed by
two of their own men, Castus and Cannicus (Liv. *Per.* 97;
Frontin. *Strat.* 2.4.7, 5.34; Plut. *Crass.* 11.2).[26] Spartacus commanded the rest.[27] They made their way into Lucania before

---

taking command of the war. Moreover, neither Pompey nor M. Lucullus
was near enough to give any immediate aid. Crassus seems, therefore, to
have been the victim of political maneuverings at Rome. Of course, the
order of events could have been the reverse of the one suggested. First,
the *optimates* could have maneuvered in the Senate to obtain a motion
empowering M. Lucullus to intervene as soon as he could, in order to
strengthen their hand. Such a maneuver then could have roused Pompey's supporters to obtain, if not from the Senate, then from the People,
a countermeasure that would have allowed him to intervene at the expense of both the *optimates* and Crassus.

25. Appian (*BC* 1.14.120) says that Spartacus got his whole army
across. Plutarch (*Crass.* 10.6) reports that a third of his army broke
through in the manner described. There need be no basic contradiction
here, since a third of Spartacus's men behind Crassus would have forced
the latter to abandon his siege and would have freed the rest of Spartacus's forces.

26. Holmes, citing A. T. Holder (*Altceltischer Sprachschatz* 1, pp.
735–36), claims that Cannicus is more correct than the spelling "Ganni-
cus" found in the texts of Livy and Frontinus: RR 1, p. 386, n. 6.

27. Plutarch (*Crass.* 11.1) claims that the split had occurred as the
result of a quarrel (cf. Sall. *Hist.* 4.37 M). More likely, the rebels had
again tactically split their forces to make foraging easier and to make it
more difficult for Crassus, who had to split his forces to cover them. If
the rebel forces had parted in anger, it is not likely that Spartacus
would have come to the aid of the others later (Plut., *Crass.* 11.1), nor
would Orosius have referred to them as *auxiliatores* (5.24.6).

Crassus could catch up with them and give battle. There, however, Crassus fell upon Castus and Cannicus while they were encamped by a lake whose water, Plutach says, was sometimes sweet and at other times bitter and undrinkable (Plut. *Crass.* 11.1).[28] Crassus sent around the mountain near this lake twelve cohorts commanded by his legates, C. Pomptinus and Q. Marcius Rufus.[29] After the battle had been joined, these troops suddenly ran down from the high ground and raised a clamor behind the rebels, who became so panicked that they abandoned the battle and fled in all directions (Frontin. *Strat.* 2.4.7). Crassus was unable to follow up this advantage, however, because Spartacus suddenly appeared and forced him to break off his pursuit (Plut. *Crass.* 11.1).

Crassus did not yet venture to fight Spartacus. Most of the other group had reformed and continued north along the Via Popilia. The way lay open directly to Rome if they chose to take it. He had to stop them first. Spartacus, on the other hand, probably took the road that branched off the Via Popilia at Eburum and followed the Siler River north towards Aquilonia.[30] He probably hoped to make a junction at Aquilonia

28. Although Plutarch's description of the Lucanian lake would fit a seaside lake, considerations of the times, distances, and places mentioned in the accounts of Frontinus (*Strat.* 2.4.7, 2.5.34) and Orosius (2.24.6), as will be clear from the rest of the narrative, lead me to identify this body of water with the now dry Lago di Palo near the modern town of Buccino (ancient Volcei) not far from Polla and just off the route of the Via Popilia on the right as one travels north: cf. R. Bonghi, "L' ultima campagna di Spartaco" in *Spartaco, Atti della Reale Accademia di Scienze Morali e Politiche di Napoli* 16 (Naples, 1881), p. 65. The lake bed is about five and one-half kilometers in circumference and is surrounded by mountain slopes. Before it was drained in the 1880s, its water level fluctuated considerably with the seasons: E. Grieco, *Buccino (Antica Volcei)* (Salerno, 1959), p. 10. The fluctuating level of the lake could account for the change in taste mentioned by Plutarch as it received freshly melted snow from the surrounding mountains in the spring and became sweeter, or dried up in the hot summer and became brackish.

29. For the name Pomptinus, see Chapter Three, p. 79, n. 74. Unfortunately, there is no record of the town Calamatium (or Calamarcum), which Frontinus also mentions (*Strat.* 2.4.7). A. Dederich, following the confused version of Plutarch (see n. 31 below), identifies Calamatium as a mountain: *Sex. Iulii Frontini Strategematicon Libri Quattuor* (Lipsiae, 1855).

30. Spartacus could have left the Via Popilia and followed the valley of the Tanager to where it joins the Siler and then picked up the road to Aquilonia.

with the Via Appia to Brundisium.[31] Accordingly, Crassus split his forces into two camps. His quaestor, Tremellius Scrofa, and his legate, L. Quinctius, were detailed to monitor the movements of Spartacus (Plut. *Crass*. 11.4; Frontin. *Strat*. 2.5.34).[32] He himself pursued Castus and Cannicus.

Spartacus soon learned that M. Lucullus had landed at Brundisium and decided to make a stand against his pursuers before he became trapped between two armies (App. *BC* 1.14.120).[33] While he was fortifying a camp near the headwaters of the Siler River, Crassus caught up with Castus and Cannicus (Frontin. *Strat*. 2.5.34; Oros. 5.24.6).[34] Crassus sent

31. Such an intention would explain the mention of Brundisium in Appian (*BC* 1.14.120). Apparently Plutarch (*Crass*. 11.4) has conflated events of the two battles that were fought against Castus and Cannicus. Spartacus's movement, therefore, should be placed after he broke up Crassus's first fight with them. Nor does it make sense to follow Plutarch and have Spartacus retreat to the mountains of Petelia and then march all the way back to face Crassus at the final battle. The only known Petelia is over 100 miles from Volcei, on the east coast of Bruttium, near Croton, and reached only by a rugged cross-country march over mountains or a circuitous route by road. Many scholars, therefore, have postulated the existence of another Petelia not so far away: V. Panebianco has sought it in the region of Cilento ("A proposito della capitale della confederazione lucana," *Rassegna storica salernitata* 6 [1945], 109–23), and Bonghi has suggested a place somewhere between the Siler and Tanager, perhaps Athena Petilia ("L'ultima campagna," *Spartaco*, pp. 66–75). Given the other geographic reference points, however, neither of these places makes sense. To have headed towards them, Spartacus would have run into enemy forces. L. Pareti's suggestion that Plutarch's text involves a corrupt reference to the mountains of Picentia makes sense paleographically and strategically, and it fits well with the geographic fact that the mountains of Picentia are not far from the site of Spartacus's last battle (*Storia di Roma* 3 [Turin, 1953], p. 705).

32. Plutarch mentions no Quinctius, only a Quintus, but the confusion of these two names is very easy. For an interesting parallel, see E. Badian, "The Family and Early Career of T. Quinctius Flamininus," *Journal of Roman Studies* 61 (1971): 102–11.

33. Plutarch (*Crass*. 11.4–5) lets moralizing overcome history and says that success went to the heads of his men after a battle, and that they forced him to fight. Appian, however, makes much better sense, except that he confused M. Lucullus with his more famous brother, L. Lucullus: Gabba, *Appiani B. C.*, pp. 331–32.

34. Spartacus's camp, therefore, should be located not far from the modern town of Capo Sele. The others were probably not far from Eburum. Münzer locates Castus and Cannicus near Paestum, but there is no evidence to support him: *RE* 3A.2 (1929), 1534.68–70, s.v. "Spartacus." Frontinus places them near a town called either Cantenna or Cathena. Unfortunately, this place canot be identified. Holmes has conflated Frontinus (*Strat*. 2.4.7, 2.5.34) and Orosius (5.24.6) and located Castus and Cannicus near the headwaters of the Siler: *RR* 1, p. 160. Orosius, however, refers to Spartacus alone in connection with the

out a detachment of cavalry that engaged the enemy and then quickly retreated in order to draw Castus and Cannicus after them in pursuit. At the appropriate moment, they dashed behind the wings of the main force, which Crassus had concealed. The trap was sprung, and the forces of Castus and Cannicus were annihilated (Frontin. *Strat.* 2.5.34; Plut. *Crass.* 11.3).[35] With this victory, Crassus recovered for Rome five legionary eagles, twenty-six manipular standards, and the fasces and axes of five lictors, along with many other spoils (Frontin. ibid.).[36]

In the meantime, Spartacus engaged the Roman force covering him and defeated it. Scrofa was wounded and barely escaped with his life (Plut. *Crass.* 11.4). Crassus, however, fresh from his victory over the others, was only a good day's march away. He arrived before Spartacus could take advantage of the situation and forced him into the long-awaited decisive battle

Siler and clearly implies that the Celts and Germans were elsewhere (ibid.):

> *Inde priusquam ipsum Spartacum ad caput Silari fluminis castra metantem bello adgrederetur, Gallos auxiliatores eius Germanosque superauit, e quibus XXX milia hominum cum ipsis ducibus occidit. Novissime ipsum Spartacum disposita acie congressum maximasque cum eo fugitivorum copias perculit.*

35. Holmes has treated Frontinus, *Strat.* 2.4.7 and 2.5.34 as merely separate accounts of the second battle against Castus and Cannicus: *RR* 1, p. 160. Clearly, 2.5.34 refers to a different battle from that mentioned in 2.4.7. First, Frontinus names a different town in each passage, Cathena and Calamatium (Calamarcum) respectively. Dederich's emendation (*Sex. Iulii Frontini*) of Cathena in Frontinus, *Strat.* 2.5.34, is unwarranted. Second, in 2.4.7, Crassus sends twelve cohorts to ambush the enemy from behind, whereas in 2.5.34, he uses cavalry to decoy the enemy into an ambush from the front. Third, the first account says only that the enemy was put to flight and battle was not joined; in the second account, the forces of Castus and Cannicus are completely wiped out.
Plutarch (*Crass.* 11.3–4), who inserted a digression between his accounts of the two battles, also seems to have done some conflating. His 6,000 ambushers in the second battle may correspond to the twelve cohorts of ambushers in Frontinus's account of the first battle.
36. As usual, casualty figures differ widely. Frontinus (*Strat.* 2.5.34) and Livy (*Per.* 97) give 35,000 dead slaves, Orosius (5.24.6) gives 30,000, and Plutarch (*Crass.* 11.3) gives 12,300. This last figure sounds most reasonable, but in the *Life of Pompey* (22.1) Plutarch uses this same figure when describing the defeat of Spartacus. Therefore, it may simply be a standard figure that was used when real knowledge was lacking.

(Oros. 5.24.6–7; Liv. *Per.* 97).[37] Realizing that this was the ultimate test, Spartacus joined the thick of it.[38] He fought bravely, but he was no match for the weight of arms that Crassus brought to bear against him. In the end, Crassus could not even recover his body, so great had been the slaughter (Sall. *Hist.* 4.41 M; Flor. 2.8.14; App. *BC* 1.14.120; Plut. *Crass.* 11.6–7; Oros. 5.24.7).[39]

Still, a number of the slaves escaped from the battlefield and fled to the mountains. There they split into several smaller bands when Crassus gave pursuit (App. *BC* 1.14.120). While he was ferreting them out, one group of 5,000 managed to elude him completely. They soon ran into Pompey's opportunistic arms as he returned from Spain, and were annihilated (Plut. *Crass.* 11.7, *Pomp.* 22.1). Pompey could not let any chance of enhancing his own reputation pass by. He wrote to the Senate that although Crassus had beaten the slaves in pitched battle, he himself had completely extirpated the war (Plut. ibid.). This claim did not fail to endear him to many

37. Cf. Appian (*BC* 1.14.120) and Plutarch (*Crass.* 11.6)) and n. 34 above. Ampelius (45.3) places the battle in Lucania, and Eutropius (6.7) locates it in Apulia. This contradiction actually adds confirmation to Orosius's location of the battle near the headwaters of the Siler. That river rises practically on the border between southwestern Apulia and northwestern Lucania. Therefore, it would have been a simple matter for one author to refer to Lucania and the other to Apulia in mentioning a battle that took place near the headwaters of the Siler.

38. C. O. Ward, perhaps drawing too great an inference from Appian and Plutarch (cf. previous note), places the armies of Pompey and M. Lucullus, as well as that of Crassus, at the last battle: *Ancient Lowly,* pp. 322–24. Any such inference is completely invalid.

39. Plutarch (*Crass.* 11.6) tells a brave story that Spartacus killed his horse before the battle and said that if he were victorious, he would have many beautiful horses, but if he were beaten, he would have no need of one. This story is probably apocryphal: cf. Brisson, *Spartacus,* pp. 237–38. It is a common dramatic topos found in descriptions of crucial battles: e.g., Sallust, *Cat.* 59.1 and Caesar, *BG* 1.25.1. Quite possibly, Spartacus did try to reach Crassus in the battle as Plutarch also claims in the same passage. Again, however, it is impossible to separate the conventional and typical from the truly historical in dealing with ancient battle accounts. Appian (*BC* 1.14.120) even adds the realistic detail that Spartacus, wounded in the thigh, dropped down to one knee and continued to fight until overwhelmed by his opponents. Who can say? The story has parallels elsewhere (cf. the death of Agis III, Diod. 17.63.4; Curt. 6.1.13–15). The only hard fact is that no one could find his body amongst the slain (App. *BC* 1. 14.120). At least Appian and Plutarch (in the *Life of Crassus*) have the good grace not to number the dead rebels. Appian says only that they were countless. Livy (*Per.* 97) and Orosius (5.24.7) give the typically exaggerated figure of 60,000.

of the Roman populace, but it sharpened an already keenly felt rivalry in Crassus.[40]

Regardless of Pompey's ungenerous behavior, the truth of Velleius Paterculus's evaluation cannot be denied: "The glory of having ended this war belonged wholly to Marcus Crassus" (2.30.6). In six months, Crassus, a specially commissioned private citizen, had accomplished what praetors and consuls had not been able to do in a year (App. *BC* 1.14.121).[41] Unwittingly, Spartacus had supplied him with the means to advance himself in the struggle for glory and honor that marked the life of a Roman noble (Vell. Pat. 2.30.6).[42]

As a visible reminder of his victory and a deterrent to further slave revolts, Crassus lined the road along his triumphant journey from Capua to Rome with 6,000 crosses bearing the bodies of crucified slaves (App. *BC* 1.14.120).[43] It is a monstrous and brutal sight for civilized men to contemplate today, but the veneer of civilization was even thinner then than now. The Romans thought it fitting.[44]

40. Adcock argues that Pompey's claiming of credit for Crassus's victory over the slaves "need not have engendered a deep-seated and lasting hostility between the two generals": *Crassus*, p. 26. More recently, B. A. Marshall has expanded upon this idea: "Crassus' Ovation in 71," *Historia* 21 (1972): 669–73. Nevertheless, Crassus had already felt the pangs of jealousy towards the younger but militarily more successful man, and he would not have been a Roman noble if he had not been angered at this attempt to steal the credit for ending the War against Spartacus. The lengths to which Crassus went to make his *ovatio* a magnificent and unprecedented one clearly indicate that he was trying to rival Pompey's triumph as much as possible.

41. Perhaps the celebration of the "Games of Highest Peace" on the first of April at Capua (*CIL* 10.2, 8070.3) was a memorial to this victory in the spring of 71: Rathke, *RBS*, p. 89 and Holmes, *RR* 1, p. 161, n. 2.

42. Brisson has suggested that without the bitter victory over Spartacus, Crassus's name might have rested indifferently with posterity: *Spartacus*, p. 242. It is likely, however, that a man of Crassus's position would have found other ways to impress himself upon the minds of future generations if Spartacus had failed to appear.

43. The number may be exaggerated, but the impact would have been hardly lessened: cf. Adcock, *Crassus*, p. 27. As for the road, it is not named in the sources. Modern authors usually identify it as the Via Appia, a reasonable assumption. The Via Latina also provided a route of about the same distance from Rome to Capua, but was not the one usually taken if Capua or other important Campanian cities were one's destination.

44. Adcock's remarks are worth quoting in full:

Those historians who condemn Crassus (as they may well do) have forgotten that no Roman aristocrat would have had a moment of

Despite the magnitude and importance of his victory, and in contrast with Pompey, a victor in a foreign war, Crassus was ineligible for a full triumph. He had to settle for an *ovatio*. It was a lesser distinction, but he was able to use his influence in the Senate to obtain the added honor of a laurel crown, traditionally reserved for a *triumphator*, instead of the myrtle crown customary for an *ovatio* (Cic. *Pis.* 58; Plin. *HN* 15.125; Plut. *Crass.* 11.8; Gell. *NA* 5.6.23).[45] Pompey would still outshine Crassus with a splendid triumph, but the race for preeminence at Rome was by no means finished.

---

pity to spare for these victims of the institution of slavery, with its ultimate sanction of ruthless terrorism. Only so could Romans feel secure from a repetition of such attempts to escape from bondage to freedom. The clemency of Caesar himself would not have preserved one of them. So too in his Res Gestae (25) Augustus takes credit for restoring 30,000 slaves, who had fought for Sextus Pompeius against him, to their masters to suffer execution (Crassus, p. 27).

45. Plutarch (*Marcel.* 22.2), in describing the *ovatio*, says that the victorious general did not ride in a four-horse chariot, nor wear a laurel wreath, nor have an accompaniment of trumpets, but walked on foot, accompanied by flutes and wearing a myrtle wreath, so that he appeared unwarlike and friendly instead of terrifying. By Crassus's day, however, the victorious general in an *ovatio* probably rode on horseback: G. Rhode, *RE* 18.2 (1942), 1898–99, s.v. "Ovatio." For an excellent study of Roman victory celebrations, see L. B. Warren, "Roman Triumphs and Etruscan Kings: The Changing Face of the Triumph," *Journal of Roman Studies* 60 (1970): 49–66. For the prestige value of Crassus's *ovatio*, see Marshall, "Crassus' Ovation in 71 B.C.," *Historia* 21 (1972): 669–73.

V

The Preliminary Struggle with Pompey, 70–65 B.C.

Rivalry with Pompey for supreme honors at Rome runs as a red thread through the rest of Crassus's career. At times, of course, accommodation or compromise was a necessity imposed by political realities, which Crassus was quick to recognize. On the long view, however, Crassus's ultimate goal was to be recognized as the leading man of the Republic, and he knew that Pompey's goal was the same. Despite temporary truces, rivalry always colored Crassus's relationship with Pompey.[1]

In 71, after he had returned to Rome from battling Spartacus and his followers, Crassus found it expedient to reach an accommodation with Pompey. Elections for the consulship were to be held later in the year. He was now eligible and planned to stand for that office, which was every aristocrat's goal.[2] Not to be outdone, Pompey, despite meeting none of the legal requirements for the office, was also aiming at the

1. This view has been accepted by numerous scholars and forms the basis of many interpretations: Plutarch, *Crassus*, 28; T. Rice Holmes, *The Roman Republic* 1 (Oxford, 1923), p. 161; M. Gelzer, *RE* 13.1 (1926), 298.55–299.8, s.v. "Licinius" (68); A. Garzetti, "M. Licinio Crasso," *Athenaeum* 20 (1942): 22; T. J. Cadoux, "Marcus Crassus: A Revaluation," *Greece and Rome* 3 (1956): 156–59. Some have sought to deny or minimize any rivalry between the two men: F. E. Adcock, *Marcus Crassus, Millionaire* (Cambridge, 1966), p. 28; K. H. Waters, "Cicero, Sallust, and Catiline," *Historia* 19 (1970): 20; B. A. Marshall, "Cicero and Sallust on Crassus and Catiline," *Latomus* 33 (1974): 809–13. Their objections to the more traditional view of a sharp personal rivalry cannot be upheld. In the light of his own failure, the older Crassus cannot but have been somewhat resentful of Pompey's much greater success in using service to Sulla for furthering his own career. Moreover, Pompey's blatant attempt to steal popular credit for ending the slave war would have offended even the most magnanimous Roman noble: cf. Plut. *Crass.* 6.4.
2. Having held the praetorship in 73, Crassus had fulfilled the requirement for an interval of three years between election to the praetorship and election to the consulship: cf. Chapter Three, p. 82, n. 84.

same goal. Even before his arrival at Rome, Pompey had sought widespread popular favor by letting it be known that he would support the restoration of full tribunician powers, which Sulla had curtailed (Sall. *Hist.* 4.45, 47 M; Plut. *Pomp.* 21.4; cf. Cic. *Verr.* 1.44–45). In the face of his great popularity and a loyal army awaiting his triumph outside Rome, the Roman Senate acceded to his demand for a special dispensation to stand for election (Cic. *Leg. Man.* 62; Liv. *Per.* 97; Plut. *Pomp.* 22.1–2; App. *BC* 1.14.121).

Crassus was in a difficult position. As already seen, there was no love lost between him and the powerful *optimates* among the nobility, despite his being compatible with them in many ways. They probably were hoping to obtain the election of someone more closely identified with themselves.[3] Regardless of his success in building up his own political and financial capital, Crassus could very well have failed in a race that included Pompey and a strongly supported *optimate*. Pompey, on the other hand, would have been very desirous of not having an optimate candidate as a colleague. For both Crassus and Pompey, the solution to their problem was clear—cooperation in support of each other's candidacy (Plut. *Pomp.* 22.1–2, *Crass.* 12.1).[4] With Crassus's personal political base and Pompey's overwhelming popularity, the results matched their hopes. They were duly elected consuls for 70.[5]

Despite their cooperation in this instance, rivalry never remained far beneath the surface. When Pompey refused to disband his army while waiting for Metellus Pius's return from Spain, Crassus refused to disband his and said that Pompey

3. Their most likely candidate was Q. Caecilius Metellus (Creticus), who was already eligible for the consulship: c.f. T. R. S. Broughton, *The Magistrates of the Roman Republic* 2 (New York, 1952), p. 108, n. 3. Significantly, he was elected consul for the year 69: ibid., p. 131.

4. In both of the passages cited, Plutarch describes their cooperation in terms that would lead one to believe that Crassus was receiving the most benefit from cooperating with Pompey. In actuality, Pompey had much to gain at this time, too.

5. The question of whether Crassus and Pompey were elected *in absentia* has been answered convincingly in the negative by J. Linderski: "Were Pompey and Crassus Elected in Absence to Their First Consulship?," *Mélanges offerts à K. Michalowski* (Warsaw, 1966), pp. 523–26. Since elections to the consulship were held outside the *pomerium*, in the Campus Martius, they could attend the election without any detriment to the one's impending ovation and the other's triumph.

should do so first (App. *BC* 1.14.121).[6] Then, when Pompey celebrated his magnificent triumph, Crassus strove not to let his lesser honor, the *ovatio*, be outshone.[7] As mentioned at the end of the previous chapter, for his *ovatio*, Crassus obtained special permission to wear the laurel crown usually reserved for *triumphatores*. Thus, he sought to make his own honor more like Pompey's in the eyes of the spectators.

Crassus also raised himself in the eyes of the Roman populace by dedicating one-tenth of his wealth to a sacrifice in honor of Hercules. This sacrifice occasioned a great public feast that the whole city of Rome shared at 10,000 tables set up for the diners. After consuming as much as possible, each Roman citizen received a three-months' supply of grain that would be a further reminder of Crassus's greatness (Plut. *Crass.* 2.2, 12.3, *Comp. Nic. Crass.* 1.4).[8]

Again, Crassus was competing with Pompey and his triumph.[9] The Roman triumph had been closely associated with the cult of Hercules from the earliest days of Rome.[10] Triumphant Roman generals had long sought to foster an association between themselves and this god in the public mind. It had become customary to dedicate one-tenth of the spoils to Hercules, often with the accompaniment of a great ritual

6. Clearly, Crassus was not willing to trust Pompey too far. For Pompey's part, Chr. Deknatel speculates that Pompey was looking for pretexts to keep his army because he wanted the command against Mithridates: *De Vita M. Licinii Crassi* (Diss., Leyden, 1901), p. 21. It is more likely that his immediate concern was fear of Metellus Pius, who was due to return from Spain soon.

7. Holmes dates Crassus's ovation before Pompey's triumph: *RR* 1, p. 164. Nevertheless, since Crassus had refused to disband his army before Pompey, it seems better to place Crassus's ovation after Pompey's triumph on the same day, 29 December 71. For the date, see Vell. Pat. 2.30.2 and M. Gelzer, *RE* 13.1 (1926), 307.31–35, s.v. "Licinius" (68). Deknatel follows App. *BC* 1.14.121 in thinking that they did not dismiss their troops until the end of their consulship. Plutarch's account, however, is to be preferred: cf. Garzetti, "Crasso," *Athenaeum* 20 (1942): 20 and A. N. Sherwin-White, "Violence in Roman Politics," *Journal of Roman Studies* 46 (1956): 6.

8. Badian has dated this whole episode to 55: *Roman Imperialism in the Late Republic* (Ithaca, 1968), p. 81. Plutarch, however, makes it clear that it occurred during Crassus's first consulship, in 70 (*Crass.* 2.2, 12.2). Just as Crassus's funds were adequate for maintaining an army in 71, so they would have been for this extravaganza in 70.

9. B. Rawson, "Pompey and Hercules," *Antichthon* 4 (1970): 30–37.

10. L. B. Warren, "Roman Triumphs and Etruscan Kings: The Changing Face of the Roman Triumph," *Journal of Roman Studies* 60 (1970): 55.

banquet held at the site of the *Ara Maxima* near the temples of Hercules Victor and Invictus.[11] The custom of the ritual banquet had fallen somewhat in abeyance and had been performed recently only by Sulla (Plut. *Sull.* 35.1).[12] At his triumph, Pompey vowed great games, probably in honor of Hercules (Cic. *Verr.* 1.31, *Pseud. Ascon. ad. Verr.* 1.31 217 St) and perhaps in imitation of Sulla's great *Ludi Victoriae Sullanae*. Crassus, therefore, countered with a vow to provide a great sacrifice and feast in honor of Hercules, in order to raise his *ovatio* even closer to the status of Pompey's triumph.[13] Clearly, this extravagant largess would also blunt the impact of Pompey's games and help Crassus in the competition for popular favor.[14]

Accounts of Crassus's activity during his consulship are varied. Plutarch says that after he and Pompey entered office, they differed and quarrelled on all points (*Pomp.* 22.3, *Crass.* 12.2). Most modern scholars accept the view that they did

11. B. Rawson, "Pompey and Hercules," *Antichthon* 4 (1970): 30–31. Cf. Warren, "Roman Triumphs," *JRS* 60 (1970): 55 and G. Dumézil, *La religion romaine archaique* (Paris, 1966), p. 424.

12. B. Rawson, "Pompey and Hercules," *Antichthon* 4 (1970): 30–31.

13. Crassus's rivalry would be even more pointed if, as Rawson (ibid.) argues, Pompey had vowed a temple to Hercules Invictus either after his earlier triumph or at the time of the present one. In the completed temple stood a statue of Hercules by the famous Greek sculptor, Myron (Plin. *HN* 34.57). Heius of Messana had also owned a Hercules by Myron, which Verres purloined (Cic. *Verr.* 2.4.5). Could it be that, in gratitude for Pompey's help in bringing Verres to justice, Heius gave this statue to grace Pompey's temple?

14. The date of Crassus's feast cannot be determined precisely within the year 70. Rawson (ibid.) argued that it was on 12 August, at the feast of Hercules Invictus. B. A. Marshall doubts that it could have taken place then, because that feast did not originate until Pompey dedicated his temple to Hercules Invictus on that date no earlier than 70: "Pompeius' Temple of Hercules," *Antichthon* 8 (1974): 80–84. Still, even if the feast had not existed earlier, provided that Pompey did dedicate his temple in 70, the day would have been set in advance, and Crassus could have timed his banquet accordingly. It is equally possible, of course, that Crassus timed his sacrificial banquet to coincide with Pompey's games, which began on 15 August (Cic. *Verr.* 1.31). In either case, it would have been an effective way of stealing some of Pompey's thunder. One might also argue that Crassus held his feast right after celebrating his *ovatio*. Nevertheless, December or January (see n. 7 above) would not be ideal months for an outdoor banquet for the Roman populace, and it would have been politically wiser for Crassus to time it so as to undercut Pompey's activities later in the year. Therefore, some date in mid-August seems to be the most reasonable time for Crassus's monumental dinner party.

cooperate in the restoration of tribunician powers and then fell into constant disagreement. They follow Plutarch (*Pomp.* 22.3) and claim that Crassus took the side of the Senate in matters other than that of the tribunician powers, while Pompey took that of the plebs.[15] Others maintain that all mention of rivalry in our sources reflects malicious propaganda from the triumviral period and that either Crassus and Pompey cooperated smoothly or that Crassus's private interests precluded participation in political rivalry with his colleague.[16]

None of these views is satisfactory. Private interests were no bar to Crassus's active participation in politics. Neither can his political activity easily be categorized as cooperation with Pompey or Pompey's senatorial enemies on all issues. Crassus shrewdly sought his own personal advantage. He maintained a flexible, independent course. When possible, he sought his own advantage against Pompey's; when expedient, he cooperated with Pompey in order to gain a share of the resultant popularity or other political advantage.[17]

The first item of business after the consuls entered office in 70 was the redemption of Pompey's popular electoral promise to restore the powers of the tribunate, which Sulla had sharply curtailed (Cic. *Verr.* 1.44–45; Liv. *Per.* 97; Vell. Pat. 2.30.4; Ascon. *Corn.* 76 C/59 St; Plut. *Pomp.* 21.4; App. *BC* 1.14.121; Pseud. Ascon. *ad Div.* 8, 189 St, *ad Verr.* 1.44–45, 220 St).[18] That Crassus did cooperate with Pompey in this endeavor is certain. Since he had been elected with Pompey on the

---

15. E.g., B. Maurenbrecher, *C. Sallusti Crispi Historiarum Reliquiae* (Leipzig, 1891), p. 173; M. Gelzer, *Pompeius,* ed. 2 (Munich, 1959), p. 65.

16. E.g., Adcock, *Crassus,* pp. 28–31; K. H. Waters, "Cicero, Sallust, and Catiline," *Historia* 19 (1970): 20. Previously I also expressed approval of the view that Crassus's private interests kept him politically inactive: "Cicero and Pompey in 75 and 70 B.C." *Latomus* 29 (1970): 66.

17. Garzetti overemphasizes Crassus's moderation here: "Crasso," *Athenaeum* 20 (1942): 15–20.

18. Under earlier legislation proposed by C. Aurelius Cotta, the tribunes had been restored the right to seek higher magistracies after their terms of office, but their powers as tribunes had been left as restricted by Sulla. Although the exact nature of these restrictions is a matter of debate, the most important aspects seem to have been strict limits on the power of vetoing legislation and the inability to move legislation without the prior approval of the Senate (Cic. *Verr.* 2.1.155; Liv. *Per.* 89; CIL 1.204/C. G. Bruns, *Fontis iuris romani antiqui* ed. 7, O. Gradenwitz [Tübingen, 1909], 14): cf. H. Last, *CAH* 9 (1932), pp. 292–93, 896, n. 3.

strength of the tribunician issue, he would not have dared to do otherwise. He would have lost needed popular favor and left it all to Pompey. The actual law, however, seems to have borne Pompey's name alone.[19]

Crassus also cooperated with Pompey in reviving the censorship after a long lapse (Cic. *Div. Caec.* 8, *Verr.* 2.5.15, *Cluent.* 117–34, *Flac.* 45, *Dom.* 124; Plut. *Pomp.* 22.5). Since both consuls had to agree to hold censorial elections (Cic. *Att.* 4.2.6), Crassus must have cooperated with Pompey in this instance. It was a very popular measure (Cic. *Div. Caec.* 8), and he was willing to oppose the conservative oligarchs in the Senate to gain popular favor by supporting it.

Although Sulla had not formally abolished the office of censor, he and his oligarchical followers had for all practical purposes, abandoned it. They wanted the new Italian citizens, who had not been enrolled right after the Social War and were a bloc of voters potentially dangerous to their political control of Rome, to remain unenrolled and thereby ineligible to vote.[20] Clearly, the revival of the censorship in 70 was part of a plan to undercut the power of the optimate oligarchs in the Senate.[21]

The men elected censors under the consuls' supervision were two friends of Pompey, Cn. Cornelius Lentulus Clodianus and L. Gellius Publicola.[22] The result of their work was a huge enrollment of new citizens (almost twice as many as in the previous, successful *lustrum*, in 86) full of gratitude to those who had made it possible.[23] Moreover, they struck sixty-four members from the rolls of the Senate (Liv. *Per.* 98), many of

---

19. W. C. McDermott argues that the only firm evidence for double sponsorship (Ascon. *Corn.* 76 C/59 St) is Cicero's perversion of the facts when he spoke while Crassus sat as *iudex* in the trial of Cornelius: "LEX POMPEIA DE TRIBUNICIA POTESTATE (70 B.C.)," *Classical Philology* 72 (1977): 49–51.

20. T. Frank, *Economic Survey of the Roman Empire* 1 (Baltimore, 1933), p. 255; E. Gabba, "Il ceto equestre e il senato di Sulla," *Athenaeum* 34 (1956): 137–38; L. R. Taylor, *Party Politics in the Age of Caesar* (Berkeley and Los Angeles, 1949), p. 52, and *The Voting Districts of the Roman Republic* (Rome, 1960), p. 120; T. P. Wiseman, "The Census in the First Century B.C.," *Journal of Roman Studies* 59 (1969): 59–75.

21. Despite Chr. Meier's denial: *Res Publica Amissa* (Wiesbaden, 1966), p. 269, n. 22.

22. For these two men and their association with Pompey, see E. Badian, *Foreign Clientelae (264–70 B.C.)* (Oxford, 1958), pp. 281–82.

23. Wiseman, "Census," *JRS* 59 (1969): 65.

whom probably had been appointed by Sulla and may have remained unfriendly to Crassus after he had lost favor among Sulla's political heirs. No doubt he would have enjoyed seeing such men diminished in status, while he reaped the gratitude of those who had been newly enfranchised.

Other reasons may also be seen for Crassus's support of the revived censorship. The new censors were the men whom he had supplanted in command of the war with Spartacus. Supporting this office for them would have helped them to recover lost dignity and earned their support for the future. More importantly, in helping to reestablish the censorship, Crassus may well have been looking ahead to the time five years later, when he would be able to hold the office and, hopefully, manipulate it to his further advantage in the race for supremacy at Rome.

Clearly, then, Crassus cooperated with Pompey on at least two issues in their consulship of 70. But, if Pompey ever did expect Crassus to be his junior colleague and dutiful supporter in all cases, as Sallust reports (*Hist.* 4.48 M), he was surely disappointed. That they quarreled over certain issues is clear (Sall. *Hist.* 4.51 M; Plut. *Pomp.* 22.3; *Crass.* 12.2; App. *BC* 1.14.121). It is fruitless to deny completely the sources' statements. Sallust, from whom much of the tradition derives, was sixteen at the time of the events described and wrote when others who remembered them were still alive.[24] There must have been some factual basis for his account or it would have lost all credibility for his audience.

The major issue that brought Crassus into opposition against Pompey may have been that of jury reform. The *optimates* had helped to maintain their oligarchic control of Roman political life through their dominance of the law courts. Juries had been composed solely of senators since the time of Sulla. Because of their influence with the jurors, leading senators were able to secure their friends' acquittal from the charges of their enemies and to obtain the condemnation of those enemies whom they themselves subjected to prosecution.[25] This

24. For Plutarch's and Appian's use of Sallust for other information on Crassus, see G. Rathke, *De Romanis Bellis Servilibus* (Diss. Berlin, 1904), pp. 49–62.
25. Cf. Cic. *Div. Caec.* 24; *Verr.* 1.17.35, 40; 2.1.155; Pseud. Ascon. *ad Verr* 1.35, 218 St.

scandalous manipulation of the senatorial juries had produced popular pressure for reform (Cic. *Verr.* 1.36–47). Indeed, Pompey had treated the subject in his very first public address as consul-elect and had been greeted with much enthusiasm (ibid., 1.45). Reform itself was a very difficult matter, however, and specific legislation was not enacted until September of 70, after Cicero had forced the infamous Verres into exile.[26]

The final solution was a compromise proposed by L. Aurelius Cotta. His bill divided the juries equally among the Senate, the *Equites*, and the *Tribuni Aerarii* (Ascon. *Corn.* 67 C/54 St).[27] It has been suggested that Crassus was the architect of this compromise, while Pompey pressed for the complete elimination of senatorial jurors.[28] On the contrary, this compromise seems to reflect the thinking and wishes of Pompey.

Two of those who strongly favored Cotta's bill may well have been Pompey's friends, M. Lollius Palicanus, praetor-elect in 70 (Schol. Gron. 328–29 St), and Cicero.[29] Despite his activity in restoring the full powers of the tribunate and

26. Cf. Cic. *Verr.* 2.7.177, M. Gelzer, *RE* 7A.1 (1939), 857.19–36, s.v. "Tullius" (29), and the discussion in Chapter One, Appendix C, p. 45.

27. The identification of the *Tribuni Aerarii* has been quite vexed. The recently prevailing view has been that they were men of equestrian census but not of the *Ordo Equester*: cf. H. Hill, *The Roman Middle Class* (Oxford, 1952), pp. 155–56; M. I. Henderson, "The Establishment of the 'equester ordo,'" *Journal of Roman Studies* 53 (1963): 63–64; C. Nicolet, *L'Ordre équestre à l'Epoque Républicaine* 1 (Paris, 1966), pp. 598–608; T. P. Wiseman, "The Definition of 'eques Romanus' in the Late Republic and Early Empire," *Historia* 19 (1970): 79–80. Most recently E. Badian has forcefully defended this position: "Marius' Villas: The Testimony of the Slave and the Knave," *Journal of Roman Studies* 63 (1973): 126 and n. 33. A.H.M. Jones has, however, argued with considerable point that whether or not the scholiast of Bobbio is correct in saying that the *Tribuni Aerarii* had a census qualification of 300,000 HS as opposed to 400,000 for the *Equites*, there must have been some minimum census qualification to distinguish the *Tribuni Aerarii* from those empanelled as *Equites*: see *The Criminal Courts of the Late Roman Republic and Principate* (Oxford, 1972), pp. 87–88. Nevertheless, their interests would have coincided more with the *Equites* than with the senators, so that the equestrian class would have had the practical balance of power on the juries.

28. Garzetti, "Crasso," *Athenaeum* 20 (1942): 17–19, and Taylor, *PP*, p. 219, n. 44. Cf. also, Deknatel, *Vita*, pp. 18–19. W. Drumann saw Crassus cooperating with Pompey on this issue: *Geschichte Roms* 4, ed. 2, P. Groebe (Berlin and Leipzig, 1908), p. 96.

29. For Palicanus, see Cic. *Verr.* 2.2.100 and R. Seager, "The Tribunate of Cornelius, Some Ramifications," *Hommages à Marcel Renard* 2 (*Collection Latomus* 101) ed. J. Bibauw (Brussels, 1969), pp. 683–84.

reviving the censorship, Pompey did not wish to mount an attack on the Senate as a whole. In the two former cases, there was no room for compromise if he wished to maintain his popularity among the populace, but in the case of jury reform it was sufficient for Pompey simply to reform the courts by ensuring that they would not be under the control of his enemies, the optimate *pauci*, who made up a powerful minority of the Senate. Such a reform would have been popular without offending all senators.

Indeed, in the *Verrines*, Cicero seems to have acted as Pompey's apologist before the senatorial order and assured them that Pompey was not behind any radical attempt to remove senators entirely from the juries. He described Pompey and the staunch optimate Catulus as agreeing that the laxity of the senatorial courts had fostered demand for the restoration of tribunician powers (Cic. *Verr.* 1.44). He claimed that the more radical proposal to eliminate senatorial jurors altogether came not from a junior senator or an equestrian, but from a member of the highest nobility (ibid., 2.2.174). This man may have been Crassus.[30]

The more radical proposal was that the courts should be placed entirely in the hands of the *Equites* (ibid., 2.3.223–24).[31] Of the powerful figures at the time, Crassus is the one most likely to have pushed vigorously for the completely equestrian juries. Although he had adherents among the senators at this time, they were usually among those of second rank, and not the powerful *optimates* who dominated senatorial politics. His policy was to rely primarily on financial power as a means to political success.

While members of the senatorial aristocracy were limited, albeit not always effectively, in the extent to which they could engage in business or commerce and preferred to invest in

30. Elsewhere, I suggested that it was the praetor L. Aurelius Cotta: "Cicero and Pompey," *Latomus*, 29 (1970): 69, n. 1. Cicero could, however, have been thinking of the consul Crassus in *Verr.* 2.3.174, although the reference in 2.5.177 is very probably to Cotta.

31. By these, I take Cicero to mean anyone who met the equestrian census qualification. Cf. Jones, *Criminal Courts*, pp. 86–90. If the praetor mentioned by Cicero is not Cotta, whose position Cicero was rhetorically overstating, as I previously suggested (see previous note), then this praetor could have been a man loyal to Crassus. None of the known praetors of 70 seems a likely choice, but two remain unnamed.

agriculture, the major source of financial power at Rome was in the men of the equestrian census class. Here were found the many traders, businessmen, and tax farmers who exploited the resources of Rome's growing empire. They were particularly anxious to regain a monopoly of the law courts, which C. Gracchus had first given them,[32] and which Sulla had finally abolished.[33] Control of the courts would ensure them power over magistrates and pro-magistrates who might seek to interfere in their exploitative ventures.[34]

Crassus can be expected to have had a greater degree of sympathy than many senators for this group and to have sought their support.[35] Pompey, too, however, had cultivated the *Equites* with great success. By supporting their desire for complete control of the juries, Crassus might have attached more of them to himself in competition with Pompey. Therefore, it is quite possible that differences over jury reform caused considerable disagreement between Crassus and Pompey in the latter part of their consulship.

Indeed, Crassus's ties with the *Equites* at this time can be seen in the story of his public reconciliation with Pompey at the very end of their term of office. According to Plutarch, when they were addressing a public assembly upon retiring from their consulship, a certain Gaius Aurelius, a man with equestrian census qualifications, mounted the rostra and claimed that Jupiter had appeared to him in a dream and commanded him to tell the people not to let the consuls lay down their office until they had become friends. Whereupon, the people shouted their approval, and Crassus took the initiative by running up to shake the hand of a surprised Pompey. At the same time, he proclaimed that it was neither undignified nor unworthy for him to initiate goodwill and friendship towards Pompey, whom the people had called "Great" even as a young man and whom they had granted a triumph before

32. Cf. Vell. Pat. 2.6.3, 13.2, 32.3; Tac. *Ann.* 12.60; Diod. 34/5.25; App. *BC* 1.3.22; Bruns, *FIRA*[7] 1.7, 11.12–17.
33. Cf. Cic. *Verr.* 1.37, Vell. Pat. 2.32; Tac. *Ann.* 11.22.
34. Cf. the famous case of P. Rutilius Rufus (Liv. *Per.* 70; Vell. Pat. 2.13.2).
35. The situation seems similar to Crassus's energetic support of the tax farmers in 60, when they requested a revision of their contract for the taxes of Asia (Cic. *Att.* 1.17.9): see Chapter Eight, p. 211.

he had even entered the Senate (*Pomp.* 23.1–2, *Crass.* 12.3–4; App. *BC* 1.14.121).

There is no need to question the basic validity of this story, as some do.[36] The main facts in different accounts agree, and it is significant that the name and rank of the man who proposed the reconciliation are preserved.[37] Plutarch's story is based on Sallust's contemporary account.[38] It is not likely that he would have found a fictitious name, which Sallust's readers would have spotted. Rather, it looks as if Crassus, in a bid for popular favor, had staged this dramatic little scene with the help of his equestrian friends. Pompey was obviously caught off guard (Plut. *Pomp.* 23.2), while Crassus completely stole the limelight from the popular hero by magnanimously praising him.[39] When the people left the Forum, it was Crassus's name, not Pompey's, that would have been first on everyone's lips.

It has also been suggested that Aurelius was related to Julius Caesar, and that Caesar had a hand in this reconciliation.[40] The only evidence adduced, however, is that Caesar's mother was an Aurelia, and Gaius Aurelius, therefore, may have been from a non-senatorial branch of the same *gens*. That is very flimsy evidence on which to build a case for Caesar's involvement in Aurelius's plea for reconciliation between Crassus and Pompey. It does not seem very probable. Nevertheless, the possibility cannot be ruled out entirely, as

36. E.g., Adcock, *Crassus*, p. 31; Waters, "Cicero, Sallust, and Catiline," *Historia* 19 (1970): 209.

37. Appian in his haste has conflated this story with the dismissal of their armies and places it at the beginning of their consulship. In *Crassus* 12.3, Plutarch apparently gives Aurelius the praenomen ὀνάτιος, but that reading is probably a corruption of ὀνόματι Γάιος. In the same passage, the description of Aurelius as rustic and uncouth seems to be a fictional embroidery added to impart "human interest" to the historical narrative. In his *Pompey* (23.1), Plutarch describes Aurelius more soberly as a man who had kept free of public affairs.

38. Cf. Maurenbrecher, *C. Sallusti Crispi*, p. 157.

39. Crassus stole a march on Pompey in a somewhat similar situation in 61 by praising Cicero's consulship (Cic. *Att.* 1.14.3, *Phil.* 2.12). It should be pointed out, too, that Crassus's praise of Pompey here is twoedged. In referring to Pompey's title Magnus and his winning a triumph before holding a senatorial office, Crassus emphasized those things that had aroused fear and jealousy among the beneficiaries of Sulla's constitution.

40. Drumann, *Geschichte* 4, p. 96.

the following discussion of Caesar's early career will demonstrate.

Caesar's early career was marked by inconsistent actions, for he was not yet openly a supporter or opponent of the Sullan oligarchy. In 81, as a nephew by marriage of Marius and son-in-law of Cinna, Sulla's old enemies, his positon had been precarious. He escaped the wrath of Sulla through the aid of Mam. Aemilius Lepidus and C. Aurelius Cotta (Suet. *Iul.* 1.2–3; Plut. *Caes.* 1.1). He then was sent as an envoy by M. Minucius Thermus to collect a fleet from Nicomedes IV of Bithynia, and in the following year he received the *corona civica* for conspicuous bravery at the siege of Mytilene (Suet. *Iul.* 2, 49; Dio 43.20.2; Aurel. *Vir. III.* 78.1). He stayed in the East and served next with P. Servilus Vatia until Sulla died in 78 (Suet. *Iul.* 3). Upon returning to Rome, he had remained aloof from M. Aemilius Lepidus's abortive revolt, but in 77 and 76, he had served notice of his ambitions by prosecuting two well-known members of the Sullan oligarchy, Cn. Cornelius Dolabella and C. Antonius Hibrida. The prosecutions failed, however, and in 75, Caesar departed from Rome for rhetorical training at Rhodes (Suet. *Iul.* 4.1; Plut. *Caes.* 3.1).[41]

Caesar's plans were rudely interrupted when he was captured by pirates.[42] Having procured his release by ransom, he gathered forces on his own private initiative and defeated the pirate band (Suet. *Iul.* 2.1–2; Plut. *Caes.* 2.3–4, *Crass.* 7.5). Shortly thereafter, when Mithridates resumed hostilities with Rome in 74, Caesar crossed from Rhodes to Asia Minor again, gathered another force and drove the invaders out of the province of Asia (Suet. *Iul.* 4.2). In view of his obvious ability and despite his earlier prosecution of Hibrida, his commander's brother, he seems to have been subsequently assigned as a legate to M. Antonius Creticus, who was placed in charge of

41. Cf. M. Gelzer, *Caesar, Politician and Statesman*, trans. P. Needham (Cambridge, Mass., 1968), pp. 21–23.
42. Plutarch's report of Caesar's exclamation that Crassus would be happy to hear of his capture seems clearly apocryphal (*Crass.* 7.5): see H. Strasburger, *Caesars Eintritt in die Geschichte* (Munich, 1938), p. 64; Adcock, *Crassus*, p. 11. For the date and details of this episode, see A. M. Ward, "Caesar and the Pirates II: The Elusive M. Iunius Iuncus and the year 75/4," *American Journal of Ancient History*, forthcoming.

a new campaign against piracy in 74.[43] He cut this service short, however, when he was co-opted into the college of pontiffs to replace his deceased cousin, C. Aurelius Cotta, and he returned to Rome in 73.[44]

This college was dominated by the oligarchic heirs of Sulla.[45] Perhaps on the advice of his mother's relatives, his old commander, P. Servilius Vatia Isauricus, and other pontiffs like Mam. Aemilius Lepidus thought that they were co-opting him safely into the bosom of the oligarchy.[46] In the security of the pontificate, however, Caesar soon played them false. On the strength of his existing popularity, he was elected military tribune probably for 72 or 71 (Suet. *Iul.* 5; Plut. *Caes.* 5.1), and aligned himself with those who were seeking power outside the circles of the *optimates*.[47]

The two most important such figures at the time were Crassus and Pompey. Caesar constantly appears as favoring the same causes as they did. No doubt, he hoped to be able to call on either of them for a return favor in the future, while he shared in their general popularity for the present. He vigorously supported the proposal to restore the powers of the tribunes (Suet. *Iul.* 5). In 70, he further supported the tribune, Plautius, who seems to have been an adherent of Pompey, in pressing for a complete amnesty for the followers of Lepidus and Sertorius (ibid.; Gell. *NA* 13.3.5; Dio 44.47.4).[48] There-

43. Gelzer, *Caesar*, p. 25.
44. L. R. Taylor, "Caesar's Early Career," *Classical Philology* 36 (1941): 117–20.
45. Ibid.
46. Ibid. Cf. also L. R. Taylor, "The Rise of Julius Caesar," *Greece and Rome* 4 (1957): 13–14.
47. Gelzer places Caesar's military tribunate in 72: *Caesar* (trans. Needham), p. 29. The year 71 is equally possible however: cf. Taylor, "Caesar's Early Career," *CP* 36 (1941): 120–21; Broughton, *MRR* 2, pp. 125, 126, n. 5. In either case, there is also a possibility that Caesar served under Crassus against Spartacus (cf. Caes. *BGall.* 1.40.5), but more than that cannot be said.
48. Plautius's legislative activity was, of course, made possible by the law restoring tribunician powers. The law providing amnesty for the followers of Lepidus and Sertorius would have fallen in with Pompey's desire to increase his popularity by appearing as lenient as possible towards those very opponents of the Sullan regime whom he had recently fought. Plautius also brought in a law, apparently at Pompey's instigation, to provide land for the veterans of the Sertorian war (Cic. *Att.* 1.18.6); cf. Plut. *Lucul.* 34.4; Dio 38.5.1–2, and R. E. Smith, "The *Lex Plotia Agraria* and Pompey's Spanish Veterans," *Classical Quarterly* 7 (1957): 82–85.

fore, in view of his attempts to ingratiate himself with those men who sought political advancement outside of the oligarchy, it is not difficult to think of Caesar as participating with friends of Crassus in a scheme to produce the public (albeit empty) reconcilation with Pompey at the end of 70. It would stand him in good stead with the powerful Crassus and even with Pompey, when the latter had a chance to reflect.

After 70, neither Crassus nor Pompey accepted a provincial governorship (Vell. Pat. 2.31.1; Plut. *Pomp.* 23.3). Pompey was biding his time and keeping a low profile (Plut. ibid.), while he hoped through his supporters to gain an overriding command, perhaps as successor to Lucullus in the East.[49] Crassus, of course, had no need to mulct a fortune out of a province in order to carry on political battles at Rome, as others did. It was much more useful for him to remain there, where he could keep watch over Pompey's maneuvers, while he furthered his own interests.[50]

There are no major events in 69 or 68 to highlight specific details of Crassus's activity, but he certainly did not remain inactive politically, as has sometimes been thought.[51] We can be sure that, along with managing his extensive financial affairs, he resumed his familiar routine of earning gratitude as an advocate (Plut. *Pomp.* 23.3). More particularly, he may have begun to show an interest in the career of Cn. Calpurnius Piso, who seems to have earned some notoriety for a violent outburst of anti-Pompeian sentiment in either 69 or 68 (Val. Max. 6.2.4).[52]

By 67, the interests of Crassus and the *optimates* had converged in opposition to Pompey. Many of the oligarchs were probably willing to overlook past activities on the side of popular reform as they searched for weapons against Pompey.[53] Through the tribune Aulus Gabinius, Pompey was seek-

49. Cf. Holmes, *RR* 1, p. 166.
50. Cf. Gelzer, *RE* 13.1 (1926), 308, s.v. "Licinius" (68); Garzetti, "Crasso," *Athenaeum* 20 (1942): 21.
51. See n. 16 above.
52. E. S. Gruen, "Notes on the 'First Catilinarian Conspiracy'," *Classical Philology* 64 (1969): 24 and "Pompey and the Pisones," *California Studies in Classical Antiquity* 1 (1968): 159–61.
53. It is possible that recognition of this common interest was actively signified by a marriage between Crassus's son, Marcus, and the daughter

ing an extraordinary commission to combat piracy with *imperium* over the whole Mediterranean Sea and its shores up to a distance of fifty miles inland. Crassus, who, ironically, had cooperated in giving back to the tribunes the power that had made Gabinius's action possible, now surely was at one with the optimate senators, who vehemently opposed the passage of this law (cf. Plut. *Pomp.* 25.4; Dio 36.24.1–3).[54]

Hortensius and Catulus had been unable to persuade the *Concilium Plebis* not to give the command to Pompey (Cic. *Leg. Man.* 52; Plut. *Pomp.* 25.5–6; Dio 36.30.5–36a). The *optimates* then used two tribunes in an attempt to block passage of the measure. The first, Trebellius, sought to interpose a veto on the proceedings, but Gabinius followed the example of Tiberius Gracchus and almost succeeded in having the Assembly remove him from office before he desisted (Dio

---

of Q. Caecilius Metellus Creticus. Record of the marriage is preserved on the grave monument of Caecilia (*CIL* 6, 1274/Dessau, *ILS*, 881). Cf. F. Münzer, *RE* 3.2 (1899), 1235, s.v. "Caecilia" (136) and E. Groag, *RE* 13.1 (1926), 270, s.v. "Licinius" (58). For the significance of this marriage as a link between Crassus and the *optimates*, see R. Syme, *The Roman Revolution* (Oxford, 1939), p. 22 and "Review of Gelzer," *Journal of Roman Studies* 34 (1944): 96; Taylor, *PP*, p. 222, n. 12; E. J. Parrish, "Crassus' New Friends and Pompey's Return," *Phoenix* 27 (1973): 357–80.

Elsewhere, however, I shall argue that this marriage is better dated to 62 or 61 (Chapter Eight, p. 203 and n. 35). Therefore it is dangerous to build any argument for close cooperation between Crassus and the *optimates* in the early 60s on the basis of this marriage. Actually, as it will soon be apparent, the commonality of interest between Crassus and the *optimates* at this point was not of long duration and had passed by early 65.

54. Cf. Deknatel, *Vita*, p. 24; Drumann, *Geschichte* 4, p. 97; Garzetti, "Crasso," *Athenaeum* 20 (1942): 23. Gelzer believes that Crassus took no part in the battle over the *lex Gabinia*: *RE* 13.1 (1926), 308, s.v. "Licinius" (68). He bases his argument on the absence of any specific references to Crassus in the scanty sources for the law, especially in Cicero's speech for the *lex Manilia* in 66. But in this speech, Cicero refers to only the public spokesmen for the opposition, Hortensius and Catulus (*Leg. Man.* 51–68). That does not mean that no other important senators were unfavorable to Gabinius's bill. For example, Cicero did not mention the opposition of C. Calpurnius Piso (Dio 36.24.1–3). Many others opposed it in meetings of the Senate or with their friends (Plut. *Pomp.* 25.4).

Adcock, on the other hand, saw Crassus as being in favor of the *lex Gabinia* in order to get Pompey out of Rome. That view is too Machiavellian. It was to Crassus's utmost advantage to prevent Pompey from increasing his military laurels and to keep him at Rome, where his military glory would tarnish from disuse and where he would be at a disadvantage in the infighting of civilian politics (cf. Plut. *Pomp.* 23.3–4).

36.24.4, 30.1–2; Ascon. *Corn.* 71–72 C/57 St). In a desperate move, Trebellius's colleague, Roscius Otho, fearing to speak, used hand signals to propose that the people should choose not one but two consulars to conduct the war. The voters rejected the proposal so vociferously that he ceased from further action, and the Gabinian law eventually passed (Plut. *Pomp.* 25.6, 26.1; Dio 36.3–5, 37.1).[55]

Crassus may well be the one whom Roscius had in mind to be Pompey's colleague against the pirates.[56] Of the living ex-consuls, Crassus was the only one who might have been considered as having a chance of being Pompey's colleague. The others had the following disabilities in various degrees and combinations: they were too old; their military records were poor or non-existent; they were already occupied; they were long-standing members of the optimate oligarchy opposed to Pompey and, therefore, unacceptable to the people; or they favored Pompey and were unacceptable to the *optimates*.[57]

For his part, of course, Pompey was doing everything he

55. Apparently, opponents of the bill had one more arrow in their quiver. Plutarch (*Pomp.* 25.7) and Dio (36.30.3) report that when the crowd shouted its thunderous disapproval of Roscius's proposal, a crow that was flying overhead dropped dead into the Forum. After commenting on the adverse physiological effect upon the crow of an air mass rapidly propelled by the shout of a crowd, Plutarch goes on to say that the assembly was dissolved and that Gabinius's law was passed at a later meeting (*Pomp.* 26.1). There is a lacuna in the text of Dio, so that it is impossible to see whether he set the voting of Gabinius's law on the same day. On the other hand, while Plutarch has Catulus make his speech earlier, Dio introduces a long rhetorical composition as Catulus's speech after the death of the crow (36.31.1–36a). Plutarch's order is to be preferred. Dio places the speech attributed to Catulus at the end of the episode in order to entertain and impress the reader with his own rhetorical skill. The sudden appearance of a dead crow in the Forum would have been a dire enough portent to stop all proceedings. No doubt, the crow did not fall as it was flying overhead. Some anti-Pompeian partisan, seeing his cause hopelessly overwhelmed at this point and having readied the crow beforehand, had probably tossed it into the Forum from some nearby vantage point to stop the meeting and gain time.

56. Deknatel, *Vita*, p. 24. If Roscius were working on behalf of Crassus, he may already have tried to cement an alliance with Crassus's friends among the *Equites* and siphon away support from those who favored Pompey. Roscius was the one who carried a bill to give the honor of occupying the first fourteen rows of seats at the theater to the *Equites*. Livy (*Per.* 99) indicates that this bill preceded his motion at the meeting on the *lex Gabinia*. For other references, which give no indication of the order of Roscius's actions, see Broughton, MRR 2, p. 145. Cicero shows how significant this preference in seating was (*Att.* 2.19.3).

57. Cf. the treatment of the various consuls from 80 to 68 in Appendix B of Chapter One.

could to weaken the power of his opponents. The spearhead of the attack was the tribune C. Cornelius, a former quaestor of Pompey (Ascon. *Corn.* 57 C/47–48 St, 61 C/50 St).[58] His first bill, to forbid loans to representatives of foreign states in Rome, was defeated.[59] By making such loans, powerful senators not only enriched themselves at high rates of interest,[60] but also turned foreign states into personal clients to be used in the struggle with their political rivals. Cornelius tried to eliminate another abuse by forbidding the senatorial practice of voting exemptions from the laws for individuals and by placing the right to do so in the hands of the people alone. He failed in this case, too, but he did effect a compromise bill that two hundred senators had to be present at senatorial meetings for voting such exemptions. In this way, he could prevent a very small group from giving preferential treatment to its political friends. He also succeeded in making the manipulation of existing laws more difficult by carrying a law that forced praetors to follow their *edicta perpetua*. Finally, while several other bills are not specifically described, he pushed for a tough bribery law that led to the acceptance of C. Calpurnius Piso's milder compromise law on bribery. Thus he forced the *optimates* to adopt new restrictions on one of their weapons in legal and electoral contests.[61]

In the following year, 66, another tribune, C. Manilius, took over Pompey's legislative program against his opponents by bringing forth two important laws. The annulment of Manilius's first bill brought him into direct hostility with Crassus. This law had been designed to increase the power of freedmen in the *Comitia Tributa* by distributing their votes among all thirty-five tribes of voters, instead of confining them to the four urban tribes (Ascon. *Mil.* 45 C/39 St, *Corn.* 65 C/53 St; Dio 36.42.2–3). This law would have earned Pompey a powerful bloc of supporters for passing legislation favorable

---

58. For the sources on Cornelius's actions, see Broughton, MRR 2, p. 144.

59. For the chronology of Cornelius's tribunate, see M. Griffin, "The Tribune C. Cornelius," *Journal of Roman Studies* 63 (1973): 196–203.

60. Cf. Brutus's loan to the city of Salamis on Cyprus (Cic. *Att.* 6.1.5).

61. For a discussion of the subsequent prosecution of Cornelius, see Chapter Six, pp. 141–43.

to him.[62] The law had been carried, however, with undue haste and the aid of considerable violence (ibid.). When the law's opponents were able to arouse plebeian opposition to it (on the ground, no doubt, that it would dilute the political and monetary value of the vote among free-born citizens), Manilius tried to shift the blame for originating the proposal onto Crassus, and he acquiesced in the annulment of his own law (ibid.). Crassus must have resented Manilius's cheap shot, but he could console himself with the knowledge that no one believed Manilius's story (Dio 36.42.4).[63]

Unfortunately for Crassus, however, Manilius's second law succeeded. That was the famous law that gave Pompey control of the great war against Mithridates.[64] It was a tremendously popular proposal and enjoyed the vigorous support of a skillful orator and rising political figure, Marcus Tullius Cicero, who had now reached the praetorship (Cic. *Leg. Man.*, passim). This instance was but one of many in which Crassus would find his interests and Cicero's clashing during the next few years. By itself, Cicero's support of the bill would not have endeared him to Crassus, for even though Crassus himself took no public stand against it, he could not have approved more power being given to Pompey. But, Cicero added insult to injury by completely ignoring Crassus's role in ending the war against Spartacus, while he emphasized Pompey's (*Leg. Man.* 30).

Later in that year, Crassus was thwarted by Cicero during the trial of C. Licinius Macer, an orator and historian who had gained great popularity by supporting such causes as the restoration of the tribunician powers (Sall. *Hist.* 3.48 M). Crassus, following his custom of earning popularity and friends through his services as an advocate, defended Macer on a charge of extortion before Cicero, who was presiding over the *quaestio de repetundis*. Macer hoped to win his case as much

62. Cf. L. R. Taylor, VDRR, pp. 144–45.
63. Dio does not link Manilius with Pompey until after the failure of his initial legislation. He represents Manilius as turning to Pompey then in the hope of enjoying the same good fortune that Gabinius had had. That is incorrect. Cornelius had asked Manilius to take up the issue at the end of the previous year (Ascon. *Corn.* 64 C/52 St). Clearly, Manilius started out as one of Pompey's supporters among the tribunes of 66.
64. See Broughton, MRR 2, p. 153 and references.

by favoritism and influence as by justice. Cicero was a model of propriety in conducting the trial, however, and Macer was so shocked at his conviction that he died of a heart attack or committed suicide. Crassus had achieved little for himself, therefore, by defending Macer, but Cicero found himself enjoying a great reputation for honesty at their expense (Cic. *Att.* 1.4.2; Val. Max. 9.12.7; Plut. *Cic.* 9.1–2).

Cicero was from a successful non-senatorial family of Arpinum (Cic. *Mur.* 17, *Planc.* 59, *Leg.* 1.1, 2.3, 3.36). By background and temperament, he basically favored the conservative Sullan constitution, while he always counselled moderation on the part of those who ruled in its name (*Verr.* 1.46–51). His political actions showed a constant attempt to strike a mean between the two political extremes of the conservative, oligarchic *optimates* and the opportunistic, demagogic *populares,* who sought personal power through support of popular programs.[65] In short, as Boren has justly observed, Cicero advocated, with appropriate modifications, the traditional Roman policy of *Concordia:* a powerful, but enlightened, Senate should run the State for the benefit of all classes (*ordines*) and, in a spirit of compromise, should extend its prerogatives to the lower orders as conditions change, in order to maintain political equilibrium and avoid factional strife.[66]

In 80, although he had not used the word *concordia* itself, Cicero had already expressed the traditional theme of this policy during his speech for Roscius of Ameria. He had shown that he favored a course of moderate compromise when he mourned the tragic death of Scaevola, who had vainly tried to bring about a compromise between the *optimates* and *populares* in 82 (*Rosc. Am.* 33). On the one hand, he himself adamantly opposed permitting the opportunistic *populares* to gain control of the State (ibid., 136). On the other hand, he issued a stern warning to the smug *optimates* about the way

65. Cf. R. Heinze, "Ciceros politische Anfänge," *Abhandlungen der Akademie der Wissenschaft zu Leipzig, Philologische-historische Klasse* 27 (1909), pp. 945–1010 and *Vom Geist des Römertums* (Leipzig and Berlin, 1938), pp. 59–141; and H. Strasburger, *Concordia Ordinum* (Diss. Borna and Leipzig, 1930).

66. H. C. Boren, "Cicero's *Concordia* in Historical Perspective," *Studies in Memory of Wallace Everett Caldwell: The James Sprunt Studies in History and Political Science* 46 (1964): 51–62.

in which they should use the high position that they had recently regained if they wished to maintain it. He said that they would have to be fair and benevolent rulers, for if they should be greedy, selfish, and repressive, they would have to forfeit their position to others more worthy than they (ibid., 139).

Cicero's great desire was to join the ranks of the consular nobility. From this vantage point he hoped to guide senatorial government to realize fully the potential for wise rule that he thought it to have. As is so often the case with such men, the establishment figures whom he sought to join and support did not reciprocate his feelings. While it was difficult for even a senator whose family had not boasted a recent consular in its ranks to reach the consulship,[67] it was next to impossible for a man from a non-senatorial family.[68] As a result, Cicero had to look elsewhere for necessary support in furthering his political career.

By following a career in the courts, he was able to earn widespread recognition as an orator second to none. In this way, he created his own personal following, but that was still not enough. He found his greatest source of strength in supporting the powerful Pompey, military hero and darling of the Roman populace, who had successfully defied the power of the *optimates* during his rise to personal eminence. He had known Pompey since his earliest days.[69] In 70, after he had agreed to support Pompey against the leading Metelli and their friends in the trial of Verres, he was elected plebeian aedile at the head of the poll (Cic. *Verr.* 1.23–25, 2.1.19, *Pis.* 2).[70] In 69, he defended Pompey's interests in the trial of M. Fonteius and, perhaps, also in that of P. Oppius.[71] In 67, probably

67. Cf. the case of M. Aemilius Scaurus, consul in 115 (Cic. *Scaur.* 1.1; Ascon. *Scaur.* 22 C/25 St).

68. M. Gelzer, *The Roman Nobility*, trans. R. Seager (Oxford, 1969), pp. 50–52.

69. A. M. Ward, "The Early Relationships between Cicero and Pompey until 80 B.C.," *Phoenix* 24 (1970): 119–29.

70. For the interest of Pompey and the senior Metelli in this trial, see Chapter One, Appendix C. For the influence of the powerful on the elections of lower magistrates, see Cicero, *pro Plancio*, passim.

71. A. M. Ward, "Cicero's Support of Pompey in the Trials of M. Fonteius and P. Oppius," *Latomus* 27 (1968): 802–9. E. S. Gruen is probably quite right that Pompey had no hand in Oppius's insubordination to M. Aurelius Cotta: "Pompey, Metellus Pius, and the Trials of

after supporting the *lex Gabinia* for Pompey's command against the pirates, Cicero was elected to the praetorship, again at the head of the poll.[72] In 66, he showed his gratitude and piled up credit for his consular campaign two years ahead by his support of the *lex Manilia* for Pompey's command against Mithridates. Thus, Cicero helped to deal Crassus a severe setback in his struggle to outshine Pompey at Rome when the *Concilium Plebis* enthusiastically endorsed Manilius's proposal.

Crassus also may have suffered a setback in the consular elections of 66. Although there is no evidence that he supported any particular candidate in these elections, it is difficult to imagine that he was neutral and took no interest in earning gratitude among any of the contestants. It is possible that he gave his backing to the two who were chosen first, P. Autronius Paetus and P. Cornelius Sulla (Cic. *Sull.* 49; Sall. *Cat.* 18.1–2; Ascon. *Corn.* 75 C/59 St, 88 C/68 St).[73] But, if Crassus had placed any hopes upon the elections of these two men, they were soon dashed. After prosecutions for bribery, the consuls designate were stripped of their right to enter office (ibid.).

Crassus, however, could comfort himself with the prospect in the following year of obtaining the censorship, the highest regular office to which a Roman aristocrat could hope to be elected. Pompey, despite his part in reviving this office with Crassus in 70, never held it, nor did Julius Caesar, who chose the dangerous dictatorship instead.[74] Perhaps even the *optimates*, with whom Crassus shared a common interest against

---

70–69 B.C.: The Perils of Schematism," *American Journal of Philology* 92 (1971): 13–15. But, by claiming that he had acted to help Pompey gain the Mithridatic command, Oppius could have aroused the sympathy of Pompey's supporters, which Cicero could have hoped to exploit for his own benefit.

72. It appears that the *optimates* had sought to manipulate this election but failed. Cicero reports that he was returned at the head of the poll three times, despite his having the elections invalidated the first two times (*Leg. Man.* 2). Cicero could hardly have demonstrated such popularity if he had opposed the *lex Gabinia*, and it is unlikely that he would have avoided a chance to win the favor of Pompey's large following and would not have supported it at least with his vote. Cf. A. M. Ward, "Cicero's Support of the *Lex Gabinia*," *Classical World* 63 (1969): 8–10.

73. Cf. Appendix B of Chapter One for the year 66.

74. As dictator, of course, he held censorial power, but the dictatorship was not a regular office and not one to which a Roman noble usually aspired in this period. Indeed, it provoked great distrust when Caesar assumed it.

Pompey, had assured him of their support. He was elected along with Q. Lutatius Catulus, one of Pompey's staunchest optimate foes in the debates over his extraordinary commands. Once having been elected, however, Crassus and Catulus found nothing else on which to agree, except to disagree, and they formally resigned without accomplishing their appointed tasks (Plut. *Crass.* 13.1; Dio 37.9.3).[75]

In 65, if he had entertained any previous hopes of significant cooperation with the *optimates,* Crassus now saw that to gain personal preeminence at Rome in competition with Pompey, he would have to do it without their support. In the long run, they would not tolerate his ambitions any more than they would Pompey's. Instead, he struck out on an independent path once more and probably enlisted the aid of Julius Caesar, who had just embarked upon his controversial aedileship.

From 71 onwards, Caesar followed a consistent policy. That was to take up the standard knocked from the hands of Marius and Cinna. He established himself as the heir and leader of the considerable following that still remained loyal to their names. In 70, he had called conspicuous attention to the fact that he was Cinna's son-in-law when he worked for the recall from exile of his brother-in-law, Lucius Cinna (Suet. *Iul.* 5; Gell. NA 13.3.5; Dio 44.47.4). Further, of course, he had supported popular legislation favored by Pompey—the restoration of tribunician powers, and the recall of the supporters of Lepidus and Sertorius.[76] In 69, the year of his quaestorship,[77] he further brought Cinna to mind in an unprecedented funeral oration for his deceased wife, Cinna's daughter, Cornelia (Suet. *Iul.* 6.1; Plut. *Caes.* 5.2–3). Already in the same year he had advertised himself as the heir of Marius at the funeral of his aunt Julia, Marius's widow, when he had effigies of him

75. Plutarch (*Crass.* 13.1) says that it was the question of annexing Egypt that led to their mutual resignation. As Adcock has pointed out, however, this question had no relation to their official duties: *Crassus,* pp. 35–36. Possibly Crassus was involved in the Egyptian question contemporaneously with that of enfranchising the Transpadanes and thereby stiffened Catulus's resistance to the latter. Both of these matters will be discussed in detail later.

76. See p. 111 above.

77. This year is the one accepted by Broughton: *MRR* 2, pp. 132, 136, n. 7. Gelzer seems to concur: *Caesar,* p. 31, n. 1. Cf. Taylor, "Caesar's Early Career," *CP* 36 (1941): 124.

carried in the funeral procession, contrary to decrees long ago laid down by Sulla (Suet. ibid.; Plut. *Caes.* 5.1).

In his aedileship, Caesar even made so bold as to have images of Marius and the trophies of his victories set up on the Capitoline Hill (Vell. Pat. 2.43.4; Suet. *Iul.* 11; Plut. *Caes.* 6.1–4). Unrepentant Marians rejoiced, but the *optimates* were enraged. He further antagonized them when he completely overshadowed his optimate colleague, M. Calpurnius Bibulus, by the splendor and magnificence of his independent additions to the aedilician games that they were supposed to organize. As a result, he received public recognition not only for his own share in putting on the games, but for Bibulus's as well (Caes. *BC* 3.16.3; Sall. *Cat.* 49.3; Plin. *HN* 33.53; Suet. *Iul.* 10.1; Plut. *Caes.* 5.5). In this way, Caesar continued to earn popularity in his aedileship with the same liberality that he had already demonstrated as curator of the Via Appia (Plut. *Caes.* 5.5).

In anger and in fear of his rising popularity among those loyal to the memory of Marius, the *optimates* succeeded in imposing a limit upon the number of gladiators that Caesar could use in games commemorating his dead father (Suet. *Iul.* 10.2). Some, perhaps honestly, feared a revolution, and Caesar's use of gladiators may have been viewed as a real danger in the light of what the gladiator Spartacus had accomplished fewer than ten years before. Even with the imposition of a limit, however, Plutarch reports that Caesar presented 320 pairs of combatants (*Caes.* 5.5).

The question of Caesar's relationship to Pompey from 70 to 66 is less clear than his attempts to reunite the followers of Marius under his standard. Some have suggested that the two may have been cooperating on a personal basis.[78] It will be useful to review the evidence thoroughly. In 70, Caesar supported legislation favored or promoted by Pompey. Yet, that action is no proof of cooperation, since it was legislation that Caesar would have had to support as a man who courted popular favor. Another, although by no means conclusive, link with

---

78. E.g., G. V. Sumner, "Cicero, Pompeius, and Rullus," *Transactions and Proceedings of the American Philological Association* 97 (1966): 579; L. R. Taylor, "Caesar and the Roman Nobility," *Transactions and Proceedings of the American Philological Association* 73 (1942): 11–21; Drumann, *Geschichte* 3, pp. 139–40.

Pompey appears in 69. In that year, Caesar had gone to the province of Farther Spain to serve as quaestor to the governor, Antistius Vetus. There are hints, no more, that this action was in accordance with the wishes of Pompey, whose province Farther Spain had been during the war against Sertorius. Though he had refused a provincial command himself after his consulship, he still would have been particularly interested in having a governor sympathetic to his recently acquired interests in Spain. Pompey's first wife had been Antistia, the daughter of the praetor Antistius of 86, who had connived in Pompey's acquittal of a charge stemming from his father's use of booty taken at Asculum (Plut. *Pomp.* 4.2). Unfortunately there is no evidence other than the shared *gentilicum* that this Antistius and Antistius Vetus were related, but it is possible that they were. If that were indeed the case, then Antistius Vetus may well have been serving Pompey's interests in Farther Spain and Caesar along with him.[79]

In 68, Caesar left his post in Spain early and proceeded to Cisalpine Gaul, where he championed the Transpadanes' demand for full Roman citizenship (Suet. *Iul.* 8). Marius and Cinna had championed the cause of the Italians after the Social War in their desire for full citizenship. This act fits Caesar's plan to gain the support of their old following. He may have taken this action for that reason, but he certainly was not seeking to add fuel to an armed uprising, as some have believed (ibid.).[80]

Caesar also may have been cooperating with Pompey, or at least seeking to identify himself with his interests. Pompey had a deep interest in the Transpadanes. His father had sponsored a law in 89 that confirmed the citizenship of Cispadane towns in Cisalpine Gaul, gave the Latin right to the Transpadane towns, and attached native tribes to some of them (Ascon. *Pis.* 3C/12 St; Plin. *HN* 3.138). Thus Pompey's father

79. Pompey's subsequent divorce of Antistia should be no obstacle to viewing the members of her family as remaining friendly to Pompey. The divorce was the result of Sulla's insistent wishes, and they would have understood the political realities of the situation and probably hoped to profit from Pompey's ties with the powerful Sulla.

80. Gelzer has accepted Suetonius's tendentious remark: see *Caesar*, p. 32. On the other hand, see the strictures of Syme, "Review of Gelzer," *JRS* 34 (1944): 96.

had placed himself in the relationship of a patron to the Transpadanes, and it was a relationship that later extended to his son (Cic. *Att.* 5.11.2).[81] Pompey could not but have been in favor of full citizenship for the *Transpadani,* and Caesar may have been acting, partially at least, as Pompey's agent in 68.

In that same year, soon after he returned to Rome, Caesar married Pompeia. She was the daughter of Sulla's daughter and Q. Pompeius Rufus, the son of Sulla's consular colleague of 88 with the same name (Suet. *Iul.* 6.2; Plut. *Caes.* 5.7).[82] Relationship of Pompeia to Pompey the Great and, therefore, any significance of Caesar's marriage to her for his standing with Pompey usually has been denied.[83] In fact, she probably was related to Pompey.[84] Nevertheless, the relationship was not

81. Badian, *FC,* p. 268.

82. Sulla's daughter, Fausta, by Caecilia would have been too young to have been Pompeia's mother. Pompeia must have been the child of a daughter by an earlier marriage. Plutarch names two earlier wives of Sulla, Ilia and Aelia (*Sull.* 6.10–11). These two names look like variants of the same name. Pompeia was probably the child of a daughter of an Aelia. It is significant that the nomen Ilius does not appear in the Index of Broughton, *MRR* 2, whereas Aelii abound.

83. Strasburger, *Caesars Eintritt,* p. 115; Gelzer, *Caesar,* p. 33.

84. Badian has corroborated the view that the three main branches of the Pompeii were related (E. Badian, "Notes on Roman Senators of the Republic," *Historia* 12 [1963]: 138–39), but no one has sought the exact connection. In view of his criticisms of Taylor (*VDRR,* pp. 244–45), it seems best to connect the Bithynici closely with the Rufi through Aulus Pompeius (1). (Numbers in parentheses after the names of the Pompeii refer to the number of each Pompeius as he appears in *RE* 21.2 [1952].) Furthermore, in view of the close friendship of the Bithynici with Pompey the Great and the praenomen Sextus, which appears among the Bithynici and the Magni (cf. Badian, *loc. cit.*), it seems necessary to postulate a fairly close relationship between the Bithynici and the Magni. The simplest solution is to make Cn. Pompeius (5), who founded the line of the Magni, the son of an unrecorded brother of Aulus Pompeius (1), who was the father of both Aulus Pompeius (2), the founder of the Bithynici, and Q. Pompeius, consul in 141 (12), the founder of the Rufi. This Cn. Pompeius (5) was close in age to the two sons of Aulus (1), and since the Pompeii were insignificant in these early generations, his father could easily have been a brother of Aulus (1) and escaped being recorded. Thus, the consanguinity of the Magni, the Bithynici, and the Rufi would have been collateral for each generation, and Pompey the Great would have been a first cousin (thrice removed) of the consul of 141, founder of the Rufi. Pompey's father, Cn. Pompeius Strabo, would have been a first cousin (twice removed) of the same man and a second cousin (once removed) of Q. Pompeius Rufus, consul in 88, if F. Miltner is correct that the Rufus who was consul in 88 was the son of the Pompeius who was consul in 141 (cf. *RE* 22.1 [1952], 2250.58–64, s.v. "Pompeius" [39]). If the consul of 88 was a

close, and the usual interpretation of the marriage seems best, in view of the animosity that had existed between Q. Pompeius Rufus, the consul of 88, and Pompey's father. It was only after Caesar had divorced Pompeia and after Pompey had joined the *optimates* against Caesar that her brother seems to have been associated with Pompey's supporters and served Pompey's interests as tribune of the plebs in 52 (Cic. *Sull.* 5.5; Ascon. *Mil.* 32–52 C/31–44 St; Dio 40.45, 49).[85] Therefore, there seems to be little possibility that Caesar's marriage to Pompeia signified early political cooperation between Caesar and Pompey.[86]

For the years 67 and 66, there are definite statements in the sources that Caesar supported both the *lex Gabinia* and the *lex Manilia* for Pompey's extraordinary commands (Plut. *Pomp.* 25.4; Dio 36.43.2–4). One cannot, however, unequivocally conclude that this evidence shows that Caesar was actually cooperating with Pompey. Since these bills had tremendous popular support, Caesar in his role as a popular leader in the Marian tradition could not have opposed them without endangering his base of support, as Plutarch and Dio recognized in their remarks.[87] Nevertheless, there is some doubt that Caesar supported both laws as strongly as the sources might lead one to believe. Plutarch mentions only Caesar's support of the *lex Gabinia* and then only in his *Pompey*, while Dio refers only to his support of the *lex Manilia* (ibid.). Suetonius mentions neither (*Iul.* 8–9). Suspicions are raised, therefore, that at the least Plutarch and Dio may have confused a fairly insignificant reference in their sources to Caesar's support of a tribunician bill favorable to Pompey.[88]

---

grandson of the consul of 141, as E. Badian insists ("Caepio and Norbanus," *Studies in Greek and Roman History*, Oxford [1964], p. 41), then he and Pompey's father would have been third cousins. Finally, Pompey would have been a third cousin (once removed) of Q. Pompeius Bithynicus (25), who died with him in Egypt in 48. Cf. the original version of "Caepio and Norbanus," where the relationship between the consuls of 141 and 88 is left open: *Historia* 6 (1967): 326.

85. Cf. Drumann, *Geschichte* 4, 319.

86. For the significance of Caesar's later divorce of Pompeia, see Chapter Eight, p. 205.

87. Cf. Gelzer, *Caesar*, p. 33.

88. Cf. Syme, "Review of Gelzer," *JRS* 34 (1944): 97. The similarity of Plutarch's and Dio's remarks concerning Caesar's motives lends support to this idea.

In summary, there is some evidence, albeit tenuous, that Caesar was actively cooperating with Pompey from 70 to 66. The possibility cannot be ruled out entirely. On the other hand, all that can be said with any real confidence is that on some occasions, consistently with his policy of earning popular support, his actions would have made him appear to be supporting Pompey in this period.

In 65, however, Caesar probably began actively cooperating with Crassus. Direct evidence is very scanty, to be sure, but the historical situation makes it highly probable that Caesar joined Crassus in a number of activities during the year.[89] Two factors would have made him look to Crassus. First, his aedileship was incurring him enormous debts that could not have been met from his own resources (Plut. *Caes.* 5.4–5, 11.1). Although he had recourse to other lenders, Crassus's great wealth would have proven to be of great benefit to him under these conditions (cf. ibid., 11.1). Second, having risen to only the rank of aedile, Caesar was neither powerful nor important enough to be working alone in the advancement of his career.[90] Despite his early prosecutions of Dolabella and C. Antonius, his friendly attitude towards Pompey, his identification with Marius, and his public munificence, he had not built up any real power. He still needed the help of a powerful political patron.

Certainly, in the light of his pro-Marian actions, the *optimates* were not about to give him much support.[91] Nor would he have looked to Pompey, whose cause he had publicly sup-

89. Others have suggested that they had begun to cooperate by the elections of 66: E. G. Hardy, "The Catilinarian Conspiracy in Its Context, A Restudy of the Evidence," *Journal of Roman Studies* 7 (1917): 156; Gelzer, *RE* 13.1 (1926): 309, s.v. "Licinius" (68); Garzetti, "Crasso," *Athenaeum* 20 (1942): 24. It is possible, but there is no reason to assume that Caesar could not have been elected to the aedileship without Crassus's support. He had many creditors other than Crassus (Plut. *Crass.* 7.6, *Caes.* 11.1), and the two may not have drawn together until some months later. Indeed, Gelzer seems to have softened his position on this point: *Caesar*, pp. 39–41.

90. A. Von Mess, *Caesar, Sein Leben, Seine Zeit und Seine Politik* (Leipzig, 1913), pp. 36–37.

91. Although he had been given important help in the past by such *optimates* as Mam. Aemilius Lepidus and the Aurelii Cottae (see above, p. 110), he now needed much greater and bolder support than they would have been willing to give. Cf. Taylor, "Caesar and the Roman Nobility," *TAPA* 73 (1942): 17.

ported at times in the past. If Pompey returned to Rome from a great Eastern victory without any challenge to his position as popular champion, Caesar and other ambitious men like him would have had no hope of getting out of Pompey's overwhelming shadow and obtaining a position of prestige and preeminence in their own right. Caesar was not like Cicero, who, until the sudden adulation resulting from his opposition to Catiline in 63, would have been content simply to reach the consulship and play a behind-the-scenes role as advisor to the Great Man. Therefore, Caesar had to look elsewhere for a powerful political ally.

In 65, Crassus, who was the highest-ranking senator most willing to challenge Pompey in ways not favored by the *optimates*, was just such a man. Censor in this year (Plut. *Crass.* 13.1–2), Crassus is the only man powerful enough or rich enough to whom Caesar could have turned for the necessary support in advancing his own political career. By this time, furthermore, Crassus, in his hitherto unsuccessful rivalry with Pompey, probably would have welcomed an association with the energetic Caesar, even if they may have had cool relations in the past (Plut. *Crass.* 7.5).[92] Indeed, Asconius (*Tog. Cand.* 83 C/64 St) does attest to their cooperation only a year later in 64.[93] Therefore, it is reasonable to conclude that in 65, Caesar had already begun to work with Crassus and played a part in a number of schemes that mark a new phase of Crassus's career.

Ever since Pompey tried to steal the honor for ending the war with Spartacus in 71, Crassus had to consider him a strenuous rival for power and prestige at Rome. This situation caused Crassus's career to take many twists and turns as he maneuvered for a better position. Therefore, he cooperated with Pompey out of political necessity in the consular elections for 70 and on certain issues during their term of office.

92. Gelzer sees tension between Crassus and Caesar arising earlier from Crassus's perception of him as a rival after his prosecution of Dolabella: *RE* 13.1 (1926): 302, s.v. "Licinius" (68). Rather, it would seem that any earlier coolness felt by Crassus towards Caesar (cf. Plut. *Caes.* 7.5) would have stemmed from Caesar's close ties with Marius and Cinna, at whose hands Crassus's family had suffered greatly.

93. For arguments in favor of the view of Asconius, see A. M. Ward, "Cicero's fight against Crassus and Caesar in 65 and 63 B.C.," *Historia* 21 (1972): 250.

At the same time, however, Crassus sought his own advantage wherever possible. After 70, he continued to build up his personal and financial bases of power, while Pompey maneuvered to further his own career.

In 67 and 66, Crassus's interests were similar to those of the *optimates* who opposed the moves of Gabinius and Manilius to give Pompey powerful, new military commissions. Nevertheless, his hopes were thwarted with the help of Cicero, who promoted Pompey's cause. Then, by 65, the old strains that had previously marred Crassus's relations with the leading *optimates* overcame any common interest in opposing Pompey, as witnessed by his quarrels with Q. Catulus during their abortive censorship. On the other hand, he now seems to have obtained the services of the increasingly popular Julius Caesar for building a common base of strength against the absent Pompey, Caesar's appearance of favoring Pompey notwithstanding. Soon, Crassus was to attempt some bold, new undertakings to check Pompey's growing power.

VI

Preparations for Pompey's Return

Crassus's plan was to build up a position of strength while Pompey was away, so that Pompey would be forced to take him into account upon completion of the Mithridatic War. The evidence for his actions in pursuing this plan and for Caesar's cooperation with him is, as almost always in dealing with Crassus, not what one would wish. Yet, with care and patience a reasonable picture can be painted.

Upon entering his censorship, Crassus raised again the old question of enfranchising the Transpadanes (Dio 37.9.3).[1] From a statesmanlike point of view, this move would have been beneficial by providing a rich new recruiting ground of citizen soldiers for Roman armies. Politically, however, it was not acceptable to Catulus and the *optimates*. In championing the Transpadanes, Crassus was trying to win for himself the standing that Pompey had long enjoyed among them. The *optimates*, on the other hand, had always been unwilling that any one man should reap the benefits of being the one to enfranchise this group. It would have provided the successful sponsor with too strong and dangerous a power base. When Catulus refused to back down in his opposition, Crassus remained equally adamant, and they both resigned (Dio ibid.).[2] This move was politically astute for Crassus, since his uncompromising attitude would have endeared him to many

1. Dio does not specifically say which of the two censors raised the question, but it is difficult to believe that it could have been Catulus in light of the opposition raised by the two consuls, L. Caecilius Metellus and Q. Marcius Rex, against the same proposal in 68 (Suet. *Iul.* 8).

2. Plutarch attributes their resignation to the dispute over the annexation of Egypt (*Crass.* 13.1). That problem must have contributed to their difficulties, but both of these sources of disagreement should be seen as part of a general impasse between Crassus and Catulus that led to their mutual decision to resign.

Transpadanes, despite his ultimate failure on the question of their citizenship.

Many commentators consider it no mere coincidence that Caesar had championed the same cause in 68, and it has been argued that Caesar was actively working with some tribunes in 65 to secure the requisite legislation so that Crassus, in his capacity as censor, could then proceed to enroll the new citizens.[3] Of course, rather than actually working with him, it is possible that Crassus was simply following Caesar's example and trying to succeed where he had failed. Nevertheless, the proposal would have been beneficial to both, and in the light of their mutual needs and desires, it is highly likely that they were cooperating in this matter, as well as in others, in 65.

Another project that Crassus promoted was the annexation of Egypt as a Roman province. In 65, Cicero delivered his speech *de Rege Alexandrino* in opposition to a proposal that Rome annex the kingdom of Egypt.[4] Plutarch (*Crass.* 13.1) says that Crassus advanced this scheme while he was censor. Suetonius (*Iul.* 11) claims that Caesar, with a view toward obtaining command of the operation for himself, enlisted some tribunes to make the proposal.[5] A frequent conclusion, therefore, has been that Crassus and Caesar were working together in support of this proposal, to the detriment of Pompey.[6]

That Plutarch mentions only one man, while Suetonius mentions only the other, does not inspire the greatest confi-

3. Cf. E. G. Hardy, "The Transpadane Question and the Alien Act of 65 or 64 B.C.," *Journal of Roman Studies* 6 (1916): 63–82, and T. Rice Holmes, *The Roman Republic* 1 (Oxford, 1923), p. 237.

4. For the date, see M. Gelzer, *Cicero. Ein Biographischer Versuch* (Wiesbaden, 1969), p. 66, n. 63. The purpose of the speech is clear from the scholiast: *Scholia Bobiensia, Reg. Alex.* 91.29–93.25 St.

5. Carcopino and Garzetti interpret these two statements to mean that Crassus as censor tried to get the question of annexing Egypt resolved after Caesar had failed by means of tribunician action: G. Bloch and J. Carcopino, *Histoire romaine* 2 (Paris, 1929), p. 614; A. Garzetti, "M. Licinio Crasso," *Athenaeum* 20 (1942): 30.

6. A. Von Mess, *Caesar, Sein Leben, Seine Zeit und Seine Politik* (Leipzig, 1913), pp. 28–32; E. G. Hardy, "The Catilinarian Conspiracy in its Context, A Restudy of the Evidence," *Journal of Roman Studies* 7 (1917):167; E. Meyer, *Caesars Monarchie und das Principat des Pompeius* ed. 2 (Stuttgart and Berlin, 1919), p. 12; E. Ciaceri, *Cicerone e i suoi Tempi* 1 (Milan, Genoa, Rome, Naples, 1939), p. 213; M. Gelzer, *RE* 13.1 (1926), 310.53–58, s.v. "Licinius" (68); E. T. Salmon, "Catiline, Crassus, and Caesar," *American Journal of Philology* 56 (1935): 305–7.

dence, however, and it has also been argued that Caesar, without any help from Crassus, was backing the scheme for annexation because it was beneficial to Pompey.[7] Great significance has been seen in Suetonius's statement that Caesar made his proposal, *per partem tribunorum* (*Iul.* 11), on the ground that, in 65, Pompey was at the height of popularity and few tribunes would have been unfriendly to him. Accordingly, the scheme to annex Egypt is viewed as another tribunician proposal made for Pompey's benefit, just as were the proposals of Gabinius and Manilius, one or both of which Caesar also had supported.[8]

This view is much less satisfactory than the former. It cannot validly be argued that, because it was made through tribunes, the proposal was likely to have been friendly to Pompey. That argument cuts both ways. It is improbable that even the great majority of the ten tribunes were subservient to Pompey. Surely, opponents of Pompey could have found some tribunes who would have done their bidding. In fact, the only known tribune of 65, C. Papius, may have been working with Crassus or Caesar, or both, against Pompey.

He sponsored the *lex Papia* that professed to prevent the illegal assumption of Roman citizenship by banishing from Rome all aliens who had come from beyond the confines of Italy (Cic. *Leg. Agr.* 1.13, *Arch.* 10, *Balb.* 52, *Att.* 14.18.4, *Off.* 3.47; Dio 37.9.5).[9] As in the case of similar laws, the *lex Papia* was politically motivated. Although there is not sufficient evidence to reveal conclusively who was behind Papius, either Crassus or Caesar, or both, are strong candidates.[10] Some have

---

7. G. V. Sumner, "Cicero, Pompeius and Rullus," *Transactions and Proceedings of the American Philological Association* 97 (1966):574.

8. Ibid.

9. F. Münzer, *RE* 18.3 (1949), 1076, s.v. "Papius" (5); T. R. S. Broughton, *The Magistrates of the Roman Republic* 2 (New York, 1952), p. 158. Hardy and Garzetti place this law in 64: E. G. Hardy, "The Transpadane Question and the Alien Act of 65 or 64 B.C.," *Journal of Roman Studies* 6 (1916):78; A. Garzetti, "Crasso," *Athenaeum* 20 (1942):32. The passage cited from Dio, however, is clearly to be read in the context of 65. Otherwise, he would not have begun the next sentence with the words τῷ δὲ ἐχομένῳ ἔτει τοῦ τε Θιγούλου καὶ τοῦ Καίσαρος τοῦ Λουκίου ἀρχόντων.

10. The political connections of a certain Glaucippius who was exempted from the law (Cic. *Leg. Agr.* 1.13) are unknown, and by the time of the first recorded trial under the law, that of Archias in 62

suggested that the law was originally a weapon created by Crassus's opponents in the Senate, to be used against Transpadanes who had come to Rome to support Crassus in his attempts to enfranchise all Transpadanes.[11] Similarly, another believed that senatorial opponents promoted the law against the interest of Caesar, who was also seeking favor among the Transpadanes.[12] Nevertheless, the words of Dio (τὴν νῦν 'Ιταλίαν: 37.9.5) clearly imply that the Transpadane region was to be treated as part of Italy under the terms of the law.[13] Therefore, since both Crassus and Caesar were seeking favor with the Transpadanes, Papius may well have been working with one or both of them and sought to protect their interests by including the Transpadane region as part of Italy.

On the other hand, Papius is not likely to have been working to Pompey's advantage, for his law was very dangerous to him. Pompey had a large number of extra-Italian clients, for many of whom he had obtained citizenship.[14] Some of these foreign clients had moved to Rome, where they supported Pompey in his political battles.[15] These men were probably the ones most liable to be affected by the *lex Papia,* since their patron was in Asia and unable to intervene directly in their behalf should it have been used to attack them. Thus the *lex Papia* put Pompey in a position to be deprived of some of his most valuable supporters in the political struggles at Rome. Of necessity, Pompey's supporters would have had to oppose this bill, which tacitly favored the claims of the Transpadanes, whom Pompey himself was eager to cultivate.

In this way, Papius's bill could have hoped to accomplish

(Cic. *Arch.* 10), anyone could have taken advantage of the law in settling a political score not connected with the aims of the original backers.

11. E. G. Hardy, "The Table of Heraclea and the *Lex Julia Municipalis,*" *Journal of Roman Studies* 4 (1914): 77–82; M. Cary, *CAH* 9 (1932), p. 481.

12. W. Drumann, *Geschichte Roms* 3, ed. 2, P. Groebe (Berlin and Leipzig, 1906), p. 140.

13. Broughton, *MRR* 2, p. 160, n. 2; *contra* Holmes, *RR* 1, p. 237.

14. E. Badian, *Foreign Clientelae* (264–70 B.C.) (Oxford, 1958), pp. 252–84, 302–8.

15. Cf. the early career of L. Cornelius Balbus: F. Münzer, *RE* 4.1 (1901), 1261.21–54, s.v. "Cornelius" (69); R. Gardner, "The Early Career of L. Cornelius Balbus," in *Cicero, the Speeches pro Caelio, de Provinciis Consularibus, pro Balbo,* LCL (Cambridge, Mass., and London, 1958), pp. 613–16.

a threefold purpose: 1) passage of the bill would have cost Pompey some valuable friends at Rome; 2) in trying to protect these friends, he would have compromised himself with the Transpadanes; 3) the backers of the bill would have bolstered their own claims to be patrons of this important group. Since both Crassus and Caesar were trying to gain the support of the Transpadanes and increase their power at Rome while Pompey was in the East, it would not be unreasonable to conclude that the tribune C. Papius was working with Crassus or Caesar, or both, in 65. But, no matter who was behind him, by the very nature of his law, Papius can hardly have had Pompey's interests at heart, and it may be assumed that there were other tribunes of 65 who also did not, and who could have been persuaded to propose a bill injurious to Pompey.

That the proposal to annex Egypt was not to Pompey's advantage is further indicated by Cicero's opposition to it. If it had been in Pompey's interest, Cicero would have supported it, or, at the least, remained publicly neutral. As shown in the previous chapter, Cicero, with his eye on the consulship, was counting on significant help from Pompey and his followers.[16] He would not have jeopardized this support by opposing a measure that Pompey desired.

On the contrary, that Pompey's rival, Crassus, was in fact behind the proposal and stood to gain much from it is clear from Cicero's speech.[17] Cicero names Crassus outright and refers to an argument with which Crassus supported annexation:

> *Sic est iusta causa belli, sicuti Crassus commemoravit cum Iugurtha fuisse. (fr. 6)*

That Caesar was helping Crassus is also demonstrable. To be sure, his name does not appear in either the *fragmenta* or

16. See Chapter Five, pp. 116–19. Pompey himself, of course was fighting Mithridates; hence Cicero's humorous request that Atticus inform Pompey that he would not mind if Pompey did not personally attend the elections. I see no reason, however, to agree with D. R. Shackleton Bailey that Cicero was being facetious in asking Atticus to organize the votes of Pompey's supporters on his behalf: *Cicero's Letters to Atticus* 1 (Cambridge, 1965), p. 394.

17. *Scholia Bobiensia, Reg. Alex.* 91–92 Stangl: cf. F. Schoell, *Orationum deperditarum fragmenta* (Leipzig, 1917), pp. 457–63; I. Puccioni, *Orationum deperditarum fragmenta* (Milan, 1963), pp. 65–69; Mommsen, *The History of Rome* 4, trans. Dickson (New York, 1895), p. 467, n. 1.

scholia, and the only source for his involvement with the proposal (Suet. *Iul.* 11) has been challenged as being based on unreliable and unduly prejudiced sources.[18] Lack of mention in the *fragmenta* and *scholia* is not a serious difficulty, however, since most of Cicero's speech and the scholiast's work is lost, and since Caesar would not have presented so much of a target as the powerful Crassus. Moreover, to the arguments against Suetonius, one must reply that Suetonius's evidence is often good, even in the early chapters of the *Divus Julius.* His testimony should not be rejected unless it obviously contradicts the historical situation, and the historical situation in 65 indicates that Caesar was working with Crassus.[19]

The question remains as to what Crassus and Caesar hoped to accomplish. It has been suggested that they were hoping to gain the *imperium* for the annexation of Egypt and the concomitant miltary forces in order to oppose Pompey.[20] Probably they were not so foolish as to hope to destroy him by arms, but, rather, sought to obtain a position of strength from which they could bargain for an alliance with him.[21] It is highly doubtful that they could have defeated Pompey in war, and even if they could, to have done so would have freed the *optimates* to crush them in turn. Therefore, since Crassus was not averse to striking a bargain with a rival if it seemed profitable (Plut. *Crass.* 7.5-8), and since the optimate-dominated Senate was a common enemy to his and Pompey's personal ambitions, he probably considered an equal alliance with Pompey to be the most practical course at the time.

18. H. Strasburger, *Caesars Eintritt in die Geschichte* (Munich, 1938), pp. 109–14; L. R. Taylor, "Caesar and the Roman Nobility," *Transactions and Proceedings of the American Philological Association* .73 (1942): 17. F. E. Adcock argues that Caesar could not have hoped to gain a command for annexing Egypt, because he was only an aedile: *Marcus Crassus, Millionaire* (Cambridge, 1966), pp. 37–38. This argument is invalid. Pompey had held great commands without having held any office, and Caesar had demonstrated military talent in the past.

19. See Chapter Five, pp. 125–26.

20. See n. 6 above.

21. F. B. Marsh, *A History of the Roman World, 146–30 B.C.,* ed. 3, H. H. Scullard (London, 1963), p. 163; E. T. Salmon, "Catiline, Crassus, and Caesar," *AJP* 56 (1935): 305; G. Walter, *Caesar,* trans. E. Craufurd (New York, 1952), p. 58; A. Duggan, *Julius Caesar* (New York, 1955), p. 64; H. H. Scullard, *From the Gracchi to Nero,* ed. 2 (London, 1963), pp. 110–11; and *Cicero,* ed. T. A. Dorey (New York, 1965), pp. 10–11.

The scheme to obtain the command for annexing Egypt
would have given Crassus and Caesar a powerful tool with
which to bargain for Pompey's allegiance. No doubt, Pompey,
Crassus, and Caesar had all seen Egypt's vast potential for
economic, political, and military power, which was later exploited by Caesar, Antony, Augustus, and the emperors. Furthermore, for a man who had visions of being another Alexander the Great (Plut. *Pomp.* 2.2), it is difficult to believe that
Pompey had not thought of adding Egypt to his long list of
conquests. Indeed, if Lucan can be trusted, Pompey had already visited Egypt before his fatal trip in 48:

> *Pars mundi nulla vacat; sed tota tenetur*
> *Terra meis, quocumque iacet sub sole, tropaeis:*
> *Hinc me victorem gelidas ad Phasidos undas*
> *Arctos habet; calida medius mihi cognitus axis*
> *Aegypto atque umbras numquam flectente Syene; . . .*
> (2.583–87)

Piganiol argues that Lucan's reference to Egypt in this speech
of Pompey is evidence that Pompey made a voyage there in 67,
between the end of the pirate war and the beginning of his
command against Mithridates.[22] Perhaps he has overstressed
this one passage, but his basic conjecture of a voyage to Egypt
in 67 is very reasonable. The sources give no detailed account
of what Pompey did between the defeat of the pirates and his
visit to Posidonius before the commencement of operations
against Mithridates. Plutarch does say, however, that he spent
his leisure time visiting cities: Καὶ σκολὴν ἄγοντα τὸν Πομπήιον
ἐπέρχεσθαι τὰς πόλεις (*Pomp.* 30.1). One of these cities easily
could have been Alexandria, the Egyptian capital.

During the pirate war, one of Pompey's lieutenants, Cn.
Cornelius Lentulus Marcellinus, had carried out extensive operations along the African coast (Flor. 1.49.9; App. *Mith.*
14.95). A statue was even set up in gratitude to him in the
temple of Apollo at Cyrene.[23] In all probability, while leisurely
"visiting the cities," Pompey visited Cyrene and Marcellinus's

---

22. A. Piganiol, "Un Épisode inconnu de la vie de Pompée," *Studi in
onore di Aristide Calderini e Roberto Paribeni* 1 (Milan, 1956), pp.
135–38.
23. Dittenberger, *SIG* ³, 750.

theater of operations on the African coast.[24] From there, he could easily have sailed along the coast to pay a friendly call on Ptolemy Auletes at Alexandria. Perhaps, as Piganiol suggests, Pompey and Auletes even entered into some form of friendly agreement at this time.[25]

Whether or not Pompey and Auletes met or entered into agreement in 67 is not crucial, however. In the light of Pompey's attitude to Egypt from 63 onward, it is inconceivable that while Pompey was campaigning between 67 and 63 in the other old Hellenistic kingdoms, he had not thought it desirable to establish his influence in Egypt, their rich and important sister kingdom. Appian implies that in 63, Pompey would have liked to extend his Eastern campaign to Egypt but dared not take the risk at that time (*Mith.* 17.114).

After Pompey returned to Rome in 61, he tried to help Auletes and hoped to establish his own influence in Egypt. Along with the ratification of his Eastern settlement, Pompey probably also wanted the Senate to give formal recognition to Auletes as king of Egypt. In 59, after Pompey was driven by the stubbornness of the optimate leaders of the Senate into a coalition with Caesar and Crassus, he was finally able to obtain passage of these measures (Cic. *Att.* 2.16.2; Caes. *BC* 2.2.13). When the Alexandrians expelled Auletes in 57, he stayed at Rome with Pompey and tried to obtain his restoration (Dio 39.14.3). Pompey strove to be the one entrusted with restoring Auletes, but the *optimates* constantly blocked him (Cic. *Fam.* 1.1–7), and he finally had to let his old friend, A. Gabinius, do the job in 55 (Cic. *Pis.* 48–50). Finally, of course, in 48, Pompey was cruelly deceived in his last desperate hope of trying to establish a base of power in Egypt from which he could turn defeat into victory against Caesar.

After failing to gain control of Egypt, Crassus and Caesar did not cease in their efforts to secure their positions. Asconius asserts that in 64, they supported Catiline's bid for the consulship (*Tog. Cand.* 83 C/64–65 St). Doubt has been cast on the credibility of Asconius's statement because it is based on

24. For a discussion of Marcellinus's activities and Pompey's deep interest in Cyrene, see J. Reynolds, "Cyrenaica, Pompey, and Cn. Cornelius Lentulus Marcellinus," *Journal of Roman Studies* 52 (1962): 97–103.
25. Piganiol, "Un Épisode," *Studi in onore* 1, p. 138.

Cicero's posthumously released *de Consiliis Suis*.[26] There is no denying that this document contained much bias and special pleading on Cicero's part, but there is no need to assume that he was falsifying the record when he wrote that Crassus and Caesar had supported Catiline in 64. Where Cicero probably was unfair was in using their support of Catiline in 64 to implicate them later in the Catilinarian Conspiracy of 63 and, as will be seen, to reiterate their involvement in the supposed First Catilinarian Conspiracy of 65.[27]

It appears that Crassus had already come in contact with Catiline in late 66 or in the beginning of 65, when, in addition to other things, he was trying to woo away from Pompey men who had supported him in the past. By placing a number of Pompey's old friends under obligation to himself, Crassus would have been in a better position to face Pompey upon the latter's return.

Crassus's attempts are revealed in three trials of 65, those of Manilius, Cornelius, and Catiline.[28] For 66, Manilius is regarded as a tribune who worked for Pompey's benefit. He had proposed two important laws that were detrimental to the optimate enemies of Pompey.[29] The first was designed to increase the power of freedmen in the *Comitia Tributa* by distributing their votes among all thirty-five tribes of voters (Ascon. *Mil.* 45 C/39 St, *Corn.* 65 C/53 St; Dio 36.42.2–3).[30] If Pompey were perceived as the man behind Manilius, he could have hoped to earn the gratitude of a great enough

26. Sumner, "Cicero, Pompeius, and Rullus," *TAPA* 97 (1966): 575; cf. R. Syme, *Sallust* (Berkeley and Los Angeles, 1964), pp. 62–64. For the *de Consiliis Suis*, see Dio 39.10.2–3; Cic. *Att.* 2.6.2; 14.17.6. For support of the view that Caesar was working with Crassus in this case, see Klebs, *RE* 1.2 (1894), 2578.25–47, s.v. "Antonius" (19); Garzetti, "Crasso," *Athenaeum* 20 (1942): 33; Taylor, "Caesar and the Roman Nobility," *TAPA* 73 (1942): 18; M. Grant, *Julius Caesar* (London, 1969), pp. 53–54.

27. Certainly Crassus had no interest in promoting a real revolution, but he may have hoped to take advantage of a crisis created by Catiline. See below, pp. 184–85.

28. Cf. A. M. Ward, "Politics in the Trials of Manilius and Cornelius," *Transactions and Proceedings of the American Philological Association* 101 (1970): 545–56.

29. One must be careful, of course, not to confuse the attitude of the *optimates* with that of all senators. Many were uncommitted, and some openly supported Pompey. Cf. A. N. Sherwin-White, "Violence in Roman Politics," *Journal of Roman Studies* 46 (1956): 5–9; Gelzer, *Cicero*, 60.

30. Cf. L. R. Taylor, *The Voting Districts of the Roman Republic* (Rome, 1960), pp. 144–45.

bloc of voters to dominate the *Comitia Tributa*.[31] This law had been passed with considerable violence, which the equally violent optimate L. Domitius Ahenobarbus had opposed as quaestor (ibid.). The law's opponents procured its condemnation by the Senate and were able to stir up popular resentment against it since it would have lessened the power of the freeborn plebs. Seeing that the plan had failed, Manilius tried to blame Crassus for the idea, and acquiesced in the annulment of his own law (ibid.).[32]

The second of Manilius's laws was the much more famous and successful *lex Manilia de imperio Gnaei Pompeii*, which gave Pompey command of the war against Mithridates (Cic. *Leg. Man.* passim, *Fam.* 1.9.11; Liv. *Per.* 100; Ascon. *Corn.* 65 C/53 St; Dio 36.42.4–43.2). Upon the expiration of Manilius's tribunate in December of 66, therefore, the optimate opponents of Pompey charged Manilius with extortion in political retaliation for his tribunician actions (Plut. *Cic.* 9.4; Dio 36.44.1).[33]

Manilius had counted on the aid of Cicero, who was not only a friend of Pompey and had supported the granting of Pompey's command, but was also the praetor in charge of the extortion court, *quaestio de repetundis* (Cic. *Leg. Man.* 1–2, *Cluent.* 147; Ascon. *Corn.* 62 C/50 St). Manilius asked Cicero for the customary ten-day postponement of his trial (Plut. *Cic.* 9.4; Dio 36.44.1). In this way, Cicero's praetorship would have expired and Cicero would have been free to defend him in January of 65.[34] With an eye toward his campaign for the

31. The issue of freedman membership in all thirty-five tribes in order to assure them an equal vote with other Roman citizens had been a recurrent issue. In 220, freedmen seem to have been limited to membership in only the four urban tribes (Liv. *Per.* 20), and in 169, they were further restricted to membership in only one of these tribes (Liv. 45.15.1–7; cf. Cic. *de Or.* 1.38).

32. That Manilius had tried to blame Crassus for the proposed law when it became unpopular is a further indication that it had been designed with Pompey in mind. Indeed, people refused to be taken in by Manilius's ruse (Dio 46.42.3).

33. For the criminal courts as political weapons in Rome, see E. S. Gruen, *Roman Politics and the Criminal Courts, 149–78 B.C.* (Cambridge, Mass., 1968). E. J. Phillips has convincingly argued that the preliminary hearing, *nominis delatio*, took place on 27 December: "Cicero and the Prosecution of Manilius," *Latomus* 29 (1970): 595–98.

34. Cf. Gelzer, *Cicero*, p. 60. Of course, Cicero could have defended Manilius even while he was praetor, if Manilius had been prosecuted on some other charge, just as he had defended Cluentius.

consulship, Cicero hoped to avoid giving further offense to the *optimates* without angering Pompey's supporters by actually refusing to defend Manilius. Therefore, he granted Manilius a postponement of only one day, so that the case would come to trial while he himself still presided over the extortion court (Plut. *Cic.* 9.5; Dio 36.44.1).

Cicero's plan backfired. Under intense popular pressure, he relented and consented to defend Manilius (Plut. *Cic.* 9.4–6; Dio 36.44.2).[35] He offered the rather lame excuse that he had granted Manilius a postponement of only one day because he had wanted him to have the advantage of being tried before him instead of some other, perhaps less friendly, praetor (ibid.).[36] Manilius himself, however, could no longer trust Cicero and, with Pompey away in Asia, apparently sought aid from the only other powerful figure near to hand who could or would help him, Pompey's rival, Crassus.

Crassus's aid took the form of a violent disruption of Manilius's trial when it began in 65 (Ascon. *Corn.* 60, 66

35. He must, therefore, have promised also to grant an additional extension of the case until such time as he would have been free to defend Manilius.

36. E. J. Phillips has argued that in granting a postponement of only one day, Cicero was favoring Manilius by practicing a ruse like the one attempted by the defense in Verres' trial: "Cicero and the Prosecution of Manilius," *Latomus* 29 (1970): 600–601. In this way, the trial, begun on the last day of the year, could not have proceeded beyond the first *actio* before the beginning of a new year. Therefore, the trial would have had to begin anew after the empanelling of a new court, and Manilius would have gained extra time in preparing his defense. This argument is not convincing. If Cicero had really wished to gain time for Manilius, he need not have chosen such a cumbersome means. With only two days remaining in 66, this ruse would not have gained Manilius any more time than, in fact, the granting of a perfectly usual ten-day postponement would have. It would have taken the same time to empanel a new court once the new year had begun, whether time had run out on a trial begun in 66 or a ten-day postponement had been granted. Moreover, if Cicero had been working actively for Manilius, Manilius never would have resorted to the expedient of having the trial violently disrupted, contrary to Cicero's desires, and Cicero would not have abandoned his defense in 65, as seen in the following discussion. Finally, there is no guarantee that the trial could not have been completed in the day remaining after a one-day postponement. With a well-prepared prosecutor and an ill-prepared defender, Cicero, as president of the court, could have forced the proceedings through despite the usual practice in extortion trials. Indeed, the pressure of time would have been a good excuse.

C/49, 53 St).[37] Cicero made the following statement in reference to the disruption of Manilius's trial:

Aliisille in illum furorem magnis hominibus auctoribus impulsus est qui aliquod institui exemplum disturbandorum iudiciorum rei< >p. perniciosissimum, temporibus suis accommodatissimum, meis alienissimum rationibus cupiverunt (ibid. 66 C/53 St)

The question is, who were these men to whom Cicero referred with the words *magnis hominibus auctoribus.* Asconius, of course, conjectures that they were Catiline and Cn. (Calpurnius) Piso (ibid.).[38] It has been suggested, however, that Cicero would not have used these words to describe Catiline and Piso in 65 and that Catiline was connected with men like Catulus and Cato, whose brother-in-law led a band of *optimates* in opposition to those who were seeking to terminate by violence Manilius's prosecution (Schol. Bob. *ad Mil.* 22, 119 St).[39]

On the other hand, further investigation will reveal that Crassus is still the most likely one with whom Catiline was associated in this instance. In an oration, Cicero very easily could have applied the vague words *magni Homines* to Catiline

37. It is clear that the disruption occurred only after the trial had begun in 65: see Phillips, "Cicero and the Prosecution," *Latomus* 29 (1970): 603, and A. M. Ward, "Politics in the Trials," *TAPA* 101 (1970): 548–49. The charge upon which Manilius faced trial in 65 has been the subject of some confusion. Phillips seems correct, however, in arguing that the charge was never changed to *maiestas* but remained *repetundae*: ibid., 603–5. Unfortunately, absolute certainty cannot be attained, because the position of the praetor C. Attius Celsus is not unambiguous: Ward, ibid., 548–49, n. 15.

38. At first glance, Piso, might be considered the prosecutor of Manilius because of Valerius Maximus's statements about his prosecution of one Manilius Crispus (6.2.4). There is, however, no solid evidence that the C. Manilius of this trial and Manilius Crispus are the same: cf. Münzer, *RE* 14.1 (1928), 1134.60–65, 1140.51–59, s.v. "Manilius" (10, 23). Also, E. S. Gruen has demonstrated that Piso must have prosecuted Manilius Crispus in 69 or 68: "Pompey and the Pisones," *California Studies in Classical Antiquity* 1 (1968): 160–61. Finally, had Piso prosecuted C. Manilius in 66/65, Asconius would not be likely to have considered him one of those behind the disruption of the trial. Therefore, whether or not he is right about the charge, the scholiast of Bobbio can be considered correct in identifying the prosecutor as one Cn. Minucius (Schol. Bob., *ad Mil.* 22, 119 St).

39. E. S. Gruen, "Notes on the 'First Catilinarian Conspiracy,'" *Classical Philology* 64 (1969): 20–34. In support of Asconius, see now E. J. Phillips, "Acsonius' *Magni Homines*," *Rheinisches Museum für Philologie* 116 (1973): 353–57.

and Piso. Although not strictly accurate, they would have had the psychological impact that Cicero wanted. Regardless of any friendship between Catiline and Catulus, it nevertheless seems best to link Catiline and the riots that disrupted Manilius's trial with the machinations of Crassus, Pompey's arch-rival.

Piso is the connection. He was working at this time with Crassus against Pompey. Crassus was behind Piso's pro-praetorian appointment to Spain in 65, an anti-Pompeian move —attempts to minimize it notwithstanding (Sall. *Cat.* 19.1– 2).[40] Crassus's interest in Piso probably began in 69 or 68 with Piso's violently anti-Pompeian outburst recorded by Valerius Maximus (6.2.4).[41] Therefore, although Catiline also had pre-vious Pompeian connections, his involvement with Piso in the disruption of Manilus's trial still links him with Crassus in another one of Crassus's anti-Pompeian schemes.[42]

Although Crassus had enough reason to dislike Manilus for his past deeds, support of him would have been helpful in the struggle with Pompey for popular favor at Rome: Crassus would have had an opportunity to show that his patronage was more valuable than Pompey's; and since Manilius was being prosecuted for his actions as tribune, Crassus would have been protecting the office of tribune, whose powers he had helped to restore in an earlier bid for popularity (cf. Ascon. *Corn.* 76 C/59 St).

The form of aid was to be a violent disruption of the trial to dissuade the prosecution from pressing its case. Catiline, re-gardless of his earlier connections and not necessarily having any close association with Crassus as yet, may have learned of the scheme and offered his help in the hope that the favor would be returned later, if necessary, when he himself was to

40. Cf. A. M. Ward, "Politics in the Trials," *TAPA* 101 (1970): 551, n. 22. J.P.V.D. Balsdon has correctly explained the title of Piso as *quaestor pro praetore:* "Roman History, 65–50 B.C.; Five Problems," *Journal of Roman Studies* 52 (1962): 134–35. But, Baldsdon's suggestion that this kind of appointment was not irregular is hardly useful in an attempt to argue that Crassus and Piso had not taken advantage of it for personal political reasons.
41. Gruen, "Notes," *CP* 64 (1969): 24.
42. For Catiline's links with Pompey, see R. Seager, "The First Cati-linarian Conspiracy," *Historia* 13 (1964): 344–45.

face trial for extortion.⁴³ Hence, Cicero's reference to those who desired an *exemplum disturbandorum iudiciorum . . . temporibus suis accommodatissimum* has a clear point.⁴⁴

Unfortunately for Manilius, the help of Crassus and his friends was of no avail. After the trial was disrupted upon its opening in January of 65, the prosecution did not desist. Instead, the *optimates* opened the matter to debate in the Senate. A *Senatus Consultum* resulted, which instructed the consuls to protect the court when the trial was resumed (ibid., 60 C/49 St).⁴⁵ At this point, Cicero seems to have refused to participate further in the defense.⁴⁶ Manilius completely lost heart, fled Rome, and was condemned *in absentia* (ibid.).

In the trial of Cornelius, Crassus was more successful in earning the gratitude of a former Pompeian tribune. As a tribune of the plebs in 67, Cornelius had introduced several popular reform bills that would have limited abuses practiced by a number of senators, especially the oligarchic *pauci*, the optimate enemies of Pompey (ibid., 57–59 C/47–48 St).⁴⁷ They were now using the charge of *maiestas* in retaliation.⁴⁸ The witnesses for the prosecution included many of Pompey's bitterest foes among the optimates: Q. Hortensius, Q. Catulus, Q. Metellus Pius, M. Terentius Varro Lucullus (brother of

43. For Catiline's indictment *de repetundis*, which was blocking his candidacy for the consulship, see Cic. *Att.* 1.1.1, 2.1; Ascon. *Tog. Cand.* 89 C/69 St. Of course, Torquatus and Cotta, the consuls, were in no way the objects of the violence. In fact, they did not even enter the picture until after the disruption of the trial, when the Senate passed a decree entrusting them with the future protection of the trial (Ascon. *Corn.* 60 C/49 St). The idea of a plot against them is a later fabrication: Seager, "The First Catilinarian Conspiracy," *Historia* 13 (1964): 344; cf. Syme, *Sallust*, pp. 101–2.

44. Catiline's armed appearance in the Forum on 29 December 66 (Cic. *Cat.* 1.15), far from being a move in support of Cicero, as Phillips argues ("Cicero and the Prosecution," *Latomus* 29 [1970]: 601–3), was a move to protect Manilius in case Cicero reneged and tried to force the prosecution.

45. The date of the trial's disruption probably was 5 February, the day Catiline supposedly bungled a plot to kill the consuls (Sall. *Cat.* 18.6–8).

46. A. M. Ward, "Politics in the Trials," *TAPA* 101 (1970): 552–53.

47. For Cornelius's legislative activities, see Chapter Five, pp. 114–15 and M. Griffin, "The Tribune C. Cornelius," *Journal of Roman Studies* 63 (1973): 196–203. For the optimate reaction to them, see *indigne eam Corneli rogationem tulerant potentissimi* (Ascon. *Corn.* 58 C/48 St), *invitis optimatibus* (ibid., 59 C/48 St), and *paucorum odio* (Cic. *Corn.* fr. 2.11, 424 S/64 P).

48. Gelzer, *Cicero*, p. 63.

L. Licinius Lucullus, Pompey's implacable foe), and Mamercus Aemilius Lepidus Livianus (ibid. 60 C/49 St, 79 C/62 St).[49]

The trial itself was but a renewal of a prosecution begun earlier. In 66, the year after his tribunate, P. and L. Cominius had charged Cornelius with *maiestas* for his actions concerning his proposal that dispensations from the laws be granted only by the People (ibid., 58–61 C/48–50 St).[50] The Cominii had not gone through with their prosecution in 66, however, because some thugs had threatened their lives if they would not abandon the case (ibid., 59–60 C/49 St). Finally, in 65, after Manilius had forfeited his case, the Cominii were emboldened to renew their charge against Cornelius.

Cicero, seeing a chance to earn the favor of both Pompey, with his many supporters, and moderates in the Senate, agreed to defend Cornelius.[51] The latter, taking the lesson of Manilius's trial to heart, made certain that no one would disrupt these proceedings (ibid.), but he did not do without the aid of Crassus. This time, Crassus was more politic. Instead of seeking to force abandonment of the prosecution, he sat on the jury that was hearing Cornelius's case (ibid., 76 C/59 St).

49. For discussions of these men, see Chapter One and its Appendices A and B. M. Terentius Varro Lucullus is listed as M. Lucullus in most MSS of Asconius. A variant reading of the Codex Matritensis X 81 (designated as P by Clark and Stangl), gives L. Lucullus, but the unanimity of the others seems decisive. The substitution of L. for M. may have been an erroneous emendation based on Val. Max. 8.5.4. Mamercus Aemilius Lepidus Livianus is erroneously listed as M'. Lepidus in most of the texts of Asconius, including those of Clark and Stangl. G. V. Sumner has clearly demonstrated, however, that the name required is Mamercus: "Manius or Mamercus," *Journal of Roman Studies* 54 (1964): 41–48.

50. Asconius names the second brother Gaius, but Cicero himself calls this brother Lucius (*Cluent.* 100); cf. E. Badian, review of Malcovati, *ORF* [2], *Journal of Roman Studies* 46 (1956): 200/ *Studies in Greek and Roman History* (Oxford, 1964), pp. 247–48, and W. C. McDermott, "De Luceiis," *Hermes* 97 (1969): 242, n. 2. The laws proposed by Cornelius and the events of his tribunate have been investigated by W. McDonald in "The Tribunate of Cornelius," *Classical Quarterly* 23 (1929): 196–208, and J. W. Heaton in "Mob Violence in the Late Roman Republic," *University of Illinois Studies in the Social Sciences,* 23.4 (Urbana, 1939): 49–51. The exact reason for the charge of *maiestas* is the subject of some question. The best explanation seems to be that he was charged with *maiestas* for personally reading out his proposal to the assembly when Globulus was trying to interpose a veto: R. A. Bauman, *The Crimen Maiestatis in the Roman Republic and Augustan Principate* (Johannesburg, 1967), pp. 27–30, 85–87, and Chr. Meier, "Die loca intercessionis bei Rogationen," *Museum Helveticum* 25 (1968): 87–88.

51. Cf. Ward, "Politics in the Trials," *TAPA* 101 (1970): 554–56.

Thus, Crassus was in a position to use his well-known talents of persuasion to Cornelius's benefit.[52] It would not, perhaps, be too bold to suggest that Crassus's influence had as much to do with Cornelius's overwhelming acquittal as Cornelius's own popularity and Cicero's oratory.

Although Crassus and Cicero supported Cornelius, they certainly were not cooperating with each other in the courts. In fact, it may have been Crassus's support of Catiline during his prosecution for extortion in this same year that led Cicero to abandon his contemplated defense of Catiline. As already noted, Catiline may already have helped Crassus and Caesar in support of Manilius, with the hope that he would have their aid when the need arose. At the moment, Catiline was just the sort of man that Crassus and Caesar needed. He had Pompeian connections that could have made him useful in dealing with Pompey. Cichorius has convincingly identified him as the L. Sergius who had served on the staff of Pompey's father in 89.[53] There, Catiline probably had met and formed an acquaintanceship with Pompey. Now he was being prosecuted for his recent actions as governor of Africa (Cic. *Att.* 1.2.1; Ascon. *Tog. Cand.* 89 C/69 St). By helping Catiline escape condemnation and then supporting him for the consulship, Crassus and Caesar could have hoped to have a valuable friend in facing future contingencies.

Cicero apparently had once thought so, too, but then changed his mind. In view of Catiline's previous connections with Pompey, Cicero probably thought that Pompey would be pleased if he defended Catiline and that Catiline would become a useful (although not essential) ally in his upcoming campaign for the consulship. Cicero had even laid concrete plans for the defense (*Att.* 1.2.1). Subsequently, however, he abandoned the idea. One possible reason for Cicero's failure to defend him is that Catiline, since he was a patrician and since his acquittal seemed assured, felt no need of the aspiring Cicero and his oratorical skills. Catiline may have felt that a man of consular rank, like Torquatus, who ultimately de-

52. McDonald has argued that during his tribunate Cornelius was acting as much for Crassus as for Pompey: "The Tribunate of Cornelius," CQ 23 (1929): 199. Rather, Cornelius in 65 probably turned to Crassus in the absence of Pompey, as Manilius had.

53. *Römische Studien* (Leipzig and Berlin, 1922), pp. 172–73.

fended him, would have been a more politically valuable defender than Cicero.[54]

On the other hand, a reasonable answer to the question of Cicero's failure to defend Catiline is that Catiline, as argued above, had already begun to work with Crassus and Caesar. The extensive bribery associated with Catiline's acquittal (Q. Cic. *Com. Pet.* 10; Ascon. *Tog. Cand.* 85 C/66 St) may indicate some financial aid from Crassus, although Catiline must have provided for such matters, at least in part, while he had been governor of Africa; and it seems very significant that in 64, during special proceedings with which Caesar was closely involved, Catiline was acquitted of his well-known murders during the Sullan proscriptions, whereas others were condemned (Ascon. *Tog. Cand.* 90–91 C/69–70 St; Dio 37.10.1–4; Suet. *Iul.* 11).[55] Cicero may well have decided that Catiline's interests had now become too closely linked with those of Crassus and Caesar. Since he did not wish to give them any aid in their attempts to rival Pompey in power, he no longer would have desired to defend Catiline.[56]

54. Except for a statement attributed to Fenestella, there is no mention anywhere that Cicero did go through with the defense, and Asconius says that he never did (*Tog. Cand.* 85 C/66 St). Asconius also reports that Torquatus defended Catiline (*Corn.* 66 C/53 St, *Tog. Cand.* 92 C/71 St). Catiline's obliging prosecutor was P. Clodius (Cic. *Att.* 1.2.1, *Har. Resp.* 42, 45).

55. In view of Suetonius's words *in exercenda de sicariis quaestione* (*Iul.* 11), it is usually asserted that Caesar presided over the court in this case: cf. Gelzer, *Caesar*, p. 42. On the other hand, Strasburger has denied it because of the words *multos accusavit et damnavit Sullanos* in the *Scholia Gronoviana* (*ad Lig.* 12, 293 St): *Caesars Eintritt*, pp. 117–19. E. S. Gruen has recently supported this view: *The Last Generation of the Roman Republic* (Berkeley and Los Angeles, 1974), pp. 76–77, n. 124. Contrary to his assertion, however, neither Cicero, *Lig.* 12, nor Dio, 37.10.1–2, confirms it. At the most, they are ambiguous. Therefore, Suetonius provides the crucial evidence that tends to confirm the more common opinion. Nevertheless, even if one does accept the view that Caesar was not the *iudex* in charge of the court, but only an *accusator*, it is clear that he was deeply involved in the prosecutions, and it is significant that he did not attempt to prosecute Catiline, one of the most notorious offenders, who was accused by L. Lucceius (Ascon. *Tog. Cand.* 90–91 C/69–70 St).

56. That Torquatus had links with Pompey (see Syme, *Sallust*, pp. 149, 151, n. 16) and that Clodius had helped make possible Pompey's Mithridatic command should be no bar to this interpretation. Having achieved the consulship, Torquatus would not have had to worry much about Pompey's views, and Clodius is notorious for putting his own interests above other considerations.

When Crassus and Caesar aided both Catiline and Antonius during the campaign for the consulship in 64, Cicero sought to weaken them by implicating them in the so-called "First Catilinarian Conspiracy." This "conspiracy" never existed. It was actually a fictitious creation of Cicero's subtle rhetoric.[57] By skillfully misrepresenting the events surrounding the consular elections and the prosecution of Manilius in 66 and 65, Cicero implicated Crassus, Caesar, and Catiline in a conspiracy to massacre the *optimates*. Supposedly, Cn. Calpurnius Piso, who had been sent to Spain, was privy to the plot, as were Autronius Paetus and P. Sulla, both of whom had been convicted of bribery in the consular elections for 65 and had been barred from office. It was particularly easy to drag Autronius into the supposed plot because he had been involved in an attempt to break up the *ambitus* court by violence in order to prevent his own prosecution (Cic. *Sull.* 15). Among the intended victims were claimed to be the two men who had replaced Autronius and Sulla, L. Aurelius Cotta and L. Manlius Torquatus (Sall. *Cat.* 18.1–19.5; Ascon. *Corn.* 75 C/59 St, *Tog. Cand.* 92 C/71 St).

Cicero was able to concoct the basic outline of this story because a tribune had blocked an official investigation into the disturbances of 65 (Dio 36.44.5). He achieved his purpose through his campaign speech, *in Toga Candida*, by four basic steps that are fortunately preserved in five passages quoted by Asconius. In the first passage, Cicero brought attention to Crassus's and Caesar's support of Catiline and Antonius in the current consular campaign:

> Dico, P. C., superiore nocte cuiusdam hominis nobilis et valde in hoc largitionis quaestu noti et cogniti domum Catilinam et Antonium cum sequestribus suis convenisse. (83 C/65 St)

Asconius comments:

---

57. Cf. R. Seager, "The First Catilinarian Conspiracy," *Historia* 13 (1964): 338–47. Many, however, have accepted its historicity. Garzetti, accepting Suetonius (*Iul.* 9.3), even agrees that part of the plot included an uprising of the Transpadanes: "Crasso," *Athenaeum* 20 (1942): 30. This idea is merely an accretion to the legend established by Cicero. H. Frisch has demonstrated how ridiculous it would have been for Crassus to hatch such a plot: "The First Catilinarian Conspiracy: A Study in Historical Conjecture," *Classica et Mediaevalia* 9 (1948): 10–36.

Aut C. Caesaris aut M. Crassi domum significat. Ei enim acerrimi ac potentissimi fuerunt Ciceronis refragatores cum petiit consulatum, quod eius in dies civilem crescere dignitatem animadvertebant: et hoc ipse Cicero in expositione consiliorum suorum significat; eius quoque coniurationis quae Cotta et Torquato coss. ante annum quam haec dicerentur facta est a Catilina et Pisone arguit M. Crassum auctorem fuisse. (ibid.)

Probably the house referred to was that of Crassus, the more important man, not Caesar's, but because Caesar was closely associated with Crassus at this time, he would have been implicated, too.

Attempts have been made to deny that Crassus and Caesar were supporting Catiline and Antonius. The main objections are that this idea rests on inferences and conjectures from the political situation and from only two passages of Asconius, both of which probably derive from Cicero's posthumous *de Consiliis Suis*; [58] and that in his private correspondence, Cicero never alludes to Crassus's and Caesar's backing of his competitors and never explicitly says that they were part of Catiline's plots except in his secret, posthumous memoir. [59] To be sure, the implication of Crassus and Caesar with the electoral campaigns of Catiline and Antonius does rest on inferences and conjectures based on the political situation. The point that the critics have missed is that these were the very inferences and conjectures that Cicero knew his audience, which was quite familiar with the political situation, would make. The public must have known of the connection between Crassus and Caesar. Cicero did not need to name names, and, as would any skillful politician who was planning to blacken his enemies on questionable grounds, he wished to work by insinuation and avoid names as much as possible. It is significant that in the passages quoted by Asconius, the only villain that Cicero actually names besides Catiline and Antonius is Cn.

58. The first passage reads, *coierunt enim ambo ut Ciceronem consulatu deiecerent, adiutoribus usi firmissimis M. Crasso et C. Caesare* (83 C/64 St). The second passage is the comment of Asconius that I have quoted in the text above.

59. For these arguments, see P. A. Brunt, "Three Passages from Asconius," *Classical Review* 7 (1957): 195. Cf. also B. A. Marshall, "Cicero and Sallust on Crassus and Catiline," *Latomus* 33 (1974): 804–9.

Calpurnius Piso, who was already dead (Ascon. *Tog. Cand.* 92 C/71 St).

Furthermore, even if it is granted that Asconius did derive both of his comments about Crassus and Caesar from the posthumous *de Consiliis Suis*, that is not to say that his comments are incorrect. He, who was familiar with the whole speech and who, through his studies, knew more about the political situation at the time of the speech than most of his contemporaries could have known without the benefit of similar study, was pointing out to the reader what Cicero intended here. By citing the *de Consiliis Suis*, Asconius directed the reader to a work in which Cicero thought it safe to be more specific with his charge than he was in his speech: all the principals were now dead and there would have been no need for circumspection.

Nor is it strange that Cicero himself, even in his letters, never alludes to Crassus's and Caesar's association with Catiline and Antonius. Not one letter survives for the period between the consular elections of 65 (*Att.* 1.2) and the first letter of 62 (*Fam.* 5.7), the very period during which Cicero would have been most likely to have made allusions to matters concerning Crassus, Caesar, Catiline, and his own campaign for the consulship. If Cicero was bold enough to make any such allusions in his letters of this period, either the recipients prudently destroyed them, or someone made certain that they were never published. In his speech of 64, Cicero knew that his mention of the meeting at the house of a certain well-known noble would be recognized for what it was, a reference to Crassus and, by implication, his close associate Caesar.

In the second passage taken from Asconius, Cicero gave Catiline a plausible motive for massacring the *optimates*:

> *Te vero, Catilina, consulatum sperare aut cogitare non prodigium atque portentum est? A quibus enim petis? A principibus civitatis? qui tibi, cum L. Volcacio cos. in consilio fuissent, ne petendi quidem potestatem esse voluerunt!* (89 C/69 St)

Asconius comments:

> *Paulo ante diximus Catilinam, cum de provincia Africa decederet petiturus consulatum et legati Afri questi de eo in*

senatu graviter ⟨essent⟩, supervenisse. Professus deinde est et Catilina petere se consulatum. L. Volcacius Tullus consul consilium publicum habuit an rationem Catilinae habere deberet, si peteret consulatum: nam quaerebatur repetundarum. Catilina ob eam causam destitit a petitione. (ibid.)

In 66, after Torquatus's son and Cotta had successfully prosecuted the consuls designate for 65, P. Autronius Paetus and P. Cornelius Sulla, on a charge of bribery (Sall. *Cat.* 18.1–2; Ascon. *Corn.* 75 C/59 St), the *optimates* had arranged with the consul Volcacius Tullus to bar Catiline from the supplementary election to fill the posts now forfeited by Paetus and Sulla.[60] In mentioning this event, Cicero suggested to his audience a plausible motive that prepared them for believing the charge that Catiline had been involved in a conspiracy in late 66 and early 65 to slay the *optimates*, namely, anger and frustration at their prevention of his candidature in the supplementary election of 66.

Having prepared the way for its acceptance, therefore, Cicero made the charge in the third passage:

Praetereo nefarium illum conatum tuum et paene acerbum et luctuosum rei publicae diem, cum Cn. Pisone socio, ne quem alium nominem, caedem optimatum facere voluisti. (Ascon. 92 C/71 St)

Asconius comments:

Quos ⟨non⟩ nominet intellegitis. Fuit enim opinio Catilinam et Cn. Pisonem, adulescentem perditum, coniurasse ad caedem senatus faciendam ante annum quam haec dicta sunt, Cotta et Torquato coss., eamque caedem ideo non esse factam quod prius quam parati essent coniuratis signum dedisset Catilina. Piso autem, cum haec dicerentur, perierat, in Hispaniam missus a senatu per honorem legationis. . . . Ibi quaestor dum iniurias provincialibus facit, occisus erat, ut quidam credebant, a Cn. Pompeii clientibus Pompeio non invito. (ibid.)

---

60. M. Mello has tried to argue that Torquatus and Cotta had automatically succeeded to the consulships of the convicted Sulla and Paetus: "Sallustio e le elezioni consolari del 66," *La Parola del Passato* 18 (1963): 47–54. G. V. Sumner, however, has clearly demonstrated that there were, in fact, supplementary elections to fill the posts left vacant by the condemnation of Sulla and Paetus: "The Consular Elections of 66 B.C.," *Phoenix* 19 (1965): 226–31.

No doubt, the day referred to was the day, probably 5 February 65, when Manilius's trial was supposed to resume. The common people had been outspoken in their anger with the *optimates* for their court action against Manilius in late December 66 (Plut. *Cic.* 9.5; Dio 36.44.2), and for some time the Forum had been shrouded in an atmosphere of fear and violence. Catiline had appeared in the Forum on 29 December to support Manilius with arms if need be (Cic. *Cat.* 1.15). Subsequently, he and Piso had violently disrupted the beginning of Manilius's trial in January (Ascon. *Corn.* 66 C/53 St; cf. Cic. *Mur.* 81). Now, they were on hand to disrupt it once more, if it should have been resumed; and the consuls, Cotta and Torquatus, had been instructed to protect the court, no doubt with an armed guard (Ascon. *Corn.* 60 C/49 St; Dio 36.44.4).[61] Although this situation had come to nothing because Manilius had failed to reappear, once given a plausible motive it was easy for Cicero's audience of 64 to accept the charge that a frustrated Catiline had really been planning to assassinate the consuls and stir up a popular massacre of the *optimates*.

Moreover, by his mention of Piso and studiously vague statement, *ne quem alium nominem,* Cicero further implicated Crassus and his associate Caesar, Catiline's backers during the current elections, in the alleged plot of 65. Crassus had helped arrange Piso's Spanish governorship in 65 (Sall. *Cat.* 19.1), and Asconius takes the ostensibly omitted reference as being so clear that he merely says *quos non nominet intellegitis.* In his comments on the first passage he has already pointed out the names of Crassus and Caesar. He need not repeat himself here. Thus, without actually naming them, Cicero prompted his hearers to conclude that Crassus and Caesar had been behind a plot of Catiline to murder the *optimates* in 65.

Cicero then reinforced this conclusion with bolder allusions to their mutual association. First he spoke about certain *mali cives:*

Qui posteaquam illo quo conati erant Hispaniensi pugiunculo nervos incidere civium Romanorum non potuerunt, duas uno tempore conantur in rem publicam sicas destringere. (93 C/72 St)

61. It was easy for Dio to turn this guard into a personal bodyguard for the consuls.

Asconius comments:

> *Hispaniensem pugiunculum Cn. Pisonem appellat, quem in Hispania occisum esse dixi. Duas sicas Catilinam et Antonium appellari manifestum est.* (*ibid.*)

Then Cicero said:

> *Hunc vos scitote Licinium gladiatorem iam immisisse capillum Catilinae† iudic. qua Q. ve Curium hominem quaestorium.* (*ibid.*)

Asconius comments:

> *Curius hic notissimus fuit aleator, damnatusque postea est. In hunc est hendecasyllabus Calvi elegans:*
> *Et talos Curius pereruditus.* (*ibid.*)

It is difficult to conceive at whom, other than Crassus and Caesar, Cicero could have been hinting when he talked about the *mali cives* who had tried to disrupt Spain by the "Spanish dirk" (*Hispaniensi pugiunculo*) and were trying to draw "two daggers" (*duas sicas*) against the state. Crassus had supported Piso's assignment to Spain, and he and Caesar were supporting Catiline and Antonius. Moreover, in this last passage, although the reference to Curius and Asconius's comment reveal no connection with Crassus,[62] the reference to *Licinius gladiator* is as close as Cicero could have come to the name of M. Licinius Crassus without actually saying it. The implication of the name Licinius is clear, so clear in fact, that Asconius does not comment on it: whether one reads *capillum* with Clark and Stangl or *lapillum* with Kiesling and Schoell, the implication that Crassus had helped in obtaining Catiline's acquittal in the trial of 65 seems unavoidable, since either *capillum* or *lapillum* used with *immisisse* indicates the action of voting for acquittal of a crime.[63] Thus, by reminding his hearers of the other shady dealings in which Crassus and Caesar were linked with Catiline, Cicero would have convinced many senators

---

62. This Curius was probably the bankrupt senator who joined Catiline in the real conspiracy of 63, whose mistress, Fulvia, passed information to Cicero (Sall. *Cat.* 23.1–6, 26.3; App. *BC* 2.1.3), and who later accused Caesar of complicity with Catiline (Suet. *Iul.* 17.1): F. Münzer, *RE* 4.2 (1901), 1840, s.v. "Curius" (7).

63. For the significance of *capillum*, see Plin. *Ep.* 7.27.14; for that of *lapillum*, see Ov. *Met.* 15.41.

that these two had supported Catiline in a plot against them.

By prominently mentioning Piso, Cicero also sought to achieve another objective, namely, to discredit Crassus, Caesar, and their candidates in the eyes of Pompey's supporters. As already noted, Crassus had been instrumental in sending Piso to Spain in an anti-Pompeian move (Sall. *Cat.* 19.1–2). Piso had caused trouble in Spain and had been murdered there (ibid., 3–5). Naturally, since Pompey had extensive clientage and influence in Spain, he would have regarded the trouble-maker Piso as a threat to his political security. Indeed, Sallust reports one rumor to the effect that Pompey's clients, acting under Pompey's orders, were the ones who had killed Piso (ibid., 4–5), and Asconius supports or repeats this view (*Tog. Cand.* 92 C/71 St). Certainly, Pompey, away in the East, would not have had a direct hand in the affair, but he would have heard of it with approval.[64] Pompey's supporters, therefore, would not have looked with favor upon consular candidates backed by the patron of Piso.

Thus, in four basic steps during the speech *in Toga Candida*, Cicero, by subtle, skillful use of fact, innuendo, and plausible fabrication, attempted to discredit Crassus, Caesar, and their candidates in the eyes of both the *optimates* and *Pompeiani*. It is a measure of Cicero's skill that he succeeded so well in blocking Crassus's hope of having a pair of friendly consuls for 63. A significant number of senators was clearly disturbed at the prospect presented by the elections. The Senate passed a decree limiting the number of attendants for candidates and outlawing the *collegia*, guilds often made up of slaves, which were used for political gangsterism (Cic. *Pis.* 8; Ascon. *Pis.* 8 C/15 St). Candidates backed by a man of Crassus's resources could have made great use of hordes of attendants and gangs of partisans. In the end, the *optimates* were frightened away from Catiline and Antonius. Pompey's forces also remained aloof from Catiline and Antonius and helped to return Cicero at the head of the poll.[65]

Crassus was not dismayed by this setback. After all, An-

---

64. Gruen, "Pompey and the Pisones," *Calif. Stud. in Class. Ant.* 1 (1968): 160.

65. Some have followed the view expressed by Sallust (*Cat.* 23.5–6) that the nobility joined behind Cicero to keep out Catiline: cf. D. R. Shackleton Bailey, *Cicero* (London, 1971), pp. 30–31. Cicero himself,

tonius had been elected and might still be helpful. His former legate of 71, C. Pomptinus, had been elected to the praetorship (cf. Cic. *Cat.* 3.5; Sall. *Cat.* 45), and he had also obtained the election of a number of useful tribunes, while Caesar remained his skillful ally. After the elections, Crassus and Caesar devised a concerted attack to gain ascendancy in the state before Pompey's return. The plan was to push a *popularis* program on all fronts. Several pieces of legislation were involved. The first was a land distribution scheme. As a popular measure, it was an attempt to gain support both from those who had been dispossessed in favor of Sulla's veterans and from many of those very same veterans who had gone bankrupt on the allotments that Sulla had handed out. In addition, as in the scheme to annex Egypt, Crassus and Caesar hoped to gain a powerful tool for bargaining with the returning conqueror.[66]

It is a mark of their success in obtaining friendly tribunes in the election of 64 that apparently all of the tribunes-elect for 63 were privy to the drafting of the bill in 64 (Cic. *Leg. Agr.* 2.11–13). Their main agent in promoting the bill was a man named P. Servilius Rullus. He promulgated the bill after entering office in December.

Rullus's bill is known from several speeches that Cicero delivered against it at the very beginning of his consulship in January of 63.[67] As has been pointed out, Rullus's proposal

however, indicates that the nobility did not support him (*Leg. Agr.* 2.3). Moreover, this whole section of Sallust is suspect because he has Catiline initiating a real conspiracy a year before he actually did: see Chapter Seven, n. 10 below. By Sallust's own admission, without the conspiracy, the nobility would not have supported Cicero's candidacy. On the other hand, if Cicero could write to Atticus, humorously instructing him to tell Pompey, *noster amicus*, that he would not be upset if Pompey himself could not come to the *Comitia* (*Att.* 1.1.3), the three must have been in fairly close communication about the matter. Indeed, Cicero even advertised the good will exhibited towards him by Pompey and his supporters (*Leg. Agr.* 2.49). For Antonius's support, see Appendix I-B, p. 31.

66. That the purpose of Rullus's bill was to secure a bargaining position with Pompey has been argued by several scholars: E. G. Hardy, "The Policy of the Rullan Proposal in 63 B.C.," *Journal of Philology* 32 (1912–13): 243–44, 257–60; Cary, *CAH* 9 (1932), pp. 485–86; Scullard, *From the Gracchi to Nero*, ed. 2, pp. 110–11.

67. Apparently Cicero delivered four speeches (*Att.* 2.1.3), of which two remain in part and one in full. The first was delivered on the first of January in the Senate (*Leg. Agr.* 1.26). The second (preserved in full) was spoken before the People a few days later (ibid., 2.1–5, 8–14). Presumably the others can be dated not long after the first two.

was not an isolated event, but a part of the whole great power-struggle that was taking place in Rome just before Pompey's return from the East.[68] It has usually been asserted that Crassus and Caesar were promoting this bill not simply as a popular measure, but against the interests of Pompey, which Cicero was protecting in his speeches.[69] Another theory is that Julius Caesar alone was promoting Rullus's bill on behalf of Pompey, and that Cicero was hurting Pompey's important interests by opposing it.[70] Skepticism over Crassus's involvement has arisen because Cicero was circumspect and often vague in pointing out the powers behind Rullus.[71] It has been said that Cicero "supplied a blank form which his senatorial and popular audiences could fill in according to their respective prejudices and fears." [72] On the other hand, it can be argued that in the unsettled conditions of the time, Cicero may well have found it prudent not to overantagonize Crassus and Caesar by naming names, especially in published speeches that could be used against him.[73]

68. A. Afzelius, "Das Ackerverteilungsgesetz des P. Servilius Rullus," *Classica et Mediaevalia* 3 (1940): 215. Gruen (*LGRR*, pp. 398–96) denies any serious political machinations behind Rullus's land bill, and he points out many beneficial, farsighted provisions that it contained. That it did contain provisions of this nature cannot be denied. But that fact is no reason to deny other, political motives behind the bill. The agrarian bill of Tiberius Gracchus provides an instructive parallel. It, too, attempted to meet legitimate needs, but it also was involved with very intense political rivalries, particularly between Scipio Aemilianus, who was about to return with his army from Numantia, and Ap. Claudius Pulcher, father-in-law of Tiberius Gracchus, and one of the three land commissioners appointed to administer the distribution of land: cf. Gruen, *Roman Politics and the Criminal Courts*, pp. 51–52; A. E. Astin, *Scipio Aemilianus* (Oxford, 1967), pp. 190–201.

69. Ciaceri, *Cicerone* 1, pp. 192–212; M. Gelzer, *Caesar, Politician and Statesman*, trans. P. Needham (Cambridge, Mass., 1968), pp. 42–44; *Cicero*, pp., 72–73; Scullard, *From the Gracchi to Nero*, ed. 2, p. 111; R. E. Smith, *Cicero the Statesman* (Cambridge, 1966), pp. 99–100.

70. Sumner, "Cicero, Pompeius, and Rullus," *TAPA* 97 (1966): 578–82. E. T. Sage argued that Caesar sponsored the bill in order to evoke Cicero's opposition and discredit the *optimates* with the people: "Cicero and the Agrarian Proposals of 63," *Classical Journal* 6 (1920/1921): 230–36.

71. Cf. *architecti huiusce legis* (1.11); *istis tuis harum omnium rerum machinatoribus* (1.16); *Rullus atque ii, quos multo magis quam Rullum timetis* (1.22); *hac lege agraria . . . condonari certis hominibus omnia* (2.15); *illi horum consiliorum auctores* (2.20); *ei, qui haec machinabantur* (2.23); *istis tuis auctoribus* (2.98).

72. Sumner, "Cicero, Pompeius, and Rullus," *TAPA* 97 (1966): 573.

73. W. C. McDermott has recently argued that the twelve consular speeches were published soon after delivery, rather than in the middle of

More importantly, if the previous analysis of Crassus's and Caesar's role in the proposal to annex Egypt in 65 is correct, there can be little doubt that Cicero was referring principally to them when he was addressing both the Senate and the People. In the first speech (to the Senate) and in the second speech (to the People) he asserted that the same men who wanted to obtain a command over Egypt in 65 were after the same command through Rullus's bill (*Leg. Agr.* 1.1, 2.44). Thus it seems that Cicero meant all sides to see Crassus and Caesar behind this bill, and there appears to be no reason to disagree with him, especially if it can be shown that it was detrimental to Pompey's interests.[74]

An investigation of the background of P. Servilius Rullus yields no conclusion as to whether the bill was favorable to Pompey or not. One possibility mentioned is that he is the Servilius spoken of by Plutarch (*Pomp.* 34.5) as the commander of Pompey's fleet in the Black Sea during 65.[75] In discussing Plutarch's Servilius, Münzer found only two possible candidates with whom to identify him, Servilius Isauricus and a Servilius Caepio mentioned by Florus (1.41.10) as a legate or prefect for Pompey along the Asian coast in 67.[76] Sumner does not think that either of these alternatives is especially good. He argues that the Caepio whom Florus mentions is ruled out if he is the same Caepio as Cato's younger half-brother Servilius Caepio, who perished on the way to take command of an Asian fleet in 67.[77] He also thinks that, since the younger Servilius Isauricus was praetor in 54, he must have been born in 94, retardation of his career being unlikely for a man of his background. Consequently, he would have been too young to hold an important command under Pompey in 65, when he would not yet have become a senator.[78] Therefore, Sumner

60, as had been assumed on the basis of *Att.* 2.1.3: "Cicero's Publication of his Consular Orations," *Philologus* 116 (1972): 277–84.

74. Cf. Afzelius, "Ackerverteilungsgesetz," *C&M* 3 (1940): 221, n. 5. Gelzer believes that Crassus's and Caesar's backing of Rullus is unequivocably proven by Suet. *Iul.* 9.2; Cic. *Leg. Agr.* 2.8.44; and Plut. *Crass.* 13.2: *RE* 13.1 (1926), 311.23–26, s.v. "Licinius" (68).

75. Sumner, "Cicero, Pompeius, and Rullus," *TAPA* 97 (1966): 580.

76. F. Münzer, *RE* 2A.2 (1923), 1761, s.v. "Servilius" (5).

77. Cf. Plutarch, *Cat. Min.* 11.1–3; 15.4; Münzer, *RE*, 2A.2 (1923), 1775.58–64, s.v. "Servilius" (40, 41, 42).

78. Cf. Broughton, *MRR* 2, pp. 184, 222.

thinks that Plutarch's Servilius may have been Servilius Rullus, one of Pompey's men who came back to Rome to become a tribune in order to help him, just as Metellus Nepos did a year later.

Although the argument that Plutarch's Servilius was not the Servilius Caepio of Florus seems fairly strong, his criticism of the identification of Plutarch's Servilius with the younger Servilius Isauricus is weak. For personal reasons, Pompey may well have given Isauricus an important command, despite his youth. Isauricus's father, P. Servilius Vatia Isauricus, had supported Pompey ever since he had promoted Pompey's claims for a triumph in 80 (Plut. *Pomp.* 14.5).[79] In return for this support, Pompey may have made Isauricus's son a *praefectus classis*.

Even if the younger Isauricus had been born in 94, his being a *praefectus classis* in 65, before he could have held the quaestorship, is in no way unprecedented or impossible. There are several examples of men who had been either *praefecti classis* or *praefecti equitum* at an early age and before they were quaestors.[80] Therefore, the argument that the younger Servilius Isauricus's age and lack of senatorial rank barred him from being Pompey's *praefectus classis* in 65 has no weight. In all probability, the Servilius who was Pompey's *praefectus classis* in 65 was the younger Servilius Isauricus, and the possibility that the P. Servilius Rullus who proposed the land bill of 63 can be identified as Pompey's *praefectus classis* in 65 is very slight indeed.

Nor can any conclusions about the bill's intention toward Pompey be drawn from a study of the other tribunes of 63. T. Labienus and T. Ampius Balbus are two who may appear to

---

79. He appears to have been in sympathy with the prosecution of Verres in 70 (Cic. *Verr.* 2.1.56; 3.210–11; 4.82), and he supported the *lex Manilia* in 66 (Cic. *Leg. Man.* 68).

80. As far back as 209, the elder C. Laelius had been a *praefectus classis* five years before he held the quaestorship (*MRR* 1, p. 288); in 82, Q. Lucretius Ofella was the *praefectus* in charge of the siege of Praeneste and had held no magistracy beforehand (ibid., 2, p. 72); Cicero's colleague in the consulship of 63, C. Antonius Hibrida, was a *praefectus equitum* no later than 84 (ibid., 2, p. 61), before he could have been a quaestor; Marcus Antonius was a *praefectus equitum* from 57 to 55 (ibid., 2, p. 205, 213, 220) well before his quaestorship of 52; D. Junius Brutus Albinus was a *praefectus classis* before he was eligible to be a quaestor: (F. Münzer, *RE* sup. band 5 [1931], 370.10–19, s.v. "Junius" [55a]).

have been supporters of Pompey: they brought in a law that permitted him to wear the costume of a *triumphator* at the public games (Vell. Pat. 2.40.4; cf. Dio 37.21.3–4). They did not veto Rullus's bill, however, and they may have been primarily attached to Caesar at this time. Labienus, despite Syme's demonstration of his early connections with Pompey, already may have begun the close relationship with Caesar that lasted through the Gallic wars and did not end until Caesar and Pompey became outright enemies.[81] As for Balbus, Syme admits that the only evidence that he was a "fanatical Pompeian" pertains to a time considerably later than 63.[82] Yet, even if it is granted that Labienus and Balbus were mainly associated with Pompey in 63, they may have refrained from vetoing Rullus's bill because they knew that someone else would veto it, and they did not wish to be connected with vetoing a bill whose proponents could have presented it as being favorable to Pompey, the popular hero.[83] Finally, it cannot be shown that the one tribune who did threaten to use his veto, L. Caecilius Rufus (Cic. *Sull.* 65), was acting with those specifically opposed to Pompey, rather than with those simply opposed to land distributions in general, or even with Pompey.[84] Therefore, nothing conclusive about Rullus's pro-

81. R. Syme, "The Allegiance of Labienus," *Journal of Roman Studies* 28 (1938): 113–21. After all, he and Caesar did cooperate during 63 in the prosecution of Rabirius (Suet. *Iul.* 12; Dio 37.27.1–2; Cic. *Rab. Perd.*, passim) and on the proposal to restore the election of priests to the people (Dio 37.37.1). For Labienus's defection from Caesar later, see W. B. Tyrrell, "Labienus' Departure from Caesar in January 49 B.C.," *Historia* 21 (1972): 424–40.

Others, on the testimony of Dio, also believe that Labienus and his colleague Balbus were induced by Caesar to procure for Pompey the honor of wearing the robes of a *triumphator* at the public games (37.21.4, cf. Vell. Pat. 2.40.4): e.g., Holmes, *RR* 1, pp. 284–85; Gelzer, *Cicero*, pp. 76–79 and *Caesar*, pp. 45–46. It is entirely possible in view of Labienus's cooperation with Caesar on other matters: cf. Gruen, *LGRR*, p. 80. There is no reason, however, to think that Labienus and Balbus could not have initiated this action on their own. They did not have to be told by anyone that it would be to their advantage to do Pompey a favor in anticipation of his victorious return. Caesar would have found it expedient to cooperate and express his approval of the measure, without having initiated it in any way.

82. Syme, "The Allegiance of Labienus," *JRS* 28 (1938): 118.

83. See the discussion of the bill's provisions and ambiguities, pp. 57–61.

84. He may have cooperated with Crassus at the beginning of the year. Cf. below, pp. 162–63. If so, he was very flexible in his choice of sides on

posal can be deduced from a study of Rullus and the other tribunes of 63.

It is now necessary to examine closely the most important provisions of Rullus's proposal to determine if they were unfavorable to Pompey or could have been used against him.

The following provisions, taken from Cicero's speeches *de Lege Agraria,* are the most important:

1. Ten men, decemviri, were to be elected by an assembly of seventeen tribes and were to act as a commission for implementing the law (2.16, 21).

2. As in the elections for the Pontifex Maximus, the seventeen electoral tribes were to be chosen by lot from the whole thirty-five tribes (2.18, 21).

3. The candidates for the Decemvirate had to present themselves in person for the election (2.24).

4. Power was to be conferred upon the decemviri by a lex curiata to be proposed by the praetor who had been elected at the head of the poll or, barring him, the one elected at the bottom of the poll (2.26–28).

5. No tribune could veto the lex curiata (2.30).

6. The lex curiata was to grant the decemviri praetorian power for five years (2.32).

7. In Italy, the ager Campanus and the campus Stellatis were expressly marked for distribution (1.20).

8. Money was to be obtained for the purchase of land from the sale of state property that had been designated in an unused senatus consultum of 81 (M. Tullio Cn. Cornelio consulibus) or later (2.35).

9. Land outside Italy that had become the property of the Roman People after 88 (L. Sulla Q. Pompeio consulibus) could be disposed as the commissioners wished (2.38).

10. On all the public lands outside Italy, except on the ager recentoricus in Sicily, the commissioners could impose a tax (1.10; 2.56, 57).

11. Gold and silver from booty and spoils and from crown gold that had not been paid into the public treasury nor spent on a memorial were to be handed over to the commissioners, Pompey the only one being excepted from this provision (1.12–13; 2.59–60).

---

any given issue. After all, he was a half brother of P. Sulla, who may have been cultivating favor on all sides. Cf. Chapter One, Appendix B, under the year 66.

12. After 63 (post nos consules), *the decemviri were to have the use of any money received from new* vectigalia (1.13; 2.62).

The first and second provisions, that the commissioners be elected by an assembly of seventeen tribes chosen by lot from all thirty-five, could have been detrimental to Pompey. It was important that these commissioners be friendly and accountable to him. He had a large number of veterans whom he had to supply with land in order to ensure their continued allegiance. If the land commissioners were under the control of other men, these men could hold the upper hand over Pompey: they could offer to use the land commission to fill his needs if he would cooperate with them, or they could threaten to withhold land from his veterans if he refused to do so. Cicero foresaw the danger. He plainly states that because of these provisions, the elections could easily have been manipulated to secure commissioners desired by Rullus and his backers (2.21–23).

Afzelius has supported Cicero's claim. He argues that Rullus and his backers could have controlled the election of the decemvirs by manipulating the lots for choosing the seventeen electoral tribes in such a way that the most land-hungry tribes, such as the four urban tribes and those in the areas that rallied behind Catiline, would have been a majority.[85] These tribes would have been most friendly to the authors of the land bill and would have voted for candidates favored by them and not necessarily loyal to Pompey. But, whether or not the lot for choosing the seventeen tribes could have been manipulated by Crassus and Caesar, the use of seventeen instead of thirty-five tribes in the election meant that Crassus's ample resources could have been very effectively employed to bribe the necessary majority of only nine tribes to vote for candidates favorable to himself and Caesar.[86] In either case, Pompey would have been hindered from the exercise of any direct control over a commission vitally important to his interests.

The third provision further ensured Pompey's lack of control over the commission since it successfully barred him from

85. Afzelius, "Ackerverteilungsgesetz," *C&M* 3 (1940): 224–26.
86. Gelzer, *Caesar* (trans. Needham), p. 44.

election to it by requiring that all candidates for *decemvir* be present at Rome. Sumner argues that this provision was actually favorable to Pompey because it also barred from the election several optimate generals who were enemies of Pompey and were waiting outside Rome for permission to celebrate triumphs. He says that they would not have wanted to give up their triumphs in order to present themselves for the elections.[87] Popular opposition, however, had denied triumphs to these optimate generals for a long time—since 66, in the cases of Lucullus and Marcius Rex.[88] It is difficult to imagine that popular opposition would have weakened enough to elect these generals to positions on the land commission even if they had sought them. Therefore, the only one who was in fact adversely affected by this provision was Pompey, who was away in Asia.

Afzelius also argues that the fourth provision, which stipulates that the first or the last praetor should preside over the passing of the *lex curiata*, was designed to select a man whose loyalty was to Caesar, not Pompey.[89] He finds that only two of the praetors in 63, P. Cornelius Lentulus Sura and C. Cosconius, had definite links with Caesar or appear to have supported Rullus's bill. Of the other six, five definitely reveal no connections with Crassus and Caesar, and the identity of the sixth is uncertain.[90] Lentulus, however, was married to Caesar's cousin Julia.[91] Furthermore, he was probably no friend of Pompey, since he had been expelled from the Senate by the Pompeian censors of 70 (Plut. *Cic.* 17.1; Dio 37.30.4). Cosconius is also likely to have been one of Caesar's friends.

87. Sumner, "Cicero, Pompeius, and Rullus," *TAPA* 97 (1966): 581. The generals were Metellus Creticus, L. Lucullus, and Marcius Rex (Sall. *Cat.* 30.3; Plut. *Luc.* 37.1–2; Cic. *Mur.* 69).

88. Broughton, *MRR* 2, pp. 154, 159, 163, 169. Marcius Rex died without ever obtaining his triumph; Lucullus finally obtained his in 63; and Metellus celebrated his late in May of 62: ibid, pp. 169, 176; A. Degrassi, *Inscriptiones Italiae* 13.1 (Rome, 1949), pp. 565–66.

89. Afzelius, "Ackerverteilungsgesetz," *C&M* 3 (1940): 226–27.

90. If the sixth praetor should have been L. Roscius Otho (cf. Broughton, *MRR* 2, p. 167), he might have cooperated with Crassus in supporting Rullus. For possible links with Crassus, see pp. 80–81, 114. For policy reasons, that would not have prevented Cicero from opposing the attack of 63 on Roscius's law of 67 (Cic. *Att.* 2.1.3; Plut. *Cic.* 13.2–3; Plin. *HN* 7.117).

91. Daughter of L. Julius Caesar, consul in 90: see F. Münzer, *RE* 10.1 (1918), 892, s.v. "Iulius" (543).

He employed Caesar's close associate Vatinius as a legate in 62 (Cic. *Vat.* 12, cf. *Fam.* 1.9.19) and was one of the twenty commissioners for carrying out Caesar's land law in 59 (Cic. *Att.* 2.19.4).

Afzelius thinks that Lentulus, a noble, was the praetor who had been elected at the head of the poll for 63, and that Cosconius, a lesser light, had been elected last.[92] If so, by providing that men whose main loyalty may have been to Caesar were to preside over the passage of the *lex curiata*, Rullus's bill could have thwarted any opposition to the land commission from either the *optimates* or Pompey. Likewise, provision five prevented Pompey from blocking confirmation of the land commissioners just as much as it prevented his optimate opponents from doing so.

Consequently, although the proponents of Rullus's bill could have argued that the first through the fifth provisions were designed to favor Pompey by blocking opposition from his enemies, those provisions appear actually to have been dangerous to Pompey because they effectively prevented him from having any say in the selection of the land commissioners and placed control of the commission in the hands of men whose principal loyalty would not have been to him. Pompey would hardly have felt comfortable under those circumstances.

The sixth through the twelfth provisions were even more dangerous to Pompey. Although they would not have allowed the *decemviri* to go to the ludicrous extreme of auctioning off Pompey's camp from beneath his feet as Cicero claimed they would (1.6; 2.99), Hardy has judiciously pointed out that they still would have posed considerable dangers for Pompey.[93]

In particular, the ninth provision was aimed at gaining control of Egypt, which, as seen before, would have been a powerful weapon in bargaining with Pompey.[94] Even the eleventh, although superficially favorable to Pompey, was, as Cicero does not fail to point out (2.60–62), more of an insult than anything else. It would also have aroused *invidia* against him among others who would have resented his seemingly preferential treatment. Moreover, the financial resources left to Pom-

92. Afzelius, "Ackerverteilungsgesetz," *C&M* 3 (1940): 227.
93. Hardy, "The Policy of the Rullan Proposal," *Journal of Philology* 32 (1912–1913): 234–44.
94. Ibid., p. 235.

pey, by excusing him from turning over any crown gold not given to the treasury or used for a memorial, were miniscule in comparison with those given to the commission by the other provisions. They never would have sufficed for giving his soldiers what they would have expected and claimed from him. Indeed, the twelfth would have denied Pompey even those monies that ought to have been his, as conqueror of the new lands upon which the *vectigalia* were to be levied (1.13, 2.62).[95]

Rullus's bill was as unfavorable to Pompey as it was to his optimate enemies. To be sure, it could have been favorable to him if it were in the hands of men whom he could trust. But, its very ambiguity indicates that it was not, and that the powers behind Rullus were working for themselves, not for Pompey. That these powers were Crassus and Caesar, as Cicero seems to indicate, is hard to deny. As in the case of their Egyptian scheme in 65, they probably were hoping to create a tool with which they could prevent Pompey from any possible reconciliation with the optimate-dominated Senate, as they finally did through the stupidity of optimate leaders in 60. They certainly did not want to destroy Pompey, for they needed him, his *dignitas,* and his numerous supporters too much. Rullus's bill cut two ways: it could have been used against Pompey if he did not cooperate with its authors; but it could have been very helpful to him if he did cooperate, since all the arrangements for the vital land allotments and donatives for his loyal veterans would have been at his disposal as soon as he arrived home. Crassus and Caesar probably calculated that Pompey would have preferred to join with them rather than face the opposition of both themselves and the Senate.

Again, the political needs of Pompey and Cicero met. Certainly, Pompey, the conqueror of the East, would have preferred not to have to rely on the good will of someone else in order to satisfy the desires of his own troops. In opposing

95. Ibid., pp. 243–44. Sumner argues that because the provision of using the new *vectigalia* from Pompey's recently conquered lands to buy land for allotments reappears in the Flavian land bill of 60, which was sponsored by Pompey, it is not unfavorable to him in Rullus's bill: "Cicero, Pompeius, and Rullus," *TAPA* 97 (1966): 580. This argument breaks down, however, because Pompey had control over the operation of Flavius's bill, which he would not have had over Rullus's.

Rullus's bill, Cicero helped Pompey to keep free of any entanglements that would have diminished his preeminence and independence. Therefore, Cicero could speak with confidence when he said that Pompey rejected Rullus's proposal (2.61–62), and he emphasized the aspects of the bill that were dangerous to Pompey in order to rally Pompey's supporters amongst the People and the *Equites* against it.

Crassus may have sought advantage through Caesar from three popular tribunician proposals successfully advanced by T. Labienus. It is clear, at least, that Caesar worked vigorously for them,[96] and they were measures from which Crassus could hope to profit. Labienus's first bill restored the provisions of the *lex Domitia* of 104, which entrusted the election of the priesthoods to the People (Dio 37.37.1–2).[97] The second measure, a law that set up the prosecution of Rabirius, will be discussed later. The third law was successfully cosponsored with T. Ampius Balbus. It permitted Pompey to wear the garb of a *triumphator* at the public games (Vell. Pat. 2.40.4; Dio 37.21.3–4). Dio specifically says that Caesar worked hard for it, and it should be viewed as an attempt to take advantage of Pompey's popularity after the death of Mithridates ensured that Pompey's return would not be far away.

Several other tribunes introduced bills that also fitted in with Crassus's designs, and all apparently enjoyed the support of Cicero's consular colleague, Antonius (Dio 37.25.3–4). Nevertheless, they went down to defeat before Cicero and the optimate forces in the Senate (Cic. *Leg. Agr.* 2.10, *Sull.* 62, *Att.* 2.1.3; Dio 37.25.4; Quint. *Inst.* 11.1.85). The first was introduced at the beginning of business in the Senate on the first of January, 63. It proposed that the rights of being a senator and of holding office be restored to P. Autronius Paetus and P. Cornelius Sulla, who had been convicted of electoral bribery in the consular elections for 65. If Crassus were involved in this effort, he may have hoped to gain another candidate to back in the consular elections for 62.

The tribune who proposed the bill was L. Caecilius Rufus,

96. See n. 81 above.
97. Although the office of *Pontifex Maximus* was already elective, this law probably helped Caesar gain election to that office in this same year: Gelzer, *Caesar* (trans. Needham), p. 46.

P. Sulla's half brother. Autronius, however, was held in great
suspicion by many because of his close relations with those
who advocated radical actions. Moreover, Sulla, who had connections with all camps, upon being apprised of the great
hostility towards the measure, apparently informed the praetor
Q. Caecilius Metellus Celer, that he did not want the question
put to a vote (Cic. *Sull.* 62–66). Later, of course, despite any
possible support from Crassus on this earlier proposal, Rufus,
perhaps at the urging of Sulla and others friendly to Pompey,
cooperated with Cicero and the *boni* in threatening to veto
Rullus's land bill and thereby dashed Crassus's hopes as regards that measure.[98]

Another tribune proposed to restore the right of holding
office to the sons of the proscribed, while a fourth proposed a
cancellation of debts. It is possible that Crassus was involved
with both. That he had played a prominent and selfish role
in the Sullan proscriptions would have been no bar to his
seeking the support of the victims' sons now. They probably
were content not to peer too intensely behind those more
congenial figures like Caesar, who were working with him. Nor
should one feel disbelief that Crassus, one of the biggest
creditors at Rome, would have supported a measure to cancel
debts. Such a measure would have had little chance for success, but would have earned popularity for its backers.

The opposition to these last two proposals was intense for
varying reasons. Some feared the political support that their
backers would gain, some old *Sullani* were no doubt personally
fearful of and hateful toward the sons of the proscribed; others
more generally would brook no challenge to Sulla's enactments;
and many, including wealthy equestrians, held no stomach
for a cancellation of debts. It was no trouble for Cicero, who
was suspicious of Crassus and Caesar and any sudden change
that might provoke violent reaction, to bring about the defeat
of these two items, as he had others.

The opposition's victory, however, was not necessarily a
total defeat for Crassus, Caesar, and their friends. If Rullus's
proposal had passed, so much the better. The same is true of
any of the other unsuccessful tribunician proposals, if, in fact,

98. Cf. above, pp. 156–57.

they were involved. Yet, even in defeat they had unequivocally identified themselves with all of those who were dissatisfied with the ones presently in control of the Senate and Rome. Many of them also had long looked to Pompey as their champion, but he was far away. He could not keep a continuously tight rein on affairs, and Cicero, who had steadfastly supported his cause, in the very act of defending Pompey's position against the schemes of Crassus and Caesar may have helped to turn some people towards them by opposing agrarian reform.

Another part of Crassus's political program for 63 entailed use of the courts. Crassus himself, as so often, stayed in the background. Caesar was prominent as a prosecutor, a role which Crassus always avoided.[99] In keeping with their policy of currying the favor of the Transpadanes, Caesar accused Gaius Calpurnius Piso, the optimate consul of 67, of having unjustly executed a Transpadane. Obviously, a successful prosecution would have helped Crassus and Caesar and their friends and hurt their enemies, but the oratory of Cicero procured Piso's acquittal (Cic. *Flac.* 98; Sall. *Cat.* 49.2). Again, however, defeat in this case did not necessarily mean a loss. Cicero's victory was somewhat hollow, because in the eyes of many, less sophisticated people he may have appeared to be selling out Pompey, who had been bitterly opposed by Piso and who had always favored the Transpadanes.[100] Thus, Crassus and Caesar would have helped to weaken the credibility of one of Pompey's chief supporters, Cicero, and perhaps even of Pompey himself.

A more famous contest between Caesar and Cicero was the prosecution of the elderly senator Gaius Rabirius on a charge of high treason, *perduellio*. The charge stemmed from actions thirty-seven years before, when Rabirius had taken part in the murder of the tribune Saturninus. Although the actual prose-

99. Garzetti makes a blanket statement that Crassus backed Caesar in all of his actions in 63: "Crasso," *Athenaeum* 20 (1942): 34. This position may be extreme, but the prosecutions in which Caesar's involvement is known fit in with the course that he and Crassus had been following together for some time.

100. That Cicero's actions would not have offended Pompey himself has been ably argued by D. Stockton: *Cicero, A Political Biography* (London, 1971), p. 108.

cutor was the tribune T. Labienus, whose uncle had been killed in the fracas surrounding the death of Saturninus (Cic. *Rab. Perd.* 18), and who himself had sponsored the bill setting up the special duumviral court to try the case, Caesar was the instigator of the action (Quintil. *Inst.* 5.13.20; Dio 37.26.1–28.4, 37.2; Suet. *Iul.* 12). In fact, Caesar manipulated things so that, contrary to precedent, the *praetor urbanus* appointed him and his cousin Lucius Caesar *duumviri* for trying the case (Dio 37.27.2).

Since Rabirius had been acting under the sanction of a *Senatus Consultum Ultimum*, the trial was actually an attack on the *S.C.U.* and the authority of the Senate, as Cicero claimed (*Rab. Perd.* 2; cf. Dio 37.26.1). Predictably, Caesar and his cousin declared Rabirius guilty. As consul, Cicero led the Senate to declare that the People were not bound by the antiquated penalty of crucifixion, and exile seems to have been substituted (Cic. *Rab. Perd.* 11–13, 32). Rabirius appealed his sentence to the *Comitia Centuriata,* while Cicero and the old optimate standby, Hortensius, defended him.[101] This proceeding was never completed, however, because the praetor Q. Metellus Celer lowered the red flag on the Janiculum, an act that, since ancient times, was a signal for the *Comitia Centuriata* to adjourn (Dio 37.26. 1–28.4).[102]

101. This interpretation is the usual one. It is based on Cicero, *Rab. Perd.* 18, where the word *antea* is taken as a reference to a speech by Hortensius earlier during this appeal trial. It is possible, however, that Hortensius defended Rabirius during the duumviral proceedings and that *antea* is a reference to that time.

102. According to Dio (37.27.3), it appeared that the appeal was not going to be favorable to Rabirius, but Suetonius (*Iul.* 12) claims that the obvious bias of Caesar in the earlier trial earned Rabirius great favor with the People. Contrary to Dio's assertion that no further action was taken, Gelzer has also argued that a final trial was held before the *Concilium Plebis: Cicero*, pp. 77–79. The language of the key passage invoked does not necessitate this view, however (Cic. *Rab. Perd.* 8). Rather, Labienus may have instituted parallel trials on subsidiary issues to damage Rabirius's chances of acquittal on appeal. Cicero's words *in eadem multae inrogatione* (ibid., 8) could be a reference to one of these actions and not the present trial. Holmes argued that the whole duumviral trial was quashed, that Labienus then turned a separate prosecution on another charge into a regular tribunician trial for *perduellio*, and that then Cicero gave his speech for Rabirius at a subsequent appeal from that trial: *RR* 1, pp. 452–55. This interpretation is also possible, but the passages upon which it is based (*Rab. Perd.* 10, 17) could simply refer to a change of sentence from crucifixion to exile. This reduced sentence then would have been

Contrary to the previous analysis, some have linked the prosecution of Rabirius with Pompey.[103] They argue that Pompey wished to cast doubt on the legality of the *Senatus Consultum Ultimum* through Labienus's prosecution of Rabirius, but did not intend to hurt Rabirius; therefore, Celer colluded with Caesar to abort the proceedings once the legal point had been made. To be sure, Labienus had close Pompeian connections and Metellus Celer was Pompey's brother-in-law. As argued above, however, Labienus may have already formed a close personal connection with Caesar and been acting primarily as a friend of Caesar. Nor can Labienus be denied any independence. Family enmities often smoldered for a long time at Rome, so that the personal factor of his uncle's murder cannot be completely ignored as a reason for Labienus's role in Rabirius's prosecution.

As for Metellus, there is no compelling reason to think that he was in collusion with Caesar.[104] He was also a strong supporter of senatorial authority, and would not have wanted the force of the *Senatus Consultum Ultimum* weakened.[105] Nor as a supporter of Pompey would he have wished to see Caesar's popularity increase at this point. If he was in collusion with anyone, he, as a supporter of the Senate and a friend of Pompey, cooperated with Cicero.[106]

Rabirius was saved, and the *S.C.U.* was upheld. A loss for Crassus, Caesar, and their friends? No. Once more, they had successfully advertised their championship of those who were

---

appealed in turn; cf. Ciaceri, *Cicerone* 1, pp. 230–32. For an additional discussion of these matters see now W. B. Tyrrell, "The Trial of C. Rabirius in 63 B.C.," *Latomus* 32 (1973): 288–92.

103. E.g., M. Grant, *Julius Caesar* (London, 1969), 52, probably following a suggestion by Syme, *Sallust*, pp. 98–99.

104. An idea suggested by many: e.g., Drumann, *Geschichte* 2, pp. 21–22, Cary, *CAH* 9 (1932), 490; Syme, *Sallust*, pp. 98–99.

105. For example, he vigorously opposed Catiline in 63 (Cic. *Cat.* 1.19, 2.5–6). Cary claims that Metellus was the praetor urbanus who had chosen the lots creating the duumvirs: *CAH* 9 (1932), 490. This view is also held by Ciaceri, *Cicerone* 1, p. 230. Actually, the praetor urbanus for 63 was L. Valerius Flaccus (Cic. *Flac.* 101): cf. F. Münzer, *RE* 8A.1 (1955), 33, s.v. "Valerius" (179).

106. Cf. now Tyrrell, "The Trial of C. Rabirius," *Latomus* 32 (1973): 298–300.

dissatisfied with the *status quo* and favored *popularis* programs, against whose proponents the *S.C.U.* had always been used.

From 65 to 63, Crassus, with the assistance of Caesar, had pursued a vigorous program of building support in his rivalry with the absent Pompey. There were many different facets to this program. His move as censor to enfranchise the Transpadanes was designed to earn the favor of a populous area in which Pompey had established many useful connections. The scheme to annex Egypt was designed to gain bargaining strength with Pompey and would have earned much popularity with Roman voters, who coveted the wealth of Egypt for their own.

Crassus also attempted to win over figures like Manilius, Cornelius, and Catiline, who had connections with Pompey. He seems to have aided Manilius and Cornelius during their prosecutions, which were occasioned by their pro-Pompeian actions as tribunes, and he may have helped Catiline obtain acquittal on a charge of extortion. He certainly backed Catiline for the consulship in 64.

On the legislative front, Crassus probably supported a number of bills to earn popularity and block Pompey. Certainly, he was involved in promoting the land bill of Rullus, which would have earned favor with the urban poor and denied Pompey direct control of valuable lands for distribution to his veterans. Other popular proposals that he may have backed were the restoration of political rights to the sons of those proscribed by Sulla and the cancellation of debts. Finally, in the courts, Crassus backed Caesar's attacks on the *optimates* through the prosecutions of Gaius Calpurnius Piso for unjustly executing a Transpadane and of Gaius Rabirius, who had taken part in the murder of Saturninus in 100 upon passage of the *S.C.U.*, a powerful weapon used by the *optimates* against *popularis* leaders since the time of the Gracchi.

In most of these matters, the *optimates* and Cicero, who tried to protect both Pompey and the traditionally strong powers of the Senate, succeeded in blocking Crassus from his immediate goals. Nevertheless, Crassus still gained much. The defeat of his attempts to enfranchise the Transpadanes and to annex Egypt and each legislative or judicial defeat thereafter earned popular support for the program that he pursued through Caesar and others. Now it could all be brought to bear on Crassus's central purpose, the election of people who would control important offices for him.

VII

Electoral Politics and Catiline

One of the candidates upon whom Crassus placed his hopes in 63 was his friend Caesar. As was expected, Caesar ran for the praetorship and was successful (Suet. *Iul.* 14). Before this office, however, an unexpected boon came in the form of his election to Rome's highest religious post, that of *Pontifex Maximus* (Vell. Pat. 2.43.3; Sall. *Cat.* 49.2; Plut. *Caes.* 7.1–4; Suet. *Iul.* 13).[1] Though a religious office, it was fraught with political importance. As chief of the college of pontiffs, Caesar was the principal advisor to magistrates on religious matters and had considerable say in determining the days for public festivals and the days when public business could or could not be conducted. His position as *Pontifex Maximus* may help to explain why, as consul later on, Caesar did not arouse great public indignation when he ignored the attempts of his colleague, Bibulus, to block his actions by announcing that he was observing the heavens (Dio 38.6.1–6).

Previously, Quintus Caecilius Metellus Pius, the leader of the staunchest optimate *factio*, had been the chief pontiff. Now, upon his death, the two senior consulars on the board of pontiffs were P. Servilius Vatia Isauricus and Q. Lutatius Catulus. Isauricus was a man who had shown favor to Pompey over the years, and it might be expected that Pompey's sup-

1. Dio (37.37.1–3) erroneously places this election after 5 December 63. Nor is there any basis for Last's statement that Caesar's eagerness to be elected *Pontifex Maximus* may be connected with a desire to free his name from any implication of involvement in Catiline's conspiracy: H. Last, Review of Bloch and Carcopino, *Journal of Roman Studies* 34 (1944): 118. Carcopino also seems wrong in claiming that election to the office of *Pontifex Maximus* was established by Labienus's bill on the election of priestly colleges: G. Bloch and J. Carcopino, *Histoire romaine* 2 (Paris, 1929), pp. 626–27; cf. also M. Cary, *CAH* 9 (1932), p. 487. Election of the *Pontifex Maximus* had probably remained in effect after Sulla: L. R. Taylor, "The Election of the Pontifex Maximus in the Late Republic," *Classical Philology* 37 (1942): 421–24.

porters were hoping for his success. Catulus was a senior representative of the leading *optimates,* and with their strong backing he was favored to win. Though also a member of the college, as a mere candidate for the praetorship Caesar was far below the other candidates in rank and prestige. He made up for these deficiencies, however, by his already demonstrated popularity with the masses, by his patrician family (whose founder, Iulus, had been *Pontifex Maximus* at Alba Longa according to a convenient legend), and by massive bribery paid for with loans added to an already crushing burden of debt.[2] Although it is wrong to see the open hands of Crassus supporting every Roman politician who engaged in bribery, in this case, Caesar probably had Crassus's unlimited backing. When the distressed Catulus offered Caesar a huge gift to pay off his debts if he would abandon his candidacy, Caesar only pushed on more vigorously (Plut. *Caes.* 7.1–2). When the vote was finally tallied, Caesar won easily.

The major political contest for the immediate future was of course the consular election. Here Crassus was only partially successful. The candidates were Servius Sulpicius Rufus, a respected jurist, Lucius Licinius Murena, a former lieutenant of Lucullus in Asia, Decimus Junius Silanus, a pontiff and husband of Servilia, stepsister of Cato the Younger, and Lucius Sergius Catilina, Catiline.

Sulpicius was a patrician, so that his immediate rival was Catiline, the other candidate for the one permissible patrician consulship. Syme has suggested that Caesar was backing him over Catiline, but that does not seem likely.[3] In a campaign marked by extravagant bribery, Sulpicius had the disadvantage of being an honest man. He spent so much time trying to secure passage of a tougher law against electoral bribery and collecting evidence against the other candidates that he disastrously neglected his own campaigning (Cic. *Mur.* 43–49).

Sulpicius was supported by Cicero (ibid., 7–8), as well as by the younger Cato, who was attempting to carve out a role for himself as an optimate leader now that Metellus Pius had

2. L. R. Taylor, *Party Politics in the Age of Caesar* (Berkeley and Los Angeles, 1949), p. 93.
3. R. Syme, *Sallust* (Berkeley and Los Angeles, 1964), p. 70, n. 46.

died and old age was taking its toll on those who had been the leading element of the *optimates* for so long. Cato was running for the tribunate in order to counter the candidacy of Pompey's man, Q. Caecilius Metellus Nepos, and, in accordance with his announced intention of combatting bribery, cooperated with Sulpicius in the prosecution of L. Licinius Murena, one of the successful candidates (Plut. *Cat. Min.* 20–21; Cic. *Mur.* 3–8).

Murena had been backed by the surviving elder optimate leaders. His father had served under Sulla, and he himself had served with distinction under Sulla's old lieutenant, L. Lucullus (Cic. *Mur.* 20). Many of Lucullus's veterans pointedly strengthened his consular campaign (ibid., 37–38). During his subsequent prosecution, Hortensius was one of his defenders.[4] Bribery, apparently, was the only thing that Cato had against Murena. Lucullus, Murena's benefactor, was married to Cato's niece, another Servilia, and Cato had helped him to obtain his long-delayed triumph in the face of Pompeian opposition (Plut. *Cat. Min.* 29.3–4).[5] After Murena's trial, Cato continued to help Lucullus against Pompey, and Murena physically protected Cato in a fracas with Metellus Nepos (ibid., 26.1–31.1).

Against the optimate candidates, Sulpicius and Murena, Crassus and Caesar backed Silanus and Catiline, who had both failed previously (Cic. *Att.* 1.1.2; Q. Cic. *Com. Pet.* 8–9). On the surface, Junius Silanus's relationship to Cato's family might cause one to link him with only the *optimates.* Indeed, it did save him from prosecution for bribery by Cato (Plut. *Cat. Min.* 21.2). Several other facts are more important, however. His wife was the mother of M. Brutus, and her interest in Caesar was the subject of considerable gossip (Plut. *Brut.* 5.1–3, *Cat. Min.* 24.1–3). Caesar is even said to have bought Servilia a pearl costing one and one-half million *denarii* (Suet. *Iul.* 50.2). Servilia was a powerful and strong-willed person with political designs of her own. If she could help Junius to the consulship by snaring Caesar, Junius might not have

---

4. Crassus's role in the defense will be discussed later, pp. 187–88, below. Contrary to Pareti's thesis, it is no indication that Crassus supported Murena during the election. L. Pareti, *La Congiura di Catilina* (Catania, 1934), p. 63.

5. For Servilia's relationship to Cato, see J. Van Ooteghem, *Lucius Licinius Lucullus* (Namur, 1959), p. 168, n. 4.

minded at all, given the mores of the late Republic.[6] Another fact, not of great import by itself, but perhaps significant in combination with others, is that Junius Silanus and Caesar had known each other for a long time as colleagues in the college of pontiffs.[7] Finally, at the end of the year, it was Silanus who, upon hearing Caesar propose imprisonment instead of death for the Catilinarian conspirators, hastily and rather ineptly backed off from his original proposal that they be executed (Cic. *Cat.* 4.7, *Att.* 12.21.1; Sall. *Cat.* 50.4, 51.16; Plut. *Cat. Min.* 22.3).[8]

As for Crassus's second candidate in 63, most authorities agree that he and Caesar supported Catiline. Still, the question is vexed.[9] Except for Sallust, who erroneously has Catiline seriously plotting armed rebellion by June of 64, there is a serious gap in the evidence for the time between the elections of 64 and those of 63.[10] Two facts are known. In the fall of 64, Caesar showed partiality toward Catiline durng the prosecution of those who had taken part in the Sullan proscriptions (Suect. *Iul.* 11; Dio 37.10.2; Ascon. *Tog. Cand.* 90–91 C/70 St).[11] Cicero's colleague, Antonius, who also had enjoyed the support

6. For the powerful influence exercised by Servilia in Roman politics, see R. Syme, *The Roman Revolution* (Oxford, 1939), pp. 23–24. For Silanus and Caesar, see Pareti, *La Congiura di Catilina*, p. 63.

7. Cf. T. R. S. Broughton, *The Magistrates of the Roman Republic* 2 (New York, 1952), p. 114.

8. Appian (*BC* 2.5.19) has caused a great deal of trouble because he followed the order of names as given by Sallust (*Cat.* 50.4) and took the sense to be that this order was also the order of debate: see T. Rice Holmes, *Roman Republic* 1 (Oxford, 1923), pp. 468–69.

9. The following see Crassus and Caesar behind Catiline: E. G. Hardy, "The Catilinarian Conspiracy in its Context, A Restudy of the Evidence," *Journal of Roman Studies* 7 (1917): 171–72; Holmes, RR 1, p. 256 (emphasis on Caesar); M. Gelzer, *Caesar, Politician and Statesman*, trans. P. Needham (Cambridge, Mass., 1968), p. 47; Carcopino, *Histoire romaine* 2, p. 633; A. Garzetti, "M. Licinio Crasso," *Athenaeum* 20 (1942): 34–35. Th. Mommsen, following the narrative of Sallust, mentions no backers for 63: *History of Rome* 4, trans. W. P. Dickson (New York, 1895), pp. 468–75. Cary says flatly that Crassus did not support Catiline's election in 63: *CAH* 9 (1932), p. 491. Similarly, Pareti claims that Catiline put himself at the head of a party completely divorced from Crassus: *La Congiura di Catilina*, p. 55. It should be clear from what follows, however, that Crassus still supported Catiline's candidacy in 63, but had no intention of joining any conspiracy after Catiline failed in this last electoral bid.

10. For Sallust's inaccuracy, see Hardy, "Catilinarian Conspiracy," *JRS* 7 (1917): 172–76, and Syme, *Sallust*, pp. 75–77.

11. Cf. Chapter Six, p. 144, n. 55.

of Crassus in 64, was actively promoting Catiline's cause in 63 (Cic. *Mur.* 49). These two facts point to Crassus's continued support of Catiline's election to the consulship in 63. Also, the persistence of rumors of Crassus's involvement in Catiline's attempted coup is best attributed to the plausibility lent them by his support of Catiline's candidacy before he became violently revolutionary.

Catiline's campaign was aimed at those very groups whose favor Crassus sought to gain through the legislative and judicial actions that he supported. A crowd of impoverished Sullan veterans and dispossessed farmers from Etruria was rounded up by Manlius and conspicuously promoted Catiline's candidacy (Cic. *Mur.* 49; Plut. *Cic.* 14). According to Cicero, at a meeting of his followers, Catiline portrayed himself as the *dux et signifer calamitosorum* and called for those who were unfortunate and in debt to follow him (*Mur.* 50). Although the accuracy of Cicero's report concerning Catiline's statements in a private meeting may be suspect, there should be no doubt about his report of Catiline's statement at a meeting of the Senate. There were many men in his audience who had been there. It clearly reflects Catiline's role as the candidate of the dissatisfied and discontented. Catiline said that the State had two bodies, one frail with a weak head, the other strong, but with no head; and that the latter, if it deserved well of him, would not lack a head so long as he lived (*Mur.* 51).

It is not valid to argue that Crassus, one of Rome's great creditors, would have had nothing to do with a program or candidate that held out the promise of relief to debtors. Vague and nebulous campaign promises have a way of disappointing people once they have elected a man, and politically Crassus would have laid many people under obligation who would support his further ambitions for power in the looming struggle with Pompey. For example, with favorable consuls in office, he might realize his twice-thwarted desire to gain control of Egypt. This move alone would offset any financial losses, even if some measure of debt relief were passed, as well as increase his political might.

Cicero was well aware of the implications of Silanus's and Catiline's candidacies. He wished to see Pompey return to Rome with unchallengeable prestige, ripe for an alliance with the leaders of the Senate and propertied classes. The success of Silanus, Catiline, and their backers Crassus and Caesar could have radically altered this scenario. Of the two candidates, Silanus was practically unassailable, but Catiline had some fatal weaknesses as the more vocally radical candidate. Cicero concentrated his fire on Catiline and did everything he could to block him, so that Crassus and Caesar would not control both consuls during the coming year. One move was to secure passage of a law, the *lex Tullia de Ambitu*, that stiffened the penalties for bribery and even included penalties for those who accepted bribes (Cic. *Mur.* 47 and 89, *Planc.* 83; Schol. Bob. *Sull.* 79 St, *Sest.* 140 St, *Vat.* 151 St, *Planc.* 166 St). In addition to the penalties of a fine, civil disability, and expulsion from the Senate, this law added ten years of exile (Dio 37.29.1).

Cicero, in his speech for Murena, says that he and the majority of senators were unhappy about the new law and that it had been forced upon them by the importuning of the honest Sulpicius. Therefore, Cicero claimed, he as consul dutifully, though unwillingly, shepherded the bill and lent it his name, while he helped to prune away some of Sulpicius's harshest provisions in debate (*Mur.* 46–47). Clearly, these statements constitute special pleading on the part of Cicero. He was defending Murena against Sulpicius, whose position he wished to weaken. He wanted, so far as possible, to convince the jurors that Sulpicius had vindictively pushed for the *ambitus* law with his present prosecution in mind (*Mur.* 45–47).

In reality, Cicero probably had initiated this legislation as a weapon against Catiline. He had been in favor of a similar bill aimed at Catiline and Antonius in the previous year, but it had been vetoed by the tribune Q. Mucius Orestinus (Ascon. *Tog. Cand.* 83 C/64 St). In 63, what probably happened was that Sulpicius had proposed some amendments to Cicero's own bill, which Cicero opposed because he thought them impractical or impolitic (cf. *Mur.* 47). Then in the trial of Murena, he tried to twist things in order to make Sulpicius responsible for the whole bill.

One wonders why no tribune vetoed the bill of 63 if it was

aimed at Catiline. After all, Crassus was backing him, and several of the tribunes seem to have worked with Crassus on other parts of his plans for the year. Some say that by the time the bill was introduced, Catiline had become an uncontrollable revolutionary, so that both Crassus and Caesar had dropped their support of him.[12] Conversely, another suggestion is that for Machiavellian reasons Crassus wanted to drive Catiline to desperation at this point.[13] A more likely explanation is that a veto might have produced a more negative effect on Catiline's candidacy than passage of Cicero's bill. It was Mucius Orestinus's veto of the previous year's bill that had provoked Cicero's outburst known as the *Oratio in Toga Candida* (Ascon. *Tog. Cand.* 83 C/64 St). That speech had done much to swing public opinion against Catiline. Crassus and Catiline's other supporters would not have wanted to give Cicero a similar opportunity now that he was endowed with all the prestige of the consulship.

Another section of Cicero's *ambitus* bill forbade holding, or the promise of holding, a gladiatorial show the year before and the year of a man's candidacy for office, unless directed to give a show by the will of a deceased person (Cic. *Vat.* 37, *Sest.* 133). Such shows were an indirect form of bribery, hence appropriately covered by this law. Also, these prohibitions were probably aimed at lessening the possibility of armed violence by candidates' using bands of gladiators brought to Rome under the pretext of giving games. Rumors of violence planned by Catiline were, no doubt, readily believed by the people and propagated by Cicero. Not without foundation. Witness Catiline's behavior in relation to the trial of Manilius in 65. Now, in 63, P. Sulla and Faustus Sulla had gathered together a troop of gladiators ostensibly for a show in memory of the Dictator (*Cic. Sull.* 53–54). Since one of the tribunes, Lucius Caecilius Rufus, had failed in his attempt to lift the penalties imposed on P. Sulla and Autronius, it may have been feared that these gladiators were really intended to sup-

---

12. Cf. Hardy, "Catilinarian Conspiracy," *JRS* 7 (1917): 178–79; Syme, *Sallust*, p. 70, n. 46.

13. E. T. Salmon, "Catiline, Crassus, and Caesar," *American Journal of Philology* 56 (1935): 311.

port Catiline in the hope that he as consul could succeed where the tribune Caecilius had failed.[14]

Somehow, an erroneous certainty has developed that Crassus took a public stand on the *lex Tullia de Ambitu.*[15] The text upon which this position is based will not support such a conclusion.[16] He might have said something if he attended the senatorial debate on this law, but for a man of his wealth, and in view of his links with electoral candidates, it would have been politic for him personally to have avoided the issue.

There is evidence, however, that Cicero's colleague, Antonius, did support the bill on bribery. The scholiast of Bobbio consistently refers to it not as the *lex Tullia* but as the law of Cicero and Antonius (Schol. Bob. *Sull.* 79 St, *Sest.* 140 St, *Vat.* 151 St, *Planc.* 166 St). The scholiast could be wrong, but it may well be that Antonius cooperated with Cicero on the bill as part of the deal whereby Cicero turned over to Antonius the rich province of Macedonia in return for his loyalty and support against Catiline, whose candidacy he had previously favored (Cic. *Leg. Agr.* 1.26; Sall. *Cat.* 26.4; Plut. *Cic.* 12.4).[17] Indeed, Cicero went to great

14. It is clear from Torquatus's prosecution of P. Sulla in 62 that there were strong rumors of Sulla's connections with Catiline, but Sulla's money and strong connections with powerful *optimates* were able to counteract them.

15. Hardy is not sure whether Crassus spoke for or against it: "Catilinarian Conspiracy," *JRS* 7 (1917): 179. Salmon, however, believes that Crassus stood with Cicero against some of the harsh provisions proposed by Sulpicius: "Catiline, Crassus, and Caesar," *AJP* 56 (1935), p. 311.

16. In the two cases cited in the previous note, the positions are based on Cic. *Mur.* 47–48. Nevertheless, even a cursory reading of the text will show that it in no way relates to Crassus's taking a stand on the *lex Tullia de Ambitu.*

17. There has been considerable debate as to whether Cicero made this arrangement at the very beginning of 63 or closer to the time of the elections. For example, Hardy argues that it was nearer to the elections: "Catilinarian Conspiracy," *JRS* 7 (1917): 184; cf. D. Stockton, *Cicero: A Political Biography* (London, 1971), p. 101. Holmes places it at the end of December 64, when the fight over Rullus's land bill was brewing: *RR* 1, pp. 457–58. W. Allen, Jr., has also argued that Cicero made the switch with Antonius in late 64 and then gave up Cisalpine Gaul in June of 63: "Cicero's Provincial Governorship in 63 B.C.," *Transactions and Proceedings of the American Philological Association* 83 (1952): 233–41. The texts support Holmes and Allen. Cicero (*Leg. Agr.* 1.26) and Plutarch (*Cic.* 12.4) are clear. A careful reading of Sallust (*Cat.* 26.4) will produce the same result. Although Sallust's narrative mentions the transfer of Macedonia to Antonius just before the elections of 63, his use of the pluperfect tense, when viewed in the light of the previous sentence,

lengths to ensure that Antonius played the part of a *vir bonus* throughout their year in office (Cic. *Sest.* 8).

As the effectiveness of Cicero's attack became clear, Catiline grew more desperate and more reckless in his rhetoric. Shortly before the elections he told Cato, who was threatening him with a prosecution (for bribery, no doubt) that if a fire were set against his fortunes, he would extinguish it not with water but with destruction (Cic. *Mur.* 51).[18] A short time later, one day before the scheduled elections, he held the famous *contio domestica*. On the strength of Catiline's reported utterances, plus his gathering armed partisans to overawe the centuries, Cicero persuaded the Senate to postpone the elections and interrogate Catiline as to his intentions (ibid., 50–51).[19] Although Catiline made his statement about leading the headless part of the State at this meeting, Cicero could produce no concrete evidence that Catiline's behavior constituted a grave menace to the Republic, and the elections were held after a brief postponement (Cic. *Mur.* 51; Dio 37.29.3–5, Plut. *Cic.*

---

clearly indicates that the transfer took place long before the time of the elections. True, in the *pro Murena*, 49, Cicero says that during the campaign of 63, Catiline boasted of certain *promissa* given him by Antonius. Nevertheless, this statement does not necessarily mean that Cicero had not yet made his deal with Antonius. These *promissa* could have been given Catiline in the previous year, before Antonius received Macedonia from Cicero; or Antonius could have been deceiving Catiline with vague statements of support in order to be able to favor one side or the other in a showdown; or Catiline could have been making false statements for campaign purposes.

18. Sallust (*Cat.* 31.9) incorrectly places this statement in the senatorial debate of 8 November: see Syme, *Sallust*, p. 76, n. 72.

19. Plutarch (*Cic.* 14.2–3) and Dio (37.29.2–3) say that Cicero summoned the Senate and asked for a postponement of the elections because he had learned of a plot to assassinate him during the voting. I agree with Stockton (*Cicero*, p. 106) however, that this story is unlikely. He suggests that it is a reconstruction based on Cicero's own statement about having a bodyguard and wearing a breastplate on the day of the elections (*Mur.* 52). Plutarch and Dio, or their source, probably were influenced by Cicero's charge that Catiline had wished to kill Cicero, along with the rival candidates for election (*Cat.* 1.11), and by Cicero's claim that he had checked such an attempt during the actual voting (*Sull.* 51). These two statements, however, must be treated with caution. Cicero's use of the breastplate and bodyguard was clearly an effort to frighten the voters into believing that Catiline was going to resort to violence. Later, in the light of subsequent events, it was easy to reinforce the belief that Catiline really had planned an assassination at the elections. In his *de Consulatu Suo* and *de Consiliis Suis*, which were familiar to Plutarch and Dio (Plut. *Crass.* 13.3; Dio 39.10.2), Cicero may have embellished the story even more.

14.5–6).[20] The damage had been done, however. Catiline lost. With the election of Silanus and Murena, Crassus could count only one of the consulships for the year 62 in hands friendly to himself.

After this second defeat at the polls, Catiline contemplated outright, armed revolution to obtain what he could not get by legitimate means.[21] Those who had come from the country districts went back and, under the leadership of men like Manlius in Etruria, began to recruit bands of armed revolutionaries among the distressed and discontented (Sall. *Cat.* 26.5–27.1). Catiline himself remained in the city and conferred with those who were plotting internal disturbances that would coincide with a general uprising in the country districts (ibid., 27.2). There are good accounts of Catiline's associates and the progress of the conspiracy, so that it will be unnecessary to repeat the details here.[22] The main question for this study is what role did Crassus play.

Circumstantial evidence certainly casts suspicion on Crassus. He had been involved with Catiline in the violent disruption of Manilius's trial in 65 and had supported Catiline's electoral ambitions in the two following years. In a meeting of the Senate on 4 December, after the principal conspirators in the city had been caught with the evidence supplied by the Allobrogian envoys, a man named Lucius Tarquinius actually

20. See C. John, "Die Entstehungsgeschichte der Catilinarischen Verschwörung," *Jahrbücher für Classische Philologie*, Supplementband 8 (1876), p. 762, and "Der Tag der erste Rede Ciceros gegen Catilina," *Philologus* 46 (1888): 663–64.

21. No doubt, Catiline had thought of such a contingency, but other than normal electoral trickery, it is unreasonable to assume that Catiline was seriously plotting an armed uprising before his second rejection at the polls: cf. E. Ciaceri, *Cicerone e i suoi Tempi* 1 (Milan, Genoa, Rome, Naples, 1939), pp. 248–49; Syme, *Sallust*, p. 76; F. E. Adcock, *Marcus Crassus, Millionaire* (Cambridge, 1966), p. 39; Gelzer, *Cicero*, p. 82; Grant, *Caesar*, p. 54.

22. E.g. W. E. Heitland, *The Roman Republic* 3 (Cambridge, 1909), pp. 259–88; Gelzer, *RE* 2A.2 (1923), 1693–1711, s.v. "Sergius" (23), and *Cicero*, pp. 82–104; Cary, *CAH* 9, pp. 494–502; Ciaceri, *Cicerone* 1, pp. 248–301; Carcopino, *Histoire romaine* 2, pp. 635–52; Stockton, *Cicero*, pp. 110–42. These accounts, based on the Ciceronian tradition, may make Cataline more responsible for revolutionary activity than he was. R. Seager has argued that Manlius and Lentulus were more their own men than simple subordinates of Catiline and that Catiline did not decide to join Manlius in Etruria until he had departed Rome in the face of Cicero's sharp attacks: "*Iusta Catilinae*," *Historia* 22 (1973): 240–48.

accused Crassus of sending him to warn Catiline to hasten to
Rome to save his friends (Sall. *Cat.* 48.3–4). The majority of
senators refused to believe this accusation. According to Sallust, who relates the story, various senators had different
motives: some honestly disbelieved Tarquinius; others, although they believed Tarquinius, did not want to force the
hand of so powerful a man as Crassus; and still more were
under financial obligation to Crassus and feared his revenge if
they accepted the accusation (ibid., 48.5–6). After opening
the matter to debate, Cicero moved and the Senate voted that
Tarquinius's testimony seemed false and that he should be
kept in chains, forbidden to do anything until he revealed who
was responsible for getting him to make his false charge
(ibid., 48.6).

No further record of Tarquinius exists, and speculation
clouds the issue that he raised.[23] Again according to Sallust,
there were some who thought that P. Autronius, who had
been stripped of his designated consulship in 66 and was
one of the principal conspirators with Catiline, had instigated
Tarquinius in order to force Crassus into actively protecting
the conspirators, lest he be dragged down with them, while
others believed that Cicero had done it in order to prevent
Crassus from defending the conspirators for fear of implicating
himself more deeply (*Cat.* 48.7–9).[24] The second hypothesis
has found little support.[25] Whatever Cicero may have felt
personally, he had no desire to alienate and antagonize a

23. F. Münzer suggests that L. Tarquinius may be the same man as
L. Tarquitius, mentioned by Cicero in 50 B.C. (*Att.* 6.8.4): *RE* 4A.2
(1932), 2390, s.v. "Tarquinius" (10).

24. On the latter point, Sallust's words are: *Alii Tarquinium a Cicerone
immissum aiebant, ne Crassus more suo suscepto malorum patrocinio rem
publicam conturbaret. Ipsum Crassum ego postea praedicantem audivi
tantam illam contumeliam sibi ab Cicerone impositam.*

The second sentence has generally been interpreted to mean that Sallust
had heard Crassus say that Cicero had tried to implicate him in the
conspiracy; e.g., Holmes, *RR* 1, p. 273; Syme, *Sallust*, pp. 103–4, n. 3;
Stockton, *Cicero*, p. 132. It is more probable, however, that the words
illam contumeliam refer only to Cicero's assertion that Crassus was accustomed to defend bad people. Nor should it be assumed that Cicero
made this remark at the meeting on 4 December. He could have made it
on any number of occasions. Indeed, Crassus was well known, as the words
more suo imply, for defending people that other important figures would
not (Plut. *Crass.* 3.2).

25. Garzetti is one of the few supporters of this view: "Crasso," *Athenaeum* 20 (1942): 38–39.

powerful man like Crassus at this critical juncture, nor is there any solid evidence that he tried to do so.[26]

Another reason for disbelief in any connection between Cicero and Tarquinius's attempted implication of Crassus is his attitude towards an attempt to implicate Crassus's ally Caesar. Sallust says that Caesar's personal enemies Piso and Catulus vainly tried to procure Cicero's cooperation in trumping up evidence against Caesar (*Cat.* 49.1). Plutarch further reports that Piso and Catulus denounced Cicero for not seizing the chance to get rid of Caesar (*Caes.* 7.2, 8.2–3). At one point, Cicero literally saved Caesar's life when he refused to let his bodyguard harm Caesar as he left the Senate, probably after the debate on 5 December, when Cato had tried to throw suspicion on him (ibid., and *Cic.* 21.2). Finally, when L. Vettius and Quintus Curius named Caesar as part of the conspiracy, Cicero volunteered the statement that Caesar had been instrumental in giving him information against it (Suet. *Iul.* 17.2). In light of Cicero's behavior toward a man like Caesar, it is unlikely that he had been behind Tarquinius's clumsy attempt to impugn Crassus.

That Autronius instigated Tarquinius is possible, given the picture of contorted machinations and bungling that can be formed if only half of the evidence about the conspiracy is correct.[27] Two other explanations are also possible, however, and even more likely. Crassus, as did Caesar, had powerful enemies among the *optimates*. If they were behind Tarquinius, that may explain the mystery of his disappearance from history. The second explanation is so simple that it is usually ignored: Tarquinius may have dreamed up the idea on his own in the hope of receiving clemency for information given. If so, the silence surrounding him can be explained by his having no useful information to give.

Clearly, both Crassus and Caesar must have been aware

26. Holmes, *RR* 1, pp. 470–73. What Cicero said in his posthumous *de Consiliis Suis* is another matter: cf. Plut. *Crass.* 13.3; Dio 39.10.2–3.

27. That Autronius or both Autronius and Antonius did it has been advocated by Hardy, "Catilinarian Conspiracy," *JRS* 7 (1917): 207–8; Cary, *CAH* 9 (1932), pp. 502–3; and Ciaceri, *Cicerone* 1, p. 282. Involvement of either Autronius or Antonius has been denied by Chr. Deknatel, *De Vita M. Licinii Crassi* (Diss., Leyden, 1901), pp. 39–40, and Garzetti, "Crasso," *Athenaeum* 20 (1942): 38.

that any association with Catiline and *popularis* causes would have laid them open to a charge of implication in the conspiracy, and they had sought to avert the danger. Indeed, it was Crassus who supplied Cicero with the documentary proof of the conspiracy necessary to produce the first concrete action of the Senate. The plan had been to have Manlius raise up rebellion in Etruria on 27 October, while other conspirators paralyzed the government at Rome with a massacre of leading citizens, including Cicero, on the 28th (Cic. *Cat.* 1.7; Sall. *Cat.* 30.1). Shortly before the dawn of 21 October, so the story goes, Crassus received a packet of letters that had been given his doorkeeper by some unknown messenger. They were addressed to himself and other leading men. Crassus opened the letter addressed to him and found an anonymous warning to flee the impending massacre. Summoning two other reputable men, M. Claudius Marcellus and Q. Caecilius Metellus Scipio (to whom, presumably, letters had also been addressed), Crassus went immediately to Cicero's house, roused the consul from his bed, and handed him the documents (Plut. *Crass.* 13.4, *Cic.* 15.1–2; Dio 37.31.1).

Cicero called a meeting of the Senate that day and had the letters read out. They gave visible proof that some kind of evildoing was afoot and lent substance to what Cicero had learned orally from informants like the notorious Fulvia. When he predicted that Manlius would rise up in arms on the 27th, the Senate was sufficiently alarmed to pass a decree of *tumultus* declaring a state of war in Italy.[28] This decree allowed Cicero to take the first official steps against the conspiracy by raising troops and using his magisterial powers to investigate the situation (Dio 37.31.1).[29] By giving the letters to Cicero,

28. It is not quite clear whether the seizure of Praeneste on 1 November was part of the original plan or was a substitute plan devised after the plans for Manlius's actions on the 27th were revealed (Cic. *Cat.* 1.8). I suspect the latter. It would reveal how well Cicero's informants were working.

29. I am following the analysis of John, "Der Tag," *Philologus* 46 (1888): 650–65, and Holmes, *RR* 1, p. 458, n. 5. They argue that there were two meetings: one on 21 October, at which *tumultus* was decreed, and a second, on 22 October, at which the S.C.U. was decreed. Holmes is wrong, however, in saying that Cicero predicted Manlius's uprising at the meeting on the 22nd: ibid., 260. Cicero himself says that it was on the 21st (*Cat.* 1.7). Indeed, if he had not, there would have been little reason for the Senate to have decreed *tumultus*, for, by itself, the revela-

therefore, Crassus prevented the conspiracy from building up more momentum and surprising the state before the government was prepared to take action.

Clearly, Crassus did the right thing in bringing the letters to Cicero. It has been suggested that these letters were actually forgeries ordered up by Cicero to force Crassus's hand and trick the lethargic Senate into action.[30] If Crassus did not volunteer the letters, they would have been conveniently "discovered" and Cicero would have convinced the Senate of a real plot as well as of Crassus's complicity in it. If Crassus came forward in order to cover himself, Cicero would have succeeded in driving a wedge between this powerful man and the conspirators, while he still would have convinced the Senate of danger.

This suggestion would appeal to Cicero's critics, but it probably would not have appealed to Cicero. It would have been a dangerous and risky game to play. Cicero could have lost all credibility if Crassus had called his bluff. Furthermore, nothing would have happened if Crassus had immediately burned the letters, so that Cicero's risky venture would have been for nought.

It is entirely possible that one of the many young or bankrupt aristocrats who were conspiring with Catiline honestly but foolishly sought to warn his friends of the impending danger. Not risking the chance of discovery if he or a servant of his took the time necessary to deliver all the letters, he could have taken them to Crassus in the belief that he was sympathetic with Catiline and would discreetly deliver them to the addressees.[31]

Still, an even greater possibility exists. Crassus may well have forged or solicited the letters himself with the full intention of revealing Catiline's plot now that it had matured to the point of presenting a real danger to the state.[32] This

---

tion of plans to assassinate individuals at Rome would not have necessitated such an action. Clearly, the letters indicated that a dangerous situation existed, but how serious it was would not have been clear. Only when Cicero predicted the armed uprising was the majority of the Senate willing to give Cicero enough support to take protective measures, but even then they were unwilling to give him a totally free hand.

30. Cf. Heitland, *RR* 3, p. 96 and Stockton, *Cicero*, p. 114.
31. Cf. Stockton, ibid.
32. Cf. Deknatel, *Vita*, pp. 35–36.

hypothesis is compatible with any of the interpretations that have been advanced about the relationship of Crassus with the Catilinarian conspirators.

Mommsen argued strenuously that Crassus was intimately involved with the plot.[33] Others have denied with equal vigor that Crassus had anything to do with Catiline after the elections of 63.[34] Still others believe that Crassus, although not really involved in the conspiracy, hoped to turn it to his advantage if a serious uprising took place, just as he had taken advantage of Spartacus's rebellion.[35] A fourth thesis stated by Deknatel and most fully argued by Salmon is that Crassus was playing a double game by encouraging the conspiracy up to a point and then helping conclusively to expose it.[36] This latter action would have helped to free him of any suspicion, but most important, Crassus hoped that he or his friend Caesar would receive a commission to quell the insurgents and thereby gain the necessary position and power to be able to deal with Pompey from strength upon his arrival from the East.[37]

If one accepts either of the first two theses concerning Crassus's relationship to the conspirators, then it is possible that he forged or solicited the warning letters and then revealed them to avoid being implicated in the plot. In respect to the second two interpretations, Crassus could have wanted to reveal forged or solicited letters in order to precipitate a crisis that he then would have hoped to manipulate to his own advantage. The latter seems very likely.[38] Admittedly, there is no solid evidence at all that Crassus was in any way connected with Catiline after the elections of 63.[39] Nevertheless, it is not impossible that Crassus was in contact with

---

33. *History of Rome* 4 (trans. Dickson), pp. 486–89; cf. Sall. *Cat.* 17.7.

34. E.g. W. Drumann, *Geschichte Roms* 4, ed. 2, P. Groebe (Berlin and Leipzig, 1908), p. 98; Holmes, *RR* 1, pp. 470–73; Adcock, *Crassus*, pp. 39–40; Stockton, *Cicero*, pp. 132–33.

35. E.g. Gelzer, *RE* 13.1 (1926), 313, s.v. "Licinius" (68) and Garzetti, "Crasso," *Athenaeum* 20 (1942): 37–40.

36. Deknatel, *Vita*, pp. 35–37; Salmon, "Catiline, Crassus, and Caesar," *AJP* 56 (1935): 310–15.

37. Salmon, ibid.

38. Even in the first two cases, it is possible that Crassus also wanted to precipitate a crisis to his own advantage.

39. See Holmes's detailed arguments against Mommsen: *RR* 1, pp. 470–73.

Catiline or his friends to some degree even after the elections and used any information that he obtained about the conspiracy to his own advantage.

For example, the conspirator T. Volturcius was known to Crassus's former legate, the praetor C. Pomptinus. When Cicero arranged a trap for Volturcius through the Allobrogian ambassadors, one of the two praetors whom he chose to carry out the operation was Pomptinus (Cic. *Cat.* 3.5, 14, *Flac.* 102, *Prov. Cons.* 32; Sall. *Cat.* 45). It is striking that Cicero chose a man connected with both Crassus and Volturcius.

The hypothesis that Crassus was playing a double game during the conspiracy is very attractive. He had long been trying to build up a countervailing position to Pompey's. After Catiline had failed at the polls in July, and the hope of controlling the consuls for the coming year had been darkened, Crassus must have been very anxious to find a means of securing his position. Mithridates was dead and Pompey's return imminent.[40] Given his past associations with Catiline, it would not have been difficult for him to become privy to Catiline's thinking and the plottings of his friends. Without actively participating in the plans and seriously jeopardizing himself, he could have given the conspirators vague encouragement until they had advanced to the point at which the plot could not be stopped, but a timely revelation would ensure that it would not create a danger to his own interests or the ultimate stability of the state.[41] If a controlled crisis of significant proportions could be created, Crassus or his ally Caesar might then be able to receive the task of dealing with it and thereby gain a position of legal and military power from which to deal with Pompey. What could not be foreseen, however, was the self-control of Catiline and the skill and vigor with which Cicero acted in dealing with the situation.

A decree of *tumultus* was not enough to force the situation.

40. Mithridates had died early in 63, before Pompey went to Jerusalem (Cic. *Mur.* 34; Dio 37.10.1; App. *Mith.* 111; Oros. 6.5.1–6.2). Salmon suggested that news of Mithridates's death and fear of Pompey's return prompted Crassus to drop support of Catiline before the consular elections, in the hope of driving Catiline to violent action that he could then exploit: "Catiline, Crassus, and Caesar," *AJP* 56 (1935): 309–10. I doubt that this was the case. Crassus would have preferred Catiline's election to the consulship, as long as the possibility existed.

41. Cf. Salmon, ibid., p. 314.

At a meeting of the Senate on the next day, 22 October, Quintus Arrius confirmed that troops were being raised in northern Etruria and that Manlius was waiting in the vicinity for a signal from Rome to attack (Plut. *Cic.* 15). Convinced of a grave emergency now, the senators voted the Extreme Decree, the *Senatus Consultum Ultimum*, by which they authorized the consuls to take any measure they saw fit to protect the state (Cic. *Cat.* 1.3–4; Plut. *Cic.* 15.3; Dio 37.31.2).[42] Now Crassus might have hoped that Catiline would have been panicked into action.

At some point, Caesar also supplied information about the conspirators (Suet. *Iul.* 17.2). Perhaps he had worked through Q. Arrius, who seems to have been close to both him and Crassus. Again, as so often, the evidence is ambiguous, and certainty is impossible. Nevertheless, the numerous bits of information make a significant case. First, Arrius, or a close relative of the same name, probably had served as a pro-quaestor under Crassus after Crassus had assumed command against Spartacus.[43] Second, Cicero, when describing him as an orator in the *Brutus* (242–43), describes him as *Q. Arrius, qui fuit M. Crassi quasi secundarium* ("who played second fiddle, as it were, to Marcus Crassus"). Here Cicero metaphorically indicates that Arrius often accompanied Crassus as a *subscriptor* in those numerous defenses that earned Crassus

42. See n. 29 above.
43. Q. Arrius, a praetor of 73, had been serving with the consuls of 72 (Liv. *Per.* 96), and when Crassus took over their armies (App. *BC* 1.13.114; Oros. 5.24.5), he probably continued to serve. There is great debate over the identity of this praetor of 73. The Gronovian scholiast has Arrius die on the way to assuming the governorship of Sicily in 72 or 71 (Schol. Gronov. *ad Div.* 3, 324 St). Cicero (*Verr.* 2.4.42) is ambiguous, however, and the scholiast could be wrong about Arrius's dying on the way to Sicily. Several scholars, therefore, have identified the praetor of 73 with the Q. Arrius of 63: R. Syme, "Review of Broughton, *Magistrates," Classical Philology* 50 (1955): 133 (cf. Broughton, MRR, *Suppl.,* 7); T. P. Wiseman, *New Men in the Roman Senate* 139 B.C.–A.D. 14 (Oxford, 1971), p. 214. Others, however, believe that the references are to two different men: Klebs, *RE* 2.1 (1895), 1252–54, s.v. "Arrius" (7 and 8); Broughton, MRR 2, pp. 109, 161; A. E. Douglas, ed., *Brutus* (Oxford, 1966) "Commentary," p. 179. Most recently, however, B. A. Marshall and R. J. Baker have strongly argued that the references are to the same man: "The Aspirations of Q. Arrius," *Historia* 24 (1975): 220–31. Certainty can never be totally achieved, but the probability of the last view is very great.

much favor among the people.[44] Only two years later he was clearly close to Crassus's ally, Caesar (Cic. *Att.* 1.17.11).[45] Finally, in 55, he, or a son, seems to have accompanied Crassus on his ill-fated Parthian expedition (Catullus 84).[46] Therefore, it is highly probable that Arrius was following the lead of Crassus and Caesar in divulging important information about Catiline's conspiracy in 63.

Catiline, however, was not about to be stampeded into overplaying his hand too early. Cicero desperately wanted Catiline out of the way. He feared Catiline as the standard-bearer of the discontented and was afraid that, to the advantage of Crassus and Caesar, he would succeed in his next try for the consulship, which might not be very far off, in view of the cloud hanging over the consul-designate Murena. Finally, at a meeting of the Senate on 8 November, Cicero claimed that Catiline had sought his assassination on the night of 6 November in preparation for leaving to join Manlius in Etruria (*Cat.* 1.1, 8–10, 2.6, *Sull.* 18, 52). Catiline attended this meeting and heard Cicero's ringing denunciation. In view of the Senate's hostility and the circumstantial evidence against him, protest was useless, and Catiline decided to abandon Rome that night (Cic. *Cat.* 2.1, 6; Sall. *Cat.* 32.1–2; Plut. *Cat. Min.* 22.1, *Cic.* 16.2–3; App. *BC* 2.1.3; Dio 37.33.1).[47] Still, neither he nor his friends at Rome resorted to hasty acts. Instead, he considered exiling himself to Massilia and wrote letters defending his dignity and justifying himself before his noble peers in an attempt to play upon their prejudice against the parvenue Cicero (Sall. *Cat.* 34.2–

44. Syme, "Review of Broughton," *CP* 50 (1955): 133. One could argue that Cicero is merely saying that Arrius imitated Crassus in his career, but the parallel between the first and second actors in Greek plays and the primary and secondary speakers on behalf of a client in a Roman court seems to have been uppermost in Cicero's mind; cf. *Div. Caec.* 48.

45. In 59, Arrius was bitterly disappointed that Caesar did not support him for a consulship (Cic. *Att.* 2.5.2, 2.7.3).

46. H. Bardon, *Catulli Carmina* (Brussels, 1970), *ad Cat.* 84. See also Marshall and Baker, "Aspirations of Q. Arrius," *Historia* 24 (1975): 220–31.

47. R. Seager has cast considerable doubt upon Cicero's story of an assassination attempt and has argued that Catiline actively considered exile upon abandoning Rome before he decided to commit himself to overt revolt: "*Iusta Catilinae*," *Historia* 22 (1973): 240–48.

35.6), the *inquilinus civis urbis Romanae* as he had once contemptuously called him (ibid., 31.7).[48]

At last, however, Catiline preferred action to exile and
joined Manilius's band in Etruria. Still, he refrained from any
direct military move right away. No doubt, practical concerns,
such as a lack of sufficient arms for his forces, were involved
in his decision not to resort to force immediately, but there
were two other considerations that may have made Catiline
wish to refrain from immediate attack. First, true to his
promise, Cato, along with the disappointed Servius Sulpicius
Rufus, undertook to prosecute the consul-elect L. Licinius
Murena. The case came to trial a short time after Catiline had
left Rome.[49] If Murena were to have been convicted, only one
consul would have taken office on January first, Decimus
Junius Silanus. He was to Murena what the doubtful Antonius
was to Cicero. In this situation, Catiline's chances of restoring
his political fortunes might have been greatly enhanced.[50]

The second consideration was that there was talk of recalling
Pompey to deal with the situation. If his old friend Pompey

48. The occasion of this insult is debated. In the passage just cited,
Sallust said that it was part of Catiline's response on 8 November. Cicero,
however, claimed that Catiline had remained silent on that occasion
(*Orator*, 129). Moreover, Sallust's transposition of other remarks from
another time to this one casts suspicion on his placement of this remark
too: cf. Sall. *Cat.* 31.9; Holmes, *RR* 1, p. 263, n. 1; Gelzer, *Cicero*, p. 87,
n. 171. Syme accepts Sallust's attribution here, while he points out the
error of 31.9: *Sallust*, p. 76, n. 72. Absolute proof is impossible, but it
does seem highly probable that Sallust attributed to Catiline a nonexistent
reply for dramatic reasons. The tone of the remark attributed to Catiline
is quite like that of his letter to Catulus (Sall. *Cat.* 35.1–6) and may
have been drawn from knowledge of one of the letters that Sallust does
not quote.

49. Gelzer has corrected his earlier misdating of the trial after 5 December 63: *Cicero*, p. 90; cf. RE 13.1 (1926), 312, s.v. "Licinius" (68).
In the *pro Murena* (6, 78–84), Cicero makes it clear that the trial was
after 8 November but before 3 December: cf. Drumann, *Geschichte* 4,
p. 201, and Garzetti, "Crasso," *Athenaeum* 20 (1942): 39. For the prosecution of magistrates-elect, see D. R. Shackleton Bailey, "The Prosecution of Roman Magistrates-elect," *Phoenix* 24 (1970): 162–65; E. Weinrib, "The Prosecution of Magistrates-Designate," *Phoenix* 25 (1971):
145–50.

50. This assessment is basically Cicero's (*Mur.* 82–83), and it has been
called into doubt: Stockton, *Cicero*, pp. 122–23. Nevertheless, Catiline
had not yet taken decisive action, nor had the leaders of the conspiracy
left at Rome yet been unmasked. With the conviction of Murena, Catiline
and the others could have stayed their hand, undermined Cicero's credibility, and waited until he was out of office to take advantage of whatever
the situation offered.

were recalled against him, Catiline might hope to turn the tables and join Pompey against the government at Rome, just as Pompey had formerly joined Sulla.[51] Barring that extreme situation, he might obtain Pompey's political support and gain election to the vacant consulship.

Since none of these situations would have been compatible with his desires, Crassus eagerly joined with Cicero and Hortensius in defense of Murena (Cic. *Mur.* 48). If he were going to profit from the situation, Catiline would have to be made to act fast. With Murena's consulship assured, Catiline would be unable to wait any longer before striking. The defense of Murena was perfectly suited to Crassus's needs. While it would help remove reasons for delay by Catiline, it would reestablish his own credit with the *optimates*. Yet among those of his friends who might favor Catiline, he had a perfect reply to a charge of breaking faith with them: Murena was a kinsman in serious difficulty whom he could not abandon.[52]

Crassus and his colleagues were eminently successful in procuring Murena's acquittal, and the Catilinarian conspirators could afford to wait no more. Final preparations were made for an uprising beginning on 17 December (Cic. *Cat.* 3.10, 17, *Sull.* 53; Sall. *Cat.* 39.6, 43.1–2). The conspirators in the city, however, made the mistake of seeking an alliance with the restless Gallic tribe of the Allobroges, whose envoys happened to be at Rome to protest maladministration in their province (Cic. *Cat.* 3.4; Sall. *Cat.* 40.1–3; Plut. *Cic.* 18.3). The envoys informed Cicero, through their patron, Fabius Sanga, and, on Cicero's instructions, pretended to join the conspiracy (Sall. *Cat.* 41; App. *BC* 2.2.4). Having obtained incriminating letters from the chief conspirators, they were "arrested" by prearrangement with Cicero in the early hours of 3 December as

51. Indeed, many were afraid that Pompey would return to Italy in the way Sulla once had (Plut. *Pomp.* 43.1).

52. Both Crassus and Murena were members of the great plebeian *gens Licinia*: cf. F. Münzer, *RE* 13.1 (1926), 447.34–36, s.v. "Licinius" (123). It is interesting to note that their relative, the Vestal Virgin Licinia, with whom the gossip mongers had indecently linked Crassus, was the same one who aided Murena in his consular canvass (Cic. *Mur.* 73). In view of these facts, one might well ask if Crassus had been supporting Murena from the beginning. As pointed out earlier, however, Murena was backed by another Licinius, L. Lucullus (p. 147 above). Crassus would have preferred a candidate like Catiline, who would be more obligated to him than to any other.

they approached the Mulvian bridge on their way out of Rome (Cic. *Cat.* 3.4–6; Sall. *Cat.* 45; Plut. *Cic.* 18.4).

After he received the letters that the Allobroges were carrying, Cicero took the principal conspirators into custody and summoned a meeting of the Senate for that very day. When the letters, which Cicero had left unopened, were read in the Senate, and T. Volturcius, who had been entrusted with a message for Catiline, gave state's evidence, the Senate ordered that the conspirators whom Cicero had brought before them remain in custody and sent orders for the arrest of five others still at large (Cic. *Cat.* 3.7–14). The five conspirators who were present were each placed under house arrest in the hands of a senator. Among the five senators were Crassus and his friend Caesar (Sall. *Cat.* 47.3–4).

Mommsen argued that the Senate chose Crassus and Caesar among the custodians in order to compromise them as accessories to the plot if their charges escaped, or to brand them as renegades in the eyes of those suspected of being felow conspirators if they faithfully discharged their duty.[53] That interpretation cannot be ruled out completely. If it is true, Crassus and Caesar were more than happy to prove their loyalty, as they had done before in turning over evidence to Cicero. For that very reason, however, it is more probable that they volunteered to take custody of their charges. Crassus, as a *consularis*, and Caesar, as a praetor-elect, had ample opportunity to express themselves in debate on the question. Cicero himself indicates that Caesar spoke in favor of the motion for arrest (*Cat.* 4.10). Similarly, Caesar spoke in favor of a motion to vote a *supplicatio* to Cicero for his services (ibid.). Accordingly, it is not difficult to see Crassus and Caesar each proposing to accept the guardianship of a conspirator in order to forestall any question of their involvement in Catiline's plot.

It is a mark of their success that the subsequent attempts of Tarquinius and Catulus and Piso to incriminate them were rejected. Nevertheless, Crassus, who usually was not one to push his luck, stayed clear of the debate about the punishment of the conspirators on 5 December (Cic. *Cat.* 4.10, *Att.*

53. Mommsen, *History of Rome* 4, p. 487.

12.21.1). No doubt, he did not wish to lose popularity by voting for the death of Roman citizens on the questionable
authority of the *S.C.U.* Cicero seems to have taken note of
Crassus's absence when he said that one of those senators who
wished to appear as friends of the people (*populares*) was not
present (*Cat.* 4.10).[54] Yet, for Crassus to have opposed the
death penalty in open debate would have given rise to further
allegations of his complicity with Catiline. His friend Caesar,
however, was more daring and perhaps felt more secure in
view of his position as *Pontifex Maximus* and status as praetor-
elect, the kinds of official safeguards that Crassus did not have.
Caesar proposed that the conspirators be placed in custody,
one each in the strongest Italian towns, that their property
be confiscated, and that anyone who should undertake any
move to mitigate the sentence be declared a public enemy
(Cic. *Cat.* 4.8; Sall. *Cat.* 51).

In this way, Caesar sought to avoid the stigma of condemn-
ing citizens to death without a formal trial, and, if his proposal
were to have been adopted, it might still have been possible
for a crisis to have arisen that would have been advantageous
to himself and Crassus. As Cato recognized, the conspirators
would have become the focal points of plotting in their prison-
towns and their escape would have fanned the flames of rebellion higher (Sall. *Cat.* 52.15–16). Nevertheless, Caesar's
speech had a great effect. Even Cicero's brother, Quintus,
agreed with it (Suet. *Iul.* 14.2). The consul-designate Silanus
abandoned his opening proposal for the death penalty and
supported a compromise proposal of Ti. Claudius Nero, who
advised that the guards be increased and that action be de-
ferred until Catiline had been defeated and further information obtained (Sall. *Cat.* 50.4; App. *BC* 2.1.5). Perhaps this
compromise would have carried if it had not been for the
vigorous harangue of Cato, which swayed opinion back to the
side of the death penalty (Cic. *Att.* 12.21.1; Sall. *Cat.*
52–53.1).

Cato stirred up such passions with his call for execution
and thinly veiled hints of Caesar's complicity in the conspiracy that some of the young *Equites* who made up Cicero's

54. Garzetti, "Crasso," *Athenaeum* 20 (1942): 39.

bodyguard had to be prevented from attacking Caesar (Suet. *Iul.* 14.2; Plut. *Caes.* 8.1–2).[55] Even Caesar realized that the better part of valor was discretion at this point, and he did not attend any further meetings of the Senate until he received the full protection of his praetorship (Suet. *Iul.* 14.2).[56]

The year 63 had been a very eventful one for Crassus, no less than for many others, as he continued to seek an unassailable advantage in Roman politics, particularly in rivalry with Pompey. He could rejoice that his ally Caesar had been elected *Pontifex Maximus* and praetor. He and Caesar also had successfully backed Decimus Junius Silanus for the consulship. Unfortunately, however, Cicero had mobilized insurmountable opposition to their other candidate, Catiline, whereupon, Catiline had launched his ill-fated plot to seize power at Rome.

Crassus, although he may have known about the plot from those connected with it, had not been personally involved. He had sought to clear himself of any suspicion by providing letters that exposed the conspiracy when it had matured to the point of presenting a real danger to the state. In this way, he may also have hoped to force Catiline's hand in order to precipitate a crisis that would have enabled him and Caesar to receive the task of dealing with it and thereby to gain a position of legal and military power from which to face the returning Pompey. Still, Catiline had held his hand in the hope that the prosecution of Murena would provide another opportunity for election to the consulship.

Therefore, Crassus had joined with Cicero and Hortensius to obtain Murena's acquittal. At this point, Catiline could wait no longer. The mistakes of his allies at Rome, however, had brought about their arrest before the plot could be adequately carried out. This turn of events had precluded a crisis great enough to give Crassus or his friend Caesar any chance of a military command. Instead, they had acted as custodians for two of the arrested conspirators to avoid any suspicion of

55. For Sallust's erroneous date of 4 December (*Cat.* 49.4), see Syme, *Sallust*, p. 104.

56. Plutarch (*Caes.* 8.3) reports that Caesar attended the Senate a few days later (μετ'ὀλίγας ἡμέρας), when he was praetor-elect (στρατηγεῖν μέλλοντος). Plutarch is probably referring to an incident early in his praetorship, which Suetonius has recorded more accurately (*Iul.* 16): cf. Gelzer, *Caesar*, p. 53, n. 4.

involvement in the plot. Nevertheless, Caesar had unsuccess-fully tried to keep the political pot boiling to their advantage by opposing summary execution of the culprits under the *S.C.U.* Crassus himself had taken no part in the senatorial debate on this matter and kept a very low profile as he sought to analyze the situation and contemplate his next move.

VIII

Pompey's Return and the "First Triumvirate"

In the face of Pompey's assured, triumphal return from the East and his own failure to achieve a position of equal prestige and power in the state, Crassus decided that the best move would be to attempt a *modus vivendi* with the Great Conqueror. He was by no means confident that he could do it. If Pompey revealed himself implacable and returned to Rome as a second Sulla, Crassus and his family would be prime targets for a new proscription. Crassus wanted assurances that no harm would come to them and hoped that he could salvage something from his weak political position in relation to Pompey.

At the beginning of 62, Crassus departed for a journey to Asia Minor (Plut. *Pomp.* 43.1; Cic. *Flac.* 32). Although no date is given in the sources, this trip must have taken place at the beginning of the year. From the middle of April onward, Crassus was at Rome participating in events to be described below. Probably he received a *legatio libera* from the Senate for his journey, since he availed himself of a Roman fleet operating in eastern waters (Cic. *Flac.* 32).[1]

Plutarch offers two interpretations of Crassus's journey. The first is that in the face of rumors that Pompey would return from the East to establish one-man rule by force of arms,

1. Cf. W. Drumann, *Geschichte Roms* 4, ed. 2, P. Groebe (Berlin and Leipzig, 1908), p. 99; M. Gelzer, *RE* 13.1 (1926), 313.27–33, s.v. "Licinius" (68). Chr. Deknatel cannot understand what Crassus was doing on one of Flaccus's ships: *De Vita M. Licinii Crassi* (Diss., Leyden, 1901), pp. 43–44, n. 2. He suggests that the man to whom Cicero was referring was Crassus's son Marcus, who, he thinks, could have been Flaccus's *contubernalis*. It is not at all likely, however, that Cicero would have referred to young Marcus as a *vir amplissimus* in 59, but he would have thought it quite fitting for the elder Crassus. Moreover, in 62, Crassus, if he were holding a *legatio libera*, would certainly have had the right to expect transportation from a government fleet. Plutarch's assertion that Crassus moved his family and valuables from Rome probably reflects later embellishments of the facts.

Crassus was fleeing Rome in fear. The second view, which Plutarch himself prefers, is that Crassus wished to give added strength to the rumors about Pompey and thereby undermine his popularity at Rome. Among modern scholars, Drumann believed that Crassus was really the dupe of Pompey's enemies in the Senate and had neither of the motives ascribed by Plutarch.[2] Gelzer accepted Plutarch's preferred explanation and treated it as an example of how helpless and resourceless Crassus was in the face of a superior opponent.[3] Others prefer the simple explanation that Crassus really was fleeing out of fear of Pompey.[4]

Surely, none of these interpretations will do. Plutarch's preferred explanation is Machiavellian enough to make it superficially attractive, but it is really baseless. Whatever one thinks of Crassus, one must realize that he cannot have made people more apprehensive of Pompey's return just because he, one of Pompey's chief rivals, had fled in apparent fear. Nor could he have been duped into taking a *legatio libera* that would bring him to Asia Minor, the territory of the man he supposedly feared. Likewise, he would not have gone there if he simply had wanted to escape Pompey. He would have headed west, as he had in 85, to Spain or Transalpine Gaul. He had clients and holdings in Spain, his former refuge. Transalpine Gaul was in the capable hands of C. Pomptinus, his old legate from the war against Spartacus.[5] It would have afforded him a convenient, protected vantage point from which to wait on events in Rome.

Ciaceri suggested that Crassus had simply abandoned politics at Rome for the time being and went to Asia to oversee the farming of taxes by the companies of *publicani*.[6] A con-

2. Drumann, *Geschichte*, 4, p. 99.
3. *RE* 13.1 (1926), 313.19–27, s.v. "Licinius" (68).
4. Cf. A. Von Mess, *Caesar, Sein Leben, Seine Zeit und Seine Politik* (Leipzig, 1913), p. 65; A. Garzetti, "M. Licinio Crasso," *Athenaeum* 22 (1944): 1.
5. Cf. T. R. S. Broughton, *The Magistrates of the Roman Republic* 2 (New York, 1952), p. 176 and *Supplement to the Magistrates of the Roman Republic* (New York, 1960), p. 48; T. P. Wiseman, *New Men in the Roman Senate 139 B.C.–A.D. 14* (Oxford, 1971), p. 253.
6. E. Ciaceri, *Cicerone e i suoi Tempi* 2 (Milan, Genoa, Rome, Naples, 1941), pp. 18–19. See also now E. J. Parrish, "Crassus' New Friends and Pompey's Return," *Phoenix* 27 (1973): 357–80.

nection between Crassus's trip and the Asian taxes undoubtedly existed. Now that peace had been restored to that battered province, the Senate and *Equites* were looking forward to
renewed prosperity and increased revenues. Probably there was
already talk of electing new censors before the end of the
current quinquennium, so that quick advantage could be taken
of the changed conditions and tax contracts revised accordingly.[7] By this time in Roman history, many Roman senators
had financial as well as administrative interests in the farming
of taxes, and Crassus was deeply involved.[8] A *legatio libera* for
Crassus in 62 to assess the situation of the province of Asia in
preparation for the letting of new tax contracts makes excellent sense.[9]

He was not, however, abandoning politics for finance. His
interest in the Asian taxes, though genuine, masked his real
purpose, namely, to sound out Pompey's feelings and, if possible, work out a *modus vivendi* that would guarantee himself
safety at Rome.[10] Early in 62, after arranging the affairs of the
East, Pompey had set out from Amisus on the Black Sea for
a leisurely trip down the coast of Asia Minor (Plut. *Pomp.*
42.4–5). At about the same time that he reached the Mediterranean coast, Crassus must have been crossing over to Asia
Minor from Ainos (Aenus) on the nearby coast of Thrace
(Cic. *Flac.* 32.)[11] A personal meeting between him and Pompey would have been easy and seems highly probable. With
the official protection of a *legatio libera*, Crassus would have
had nothing to fear. Injury to an official representative of the
state at this point would have given Pompey's enemies at
Rome a pretext for precipitating a dangerous confrontation. If
personal assurances of future safety were not forthcoming

7. Censors were elected in the following year and new tax contracts
let (Dio 37.46.4; Cic. *Att.* 1.17.9, 18.8, 2.1.11). The names of these
censors are unknown. Conjectures that one of them was C. Scribonius
Curio *pater* must remain just that: cf. W. C. McDermott, "Curio *Pater*
and Cicero," *American Journal of Philology* 93 (1972): 383–84, n. 7.

8. E. Badian, *Publicans and Sinners* (Ithaca, N. Y., 1972), pp. 101–12.

9. That Crassus used the fleet of Flaccus, the governor of Asia, is,
therefore, significant.

10. Cf. F. E. Adcock, *Marcus Crassus, Millionaire* (Cambridge, 1966),
p. 41, and Parrish, "Crassus' New Friends," *Phoenix* 27 (1973): 357–80.

11. For the time involved in a journey from Rome to Asia, see n. 21
below.

from Pompey, Crassus would have been free to leave and seek safety away from Rome.

By this stage of events, therefore, some scholars have already discerned the beginnings of the "First Triumvirate." [12] The case has even been made that as early as July of 63, Pompey had sent his legate and brother-in-law Q. Metellus Nepos back to Rome to negotiate with Crassus and Caesar while he also sought election to the tribunate.[13] It is difficult to see what Pompey could have hoped to gain at this point from negotiations with Crassus and Caesar. They really had nothing to offer. Pompey's popularity with the masses, the *Equites*, and many senators was still unassailable. Crassus and Caesar were only hoping to take advantage of the situation created by Catiline to place them in a more favorable position vis à vis the great man, but this attempt collapsed completely after the debate of 5 December 63.

To be sure, after failing to prevent the execution of the conspirators on 5 December, Caesar cooperated with Nepos in promoting a measure favorable to Pompey. In the beginning of January, Nepos proposed to the Senate that Pompey be recalled to crush Catiline and restore order (Plut. *Cat. Min.* 26.2, *Cic.* 23.2; Schol. Bob. 134 St; Dio 37.43.1).[14] When the Senate rejected this proposal at the urging of Cato, who declared that Pompey would not enter Rome so long as he himself was alive, Nepos and Caesar submitted it to the People. This attempt also failed, amid rioting instigated by Cato's partisans (Plut. *Cat. Min.* 26.2–28.5; Cic. *Sest.* 62; Dio 37.43.1–3; Suet. *Iul.* 16.1).

According to the Scholiast of Bobbio (*ad Cic. Sest.* 62, 134 St), Nepos and Caesar also proposed a bill to permit Pompey to stand for the consulship *in absentia*. If they did, it, too, came to nought.[15] Finally, if Dio can be believed, Caesar had

---

12. E. G. Hardy, "The Catilinarian Conspiracy in its Context, A Restudy of the Evidence," *Journal of Roman Studies* 7 (1917): 225–27; E. T. Salmon, "Cicero, Crassus, and Caesar," *American Journal of Philology* 56 (1935): 316; Adcock, *Crassus*, pp. 41–42.

13. Hardy, "Catilinarian Conspiracy," *JRS* 7 (1917): 225–27.

14. T. Rice Holmes argues that the crushing of Catiline and the restoration of order were parts of the same general proposal: *The Roman Republic* 1 (Oxford, 1923), p. 285, n. 3.

15. That such a proposal was advanced seems very probable; cf. Chr. Meier, "Pompeius' Rückher aus dem Mithridatischen Kriege und die

also proposed on 1 January 62 that the honor of rebuilding the temple of Capitoline Jupiter be taken away from Catulus and given to Pompey (Dio 37.44.1–2; cf. Suet. *Iul.* 15).[16]

None of these moves, however, indicates that any kind of an understanding had been reached with Pompey by Crassus and Caesar. Caesar was not acting as Crassus's ally in this case.[17] Rather, Caesar, who had less to fear from Pompey in the light of his earlier actions in Pompey's favor, was once more seeking to ingratiate himself with the great man after having failed to advance his own power in cooperation with Crassus.[18] This course was the only one left to him. Certainly Crassus understood Caesar's position and may have hoped to gain if Caesar succeeded. Caesar was politic and would not turn a friend into an enemy if he could avoid it.[19]

For the moment, however, Crassus had to fend for himself in relation to Pompey. Hence, his journey to the East. He certainly could not hope for any kind of alliance, however. Pompey was at the pinnacle of his prestige and he was in no mood to have any partner in power, as Cicero was learning to his bitter sorrow (*Fam.* 5.7). Neither could Crassus imitate Caesar and simply pose as Pompey's *amicus*. Crassus was closer to Pompey in age and rank and was much more compromised in Pompey's eyes. He needed some kind of an understanding with Pompey. He would have to give concrete

---

Catilinarischen Verschwörung," *Athenaeum* 40 (1962): 103–25; M. Gelzer, *Caesar, Politician and Statesman*, trans. P. Needham (Cambridge, Mass., 1968), p. 56.

16. Gelzer discounts Dio's claim that Caesar specifically proposed that the honor be given to Pompey, since Suetonius makes no mention of it: *Caesar*, p. 55. For the relationship of Caesar to the earlier measure permitting Pompey to wear the robes of a *triumphator*, see Chapter Six, p. 156, n. 81.

17. Salmon argued that Crassus fled Rome and left Caesar to make overtures to Pompey through Nepos: "Catiline, Crassus, and Caesar," *AJP* 56 (1935): 316. It is more reasonable, however, to see Caesar acting on his own at this point: Deknatel, *Vita*, p. 52; Von Mess, *Caesar*, p. 64; Garzetti, "Crasso," *Athenaeum* 20 (1942): 40; Gelzer, *Caesar*, p. 56.

18. Holmes, *RR* 1, p. 467.

19. Deknatel assumed that Caesar's friendly moves towards Pompey would have precluded any good will towards him from Crassus: *Vita*, p. 52. That would be uncharacteristic of Crassus, however. Although he was not behind Caesar's actions, he still could have hoped that Caesar, upon establishing rapport with Pompey, would have put in a good word for him. After all, it would have been to Caesar's advantage to have as many important friends as possible.

promises that he would not be Pompey's enemy and seek assurances that Pompey intended no harm to him. Apparently he was satisfied to this effect and soon returned to Rome.[20]

Soon after he returned, however, the situation changed. While Crassus had been journeying to Pompey, Caesar and Pompey's agent Metellus Nepos had been engaged in their activities on Pompey's behalf. Nepos's threats against Cicero for his activities against the Catilinarians and the disorders surrounding the proposal to recall Pompey had so alarmed the *optimates* that with Cato as their champion they had obtained passage of the *Senatus Consultum Ultimum,* and forced a suspension of the two men from their official duties as praetor and tribune. After heated exchanges on both sides, Metellus had summoned a *contio,* denounced Cato as an enemy of Pompey, and set out for Asia to apprise Pompey of the situation (Dio 37, 42, 3; Suet. *Caes.* 16.1; cf. Plut. *Cat. Min.* 20, 26–29.2, *Cic.* 23; Cic. *Fam.* 5.1, 2).

Nepos was probably nearing his destination as Crassus was leaving. Not long after Crassus reached Rome, a letter that Pompey sent to the Senate upset his plans. The letter itself is lost, but the nature of its contents can be discerned in a letter from Cicero to Pompey (*Fam.* 5.7).[21] Despite the bad

20. Garzetti says that Crassus did not return home until Pompey disbanded his army: "Crasso," *Athenaeum* 22 (1944): 2; cf. Adcock, *Crassus,* p. 42. That Crassus returned very soon, however, is seen by his participation in other events of 62 that are discussed below.

21. This letter was written most likely in May of 62: L. Constans, *Cicéron: Correspondance* 1 (Paris, 1934), p. 109. Crassus probably had returned to Rome not much earlier. Travel between Rome and Asia took six to eight weeks without any serious delays. For example, a certain Agusius arrived from Rhodes at Brundisium on 8 July 47 after having been on Rhodes at least as late as 29 May (Cic. *Att.* 11.23.2). In the same year, a freedman of C. Trebonius arrived at Brundisium from Seleucia Pieria on the 28th day of his journey (ibid., 20.1). The road from Brundisium to Rome was 360 miles (Strabo 6.3.7), and the average travel time was probably about two weeks (cf. Hor. *Sat.* 1.5). This time compares well with the extra three or four days that it would take from Rhegium to Rome, an additional distance of about 100 miles (Strabo 6.3.7). Therefore, six to eight weeks seems to be about right for the trip from Rome to Asia.

Now, Crassus was involved with Cicero in negotiating the sale of a splendid house on the Palatine about May or June 62, when Cicero received 2,000,000 sesterces towards its purchase while defending P. Sulla against charges of complicity in the Catilinarian conspiracy (Gell. *NA* 12.12.2; Cic. *Fam.* 5.6.2). The trial cannot have taken place much before June, since several months elapsed while others were tried on the same

news that he had received from Nepos, Pompey held out to
the Senate hope of peace and tranquility (*spem oti*). It was
probably in this letter, too, that instead of demanding an
extraordinary consulship *in absentia*, as he was thought to have
desired, he simply requested a postponement of the consular
elections until his lieutenant M. Pupius Piso could return and
stand for office. Not wishing to give further offense, the Senate
granted the request, and Piso was easily elected when he arrived (Dio 37.44.3).[22]

The conciliatory nature of Pompey's attitude as well as the
promise of peaceful relations between him and the senatorial
leaders who had so deeply offended the tribune Nepos, greatly
disturbed Crassus. Both he and Caesar had counted on senatorial opposition to Pompey to give them an opportunity for
maneuvering with him. If Pompey were able to maintain
harmony with the Senate, he would completely dominate the
political scene at Rome. They would remain secondary figures.
In his letter to Pompey, Cicero refers to their consternation:
*Sed hoc scito, tuos veteres hostes, novos amicos, vehementer
litteris perculsos atque ex magna spe deturbatos iacere* (*Fam.*
5.7.1).[23]

Most commentators have recognized that the words *veteres*

---

charge (Cic. *Sull.* 6–7, 10, 21, 48, 83, 92). Therefore, Crassus probably
arrived in Asia towards the end of February, after leaving Rome in early
January, and left Pompey at some time during the first two weeks of
March, so that he arrived back at Rome by early May. Nepos probably
reached Pompey towards the end of March, after leaving Rome about the
end of January.

22. Plutarch (*Cat. Min.* 30.2, *Pomp.* 44.1) says that when Pompey arrived in Italy, he asked postponement of the elections until he could reach
Rome to campaign for Piso in person, but that Cato successfully blocked
this request. Gelzer ignores this conflict: *Cicero*, p. 109. Holmes, however, follows Plutarch: *RR* 1, p. 289, n. 2. Chronologically, Plutarch's
account is impossible. Pompey did not reach Italy until December, long
after the elections would have been held (cf. Cic. *Att.* 1.12.3, 14.1–4).
When he wrote this part of the *Life of Pompey* (44.1–4), Plutarch was
clearly confused about this election and that of Afranius in 61. On the
whole, Dio's account should be preferred on this point, although Hardy,
who follows Dio, thinks that Crassus and Caesar were behind the postponement and that it was a favor to Pompey. Probably Caesar did lend
his support, but it is doubtful that Crassus did. In any case, it was a
small favor, and the majority of senators would have voted for it regardless of Crassus, Caesar, or even Cato.

23. "But know this, that your old enemies, now your new friends, lie
prostrate, completely overwhelmed by your letter and cast down from their
high hope."

hostes, novi amici refer to Crassus and Caesar.[24] They surely do not refer to the *optimates*.[25] Cicero did not wish to bring suspicion upon the *optimates*, with whom he hoped to reconcile Pompey in a union with the Senate and whom Pompey himself was trying to placate. Indeed, the *spes oti* that Pompey's letter had promised would have been very pleasing to the *optimates*. Nor, as has also been suggested, did these words refer to the victims of the Sullan proscriptions.[26] First of all, this view is based on the proposition that the Rullan land bill, from which many of these men might have hoped to benefit, was a "Pompeian" bill, which it was not.[27] Secondly, many of these same men had joined the army of Catiline (Cic. *Mur.* 49; Sall. *Cat.* 28.4, 37.9). They can hardly have been feeling very friendly to the man from whose camp a tribune had just proposed that he be recalled to crush them.

Novos amicos in this case must have an immediate reference to specific individuals who had very recently evidenced a change of attitude and were capable of working for Pompey's good or ill. Prominent among these men were Crassus and Caesar. As usual, Cicero did not wish to name names, especially in a letter that might get into the wrong hands.[28] Pompey would have been well aware of Cicero's meaning. Cicero had earlier exalted himself above Pompey in prestige after suppressing Catiline. He considered his own glory as *consul togatus* greater than that of Pompey, the *dux armatus* (*Mur.* 84).[29] He had even sent a letter in which he voluminously

24. E.g., R. Y. Tyrrell and L. C. Purser, *The Correspondence of M. Tullius Cicero* ed. 3 (Dublin and London, 1904) 1, p. 187; Hardy, "Catilinarian Conspiracy," *JRS* 7 (1917): 226; Holmes, *RR* 1, p. 288; W. W. How, *Cicero, Select Letters* 2 (Oxford, 1926), pp. 62–63; D. R. Shackleton Bailey, *Cicero* (London, 1971), p. 38, n. 4; M. Gelzer, *Cicero. Ein biographischer Versuch* (Wiesbaden, 1969), p. 108, n. 47.

25. *Contra* L. R. Taylor, "Caesar and the Roman Nobility," *Transactions and Proceedings of the American Philological Association* 73 (1942): 19.

26. *Contra* E. S. Gruen, "Veteres Hostes, Novi Amici," *Phoenix* 24 (1970): 237–43. See now T. N. Mitchell, "Veteres Hostes, Novi Amici (Cic. *Fam.* v. 7,1)," *Historia* 24 (1975): 618–22.

27. Cf. Chapter Six above.

28. Cicero often sought to disguise names that might otherwise prove embarrassing if they became revealed to one other than the addressee of a letter; cf. *Att.* 2.19.5.

29. Cf. C. Nicolet, "*Consul Togatus*: Remarques sur le vocabulaire politique de Cicéron et de Tite-Live," *Revue des études latines* 38 (1960): 236–63.

glorified the deeds of his consulship and claimed a glory greater than that of all famous generals (Schol. Bob. *ad Planc.* 85, 167 St). Pompey was gravely offended, as Cicero now realized (ibid.; Cic. *Fam.* 5.7.2–3).[30] Crassus and Caesar had gained political advantage by showing a willingness to take a back seat to the returning conqueror. Now, while moderating his own position in the hope of mollifying him, Cicero tried to plant suspicion in Pompey's mind about Crassus and Caesar. The words *veteres hostes* are meant to recall their attempt to gain control of Egypt, their backing of the Rullan land bill, and their other efforts to build up a base of power during Pompey's absence. *Novos amicos* refers to Caesar's behavior since 5 December and Crassus's recent promises of good behavior.

The unexpected prospect of cordial relations between Pompey and the optimate-dominated Senate certainly must have troubled both Crassus and Caesar. The younger man, Caesar, with more time and the consulship still ahead, decided that he could continue to act as Pompey's supporter. For Crassus, however, the situation was different. He had held all the high magistracies, so that he could not hope to advance himself through service to Pompey. Yet, he could not be much of an influence in the Senate if the leadership cooperated with Pompey after his return. His only hope was to join with them first and try to block any rapprochement with the returning conqueror.[31]

One of the steps he took was to move closer to Cicero, who had emerged as one of the leading spokesmen of the *optimates* since the suppression of Catiline. Crassus was eager to prevent Cicero from attaching himself closely to Pompey and drawing him into harmony with the *optimates*, as Cicero

---

30. The degree of Pompey's pique may be seen in the action of his ally M. Piso, in giving first place in senatorial debate to his *gentilis*, C. Piso (Cic. *Att.* 1.13.2). M. Piso had long been a friend of Cicero (Ascon. *ad Pis.* 62, 15 C/20 St; Cic. *Fin.* 4.73, 5.1, *Brut.* 240, 310). Of course, the motive of wanting to neutralize C. Piso, who had been a bitter foe of Pompey, also may have been strong. For the two Pisones, see E. S. Gruen, "Pompey and the Pisones," *California Studies in Classical Antiquity* 1 (1968): 155–70. For the question of their relationship (probably not close), see R. Syme, "Piso Frugi and Crassus Frugi," *Journal of Roman Studies* 50 (1960): 14, and E. Badian, "M. Calpurnius M. F. Piso Frugi," *Acta of the Fifth Epigraphic Congress* (1967): 214, n. 37.

31. Cf. Deknatel, *Vita*, pp. 49–50.

so fervently wished to do. One of the ways in which Crassus sought to block Cicero was through his characteristic use of financial obligation. Cicero desired a residence equal to the exalted status he had gained during his *annus mirabilis*. Conveniently, Crassus with his great real estate holdings had just the right place on the Palatine, where other great figures of the Roman nobility lived. He let Cicero buy it for much less than he could otherwise have sold it.[32]

One might even conjecture that he had something to do with getting Cicero the money to pay for it. Cicero received 2,000,000 sesterces towards the purchase price for defending P. Sulla (Gell. *NA* 12.12.2). Crassus may well have been associated with Sulla, for such an association would have helped the successful effort to link Crassus to the fictitious "First Catilinarian Conspiracy." If the two men were friends, Crassus could have been in a position to aid the transactions between Cicero and Sulla. Moreover, the rest of the money was procured from Crassus's old friend and Cicero's consular colleague, C. Antonius, while the latter was governor of Macedonia (Cic. *Att.* 1.12.1–2, 13.6, 14.7, *Fam.* 5.5).[33] Therefore, Crassus may well have tried to bind Cicero to him in a web of financial deals.

Crassus also sought to influence Cicero by playing up to his vanity. In this way, he completely won Cicero's gratitude and good will one day about the middle of February of the following year, 61, just after Pompey's return to Rome. At a meeting of the Senate, Pompey praised all the decrees of that

32. Cicero paid 3,500,000 sesterces for it, a princely sum, to be sure (Cic. *Fam.* 5.6.2). He showed understandable satisfaction, however, in another letter, where he reports that early in the following year the consul Valerius Messalla bought a house in the same neighborhood for 13,400,-000 (*Att.* 1.13.6). L. A. Constans emends ⌈CXXXIIII⌉ to read ⌈XXXIII⌉ (3,300,000), but his only reason for doing so is that 13,400,000 seems too high in the light of the price that Cicero paid for his house: *Cicéron: Correspondance* 1 (Paris, 1934), cf. *Att.* 1.13.6. That is not a good reason, however. As D. R. Shackleton Bailey points out, Pliny says that Clodius, their younger contemporary, paid 14,800,000 sesterces for his house (*HN* 36.103): *Cicero's Letters to Atticus* 1 (Cambridge, 1965), p. 306. This figure corroborates the price of Messalla's house and reinforces what a bargain Cicero received from Crassus.

33. Cf. D. Lange, "Two Financial Maneuvers of Cicero," *Classical World* 65 (1972): 152–54. It is interesting to note that Antonius's proquaestor, P. Sestius, congratulated his friend Cicero on the purchase even before it was completed (Cic. *Fam.* 5.6.2).

body and indicated approval of Cicero's consulship. Not to be outdone, Crassus got up and expatiated on Cicero's consulship in the most flattering terms and with great approval from the assembled senators. He claimed to owe Cicero his status as a senator, his citizenship, his freedom, and his life itself; he said that as often as he saw his wife, his house, and his native city he saw a gift of Cicero's, and he repeated all the alarming details of Catiline's plot, as Cicero was wont to do (Cic. *Att.* 1.14.3, *Phil.* 2.12). Pompey was visibly disturbed that Crassus was stealing such a march, and even Cicero was surprised, since he had spent so much of his career boosting Pompey at Crassus's own expense (*Att.* 1.14.3). Clearly, Crassus must have thought it very important to improve his relationship with Cicero, and Cicero responded enthusiastically: *hic dies me valde Crasso adiunxit, . . .* (ibid., 4).[34]

Another way Crassus probably moved closer to the *optimates* was through the traditional aristocratic use of marriage ties. It was probably in 62 or early 61 that his son Marcus married Caecilia Metella.[35] She was the daughter of Q. Caecilius Metellus Creticus (*CIL* 6, 1274/Dessau 881), a leading optimate general and confirmed foe of Pompey. Aside from general optimate opposition to Pompey, Creticus had

---

34. Cf. Deknatel, *Vita*, pp. 50–51.

35. E. Groag would place this marriage in about the year 67: *RE* 13.1 (1926), 270.56–64, s.v. "Licinius" (58). He is assuming, however, that in 30 B.C., when this man's son was consul, the minimum age for the consulship had been fixed at thirty-three and that this son's son was consul *suo anno* in 14, which would place his birth in 47 and would mean that his father, Crassus's grandson, could not have been born much later than 67. I think it more likely that Crassus's grandson was born in 61. Augustus had not yet set minimum ages for the magistracies in 30: R. Syme, *The Roman Revolution* (Oxford, 1939), p. 369, n. 2. At the age of thirty-one, without having held the praetorship (Dio 51.4.3), Crassus's grandson could still have been consul. Also, Augustus would have been advancing a young man in rank ahead of his time as a political favor for switching allegiance (cf. Syme, ibid., 296).

Admittedly, this dating makes Crassus's great-grandson, the consul of 14, consul at a very young age, no older than 28. Nevertheless, dispensations of this magnitude are not unknown after 29, although they were often reserved for members of Augustus's own family, whose fortunes he was promoting: Syme, ibid., p. 373 (Marcellus in 22 and Tiberius in 13, the year following that of Crassus's great-grandson, are two examples). Possibly, Augustus was willing to grant a special dispensation to the son of the man who had been denied the dedication of the *spolia opima*, in order to assuage any feelings of injured family pride and keep the support of an important aristocratic family.

come into personal conflict with Pompey during the trial of his brother-in-law, Verres, in 70. In 67, Pompey even had sought to snatch the fruits of victory from him on Crete (Vell. Pat. 2.40.6). No doubt Crassus helped his son's father-in-law finally to win approval for his long-sought triumph over the Cretan pirates in late May 62.[36]

Crassus's move towards the *optimates* certainly is revealed by his leading role with Lucullus and Cato in blocking Pompey's desires in 61 (Plut. *Luc.* 42.5). Any idea that a partnership had been formed between him and Pompey is quickly dispelled by these actions.[37] When Pompey wished to have his eastern settlement quickly ratified by the Senate, Crassus helped to frustrate him by joining with those who insisted that each point be debated separately (App. *BC* 2.2.9; cf. Dio 37.49.4–5). Thus, Crassus seemed to be emerging as one of the principal leaders of the *optimates* in throwing down Pompey from his high horse (Plut. *Luc.* 42.5).[38]

36. For the triumph and its date, see Broughton, *MRR* 2, p. 176.

37. Cf. Garzetti, "Crasso," *Athenaeum* 22 (1944): 4, although all the sources that he cites are not germane.

38. E. J. Parrish has presented a very strong case that either Crassus or his son Marcus became a pontiff in 60 with the support of conservative senior members of the college, among whom he had many friends and connections: "M. Crassus Pontifex: By Whose Patronage?" *Latomus* (forthcoming). That is certainly possible, given Crassus's opposition to Pompey at that time. Nevertheless, it does not mean that Caesar could not have supported his or his son's candidacy, too. After all, Crassus had recently helped Caesar against creditors and had agreed to help him to win the consulship. Caesar's support of Crassus or his son for the pontificate could easily have been part of a bargain. That Caesar's support could gain a candidate membership in the pontifical college at this time is shown by the case of P. Cornelius Lentulus Spinther (Caes. *BC* 1.22). Moreover, support from Caesar need not have lost Crassus or his son the favor of conservative pontiffs. Crassus's position vis à vis Pompey may have been a greater consideration for them at this time than was his relationship with Caesar. For Caesar and Crassus in this case see L. R. Taylor, "Caesar's Colleagues in the Pontifical College," *American Journal of Philology* 63 (1942): 399.

Taylor thought it likely that the Crassus who became a pontiff was not the "Triumvir," but his homonymous son, Marcus: ibid., 393–94. Her reasoning is based on the belief that Marcus was the elder son and that since Publius became an augur in 56, the elder son very well may already have had a priesthood, otherwise he should have received the augurate before Publius. Publius, however, was the elder son; cf. Chapter Three, pp. 55–57. Therefore, it is much more likely that the father held the pontificate and that the next member of the family to be honored with a priesthood was the elder son, Publius.

Unfortunately, the significance of this admission to the pontificate must remain somewhat obscured by the problem of dating. For example,

Later in 61, however, Crassus lost rapport with the *optimates*, and they parted ways. Mutual enmity towards Pompey was not strong enough to overcome other differences. They were bound to clash.[39] The first occasion for differences to arise was the trial of P. Clodius for sacrilege at the rites of the *Bona Dea* in December 62. Because Caesar was *praetor urbanus* that year, these rites had been held in the Regia, the official residence of Caesar by virtue of his also being *Pontifex Maximus*.[40] The rites were forbidden to men, but, so the story goes, P. Clodius, the lover of Caesar's wife, Pompeia, disguised himself as a woman and gained entrance with the help of a friendly maid. He ran afoul of another maid, who was not in on the scheme, was discovered, and barely escaped with the aid of the girl who had let him in (Cic. *Att.* 1.12.3, 13.3, *Har. Resp.* 44; Plut. *Caes.* 10.1–3, *Cic.* 28; Dio 37.45.1; App. *BC* 2.2.14).

The rites were reenacted properly by the Vestal Virgins, but rumors of Clodius's sacrilege spread. Caesar summarily divorced Pompeia (Cic. *Att.* 1.12.3, 13.3). The marriage was childless and perhaps also by now a political liability to him as a *popularis*, since Pompeia was a granddaughter of Sulla. For many of the *optimates*, however, the case was far from closed. Here was a chance to embarrass Caesar, but more than that, to put a stop to the career of Clodius. Clodius was an ambitious and totally unscrupulous representative of the arrogant young nobles who were making a shambles of Roman moral and political traditions (Cic. *Att.* 1.16.1). He had greatly injured his optimate brother-in-law and general, Lucullus, by undermining his military command against Mithridates

Broughton lists Crassus (or his son) and C. Scribonius Curio (*pater*) as pontiffs under the year 61; MRR 2, p. 186. G. J. Szemler is more cautious, however: *The Priests of the Roman Republic (Collection Latomus 127)* (Brussels, 1972), pp. 133–34, n. 9. All one can say is that the election took place before 57 and sometime after 61 or 60. It would seem unlikely, however, that a vacancy in the college would have been filled before the return of Caesar, the Pontifex Maximus, to Rome, in June of 60, after twelve months in Spain.

39. It has been suggested that it was their rivalry over the unofficial position of leadership left vacant by the death of Catulus that caused the clash between Crassus and Cato: Chr. Meier, *Res Publica Amissa* (Wiesbaden, 1966), pp. 274–76. Certainly, Cato had ambitions to leadership, but the reasons for not cooperating with Crassus were based on more fundamental differences between the two men.

40. Cf. Holmes, RR 1, p. 292, n. 1; Gelzer, *Caesar*, p. 59.

prior to Pompey's takeover (Cic. *Har. Resp.* 42; Sall. *Hist.*
5.11–12 M; Plut. *Luc.* 34.1–3; Dio 36.14.4). Now was the
chance for revenge.

In January 61, after the college of pontiffs, which Caesar
himself headed, declared that a sin had been committed
against the state religion, the Senate decreed that the consuls
should promulgate a bill to create an extraordinary commission
for trying the case (Cic. *Att.* 1.13.3, 14.1). All the prominent
optimates were behind it—Lucullus, Hortensius, Cato, Gaius
Piso, and the consul Valerius Messalla—although their friend
Cicero began to doubt the wisdom of pressing the matter too
much (ibid., 13.3, 14.5). After heated debates and menacing
actions by groups of thugs in the employ of Clodius, a compromise bill was passed through the agency of the tribune
Fufius. It allowed for the selection of jurors by lot rather than
by the presiding praetor. Cicero, who foresaw a disaster because of a bought jury, would have preferred to let the matter
drop (ibid., 14.5, 16.1–2).

Clodius had to have much support in order to force a compromise upon the most prestigious optimate leaders of the
Senate. Although Pompey did not wish to offend the *optimates*
and avoided taking a specific stand on the matter in public, he
certainly felt kindly toward Clodius and did not want to
alienate him. Therefore, Pompey's man in the consulship,
Pupius Piso, worked vigorously on Clodius's behalf (ibid.,
14.1–2).[41] Even Caesar, whose honor had been stained, refused to give any evidence against Clodius.[42] Obviously, his
honor had been satisfied by divorcing his wife, and now he

41. Cicero momentarily deceived himself that support of Clodius
caused a breach between Piso and Pompey (*Att.* 1.14.6), but it is more
likely that Piso was acting with Pompey's covert blessing and that there
was no breach: D. R. Shackleton Bailey, *Cicero's Letters to Atticus* 1
(Cambridge, 1965), p. 312; cf. Cic. *Att.* 1.16.12.
42. There is a question whether Caesar refused at the time of the
trial or avoided the trial altogether and went off to his province beforehand. Suetonius (*Iul.* 74.2) and Plutarch (*Caes.* 10.6) indicate that
Caesar appeared at the trial. H. Strasburger argued that he left for Spain
before the trial began: *Caesars Eintritt in die Geschichte* (Munich, 1938),
p. 111, n. 55. Gelzer concurs: *Caesar*, p. 60, n. 3. This position is supported by an earlier passage in Suetonius (*Iul.* 18.1), which says that
Caesar left for Spain before the passage of a senatorial decree confirming
the grant or praetorian provinces. The decree was passed sometime around
the 15th of March (Cic. *Att.* 1.15.1), and Clodius's trial was subsequent
to that date (ibid., 14.3, 16.1–5).

hoped to avoid making a potentially dangerous enemy when
he might put an ambitious, talented, and popular young tribune in his debt with a view toward political benefits in the
future.[43]

It was Crassus, however, who really saved Clodius. The
optimates marshalled overwhelming evidence at the trial. De-
spite Caesar's own reticence, his mother, Aurelia, and sister,
Julia, are said to have given testimony of the affair under oath
(Suet. *Iul.* 74.2; Schol. Bob. *in Clod. et Cur.* fr. 23, 89 St).
Lucullus bore witness against Clodius's character by bringing
forth female slaves to testify how Clodius had committed
adultery and incest at the same time with Lucullus's wife,
Clodius's own sister (Cic. *Mil.* 73; Plut. *Cic.* 29.2, *Luc.* 38.1,
Caes. 10.5). Finally, Cicero destroyed Clodius's alibi that at
the time of the alleged sacrilege he had been ninety miles away
at Interamna. Cicero said that he had seen Clodius in Rome
on that very day (Schol. Bob. *in Clod. et Cur. argumentum*,
85 St).[44] Even the jury, no baser crowd than which ever sat at

43. Cf. Holmes, *RR* 1, p. 297; M. Grant, *Julius Caesar* (London,
1969), pp. 64–65. Although E. S. Gruen stresses Caesar's fear of Clodius
and insists on no connection between them, there is no reason why Caesar
might not hope to make use of Clodius in the future, even if this hope
did not materialize: "P. Clodius: Instrument or Independent Agent?"
Phoenix 20 (1966): 121.

44. J.P.V.D. Balsdon has suggested an argument to support Clodius's
alibi: "Fabula Clodiana," *Historia* 15 (1966): 71–72. It centers on the
question of when Clodius called on Cicero the day of the alleged
sacrilege:

> In one passage, he [Cicero] suggests that the call was made only
> three hours before the outrage [*Att.* 2.1.5]—that is to say, late in
> the evening, which was not a usual time for calling; and if Clodius
> had in fact called at this hour, he would have been insane to plead
> that he had been at Interamna. He could have invented a far more
> plausible alibi. The Scholiast of Bobbio states that Cicero's evidence
> was of a call at the morning salutatio [*in Clod. et Cur. argumentum*,
> 85 St]. In that case, if he rode on horseback and arrived late at
> night, Clodius could easily make the 90-mile journey to Interamna
> in the day.

In reply, several comments must be made. First, the Scholiast says
only that Cicero reported receiving a *salutatio* from Clodius. There is no
indication of time of day. Second, Cicero nowhere says that he saw
Clodius only three hours before the sacrilege at Caesar's house. He may
indicate, however, that he saw Clodius only three hours before the latter
claimed to have arrived at Interamna (*Att.* 2.1.5). Presumably, Balsdon
takes the reference to night in this passage as an indication that Clodius
claimed to have entered Interamna after dark, so that Cicero, then,
would have been saying that he had seen Clodius very late in the day,

a gambling table, according to Cicero (*Att.* 1.16.3), seemed ready to convict Clodius and adjourned while they awaited senatorial action on their request for a bodyguard (ibid., 16.5).

Before they returned, however, Crassus intervened. In two days, Crassus made contact with all the jurors, summoned them to his house, and offered each one what it would take to buy his vote in favor of Clodius (ibid.). Reportedly, if Crassus's money were not enough, the favors of certain women or introductions to influential young men of noble rank were also offered (ibid.).[45] Slander and malicious gossip may be involved in these charges, but in the light of "call girl scandals" that have frequently rocked modern politics, the charge is quite believable, especially where Clodius was involved. Despite all of Crassus's resources, however, a significant number of jurors either could not be bought or pocketed their profits and voted their consciences. Clodius was acquitted by a narrow margin, thirty-one to twenty-five (ibid.).

The question is, of course, what was Crassus's motive in protecting Clodius. As in the case of Clodius and Caesar, there

---

not long before the scandalous events of that evening. Actually, Cicero was talking about Clodius's claim that he once had entered Rome at night after travelling from the Straits of Messina (approximately 450 miles away) in seven days (ibid.). The implication of this story was that he could travel at a phenomenally swift rate and, therefore, could have travelled to Interamna in a very short time. Unfortunately, according to Clodius, since on that previous trip he had entered Rome at night, there was no witness to verify the speed that he claimed. Cicero referred to Clodius's nocturnal entry on that occasion, *idem ante*, only to make a scurrilous pun on his sexual escapades (ibid.). There is no reference to any assertion by Clodius that he had arrived at Interamna in the night. Therefore, there is no contradiction between what Cicero says about seeing Clodius and what the Scholiast reports: Cicero asserted that he had received a *salutatio* at such a time that it made Clodius's alibi unbelievable.

Finally, even if Cicero only spoke of three hours to point up the ridiculousness of the speed that Clodius was claiming and never indicated that he had seen Clodius literally three hours before the latter said that he had arrived at Interamna, one cannot support Balsdon's calculations for the time in which the distance could be travelled. The average rate of overland travel was about twenty-five miles a day: cf. n. 21 above. No doubt a man in a hurry could do better, but even in the mid-nineteenth century A.D., Pony Express riders, using steel-shod horses and saddles with stirrups and changing fresh mounts approximately every ten miles, could not be expected to cover more than seventy-five to eighty miles in an eight- or ten-hour shift: cf. W. F. Bailey, "The Pony Express," *Century Magazine* 34 (New York, 1898): 889. In this light, even Balsdon's calculations seem to be impossible. The truth is, Coldius's alibi was contrived, and Cicero's honest testimony exposed its falsity.

45. See Appendix to Chapter Eight.

is no need to see any prior connection between Clodius and Crassus. Crassus was simply taking advantage of the situation to aid himself. Caesar had not the resources to guarantee Clodius's victory. Pompey, moreover, despite the maneuverings of his friend Piso, had not been willing to exert himself personally on behalf of the man who had helped make possible the command against Mithridates. By saving Clodius, Crassus could produce such gratitude in Clodius that he might deny his great rival the services of this rising political force and could hope to use him to his own benefit in the future.[46]

Whether Crassus actively cooperated with Caesar in this case or whether he worked with Clodius independently cannot be said for certain. If Caesar had already left for his province of Farther Spain before the trial, then the former is highly probable. Since December 63, Caesar had been treading a fairly independent path in trying to be friendly toward Pompey.[47] Of course he had not sought to alienate Crassus either. As Caesar was about to depart for Spain, however, Crassus seized a chance to establish a new, tighter bond with his old ally in political intrigue.[48] Caesar was 100 million sesterces in debt, and his creditors were preventing his departure by attaching his baggage. Crassus advanced him 20 percent of that amount, 830 talents, which was enough to keep the creditors at bay and allow him to depart (App. *BC* 2.2.8; Plut. *Crass.* 7.6, *Caes.* 11.1).

Whatever good will among the *optimates* Crassus had lost, especially because of his aid to Clodius,[49] he still had reason to be pleased with the way things were going. Pompey would celebrate his incredibly magnificent triumph (Vell. Pat. 2.40.3; Diod. 40.4; Plin. *HN* 7.98, 37.11, 13–16; App. *Mithr.* 17.116–17; Dio 37.21.1–2; Plut. *Pomp.* 45), but approval of his eastern settlement remained blocked, and Cato contemptuously spurned his overtures for an alliance (Plut. *Pomp.* 44.2–3, *Cat.*

46. Cf. Holmes, *RR* 1, p. 297, Grant, *Caesar*, p. 65.
47. Grant (ibid., p. 67) suggests that Caesar's relations with Pompey were strained because of his alleged illicit affair with Pompey's wife, Mucia (cf. Suet. *Iul.* 50.1). Suetonius's allegations, however, seem to stem from the later propaganda aimed at driving wedges between the members of the "First Triumvirate," as his reference to Curio indicates.
48. Cf. Garzetti, "Crasso," *Athenaeum* 22 (1944): 3.
49. Cicero's outrage is clear (*Att.* 1.16.5) and that of many leading *optimates* can be assumed.

Min. 30.2–4). Pompey's rapprochement with Cicero really did not mean as much as Cicero would have liked (*Att.* 1.16.11). Moreover, his blatant bribery on behalf of his trusted lieutenant, L. Afranius (son of Aulus), who was running in the consular elections for 60, did not enhance his reputation. Indeed, Cato and Domitius persuaded the Senate to pass two decrees aimed at stopping this maneuver, and special arrangements, including postponement of the elections, were made. The postponement was to allow the tribune Lurco to propose a stiff new law on bribery (ibid., 16.12–13; Plut. *Pomp.* 44.3). Eventually, Afranius was elected, but his colleague was Q. Caecilius Metellus Celer, who opposed Pompey at every turn (Cic. *Att.* 1.16.6, 19.4, 2.1.8; Dio 37.49.3).

By the end of the year, however, Crassus himself was hopelessly at odds with the optimate leadership of the Senate and in as much danger of losing political power as Pompey. Crassus had consistently sought favor with the *Equites,* who were a powerful force in the *comitia,* and he was intimately involved in the financial dealings of many of them.[50] At this time, the *optimates,* under the misguided influence of Cato, were giving the *Equites* grave offense and creating an irreparable breach between that order and the Senate. First, no doubt because of Clodius's trial, Cato moved and the Senate passed a decree that a law be promulgated that would make any juror who took a bribe subject to punishment (Cic. *Att.* 1.17.8, 18.3, 2.1.8). Under current statutes, equestrian jurors could not be punished for taking bribes (Cic. *Cluent.* 145–48).[51] Naturally, the *Equites* bitterly resented this loss of privilege and its implied criticism of their order (Cic. *Att.* 1.17.8, 18.3, 2.1.8). Crassus probably would have supported the *Equites* as part of his general strategy. He was particularly concerned with this case, however, because he had supplied the bribes to the jurors in Clodius's trial, who would have been the first to be prosecuted under this law.[52]

50. Badian, *Publicans and Sinners,* pp. 101–12.

51. The law probably did not pass, or if it did, it was rescinded not long afterwards (Cic. *Rab. Post.* 16–18).

52. Cicero, who was also a friend of the *Equites* and wished to preserve harmony between them and the Senate, was away at the time the decree was passed and lambasted the Senate when he found out about it (*Att.* 1.17.8, 18.3, 2.1.8).

The issue that forced Crassus's complete break with the *optimates* was that of the Asian tax contracts. Despite his trip to Asia in 62, ostensibly to assess the economic situation, the companies that bid on the tax contracts in 61 were so eager to outbid one another that the winning company overestimated the potential revenue and found itself saddled with a sum that the war-weary province could not possibly produce in taxes, let alone exceed with any profit to the investors. Late in the year, with Crassus as their patron, the troubled publicans asked the Senate to nullify their original contract. Despite his dislike of the questionable ethics behind this request, Cicero was Crassus's most vigorous ally in the Senate. He felt that the principle involved was not worth the risk of completely alienating the *Equites* from the Senate. On 1 and 2 December, Cicero tirelessly lectured the Senate on the need of maintaining the harmony of the two orders. No doubt, many other senators had more personal reasons for agreeing with Crassus, and by 5 December, it appeared that Crassus's efforts on behalf of the tax farmers would meet with success (Cic. *Att.* 1.17.9, 2.1.8).[53]

53. Parrish argues that Crassus was not really working for the interests of the equestrian order here: "Crassus' New Friends," *Phoenix* 27 (1973): 357–80. She maintains that Crassus probably had an interest in a rival company and had promoted the cause of those who had overbid simply as a red herring to delay senatorial action on Pompey's *acta*. It is an interesting argument but is ultimately unsatisfactory. First, the opposition to Pompey was supported by so many powerful nobles that it would have been clear to Crassus that confirmation of Pompey's *acta* would be delayed by intensive wrangling. A red herring would have been unnecessary.

Second, although there were equestrians and equestrians, it is not invalid to see a politician appealing to them as a single class on issues that could cut across divergent interests and subgroups within the general class. In the case of those who had overbid for the Asian taxes, a precedent beneficial to all companies of *publicani*, as well as to other contractors with the state, could have been established. Cicero indicated to Atticus that the majority of *Equites* would have been offended by an unfavorable decision, and that, therefore, he decided to support the company's request despite doubts about its intrinsic merits (*Att.* 1.17.8–9).

Third, Crassus could have been concerned about the financial ramifications involved in the collapse of an important company. Its failure could have set off a chain reaction of defaults on loans that would have collapsed credit and caused a general financial panic. Crassus would have been especially desirous of preventing that.

Fourth, the suggestion that Quintus Cicero was working for Crassus by making things difficult for the tax collectors in the province of Asia

All was brought to nought, however, through the determined shortsightedness of Cato, whose concept of senatorial power came from another age (ibid., 2.1.8).⁵⁴ As of 5 December, he had not had a chance to deliver his opinion in debate (ibid., 1.17.9). When his turn did come, he used all of his talents for obstruction against it (ibid., 1.18.7). By June, the tax farmers had still not received any relief (ibid., 2.1.8). Crassus was desperate. If the *optimates* would not let him procure relief from the Senate for his friends and supporters, he would have to get it elsewhere. Fortuitously, the means lay at hand.

Caesar had remained in Spain about twelve months—not a long time, but long enough to make sound political and financial profits. He earned the gratitude of many provincials by relieving them of several difficulties, especially the reparations imposed since the Sertorian War ([Caes.] *B.Hisp.* 42.2; Caes. *BC* 2.18.5–6, 20.2). At the same time, he secured the favor of Roman *Equites* by guaranteeing them repayment of loans that they had made to provincials (Plut. *Caes.* 12.3). He also conducted successful military operations against some recalcitrant tribesmen on the pretext that they were brigands, and besieged

---

is groundless, although he may well have had some ties with Crassus. On the question of the provincial *portoria*, Quintus did not offend the *publicani* by removing these taxes. Instead, he avoided the delicate question of what to do about the *portoria* by passing it on to the Senate for a decision, despite his brother's advice that this tax should be removed for the good of the province (Cic. *Att.* 2.16.4). If anything, therefore, Quintus Cicero sought to look out for Crassus's interests by refusing to remove the *portoria* himself. Quintus's main problem as governor was a hot temper (Cic. *Q. Fr.* 1.1.37–40), but that temper seems not to have been directed against any special target like the company of tax collectors in his province. It seared individual provincials and Roman citizens alike (ibid., 1.2.4–14). (It may be worth noting, however, that in at least one important case he acted contrary to the interests of Pompey [ibid., 10–12].)

Finally, there is no reason to see Cicero as expressing surprise in *Att.* 1.17.9 that Crassus supported the tax company's cause. Rather, he expresses extreme annoyance that, because of Crassus's urgings, the company forced him to take an unpleasant stand in its favor. Therefore, there is little reason to reject the view that in this case Crassus was supporting the *Equites* in general, a group whose support had often been useful to Pompey and which support Crassus sought to monopolize to the former's disadvantage.

54. Cato's lack of political judgment in this period is also illustrated by his attack on the agrarian law proposed by Flavius for Pompey's veterans. Neither the other optimate leaders nor Crassus dared risk the consequences of attacking such a popular measure as that (Cic. *Att.* 1.18.6). Grant erroneously says that Crassus joined in suppressing the law: *Caesar*, p. 72.

the unfortunate city of Brigantium (Dio 37.52.3–53.4; Plut. *Caes.* 12.1; Suet. *Iul.* 54.1). The latter victory had provided him with booty enough to please his soldiers and his creditors. Now, with a fair political wind behind him, he arrived outside of Rome in June 60, whereupon he was expecting to celebrate a triumph and run for the consulship (Cic. *Att.* 2.1.6–9; App. *BC* 2.2.8).

There was one problem, however. There were only a few days remaining for Caesar to declare his candidacy if he wished to run in the elections of 60. By law a candidate had to appear in person to make a declaration (*professio*) of his candidacy. But, *professio* was made inside the *pomerium*, probably on the *Comitium*. Since there was not enough time to hold his triumph before the last day possible for making his *professio*, Caesar would have had to forfeit his *imperium* and the right to a triumph if he were to comply with the law.[55] Therefore, he petitioned the Senate to allow him to make a *professio in absentia* through some friends. Cato, however, with his usual myopia, effectively blocked the request by a filibuster. Accordingly, Caesar forfeited the triumph and ran for the consulship (Suet. *Iul.* 18.1; Plut. *Caes.* 13.1–2, *Cat. Min.* 31.2–3; App. *BC* 2.2.8; Dio 37.54.1).

The *optimates* used extensive bribery in an attempt to prevent Caesar's election, or at least to secure election of a colleague who might block his actions. Even Cato, that usually strait-laced paragon, consented to a massive bribery fund to assure the success of one optimate, M. Calpurnius Bibulus (Suet. *Iul.* 19.1). Caesar made a very advantageous pact with the wealthy non-noble candidate, Lucceius, whereby the popular Caesar would campaign on behalf of both and Lucceius would similarly distribute bribes.[56] The result was that Caesar and Bibulus were elected and Lucceius was left poorer (ibid.).

Crassus probably lent Caesar his support, too. No doubt,

---

55. That it was Caesar's presence at the *professio*, and not the election, which was held in the Campus Martius outside the *pomerium*, that was the problem has been clearly demonstrated by J. Linderski, "Were Pompey and Crassus Elected in Absence," *Mélanges offerts à K. Michalowski* (Warsaw, 1966): 523–26. Cf. Holmes, *RR* 1, p. 309, and M. Cary, *CAH* 9 (1932), p. 513.

56. This Lucceius was the son of a Marcus, to be distinguished from the scholarly son of Quintus: W. C. McDermott, "De Lucceiis," *Hermes* 97 (1969): 234–46.

Crassus had already looked ahead to Caesar's campaign when he secured his release from importunate creditors, and in view of Caesar's friendly action towards the equestrian creditors in Spain, he could expect a sympathetic attitude from Caesar toward the plight of the Asian tax farmers. One might argue that Caesar would not have needed Lucceius's money if Crassus supported him,[57] but that is not necessarily true. Why should Crassus spend money if Caesar could find another to do it? Indeed, Lucceius sought his *coitio* with Caesar through Arrius, Crassus's close friend, in late 61 (Cic. *Att.* 1.17.11).[58] Probably, Crassus hoped that they would both get elected. In this way he could hope to acquire what the *optimates* had prevented him from obtaining in the Senate.

Another mark of cooperation between Crassus and Caesar may be Crassus's election to the pontificate. A vacancy had occurred in the College of Pontiffs through the death of Catullus in late 61 or early 60, at the latest (Cic. *Att.* 1.16.5, 20.3; Dio 37.46.3). In return for his support of Caesar's election to the consulship, Crassus probably received Caesar's support for election to the pontificate.[59]

Caesar surely also enjoyed the good will of Pompey in the elections. Pompey needed a man who would support his optimate-thwarted desires, and Caesar had pointedly taken stands favorable to Pompey in late 63 and early 62. Accordingly, Pompey, as well as Crassus, hoped to enlist his support as consul (App. *BC* 2.2.9).[60] To argue, however, that Pompey also supported Caesar in no way implies that the coalition of Crassus, Pompey, and Caesar, often designated as the "First Triumvirate," had already come into existence by the elections of 60.[61] At that point, Caesar was dealing with

57. E.g., Grant, *Caesar*, p. 70.
58. Cf. Shackleton Bailey's comment: *Cicero's Letters to Atticus* 1, p. 328.
59. See note 38 above.
60. Caesar's co-candidate, Lucceius, was an ardent Pompeian later in life, but there is no evidence to connect him with Pompey at this stage of his career: Shackleton Bailey, *Cicero's Letters to Atticus* 1, pp. 350–51.
61. Many scholars have seen the coalition in existence by this time: e.g., Th. Mommsen, *History of Rome* 4, trans. W. P. Dickson (New York, 1895), p. 505; C. Merivale, *The Roman Triumvirates* (New York, 1886), p. 70; H. A. Sanders, "The So-Called First Triumvirate," *Memoirs of the American Academy in Rome* 10 (1932): 55–68;

Crassus and Pompey, each independently of the other, and there seems to have been no contact or cooperation between these two old rivals (Vell. Pat. 2.44.1; Dio 37.54.3–4, 56.1; Suet. *Iul.* 19).

No agreement was worked out by all three in relation to one another until later in 60 or possibly even in the first few days of 59. After being elected, Caesar realized that he could not satisfy the hopes of either his two major supporters or himself unless the former were willing to cooperate actively with each other against the opposition of Cato and the other *optimates* (Plut. *Crass.* 14.2; Dio 37.55.1–57.1).[62] He also hoped to make

Carcopino, G. Bloch and J. Carcopino, *Histoire romaine* 2 (Paris, 1929), p. 676–77; Scullard, *From the Gracchi to Nero* ed. 2, pp. 117–18. Sanders (ibid., n. 60) has argued extensively that there must have been a secret agreement among all three before Caesar's election, otherwise Crassus and Pompey each would not have supported him. That is an unwarranted assumption. So long as Caesar promised each one to obtain what he wanted, each would have supported his election in spite of the other: cf. Deknatel, *Vita*, p. 60 and Meier, *RPA*, p. 19.

Most recently, G. R. Stanton and B. A. Marshall have argued for the early existence of an active coalition between Pompey and Crassus behind Caesar: "The Coalition between Pompeius and Crassus, 60–59 B.C.," *Historia* 24 (1975): 205–19. They claim that Crassus's and Pompey's support of Caesar's consular candidacy in 60 must reveal the existence of a coalition that Caesar's offer *ut cum Pompeio Crassum coniungeret* in December of 60 may refer to some other matter than forming a coalition, and that since L. Lucceius and Q. Arrius were connections of Pompey and Crassus, respectively, a coalition between Pompey and Crassus is revealed when Caesar worked through Arrius to make an electoral *coitio* with Lucceius.

On the contrary, that Crassus and Pompey both supported Caesar in the elections of 60 is no proof that they were actually cooperating with each other at that time. Those ancient authors who say that they were, probably based their statements on a deduction from that fact that each supported Caesar. Therefore, the traditional interpretation of Caesar's December offer (Cic. *Att.* 2.3.3) is stronger. The evidence that Lucceius was connected with Pompey in 60 rests on only the evidence of two letters dated not long before 58, and perhaps as late as 48 (Cic. *Fam.* 41, 42: cf. McDermott, "De Lucceiis." *Hermes* 97 (1969): 234–46. If Lucceius had been a partisan of Pompey in 60, Caesar would not have had to work through Crassus's man Arrius to form an electoral *coitio*. He would have worked through Pompey.

62. Cf. Drumann, *Geschichte* 4, p. 100 and Gelzer, *Caesar*, p. 68. At this point, Crassus and Pompey were more worried about optimate opposition to their desires than about each other, as their willingness to acquiesce in each other's backing of Caesar demonstrated. After the election, Caesar had realized that he would have to have more than just the quiet acquiescence of each to his efforts on behalf of the other, and persuaded them to pledge mutual cooperation: see R. Hanslik, "Cicero und das erste Triumvirat," *Rheinisches Museum für Philologie* 98 (1955): 224–34.

Cicero a fourth partner. Cicero's oratorical skill would be in-valuable, his feelings for Pompey were obvious, and his dis-enchantment with Cato must have been clear from his speeches against Cato's motions in the Senate, his departure from Rome (*Att.* 1.20.2–3, 2.1.8), and the breakdown of the concord between Senate and *Equites* that he had prized so greatly.

In late December, Caesar's and Pompey's friend, L. Cornelius Balbus, brought Caesar's proposal to Cicero. In return for Cicero's cooperation, especially on the land bill, Caesar promised that he would follow Cicero's and Pompey's advice in all things and would attempt to unite Crassus with Pompey (Cic. *Att.* 2.3.3). Cicero was tempted. Here was the chance for the close association with Pompey that he had desired since Pompey's return, the opportunity to win the friendship of Caesar, and the prospect of reconciliation with his enemies Crassus and Clodius, with whom he had been on bad terms since Crassus's rescue of Clodius during the *Bona Dea* trial.[63] On the whole, he would be able to be popular with the common people and enjoy a peaceful old age (ibid., 4). Yet, in the end, Cicero decided to stand on principle and resist Caesar's tempting offer.

On the a priori assumption that Crassus, Pompey, and Caesar must have secretly formed a mutual union before Caesar's election, it has been argued that *ad Atticum* 2.3 shows Caesar still attempting to keep it secret by having Balbus say that he would try to unite Crassus with Pompey.[64] It is possible that

63. Cicero himself did not name the "enemies." Sanders equates the word enemies (*inimicis*) with only Clodius: "The So-Called First Triumvirate," *MAAR* 10 (1932): 60. Despite the terrible prospect of prosecution, which Clodius threatened, it seems unlikely that Cicero would have referred to him in the plural. Probably Cicero is referring to both Clodius and his protector, Crassus. Any good will that Crassus had received from Cicero as a result of his laudatory speech in early 61 had been dissipated as a result of his rescue of Clodius later that year. Therefore, Cicero resumed his suspicious hostility towards Crassus.

64. Sanders, "The So-Called First Triumvirate," *MAAR* 10 (1932): 60. Although Dio (37.58.1) says that the "triumvirs" kept their agreement secret for a long time by feigning animosity towards each other, he cannot be used to support this argument. Dio's statement seems to have been predicated upon a desire to moralize as shown by the succeeding material on heavenly portents that would have revealed the existence of the "Triumvirate," if people had paid attention (37.58.2–4). For further arguments against Dio, see E. S. Gruen, "P. Clodius: Instrument or Independent Agent?" *Phoenix* 20 (1966): 126.

Caesar had effected the union by the date of this letter and did not wish to reveal his plans any more than necessary.[65] Perhaps Cicero and the *optimates* would not have believed that Caesar could reconcile these two men without the help of Cicero himself. Nevertheless, if Caesar had already reconciled them, he certainly revealed what he was planning, and his enemies were put on guard if they had a mind to be. Accordingly, his secrecy would have had little point.

On the other hand, it seems more likely that Caesar had not yet worked out an agreement with Crassus and Pompey in concert and was seeking real help from Cicero. Again, Cicero and the *optimates* may have thought that such an agreement could not be made. Nevertheless, a short time later, in the light of Balbus's conversation with Cicero, they saw that Crassus had joined with Pompey in support of Caesar to their undoing.

In January, true to the agreement with his partners, Caesar introduced in the Senate the land bill that Pompey needed in order to satisfy his veterans.[66] Although Caesar tried to make

65. Garzetti argues that the existence of Varro's *Tricaranus*, in combination with Cicero's letter, shows that the "Triumvirate" existed and was known at this time: "Crasso," *Athenaeum* 22 (1944): 10–11. Appian (*BC* 2.2.9), the source of knowledge of Varro's *Tricaranus*, does not provide the kind of chronological exactitude necessary to be certain on this matter, however.

66. L. R. Taylor dates Caesar's action to January; "On the Chronology of Caesar's First Consulship," *American Journal of Philology* 72 (1951): 254–68. This view is based upon the assumption that Caesar held the *fasces* in January because he had been elected at the head of the poll. J. Linderski has argued that since Bibulus postponed the curule elections in July, he, not Caesar, was elected first and held the *fasces* in January, which, like July, is an odd-numbered month: "Constitutional Aspects of the Consular Elections in 59 B.C.," *Historia* 14 (1965): 423–33. L. R. Taylor and T.R.S. Broughton have rebutted his arguments: "The Order of Consuls' Names in Official Republican Lists," *Historia* 17 (1968): 166–72; and L. R. Taylor, "The Dating of Major Legislation and Elections in Caesar's First Consulship," *Historia* 17 (1968): 173–76. That Caesar held the *fasces* in January is confirmed by his giving Crassus priority in debate at the Senate's first meeting of 59 (Suet. *Iul.* 21; Gell. *NA* 4.10.5), a fact that seems to have been overlooked in all previous discussions.

Therefore, two conclusions are possible concerning the relative positions of the consuls Caesar and Bibulus: either Caesar held the *fasces* in January because he was elected at the head of the poll and Bibulus was able to postpone the elections of curule magistrates in July for some other reason; or Bibulus was elected first and, thereby, received charge of the July elections, and Caesar held the *fasces* in January for some other reason.

the bill as fair as possible and proceeded with utmost caution
regarding the feelings of the Senate, the *optimates,* spear-
headed by Cato, Bibulus, and Pompey's arch foe, Lucullus,
vigorously obstructed any favorable action (Plut. *Caes.* 14.1,
Cat. Min. 31.3; App. *BC* 2.2.10; Dio 38.1–3.1).[67] When
Cato made it clear that he would provoke martyrdom in prison
rather than yield, Caesar despaired of obtaining a favorable
decree from the Senate and took his bill directly to the People
(Plut. *Caes.* 14.2–5; Gell. *NA* 4.10.8; Dio 38.3.2–3; App. *BC*
2.2.10).[68] When Bibulus and Cato continued their opposition
in the Forum, Caesar summoned Crassus and Pompey to the
Rostra. Pompey spoke at length about the advantages of the
bill and, when asked if he would assist Caesar against the bill's
opponents, indicated that he would call upon his veterans if
the need arose (Plut. *Pomp.* 47.4–48.1; Dio 38.4.4–5.5). Crassus spoke in a similar vein and stated his agreement with Pompey (Dio 38.5.5). Clearly, Cicero and the *optimates* now had
proof positive that Caesar had reconciled Crassus with Pompey
in a common cause.[69]

At first, Crassus's role in the partnership appears to have
been equal to those of Pompey and Caesar. During the first
meeting of the Senate in January, Caesar honored Crassus by

67. In *Cat. Min.* 31.3, Plutarch adds the name of Cicero, but the
evidence is unclear. In the letter of December 60, Cicero bravely asserts
that his course will be "to fight for the fatherland" (*Att.* 2.3.4). Nowhere,
however, does he say that he overtly opposed the measure. Later, in
explaining Caesar's anger with him, he says that it was because of some
remarks that he had reportedly made in defending his old colleague
Antonius (*Prov. Cons.* 41, cf. *Cael.* 47; Suet. *Iul.* 20.4; Dio 38.10.4).
Of course, if he had opposed the bill, he would not have wished any
record of it to survive.

68. Chr. Meier has dated the passage of this law after 18 February:
"Zur Chronologie und Politik in Caesars ersten Konsulat," *Historia* 10
(1961): 69, n. 2. Taylor has argued more convincingly, however, for
29 January: "The Dating of Major Legislation," *Historia* 17 (1968):
173–82. Plutarch (*Cat. Min.* 33.1–2) and Valerius Maximus (2.10.7)
erroneously connect Cato's arrest with other incidents.

69. Dio (38.5.5) says that the common people were impressed by
Crassus's expression of agreement with Pompey because they did not
realize that they were acting in concert. That may be a fiction in keeping
with Dio's theme of secrecy, but it is possibly true, for the average man
in the street did not have the information on political maneuverings
among the elite that a senator would have. Later, however, the populace
became angry over the control that Caesar exercised with the help of his
friends, especially Pompey (cf. Cic. *Att.* 2.18.1–2, 19.2–3, 20.3–4,
21.1–5).

giving him the right to voice his opinion first in senatorial debate (Suet. *Iul.* 21; Gell. NA 4.10.5). He also made Crassus one of the twenty commissioners for carrying out the provisions of the land bill, a position that would make Crassus a benefactor of many grateful recipients (Dio 38.1.3). In March or April, after having gained passage of the land bill for Pompey, Caesar duly obtained passage of a law to reduce the Asian taxes by one-third, as Crassus had desired in return for his participation in the coalition (Cic. *Att.* 2.16.2, *Planc.* 35; Suet. *Iul.* 20.3; Dio 38.7.4; App. *BC* 2.2.13; Val. Max. 2.10.7).[70]

Crassus probably also participated equally in the decision to effect Clodius's adoption into a plebeian family, which the three allies had previously refused to do. This move was bound to affect Cicero adversely, but he had precipitated it by his own actions. In the first few months of 59, the three had supported a prosecution of C. Antonius upon his return from Macedonia (Cic. *Att.* 2.2.3).[71] In this way, they earned popularity with those who mourned Catiline, whom Antonius had abandoned in response to Cicero's blandishments (Cic. *Flacc.* 95). In recognition of Antonius's service, Cicero defended him and during the course of his speech, revealed his dislike of the political situation at Rome (Suet. *Iul.* 20.4; Dio 38.10.4). That same day, Caesar, as *Pontifex Maximus,* and Pompey, as *augur,* hastily carried out the adoption, so that by Clodius's threat to run for a tribunate and prosecute Cicero they might muzzle further outbursts from the great orator (Cic. *Att.* 2.12.1–2,

70. Cf. Schol. Bob. *ad Planc.* 31, 35, pp. 157, 159 St. Holmes argues that Caesar had not acted on the reduction of the Asian taxes until after July: *RR* 1, p. 323, n. 2. Meier argues more convincingly that the reduction was obtained earlier: "Zur Chronologie," *Historia* 10 (1961): 70.

71. Pompey was already threatening prosecution upon returning from Asia (Cic. *Att.* 1.12.1). M. Gelzer dates the trial in March: "Die Lex Vatinia de imperio Caesaris," *Hermes* 63 (1928): 121. There is a great debate over the charge against him. Some say that it was *vis* (violence): R. Heinze, "Ciceros Rede Pro Caelio," *Hermes* 60 (1925): 211; Ciaceri, *Cicerone* 2, pp. 40–42. Others say *maiestas* (treason): e.g., W. E. Heitland, *The Roman Republic* 3 (Cambridge, 1909), p. 132. Still others say *res repetundae* (extortion): e.g., Holmes, *RR* 1, p. 317; Gelzer, *Caesar,* p. 76. Broughton says both of the latter: *MRR* 2, pp. 175–76. I doubt that, but which of the charges it was must remain uncertain, although E. S. Gruen has argued the case for *res repetundae* as fully as possible: "The Trial of C. Antonius," *Latomus* 32 (1973): 301–10.

Dom. 41, *Prov. Cons.* 45–46; Suet. *Iul.* 20.4).[72] Cicero himself referred to the plans of the three dynasts when he wrote to Atticus in mid-April: "Indeed if the Senate's power was hateful, what do you think the situation will be now that power has been concentrated in the hands of three unfettered individuals?" (*Att.* 2.9.2).[73]

After the initial recognition of Crassus, however, the partnership became more and more unequal to the disadvantage of Crassus. From May 59 until the conference at Luca in April 56, Crassus's influence on Pompey and Caesar became minimal. During this period, a so-called triumvirate can hardly be said to have existed.[74] The turning point seems to have been the passage of the *lex Vatinia,* which gave Caesar command of Cisalpine Gaul and Illyricum as his provinces (Cic. *Vat.* 36, *Prov. Cons.* 36–37; Liv. *Per.* 103; Vell. Pat. 2.44.5; Suet. *Iul.* 22.1; Plut. *Pomp.* 48.3; Dio 38.8.5).[75] Crassus's key assets in

72. Gruen has argued that Clodius was not the mere instrument of Crassus, Pompey, and Caesar and was not engaged by them for the purpose of exiling Cicero: "P. Clodius," *Phoenix* 20 (1966): 122. True enough, but they certainly were using Clodius's well-known hatred of Cicero to frighten Cicero at this point, and they succeeded very well. As for Pompey's earlier refusal to countenance Clodius's *transitio* (Cic. *Att.* 1.18.4–5, *Har. Resp.* 45), that was before the formation of the coalition with Crassus and Caesar, and he probably feared Clodius as a friend of Crassus.

73. Sanders argues that the *tres homines immoderatos* are Pompey, Caesar, and Clodius: "The So-Called First Triumvirate," *MAAR* 10 (1932): 61. The next line of the letter, "Let them make consuls and tribunes whomever they want . . . ," seems to show that Cicero was not referring to Clodius among the three. Clodius was one of those whom the three principal actors were going to place in positions useful to them.

74. Cf. D. Stockton, *Cicero: A Political Biography* (London, 1971), p. 182 (although he does not see the coalition weakened until 58) and R. J. Rowland, Jr., "Crassus, Clodius, and Cicero in the Year 59 B.C.," *Historia* 15 (1966): 217–23. Sanders's argument that the existence of the "Triumvirate" was unknown to Cicero because his letters during this period bring only Caesar and Pompey, but not Crassus, into the picture is, therefore, unconvincing: "The So-Called First Triumvirate," *MAAR* 10 (1932): 61–68.

75. Meier has convincingly dated the passage of the *lex Vatinia de Caesaris Provincia* to March or early April of 59: "Zur Chronologie," *Historia* 10 (1961): 69–88; cf. Shackleton Bailey, *Cicero's Letters to Atticus* 1, p. 408. L. R. Taylor, defending her earlier position, argued that the bill was only promulgated by fairly early March, but was not voted until one of the first comitial days in the second half of May: "On the Chronology of Caesar's First Consulship," *American Journal of Philology* 72 (1951): 254–68; "The Dating of Major Legislation and Elections in Caesar's First Consulship," *Historia* 17 (1968): 182–87. Her main arguments are that while, according to Suetonius (*Iul.* 22.1),

the original coalition were his influence with the *Equites* and, to some extent, his financial support. The strength of these assets was easily diluted, however: Pompey, too, had considerable support among the *Equites*; after Caesar obtained passage of the tax bill, in his own name, he could have hoped to count on the good will of many *Equites* for himself; [76] Pompey could easily rival Crassus's financial resources because of his Eastern conquests; [77] and Caesar gained financially as a result of an immense bribe that he received from Ptolemy Auletes in return for the passage of a law recognizing the latter's right to the ancient throne of Egypt (Suet. *Iul.* 54.3; Dio 39.12.1). Finally, after the passage of the *lex Vatinia* guaranteed him military power, Caesar no longer needed Crassus's support. Pompey, on the other hand, was still a force with which to be reckoned. He had the armed strength of his loyal veterans, which could be very dangerous to Caesar if his cooperation were not secured. Moreover, Pompey wanted loyal

---

Caesar's father-in-law, L. Piso, and his son-in-law, Pompey, helped to obtain passage of the law, these marriage alliances were not made until the end of April or the first few days in May (Cic. *Att.* 2.16.1), that Cicero's reference to Caesar's army in a letter of 29 April or 1 May refers to the army that Vatinius's law would give him when finally passed, and that the *supplicatio* for Pomptinus had nullified the comitial days that ordinarily would have been available for a vote on the *lex Vatinia* in late March or early April. To the first point, it must be replied that the sequence of events in Suetonius, *Iul.* 21 and 22, is all confused. He places the marriages at about the same time as the Vettius affair, which Taylor would date no earlier than late July: "The Dating of Major Legislation," *Historia* 17 (1968): 190–93. Therefore, the accuracy of his details is open to question. Furthermore, after saying that with the support of his father-in-law and son-in-law, Caesar chose the Gauls as his province, Suetonius backtracks and says that first, by the *lex Vatinia*, he received only Cisalpine Gaul and Illyricum. Therefore, it is quite possible that the support of the two in-laws should be connected with only the later grant of Transalpine Gaul. Secondly, Cicero's reference to Caesar's army is so concrete that it seems more probable that the first two provinces, with their three legions, had already been voted: cf. Shackleton Bailey, *Cicero's Letters to Atticus* 1, p. 408. As for the third point, the protest that Caesar's men made over the *supplicatio* of Pomptinus is connected with its implication of a military victory, which would make a special assignment of Transalpine Gaul to Caesar appear unnecessary, rather than with the loss of comitial days (cf. note 83). For the same reason, Caesar's partisans held up the grant of Pomptinus's triumph until 54, when Caesar and Pompey were away from Rome: Broughton, *MRR* 2, p. 225.

76. His later anger when the *Equites* offended him in the theater can be readily understood (*Att.* 2.19.3).

77. E. Badian, *Roman Imperialism in the Late Republic* (Ithaca, N. Y., 1968), p. 82.

men with power to help him dominate Roman politics. Caesar could be useful to him, but he would not trust Crassus, who was more his equal in rank and dignity.

As a result, Crassus saw Caesar move away from him and establish closer ties with Pompey. Pompey and Caesar began to manage affairs so much to their own liking, without regard to Crassus, that it would be more accurate to say that Rome was under the domination of an informal duumvirate of Pompey and Caesar.[78] First of all, Caesar forged a much stronger bond between himself and Pompey than ever existed between him and Crassus. In late April, shortly after the adoption of Clodius, Caesar suddenly made Pompey his son-in-law through marriage to his daughter, Julia (Cic. *Att.* 2.17.1; Suet. *Iul.* 21; Plut. *Caes.* 14.4, *Pomp.* 47.6; App. *BC* 2.2.14; Dio 38.9.1). Concomitantly, and contrary to all precedent, Caesar began to call on Pompey first in senatorial debate instead of Crassus, to whom he had given the honor at the start of the year (Suet. *Iul.* 21; Gell. *NA* 4.10.5).

Crassus soon found himself denied other political spoils as well. Earlier in April, it had been rumored by some that the consuls of 58 were to be Pompey and Crassus (Cic. *Att.* 2.5.2). Though they probably were not planning to hold office themselves, it is a mark of how they were working together early in the year for people to consider it possible. Clearly, Crassus's good friend Arrius did expect to be rewarded with one of the consular posts, probably along with Pompey's loyal partisan A. Gabinius. Suddenly, however, he found himself thrust aside in favor of Caesar's new father-in-law, L. Calpurnius Piso (Cic. *Att.* 2.5.2, 7.3; Suet. *Iul.* 21; Plut. *Caes.* 14.5, *Cat. Min.* 33.4, *Pomp.* 48.3). Caesar wanted a man loyal to him alone in office while he was away on his provincial command. Crassus was less to be feared than Pompey. Therefore, Caesar was willing to abandon Crassus's candidate to reach his goal.

Caesar's ambitions also led him to run roughshod over Crassus's interests in the matter of Transalpine Gaul. The *lex Vatinia* had given Caesar command of only Cisalpine Gaul and Illyricum with three legions (Suet. *Iul.* 22.1; Plut. *Pomp.*

78. Cf. R. J. Rowland, Jr., "Crassus, Clodius, and Cicero," *Historia* 15 (1966): 220.

48.3; Dio 38.8.5).[79] These provinces and legions would have given him a powerful position but one still short of his and even Pompey's desires. The real opportunity lay in the provincial command of the region beyond the Alps. He could capitalize on unrest there and in the Gallic states beyond the province of Gallia Transalpina to create an emergency and justify a great war for his own aggrandizement.

The revolt of the Allobroges and the movements of Germans and Helvetians in the regions beyond had already prompted the Senate to decree in March 60 that the consuls, Metellus Celer and Afranius, should recruit armies and cast lots for the two Gallic provinces (Caes. *BGall.* 1.31.3–11; Cic. *Att.* 1.19.2). Pompey's man, Afranius, probably took command of Cisalpina in 59,[80] but Celer died suddenly in April 59 without having left Rome. Caesar and Pompey seized upon the death of the assigned governor to have Transalpina reassigned to Caesar himself, with the power to protect Roman interests in the Gallic lands beyond (Suet. *Iul.* 22.1; Cic. *Att.* 8.3.3).[81]

Up to this point, Pomptinus, who had been Crassus's legate in 71, had been governing Transalpina as pro-praetor.[82] Caesar obtained the province at his expense. In the ordinary course of events, Pomptinus probably would have had his command prorogued upon the death of his ill-fated successor, Celer. No doubt, Crassus, too, who had no military power, in contrast with Pompey and Caesar, would have preferred that his friend Pomptinus retain control of that strategic province. Pompey and Caesar, however, mounted a campaign to discredit him.

Pomptinus had successfully put down the rebellion of the

79. Plutarch (*Caes.* 14.6) does not distinguish between the grants of the two Gauls, and he lists four legions. Dio (38.8.5) gives a figure of three legions in connection with Cisalpina and Illyricum. The fourth legion probably was added with the later grant of Transalpina. Orosius (6.7.1) says that the *lex Vatinia* gave him the three provinces and seven legions. This figure appears to be a conflation of Plutarch's and Dio's.
80. Broughton, *MRR* 2, p. 190.
81. Pompey's tribune, Flavius, had threatened to deny Transalpina to Celer (Dio 37.50.4). Apparently, however, he had not carried out his threat, for the death of Celer would not have mattered if he had. Concerning the reassignment of the province, Suetonius refers to Gallia Comata, which is the term applied to the hitherto independent Gallic states beyond Transalpina; cf. Holmes, *RR* 1, pp. 325–26.
82. Broughton, *MRR* 2, p. 176.

Allobroges (Dio 37.47.1–48.2; Cic. *Prov. Cons.* 32; Caes. *BGall.* 1.31.3–11), and the Senate had gratefully decreed a *supplicatio* in his honor (Cic. *Vat.* 30). A *supplicatio* included public worship of the state gods and, upon a great victory, large-scale festivities (*Liv.* 22.10.8; Plut. *Caes.* 21.1–2). As part of the festivities during Pomptinus's *supplicatio*, Crassus's friend Q. Arrius, who was then hoping for a consulship, put on a public banquet in honor of his deceased father (Cic. *Vat.* 30; Schol. Bob. *ad Vat.* 30, 149–50 St). Arrius's expenditures were so great that this banquet became proverbial for its lavishness (Hor. *Sat.* 2.3.85–86).

Caesar undermined the impact of these events and belittled Pomptinus's accomplishments through both his friend, the tribune Vatinius, and others. They publicly showed contempt for the *supplicatio* and festivities sponsored by Arrius when they appeared in black at the temple of Castor during Arrius's banquet. Protocol demanded white for such occasions (Cic. *Vat.* 30–32; Schol. Bob. *ad Vat.* 30, 149–50 St). By publicly derogating Pomptinus's *supplicatio*, Caesar wished to advertise his claim that there was still an emergency in Transalpine Gaul that would justify adding it to his command of Cisalpina and Illyricum.[83] Thus Crassus's men were sacrificed to the ambitions of Pompey and Caesar. Crassus himself was clearly falling into a position inferior to that of his erstwhile partners.

Already, by mid-April, Cicero at Antium suspected that all was not well among the three (*Att.* 2.7.3). He saw that one possible source of division was over the question of what to do with Clodius. It seemed that Caesar was reneging on several promises, including a tribunate.[84] He also noted the disap-

---

83. Cf. Gelzer, *Caesar*, p. 86. Taylor argued that Caesar was not challenging the validity of Pomptinus's victory but was protesting the loss of comitial days for his legislative program: "The Dating of Major Legislation," *Historia* 17 (1968): 186–87. Her argument is that if he had been attacking the basis of the *supplicatio*, he would have opposed its granting; he did not, because Pomptinus was Crassus's friend. She goes on to assert that Caesar's loyal tribune, Vatinius, disgraced the *supplicatio* in protest over the loss of comitial days. The argument cannot work both ways. Caesar can hardly have been concerned about Crassus's feelings if he let the latter's friends, Pomptinus and Arrius, be publicly disgraced.

84. . . . subcontumeliose tractatur noster Publius, primum qui, cum domi Caesaris quondam unus vir fuerit, nunc ne in viginti quidem esse potuerit; deinde alia legatio dicta erat, alia data est. illa opima ad exigendas pecunias Druso, ut opinor, Pisaurensi an epuloni Vatinio reservatur; haec ieiuna tabellari legatio datur ei cuius tribunatus ad

pointed expectations of Arrius and the anger of a certain Megabocchus, who was one of Crassus's youthful supporters (ibid.).[85] He further took heart when Atticus hinted at disagreement among the members of a certain board of *quinqueviri* (*Att.* 2.7.4). On 19 April, he still considered the three men as a unit (*Att.* 2.9.1–2).[86] Then, after the marriage between Pompey and Julia in late April, the alienation of Crassus was clear (*Att.* 2.17.1, 21.1–4).[87] The "Triumvirate" seemed to be breaking apart.

The years from 62 to 59 marked a series of compromises and shifts by which Crassus sought a position for furthering his political ambitions in the face of Pompey's return to Rome. In 62, he boldly negotiated a *modus vivendi* with Pompey, only to see his plans shattered by Pompey's unexpected considerateness towards the optimate-dominated Senate. Consequently, Crassus himself sought the cooperation of the *optimates* and Cicero, with whom he had often been at odds as he sought political eminence at Rome. In this way, he hoped to prevent Cicero from drawing Pompey into harmony with the *optimates*.

This shift in tactics is evidenced in several ways. First, he helped Cicero purchase a house that he owned on the Palatine for much less than he otherwise could have sold it. More importantly, in 61, he gave a public speech that strongly praised Cicero's consulship and earned the orator's surprised gratitude. Also, probably in 62 or early 61, Crassus married his son, Marcus, to the daughter of Q. Caecilius Metellus Creticus, an optimate foe of Pompey. Finally, he cooperated with two lead-

---

istorum tempora reservatur. incende hominem, amabo te, quoad potest. una spes est salutis istorum inter ipsos discensio; cuius ego quaedam initia sensi ex Curione.

In this passage the word *istorum* refers to the "triumvirs."

85. Cf. Rowland, "Crassus, Clodius, and Cicero," *Historia* 15 (1966): 221 and Shackleton Bailey, *Cicero's Letters to Atticus* 1, p. 366.

86. Cicero's words *his dynastis* and *tres homines immoderatos* are clear references to the "triumvirs."

87. Sanders took this reference to Crassus's enjoyment of Pompey's ill-repute as proof that Cicero was unaware of Crassus's union with Pompey and Caesar: "The So-Called First Triumvirate," *MAAR* 10 (1932): 61–62. Rather, it ought to be taken as an indication of Crassus's rupture with his former colleagues. Only three other letters of Cicero intervene between *Att.* 2.17 (written in early May) and *Att.* 2.21 (written after 25 July). If there were more, earlier specific confirmations of Crassus's difficulties with the other two probably would be found.

ing *optimates*, L. Lucullus and M. Cato, to block confirmation of Pompey's *acta* in the East.

Unfortunately, later in 61, he seriously jeopardized himself with the *optimates*, when he corruptly obtained the acquittal of P. Clodius on a charge of sacrilege in the infamous *Bona Dea* affair. A complete break with the *optimates* came in 60, when Crassus supported the revision of the tax contracts for the province of Asia. To overcome the shortsighted opposition of Cato and other *optimates* on this question, he supported the election of his old ally Caesar to the consulship, after the latter had returned newly strengthened from governing Spain.

Independently, Caesar also obtained Pompey's support by promising to overcome the *optimates'* opposition to his desires. Late in 60, or possibly in the first few days of 59, Crassus made his greatest compromise thus far, when he agreed, through Caesar's good offices, to cooperate with Pompey, and the three men formed the coalition known as the First Triumvirate. As a result, Crassus finally gained the relief that he desired for the collectors of the Asian taxes.

Not long thereafter, however, Crassus found that Pompey and Caesar were concentrating more and more on their interests to the detriment of his. After the passage of the *lex Vatinia*, Caesar did not really need Crassus's support, and Pompey always distrusted him. Their alienation of Crassus can be seen in the marriage of Caesar's daughter to Pompey and in Caesar's disregard of the ambitions of Crassus's friends, Pomptinus and Arrius. Now, Crassus had to deal with two dangerous rivals.

Appendix VIII

Calvus ex Nanneianis

Nosti Calvum ex Nanneianis illum, illum laudatorem meum,
de cuius oratione erga me honorifica ad te scripseram. Biduo
per unum servum et eum ex ludo gladiatorio confecit totum
negotium: arcessivit ad se, promisit intercessit dedit. Iam vero
(o di boni, rem perditam!) etiam noctes certarum mulierum
atque adulescentulorum nobilium introductiones non nullis
iudicibus pro mercedis cumulo fuerunt. (Cic. Att. 1.16.5)

Many scholars have tried to identify the *Calvus ex Nanneianis*
in the passage above, where Cicero explains how P. Clodius
escaped conviction at his trial for sacrilege in the infamous
Bona Dea affair. A large number have identified him with
Marcus Crassus: *Calvus,* if meant with a small "c," may refer
to a prominent physical characteristic of Crassus; with a
capital "C," it also is a cognomen of one branch of Crassus's
gens, the Licinian; and most accept the mention of the
honorific speech as a clear reference to Crassus's praise of
Cicero earlier in 61 (Cic. *Att.* 1.14.3). The phrase *ex Nanneianis,* therefore, is explained as a reference to one of Crassus's notorious purchases during the Sullan proscriptions.[1]

Frank and Hathorn, however, have seen this reference as
one to Crassus's younger contemporary, the neoteric poet C.
Licinius Macer Calvus.[2] Their arguments are weak. Frank
conjectured that the word *Nanneianis,* derived from the Greek

1. For Bosius, Casaubon, Gronovius, and Manutius, cf. the *variorum*
edition of 1684. For more modern writers, cf. Chr. Deknatel, *De Vita*
M. Licinii Crassi (Diss., Leyden, 1901), pp. 50–51; R. Y. Tyrrell and
L. C. Purser, *The Correspondence of M. Tullius Cicero* 1 (Dublin and
London, 1904), pp. 212–13; L. A. Constans, *Cicéron: Correspondance*
1 (Paris, 1934), #22 and p. 284; A. Garzetti, "M. Licinio Crasso,"
Athenaeum 22 (1944): 3, n. 4; M. Gelzer, *Caesar, Politician and States-*
man, trans. P. Needham (Cambridge, Mass., 1968), p. 60; D. R.
Shackleton Bailey, *Cicero's Letters to Atticus* 1 (Cambridge, 1965),
pp. 316–17; D. Stockton, *Cicero: A Political Biography* (London, 1971),
p. 160, n. 36.
2. T. Frank, "Cicero and the Novi Poetae," *American Journal of*
Philology 40 (1919): 396–98; R. Y. Hathorn, "*Calvum ex Nanneianis,*"
Classical Journal 50 (1954): 33–34.

word νάννος (which is the equivalent of the Latin *barbatus*), was a translation of the Latin *barbatulis* in reference to the short beards affected by the fast set of young men with whom the *Novi Poetae* were associated (cf. Cic. *Att.* 1.14.5, 16.11). Hathorn rightly rejected this argument as being farfetched. Nevertheless, his own conjecture, that *Nanneianis* signifies the New Poets by an allusion to Nanno, mistress of the Greek poet Mimnermus, though it makes more sense, fails linguistically. The diphthong *ei* represents a long *i*. An adjective derived from Nanno would be *Nannianus* with a short *i* as in *Ciceronianus*.[3]

While he has ignored several telling points against the identification with Licinius Macer Calvus,[4] Wiseman has adduced several other weak arguments in favor of it. He claims that if the reference were to Crassus, the word *Calvus* would contain an almost obscene double entendre to which Cicero would not have stooped.[5] Those who know the *scurra consularis*, however, have no qualms about believing Cicero to be capable of an occasional well-placed obscenity (e.g., *Att.* 2.1.5).[6] Similarly untenable is the argument that it would not have been compatible with Crassus's *dignitas* and good reputation for him to have been personally involved in these sordid dealings.[7] Crassus was no Victorian gentleman.[8] Furthermore, Cicero makes it clear in the passage quoted that at least part of the dirty work was carried out by a slave.

Finally, it is difficult to accept Wiseman's hypothesis about the textual corruption of the Greek NEANÍAIΣ (which would have been written in Roman characters, as so often with Greek words in the manuscripts of Cicero's letters) to NEANIANIS (to make it look like a normal Latin ablative) and then further

---

3. Cf. C. D. Buck, *A Comparative Grammar of Greek and Latin* (Chicago, 1933), p. 86. Or the adjective might have been Nannicus: T. P. Wiseman, "Two Friends of Clodius in Cicero's Letters," *Classical Quarterly* 18 (1968): 299.

4. Cf. I. Trencsényi-Waldapfel, "Calvus ex Nanneianis," *Athenaeum* 43 (1965): 42–51.

5. Wiseman, "Two Friends of Clodius," *CQ* 18 (1968): 297–98.

6. Cf. W. C. McDermott, "In Caelianam," *Athenaeum* 48 (1970): 408–9; "Cicero: The Human Side," *Classical Bulletin* 49 (1972): 17–25. That there was any obscenity intended here, however, may be doubted: P. W. Fulford-Jones, "Calvus ex Nanneianis," *Classical Quarterly* 21 (1971): 183–84.

7. Wiseman, "Two Friends of Clodius," *CQ* 18 (1968): 297.

8. Of course, the account of the activities surrounding the subversion of the jurors was probably slanderously exaggerated: cf. Fulford-Jones, "Calvus ex Nanneianis," *CQ* 21 (1971): 185.

corrupted to NANNEIANIS.[9] Although his explanation seems to be a reasonable one for the end of the word, it seems highly unlikely that the E would have dropped out in the first syllable. Moreover, if such a process had taken place, one might expect to find some evidence for it in the textual tradition. The manuscripts, however, show no trace of it.[10]

It is still best to see *Calvum ex Nanneianis* as a reference to Crassus. The probability in favor of this interpretation is greater than any other because of Cicero's reference to the honorific speech about which he had written earlier in the year.[11] In February, Cicero wrote to Atticus and expressed his pleasure at a very flattering speech that Crassus had delivered concerning his services as consul (*Att.* 1.14.3). The letter currently in question was written some months later, in July (*Att.* 1.16). It is possible that other letters besides 1.15 intervened, but Trencsényi-Waldapfel has clearly demonstrated that Licinius Macer Calvus was in no position to make a speech honoring Cicero.[12] Therefore, the most likely way in which Cicero's mention of the *oratione erga me honorifica* can be taken is as a reference to the speech of Crassus described in *Att.* 1.14.3.

In this case, however, the meaning of *ex Nanneianis* has been interpreted in two different ways. One has been set forth recently by Trencsényi-Waldapfel. He has equated *Nanneianis* with an adjective derived from Nannion, a common name for courtesans in Greek and the title of a comedy by Eubulus (or Philippus), so that *ex Nanneianis* would be translated as "one of the affiliates of Nannion."[13] He supports this conjecture with a fragment of the play to show that such a description as this would befit the protector of Clodius.

Cicero's correspondence with Atticus is replete with allusions to Greek literature, and it is not at all difficult to imagine

9. Wiseman, "Two Friends of Clodius," *CQ* 18 (1968): 299. That it was a corrupted Greek word was suggested by Boot and Tyrrell and Purser: cf. Tyrrell and Purser, *Correspondence* 1, p. 213.

10. Cf. L. C. Purser, M. *Tulli Ciceronis Epistulae* 2.1 (Oxford, 1903), *App. Crit. ad Att.* 1.16.5.

11. Fulford-Jones, "Calvus ex Nanneianis," *CQ* 21 (1971): 183–84. E. S. Gruen has rejected this interpretation rather summarily, without taking into account the number of points in its favor: "P. Clodius: Instrument or Independent Agent?" *Phoenix* 20 (1966): 121–22; *The Last Generation of the Roman Republic* (Berkely and Los Angeles, 1974), p. 275, n. 58.

12. Trencsényi-Waldapfel, "Calvus ex Nanneianis," *Athenaeum* 43 (1965): 42–47.

13. Ibid., pp. 49–51.

Atticus perceiving a reference to a famous Attic comic poet. That Cicero may have had Greek literature in mind even at this point in the letter is indicated by the quotation from the *Iliad* with which he opened this segment of the letter. It is also interesting to note that one of the characters in the *Nannion* is the nauarch, Kydias. He has been interpreted as a parody of the man who was working for the colonization of Samos by Athens in the middle of the fourth century.[14] That raises the question of a possible parallel with Crassus and his efforts to procure the annexation of Egypt in 65.

Nevertheless, Trencsényi-Waldapfel's derivation of *Nanneianis* ultimately must be rejected on linguistic grounds. It does not seem likely that the short iota of the name Nannion in Greek would yield a Latin adjective *Nanneianus* with an *ei* diphthong.[15] Therefore, the other explanation of *ex Nanneianis* as a reference to Crassus is the preferable one.

This explanation has already been mentioned, namely, that it is a reference to the proscription of a certain Nannius (Q. Cic. *Com. Pet.* 9), from which Crassus had probably benefited financially. The incident may well have been so infamous that people who had benefited from the proscription of Nannius and others had become proverbially identified as *Nanneiani*. There is no problem in equating the *Nanniorum* in the MSS of the *Commentariolum Petitionis* with the genitive plural of *Nanneius*, the root of *Nanneianis*. In this period there was great ambiguity between the use of the diphthong *ei* and long *i*.[16] Therefore, the name *Nannius* is probably the same as that of *Nanneius* found on several inscriptions (CIL 6.37484–5, 38700a, 10.498), and Watt justifiably prints *Nanneiorum* (with a reference to Cic. *Att.* 1.16.5) instead of *Nanniorum* in his edition of the *Commentariolum Petitionis*.[17]

In conclusion, the traditional interpretation of *Calvus ex Nanneianis* as a reference to Crassus is the strongest possible explanation of the phrase, and Crassus should be seen as the prime mover behind Clodius's scandalous acquittal in the *Bona Dea* affair.

14. Cf. G. Kaibel, *RE* 6.1 (1907), 878, s.v. "Eubulos" (14).
15. Cf. Buck, *Grammar*, p. 86.
16. Ibid.
17. W. S. Watt, *M. Tulli Ciceronis Epistulae* 3 (Oxford, 1958), p. 195.

IX

Outmaneuvering Pompey and Caesar

After being pushed aside in 59, Crassus strove to recover his position against Pompey and Caesar until the "Triumvirate" was renewed on a basis more equitable to him in April 56. By harassing Pompey and weakening his position at Rome, Crassus helped drive him to seek closer ties with Cicero and with Caesar's enemies in the Senate. Thus a wedge was driven between Pompey and Caesar. Crassus was then able to persuade Caesar to help force Pompey into an arrangement more to Crassus's own liking.

Ironically, it was to Crassus's advantage that he had fallen into the background, as compared with his supposed partners. He escaped the unpopularity that the other two suffered as 59 progressed (cf. Cic. *Att.* 2.19). Accordingly, he hoped to utilize and increase their unpopularity to his benefit. To this end, he was aided by two ambitious and talented young nobles, P. Clodius and C. Scribonius Curio the Younger, son of the consul of 76.

Crassus's connection with Clodius may be seen as early as 61 in the role that he played in saving Clodius from condemnation in the trial for profaning the rites of the *Bona Dea*. In 59, within a few weeks prior to late April, he probably had also supported Clodius's adoption into a plebeian family, so that the latter could run for the tribunate.

Curio's connection with Crassus can be seen through Clodius. He was a close friend of Clodius. His father had supported Clodius in the Senate and defended him at his trial in 61 (Cic. *Att.* 1.14.5, 16.1),[1] and he himself had led a band of young Turks who had demonstrated for Clodius at the as-

---

1. For a recent study of the career of Curio *pater*, see W. C. McDermott, "Curio *Pater* and Cicero," *American Journal of Philology* 93 (1972): 381–411.

sembly (ibid., 14.5). In 59, he was a close confidant of Clodius (Cic. *Att.* 2.7.3, 8.1, 12.2) and later married his widow, Fulvia (Cic. *Phil.* 2.11, 115).[2]

That is not to say that either of these men was the tool or henchman of Crassus. In particular, the question of Clodius's relationship with other leading figures during this period has exercised students of Roman history for a long time. One scholar or another has viewed him as a loyal subordinate of Crassus, Pompey, and Caesar either separately, together, or in combinations with two of the three; still others have viewed him as a completely independent agent working for his own ends.[3] Clearly, Clodius had built up a powerful political position based on a following of young nobles and the urban plebs from 63 onward.[4] Certainly he was a power in his own right and had goals of his own to pursue.[5] As would any politician, however, he made alliances with others whose interests were similar or who were willing to cooperate with him in return for

2. C. Babcock sees the marriage as taking place most likely between April and August of 51: "The Early Career of Fulvia," *American Journal of Philology* 86 (1965): 9, n. 19. For Curio's relationship with Clodius, see R. Seager, "Clodius, Pompeius, and the Exile of Cicero," *Latomus* 24 (1965): 522–23.

3. Agent of Crassus: Chr. Deknatel, *De Vita M. Licinii Crassi* (Diss., Leyden, 1901), pp. 78–79; F. B. Marsh, "The Policy of P. Clodius from 58–56 B.C.," *Classical Quarterly* 21 (1927): 30–36; R. Syme, *The Roman Revolution* (Oxford, 1939), p. 36; R. J. Rowland, Jr., "Crassus, Clodius, and Curio in the year 59 B.C.," *Historia* 15 (1966): 217–23. Caesar: L. G. Pocock, "Publius Clodius and the Acts of Caesar," *Classical Quarterly* 18 (1924): 59–65; M. Grant, *Julius Caesar* (London, 1969), pp. 90–93. Crassus and Caesar: T. J. Cadoux, "Marcus Crassus: A Revaluation," *Greece and Rome* 2nd ser. 3 (1956): 158; M. Cary, *CAH* 9 (1932): 522. All three: R. Syme, *Sallust* (Berkely and Los Angeles, 1964), p. 24; A. Garzetti, "M. Licinio Crasso," *Athenaeum* 22 (1944): 14. Independent: G. Bloch, *La république romaine: les conflicts politiques et socieux* (Paris, 1919), p. 319; E. S. Gruen, "P. Clodius: Instrument or Independent Agent?" *Phoenix* 20 (1966): 120–30; A. W. Lintott, "P. Clodius Pulcher-*Felix Catilina?*" *Greece and Rome* 14 (1967): 157–69.

4. A. W. Lintott, *Violence in Republican Rome* (Oxford, 1968), pp. 193–200. Cf. E. S. Gruen, "P. Clodius: Instrument or Independent Agent?" *Phoenix* 20 (1966): 120–30.

5. For example, although Crassus, Pompey, and Caesar all had reasons for not wanting Cato in Rome, there is no necessity to argue, as Oost does, that Clodius was working for them in sending Cato to Cyprus: S. I. Oost, "Cato Uticensis and the Annexation of Cyprus," *Classical Philology* 50 (1955): 98; cf. Plutarch, *Cat. Min.* 34. Cato was as much of a threat to Clodius as he was to any of the other three: cf. Lintott, "P. Clodius," *G&R* 14 (1967): 166.

some useful service on his part.[6] Of course, when an alliance was no longer to his benefit, he would not hesitate to switch his allegiance.[7]

After April 59, Clodius shared a common interest with Crassus—dislike of the dominant position being assumed by Pompey and Caesar. Just as they had shoved Crassus into the background, so they had tried to clip Clodius's budding wings. After having successfully frightened Cicero by effecting Clodius's adoption in March, Pompey and Caesar decided that he might be too dangerous to themselves if his ambitions were left unchecked.[8] By mid-April, Caesar already had denied him a position on the board of twenty land commissioners, and he and Pompey sought to gain veto power over his tribunician plans by sending him off on a *legatio* to Tigranes of Armenia (Cic. *Att.* 2.7.2–3). It was a second-rate post at that, and a better one that had been originally offered was now destined for one of Caesar's close friends like Vatinius (ibid.). It has even been suggested that an embassy to Tigranes, Pompey's client, could have meant more than mere delay for Clodius if they thought it expedient.[9] When Clodius did not subordinate himself to their desires, they went so far as to deny that they had taken part in any adoption and thereby sought to cast doubt on the legality of his campaign for the tribunate (Cic. *Att.* 2.12).

Not to be cowed so easily, and confident of his own strength, Clodius campaigned as Caesar's enemy. He threatened, if elected, to rescind Caesar's legislation (ibid.). If this threat were carried out, Crassus would have little to lose and much to gain. The piece of legislation that had been of intense interest to him was the law revising the Asian taxes for his friends the tax farmers. The only other loss would have been the potential *gratia* of those who would have benefited from his work on the land commission. Pompey, however, would have lost the land for his veterans and the confirmation of his Eastern

6. Lintott, *Violence in Republican Rome*, pp. 191–95.
7. Lintott, "P. Clodius Pulcher," *G&R* 14 (1967): 162; Gruen, "P. Clodius," *Phoenix* 20 (1966): 130.
8. Lintott, ibid.; Gruen, ibid., 123; R. Seager, "Clodius, Pompeius, and the Exile of Cicero," *Latomus* 24 (1965): 520–22; D. Stockton, *Cicero: A Political Biography* (London, 1971), p. 179.
9. Seager, ibid., 521, n. 1.

settlement, while Caesar would have lost his provinces and all-important legions.[10]

To counter Clodius, Caesar now sought to protect Cicero, whom he had previously intimidated by sanctioning Clodius's transfer to plebeian status. He offered Cicero a legateship, a free embassy, or a position on the new land commission (ibid., 2.18.3, 19.4–5). Still, as Clodius continued his attacks, a rising tide of hostility towards Caesar and Pompey was obvious (ibid., 2.18.1–2).[11] Caesar's opposition to Clodius's election was blocked by three important individuals: the younger Curio, the praetorian candidate C. Memmius, and, apparently, Metellus Nepos, Pompey's former brother-in-law and Clodius's cousin or stepbrother (ibid., 8.1, 18.1–2).[12] They reveal the strength of Clodius's support. Curio was particularly prominent. He was heartily applauded and greeted with great honor in the Forum; even the *optimates* looked on with favor (ibid., 18.1).

By early July, popular discontent had risen very high (ibid., 19.2). At the gladiatorial games, the sponsor, probably Pompey's consular candidate, Gabinius, was hissed (ibid., 19.3).[13]

10. Seager (ibid.) argued that Caesar was not threatened because the laws benefiting him had not yet been passed. As stated earlier, Meier has shown that the *lex Vatinia* giving Caesar command of Cisalpine Gaul and Illyricum had been passed by early April: Chapter Eight, p. 220, n. 75. Nor did Clodius threaten only the *leges Iuliae* at this time, but everything—*omnia* (Cic. *Att.* 2.12.2). Marsh argued that the tax farmers had already received their profits and would not have suffered from repeal: "The Policy of Clodius," *CQ* 21 (1927): 33. Since the contract was for five years, however, Crassus's friends among the contractors for the Asian taxes still may have been in jeopardy. Nevertheless, it would have been a small price for Crassus to pay compared with the losses to be suffered by Caesar and Pompey.

11. He also attacked the opponents of Caesar and Pompey, a fact that left Cicero confused (*Att.* 2.27.1). These moves were not primarily intended as a smoke screen to leave Cicero in uncertainty, however, but were part of his program of currying popular opinion, which was running unfavorably against both camps (cf. ibid., 22.1).

12. Memmius was related to Curio. According to Seager, Memmius at one point gave his daughter in marriage to either Curio or Curio's son: "Clodius," *Latomus* 24 (1965), 523. That view seems incorrect. Rather, Curio was related to Memmius through his mother: T. P. Wiseman, "Lucius Memmius and his Family," *Classical Quarterly* 17 (1967): 164–67. Interestingly, Metellus Nepos is also found intriguing for Clodius's election to the aedileship in 57 (Cic. *Att.* 4.3.3–4, *Dom.* 13, *Sest.* 89; Dio, 39.7.4).

13. D. R. Shackleton Bailey, *Cicero's Letters to Atticus* 1 (Cambridge, 1965), pp. 389–90.

At the *ludi Apollinares*, the actor Diphilus was vociferously applauded when he delivered lines that seemed aimed against Pompey. A hush of silent disapproval greeted Caesar when he took his seat. Curio, conversely, was given a hero's hand, and the *Equites*, who held the first fourteen rows of seats as a mark of honor, even rose to their feet (ibid.). Many of these men were Crassus's friends. Indeed, the *lex Roscia*, which had given them their seats of honor may have been inspired by Crassus.[14]

Caesar immediately sent a letter to Pompey, who was overseeing land distribution in Campania, to apprise him of their deteriorating situation. Rumors of retaliation spread. It was said that they were planning to repeal the *lex Roscia* as a punishment for the *Equites* and abolish or limit the distribution of grain for the urban plebs (ibid.). Pompey quickly returned and sought to restore his prestige, but to little avail. When he addressed a *contio* on 25 July to defend himself against the abusive edicts of Bibulus, he cut a sorry and pathetic figure. Crassus was delighted (ibid., 21.3).

Everything was working out to Crassus's advantage. It looked as if the electoral candidates put up by Pompey and Caesar would fall before the swelling tide of hostility. Bibulus postponed the election of curule magistrates to give this hostility time to grow, and Caesar found it impossible to stir up a public protest against his action (ibid., 5).[15] Pompey and Caesar were in serious trouble.

Pompey was moved to seek whatever remedy he could to restore his sagging fortunes. Cicero feared that in bitterness and unhappiness he might resort to violence (*Att.* 1.21.1–5, 22.6). Pompey made continued assurances to Cicero that he would prevent him from coming to any harm at the hands of Clodius (ibid., 19.3, 20.2, 21.6, 22.1–2), and he openly sought advice from Cicero on how to find a way out of his own difficulties (ibid., 23.2). These remarks were signals that he was willing to cooperate with the *optimates*, but they re-

14. See Chapter Five and E. S. Gruen, *The Last Generation of the Roman Republic* (Berkeley and Los Angeles, 1974), p. 187.

15. L. R. Taylor, "The Dating of Major Legislation and Elections in Caesar's First Consulship," *Historia* 17 (1968): 189–93. Cf. Chapter Eight, p. 217, n. 66.

fused the offer, as Cicero foresaw (ibid.).[16] They were naturally suspicious of Pompey and thought that it was the time to break his power permanently.[17]

Then in August came the notorious "Vettius Affair" and with it, an abrupt improvement in the political fortunes of Pompey.[18] Briefly, Lucius Vettius, an *eques* of rather unsavory character, had approached the young Curio with a plan to assassinate Pompey; Curio reported Vettius's remarks to his father, who then informed Pompey. Thereupon the matter was laid before the Senate, and Vettius was brought in for interrogation. At first he denied even meeting Curio and then asked for immunity in return for revealing the plot. He claimed that Curio had formed a group of young men who included L. Aemilius Paullus, M. Junius Brutus (Caepio), and L. Cornelius Lentulus (with his father's knowledge), as well as C. Septimius, who brought a dagger from Bibulus, to whom he was a secretary. The Senate did not believe his story and decreed that he be locked in prison (Cic. *Att.* 2.24.2–3).

The next day, Caesar placed Vettius before a *contio* to give his story to the assembled people. Only this time, his story was

16. Cf. Seager, "Clodius," *Latomus* 24 (1965): 524.
17. Cf. Lintott, *Violence in Republican Rome*, p. 192.
18. Cf. Cic. *Q. Fr.* 1.2.15. The dating of this incident has caused no little debate. The traditional dating of the letter in which Cicero describes it is some time in August or possibly September (*Att.* 2.24). L. R. Taylor attempted to date this letter and the previous one to mid-July: "The Date and Meaning of the Vettius Affair," *Historia* 1 (1950): 45–51; "On the Date of *Ad Atticum* 2.24," *Classical Quarterly* 4 (1954): 181–82; "The Dating of Major Legislation and Elections," *Historia* 17 (1968): 191–92. Several others have accepted her revision: W. C. McDermott, "*Vettius ille, ille noster index*," *Transactions and Proceedings of the American Philological Association* 80 (1949): 358–59; W. Allen, Jr., "The Vettius Affair Once More," *Transactions and Proceedings of the American Philological Association* 81 (1950): 153; M. Gelzer, *Caesar, Politician and Statesman*, trans. P. Needham (Cambridge, Mass., 1968), p. 90, n. 2. Many others have rejected her arguments, however, and I remain convinced by the traditional dating: cf. P. A. Brunt, "Cicero: *Ad Atticum* 2.24," *Classical Quarterly* 3 (1953): 62–64; Chr. Meier, "Zur Chronologie und Politik in Caesars ersten Konsulat," *Historia* 10 (1961): 89–93; Seager, "Clodius," *Latomus* 24 (1965): 525, n. 1. S. I. Oost disputes Taylor's dating and argues that *Att.* 2.23 was written before the tribunician elections but that the elections were held at about the same time as the elections for regular magistracies, which had been postponed until October: "The Date of the *Lex Julia de Repetundis*," *American Journal of Philology* 77 (1956): 25–26. There is no reason for believing that the tribunician elections were postponed along with those of the curule magistracies, however: cf. Meier, "Chronologie," *Historia* 10 (1961): 89–93.

radically different. He left out mention of Caesar's friend Brutus and inserted a host of others never mentioned before: L. Lucullus, C. Fannius, L. Domitius, Cicero (by implication), Cicero's son-in-law Piso, and the one-time optimate candidate for tribune, M. Laterensis. He was then put up on a charge of *vis*, but his case never came to court. Instead, Vettius died mysteriously in prison. (Cic. *Att.* 2.24.3–4, *Vat.* 26; Suet. *Iul.* 20.5).[19]

Most scholars have concluded that Vettius was an *agent provocateur* of Caesar or his associates, especially Vatinius.[20] The object of the affair has been variously interpreted in relation to Pompey, the major figure of the time. One scholar adduced several objectives: to guarantee Pompey's estrangement from the *optimates* and further indebt him to Caesar; to warn the older *optimates* against continued opposition to the triumvirate; and similarly to warn its younger opponents, but with a view to long-term efforts to win them over.[21] Others have stressed Caesar's desire to break the growing popularity of young Curio, who was leading a successful campaign of opponents to his own candidates in the upcoming elections.[22] Still another scholar emphasized Caesar's desire to destroy the influence of Cicero with Pompey and make Pompey fearful of any movement towards the *optimates*.[23]

More recently, a quite different interpretation of the affair's origin has been advanced. It is argued that Clodius was the real instigator of Vettius because he wished to dissuade Pompey from rapprochement with the *optimates* and from giving aid to Cicero, ideas that Pompey entertained because of the earlier attacks of Clodius and Clodius's friend Curio.[24] This analysis suffers from two major faults, however. It fails to

19. For a comparison and evaluation of the ancient sources, see McDermott, "Vettius ille," TAPA 80 (1949): 351–58.
20. For an extensive summary of opinion up to 1949, see McDermott, ibid.
21. Ibid., p. 366.
22. Taylor, "Date and Meaning," *Historia* 1 (1950): 48–51; Rowland, "Crassus," *Historia* 15 (1966): 223; Gelzer, *Caesar*, p. 91, and *Cicero, Ein biographischer Versuch* (Wiesbaden, 1969), p. 129. Meier rejects Taylor's chronology, but essentially agrees with her on Caesar's purpose: "Chronologie," *Historia* 10 (1961): 89–93.
23. Allen, "The Vettius Affair Once More," TAPA 81 (1950): 153–62.
24. Seager, "Clodius," *Latomus* 14 (1965): 525–31.

explain why Clodius would implicate his friend Curio in the alleged plot and, hence, expose him to possible prosecution. In addition, most of the other names of alleged conspirators upon which much of this argument depends come from the list supplied by Vettius after Caesar's intervention.

It is much more reasonable to see Pompey himself behind Vettius in an attempt to reinflate his rapidly collapsing popularity. In fact, Plutarch reports widespread belief that Vettius had been suborned by the partisans of Pompey (*Luc.* 42.7). If Vettius had been put up by Caesar, he would not have mentioned Servilia's son, Brutus, in his first version of the plot. Nor does it make sense to see Caesar (or Clodius) trying to drive a wedge between Pompey and the *optimates*. They had rebuffed Pompey's overtures earlier (Cic. *Att.* 2.21.3–5, 23.2).[25] On the other hand, by his own admission, Pompey was desperate and willing to try anything (ibid.). Bibulus had forced postponement of the curule elections until 18 October in the hope that the popular indignation that Crassus and others were promoting against Pompey and Caesar would bring defeat of their candidates. Pompey had to do something dramatic to hurt his enemies and recoup his popularity. Caesar could look forward to his proconsulship for fulfilling his needs. A faked assassination plot would have been just the right thing for reminding the populace of their old devotion to Pompey. Rumors of plottings against his life already existed, so that he could expect people to believe Vettius's story.

Indeed, there is good reason to link Vettius with Pompey. Despite Orosius's description of him as a Paelignian (6.6.7), he may well have been from Pompey's home district of Picenum. He was closely associated with Pompey as a fellow member of the staff that accompanied Pompey's father at Asculum during the Social War (*CIL* I² 709 = Dessau 8888). He may also be the Vettius Picens who, along with Pompey, served Sulla during the Civil War.[26]

Vettius was also accustomed to political intrigue. He had first joined and then informed upon the Catilinarian conspirators (Dio 37.41.2–3). In 62, he had sought political profit from

25. See above, pp. 235–36.
26. Cf. Sall. *Hist.* 1.55.17 M and C. Cichorius, *Römische Studien* (Leipzig and Berlin, 1922), pp. 161–62. Gruen also indicates the possibility that Vettius was working on Pompey's behalf: *LGRR*, p. 96.

Caesar's enemies by accusing him of complicity with Catiline and served time in prison for his pains (Suet. *Iul.* 17.1–2).[27] Pompey could trust him to handle the arrangements for the scheme that he was making.

Apparently, Pompey's original plan was to lead certain of his most vocal or visible opponents into a compromising situation and then expose the "plot." These people were those on Vettius's first, or "short," list (Cic. *Att.* 2.24.2). The younger Curio was an obvious choice as ringleader of a group of young hot-bloods out to assassinate Pompey. In the preceding months, he had prominently waged a successful campaign against Pompey's interests. It certainly made sense to include L. Aemilius Paullus in the group. He was the son of M. Aemilius Lepidus, consul of 78, whom Pompey had betrayed and then hunted down. The case of Brutus is similar. His father, Lepidus's legate, had suffered the same fate as his commander.[28] No doubt, all of these young men had been attracted to Clodius and Curio because of their attacks on Pompey. Similarly, L. Cornelius Lentulus, whose father was competing against the candidates backed by Pompey in the consular elections, probably had associated himself with Pompey's detractors and was a logical choice for inclusion in a "plot." [29]

Doubt has been expressed as to why the son and not the father was named. The reason is that the actual assassination "plot" involving physical exertion and danger was to be carried out by young men while older men simply backed them. Hence, Bibulus is brought into the "plot" not as a member of the assassination squad but as a supplier of the murder weapon. Surely, he is a logical one to implicate, since his scurrilous edicts had reduced Pompey to abject rage (Cic. *Att.* 2.19.5). Because his attacks on Pompey had intensified since

27. McDermott ingeniously argued that in 62, Vettius was actually cooperating with Caesar in an attempt to force Cicero to put an end once and for all to rumors of Caesar's involvement with Catiline: "Vettius ille," *TAPA* 80 (1949): 362. Caesar's harsh punishment of Vettius in this incident makes it impossible to accept this view, however: Suet. *Iul.* 17.2; cf. Gelzer, *Caesar*, pp. 58–59.

28. Cf. Seager, "Clodius," *Latomus* 24 (1965): 526. Seager also suggested that Brutus was inimical to Pompey because his adoptive father had already been betrothed to Caesar's daughter, Julia, before Caesar reneged and gave her to Pompey. The exact relationship here is unclear, however: cf. Shackleton Bailey, *Cicero's Letters to Atticus* 1, p. 400.

29. Seager, ibid.

he warned Pompey of an assassination plot on 13 May, the general public probably would not have considered his inclusion in the plot as so much of a discrepancy as did the Senate (Cic. *Att.* 2.24.2).[30]

That neither Crassus nor Clodius was named by Vettius is probably related to Clodius's popularity and soon-to-be-assumed tribunate, both of which he, if offended, could use with great effectiveness against Pompey in the following year. Where Pompey and Vettius had miscalculated was in not confiding in Caesar about their plans and in not foreseeing Curio's consultation with his father, who prematurely revealed the "plot" to Pompey himself. Both errors are understandable, however. Vettius certainly would have had no desire to work with Caesar. Curio's relations with his father had been very poor,[31] and it should not have seemed likely that Curio would confide Vettius's offer to his father. Nevertheless, Pompey probably calculated that the premature revelation of the "plot" would still accomplish his purpose, and he let events take their course in the Senate.

Things may well have turned out entirely as originally planned if Vettius had not panicked. Apparently Vettius had not had time to consult with Pompey before he was brought before the Senate and thought that, since Curio had betrayed him, he could not successfully accuse Curio of involvement in a current plot. Therefore, he tried to backdate the assassination attempt to the time of the games in early July, when Curio had been so bravely applauded. The decisive flaw in this story was that one of the alleged chief conspirators, L. Aemilius Paullus, had not returned by then from Macedonia, where he had been serving as quaestor to the governor, Octavius, since the beginning of the year (Cic. *Att.* 2.24.3, *Vat.* 25; Schol. Bob. *ad Vat.* 25, 149 St).[32] Accordingly, the Senate decreed

30. Bibulus's purpose in "warning" Pompey was probably to sow in Pompey's mind as much fear and suspicion as possible in order to strain his relationships with political associates.

31. Cf. McDermott, "Curio *Pater* and Cicero," *AJP* 103 (1972): 401–3.

32. The language of Cicero's letter indicates that Paullus was at Rome when he wrote the letter but not at the time to which Vettius dated the "plot": . . . *in eo principem Paulum* [*sic*] *fuisse, quem constabat eo tempore in Macedonia fuisse.* The later reference in the *in Vatinium* is either made from the point of view of the time of the plot itself and not

Vettius's testimony to be false and ordered him thrown into prison, with the proviso that anyone seeking his release would be acting against the state (Cic. *Att.* 2.24.3).

At this point, Caesar and his friend Vatinius intervened to capitalize on the situation (ibid.). After coaching Vettius on the night when he was incarcerated, Caesar summoned a *contio* the next day and led Vettius to the *rostra* to expatiate on the alleged plot once more.[33] First, Vettius dropped Servilia's son from the list, then he added several others, some only after Vatinius had summoned him back to speak as the *contio* was breaking up.

All of the additional cast of characters were men whom Caesar would have liked to see placed in a compromising situation. The name of Lucullus, a bitter enemy of Pompey, would give more credibility to the plot in the eyes of the public and would discredit one of the mainstays of the optimate cause. Both C. Fannius, the tribune, and L. Domitius Ahenobarbus, candidate in the praetorian elections, were enemies of Caesar (Cic. *Sest.* 113). As for the mention of Cicero's son-in-law, Piso, the reference to his friend, M. Juventius Laterensis, and other innuendoes against Cicero himself, Caesar hoped thereby to undermine Cicero's popularity and force the orator to seek refuge with him.[34]

It was enough to have made charges against these men. To have had them tested in court would have been dangerous. From Caesar's point of view, Vettius must have seemed entirely untrustworthy (cf. Cic. *Att.* 2.24.4). He was a man of few scruples and could prove very embarrassing if he decided to reveal the true nature of events under the pressure of prosecution. Before the case could come to trial, Vettius was found dead in jail (Suet. *Iul.* 20.5; Plut. *Luc.* 42.8; Dio 38.9.4; App. *BC* 2.2.12).[35] Those whom Vettius had named were never

---

the time of the accusation, or else it is simply less precise, given the passage of time. Paullus had probably returned to Rome later, in July, to sue for a triumph on behalf of Octavius for the latter's victory over the Bessi (cf. Vell. Pat. 2.59.2; Suet. *Aug.* 3.2, 94.5).

33. Later, Cicero did not mention Caesar and said it was Vatinius (*Vat.* 24), but then he was tailoring the facts to suit his own purposes.

34. Cf. McDermott, "*Vettius, ille,*" *TAPA* 80 (1949): 364.

35. Stockton argued that Caesar had nothing to gain by silencing Vettius: *Cicero*, p. 185. Actually, both he and Pompey had little to lose and everything to gain.

charged, but the damage to their cause had been done. Pompey's popularity increased greatly, and the consular candidates backed by him and Caesar won.

In this way, Crassus was frustrated in his attempt to break the political domination of his erstwhile partners, especially Pompey. Having failed to block the election of the others' candidates by encouraging the attacks of Clodius, Curio, and others, Crassus, therefore, sought to nullify the election of Pompey's man, Gabinius, by backing his prosecution for electoral bribery (*ambitus*). If the prosecution should have succeeded, Gabinius would have been denied admission to office, and a man loyal to Crassus might have become his replacement in a supplementary election.

The man who was to handle the job was C. Porcius Cato, "a young man of no wisdom but a Roman citizen and a Cato nonetheless" in Cicero's estimation (*Q. Fr.* 1.2.15). A quotable, yet no doubt biased view. This Cato seems to have been another of the young men surrounding P. Clodius. As tribune in 56, he aided Clodius's attempt to be elected aedile and helped Clodius and Crassus attack Pompey.[36] Therefore, although evidence from later actions is not conclusive, Clodius, with encouragement from Crassus, probably recruited Cato to prosecute Gabinius. In a dangerous prosecution such as this one, it made sense to make use of a relatively unknown man of little rank.[37]

How dangerous a task it was soon became clear. Pompey sought to block the prosecution, and no praetor would grant a preliminary hearing. When Cato in frustration called Pompey a dictator at a public meeting, he was nearly murdered (Cic. *Q. Fr.* 1.2.15). Once more, Crassus's plans were sidetracked, and he was unsuccessful in challenging the power of his rival, Pompey, as the year 59 came to a close.

At this point, Crassus sought to cover himself by reestablishing good lines of communication with Caesar. Although they both had suffered from each other's recent maneuverings, Caesar found it expedient to keep the door open between them, especially since he was going to be absent from Rome. Ac-

36. See below, p. 257.
37. Cf. Cicero's prosecution of Verres.

cordingly, when Caesar left for his province in 58, he took Crassus's son Publius with him (Caes. *BGall.* 1.52.7).

Crassus also tried to remain on good terms with another important figure, Cicero. Just as Caesar, who did not leave for Gaul until Cicero had rejected his offers of help and gone into exile, so Crassus realized that Cicero could have been a useful friend. The problem that clouds their relationship is, of course, Clodius's adamant demand for Cicero's removal from the political scene. Those who see Clodius as the tool of Crassus or of Crassus and Caesar together naturally view Crassus as hostile to Cicero during this great crisis in the orator's life.[38] Cicero himself had his suspicions (*Fam.* 14.2.2).

This view is largely the result of Clodius's own propaganda, however. He publicly proclaimed that he had the backing of Crassus against Cicero, but he was simply taking advantage of Crassus's understandable reluctance to offend him, a man who was often so useful, by opposing his desires in this matter too strongly (Cic. *Sest.* 39–41).[39] A close look at Crassus's actions both before and after Cicero's exile will show that Crassus tried to restrain Clodius until it became clear that a disastrous fight could not be avoided if he continued. In 59, when Clodius was making his first threats against Cicero, Crassus tried to intercede with Clodius for him (Cic. *Att.* 2.22.5).[40] Later, Crassus's son Publius worked assiduously on

38. E.g., W. Drumann, *Geschichte Roms* 4, ed. 2, P. Groebe (Berlin and Leipzig, 1908), p. 101; Pocock, "Publius Clodius," *CQ* 18 (1924): 61; Marsh, "The Policy of P. Clodius," *CQ* 21 (1927): 32–33; Rowland, "Crassus," *Historia* 15 (1966): 222–23. Plutarch (*Crass.* 13.4) and Dio (38.17.3) were probably influenced in their views by Cicero's own suspicions and charges, especially as expressed in his defamatory *de Consiliis Suis*.

39. Cf. Gruen, "P. Clodius," *Phoenix* 22 (1966): 127, and Lintott, "P. Clodius Pulcher," *G&R* 14 (1967): 165.

40. Unfortunately, the text of this passage is corrupt at the most crucial point. It reads *Puto Pompeium Crasso urgente si tu aderis, qui per* βοῶπιν *ex ipso intellegere possis qua fide ab illis agatur, nos aut sine molestia aut certe sine errore futuros.* The crux is *Pompeium Crasso urgente:* J. S. Reid, "On *Att.* I–II," *Hermathena* 13 (1905): 391. Shackleton Bailey suggests that something like *vacillare, sed* has dropped out of the text after *urgente: Cicero's Letters to Atticus* 1, p. 397. This reconstruction is based on the erroneous assumption that Crassus was unfriendly to Cicero and in league with Caesar and Clodius against him. As Shackleton Bailey himself admits, Watt's emendation, *Pompeio eum* [meaning Clodius] *et Crasso,* is paleographically more reasonable (ibid.), and that is the way in which it should be taken.

Cicero's behalf and put on mourning to show his sympathy for Cicero when Clodius promulgated legislation aimed against him (Plut. *Crass.* 13.4; *Cic.* 33.5; Dio 38.17.3).[41]

Even while Cicero was gone, Crassus maintained a friendly attitude towards him. In June 58, Cicero was confident enough of Crassus's good will to recommend that his brother, Quintus, if threatened with any prosecution for provincial misgovernment, seek Crassus's support (*Q. Fr.* 1.3.7).[42] In the same month, it seems that Crassus's friend Q. Arrius had been working with Hortensius to aid Cicero, although at that moment Cicero was so distressed that he was not certain about either Hortensius or Arrius (ibid., 1.3.8).[43] Crassus also kept in touch with Cicero. The Axius who informed Cicero of events at Rome by letter was probably a close friend of Crassus (Cic. *Att.* 3.15.3).[44] In July or very early August 58, one of Crassus's own freedmen reported to the exile in person (ibid., 1–3).[45]

41. He should not be confused with the praetor P. Licinius Crassus Dives, who also worked on Cicero's behalf (Cic. *Red. Sen.* 23).

42. Deknatel conjectured that Cicero was referring to Crassus's son, Publius, Crassus Dives, or some unknown Crassus: *Vita*, pp. 79–80. The first and last suggestions appear highly unlikely, but Crassus Dives cannot be ruled out entirely. In the letter cited, only the name Crassus is given, but it does appear in conjunction with that of M. Calidius, who, as a colleague in the praetorship of 57, worked with P. Crassus Dives for Cicero's restoration (Cic. *Fam.* 4.8.4, *Red. Sen.* 23). Therefore, the suggestion that Cicero meant Crassus Dives has some strength. On the other hand, Cicero does usually distinguish between the two Crassi by mentioning P. Crassus's praenomen or cognomen to distinguish him from the older, more famous Marcus (cf. *Att.* 2.13, 24.4, *Red. Sen.* 23). One could argue that Cicero's brother would need no such differentiation here. Nevertheless, Marcus Crassus seems the one intended, for it seems that Quintus was on fairly good terms with Crassus in 55. Crassus acted favorably in procuring some honor for Quintus (*Q. Fr.* 2.9.2). Cf. W. C. McDermott, "Q. Cicero," *Historia* 20 (1971): 707.

43. There is no evidence, other than Cicero's fevered perceptions, at this time to suggest that Arrius's efforts were not sincere, contrary to the views recently expressed by B. A. Marshall and R. J. Baker: "The Aspirations of Q. Arrius," *Historia* 24 (1975): 228–29.

44. Shackleton Bailey, *Cicero's Letters to Atticus* 2, p. 151 and 1, p. 298. Cf. Chapter Eleven, p. 292, note 11.

45. In the opening line of the third paragraph of *ad Atticum* 3.15, Cicero says, *Crassi libertum nihil puto sincere locutum.* Shackleton Bailey translates this sentence as, "I imagine that Crassus's freedman spoke only in malice.": *Cicero's Letters to Atticus* 2, p. 31. Perhaps he takes it as Cicero's comment upon the distressing report that this freedman made to Atticus concerning Cicero's health. This report is referred to in the very first paragraph, however, and is dropped as a subject half way through paragraph two. In paragraph three, Cicero deals with conflicting reports on the status of the movement at Rome to secure his recall from

As time went on, Cicero became doubtful of Crassus's position regarding his recall. Writing to his wife, Terentia, on 5 October 58, he expressed hope in the new tribunes for 57, if they could rely on Pompey's friendliness, but he was afraid of Crassus (*Fam.* 14.2.2). Cicero's suspicion is understandable, for Crassus was in an awkward position. He wanted to remain on good terms with Clodius, who had attacked Pompey furiously for the favor he was showing Cicero (*Sest.* 69, *Har. Resp.* 49, *Pis.* 28–29). It would have been dangerous for Crassus to oppose Clodius too openly, since the attacks on Pompey were useful and he did not want to incur Clodius's wrath. He continued, however, to cooperate with Cicero's friend Atticus, who was working diligently for the orator's recall (*Att.* 3.23.5). Therefore, Cicero's fears concerning Crassus were not borne out.

Crassus was friendly towards Cicero's recall not out of any great love for the man who had consistently blocked many of his plans in the past, but simply because Cicero was more useful to him at this point in Rome rather than in exile. It long had been Cicero's desire to unite Pompey with the optimate leadership of the Senate. If Cicero could succeed, a breach between Pompey and Caesar would be inevitable, to the great advantage of Crassus. Therefore, Crassus played a double game in an attempt to effect this result. On the one hand, by encouraging Clodius's attacks upon Pompey, he made Pompey's position intolerable and rapprochement with Cicero and the *optimates* more desirable. On the other hand, he tried to ensure that it took place by working discreetly for Cicero's recall.

Clearly, Clodius's attacks upon Pompey were harsh, and they forced him to look more and more to Cicero and the *opti-*

---

exile. Actually, Atticus's reports seem to have been more optimistic than those of others, and Cicero seems to have been twitting Atticus about this discrepancy in paragraph three. In the paragraph's fourth and fifth sentences, when referring to the difference between Atticus's and Axius's accounts of a speech by Curio, Cicero says rather sarcastically, *At potest ille aliquid praetermittere; tu nisi quod erat, profecto non scripsisti.* Therefore, it is better to treat the reference to Crassus's freedman in sentence one of the paragraph as another dig at Atticus when juxtaposed with the second sentence, *In senatu rem probe scribis.* Cicero's intent would be clearer than if "spoke untruthfully" were substituted for Shackleton Bailey's "spoke only in malice."

mates.[46] First of all, Clodius sought to undermine the loyalty of the consuls, Piso and Gabinius. In this effort he temporarily succeeded by procuring special legislation granting them lucrative provinces: Macedonia for Piso, for Gabinius, first Cilicia and then Syria.[47] He also attempted to interfere with Pompey's clients. For example, Pompey sought to influence affairs in the East through Tigranes, king of Armenia. To ensure the king's loyalty and devotion, Pompey held his son, the younger Tigranes, as a hostage at Rome. Clodius contrived the escape of the prince and his safe return to Armenia, and thereby weakened the hold that Pompey had on that important kingdom (Ascon. *Mil.* 37, 47 C/40–41 St; Dio 38.30.1–3).[48]

In May, greatly disturbed by his deteriorating position at Rome and the indignity suffered at the hands of Clodius, Pompey made overtures to the *optimates* and started action on Cicero's recall (Cic. *Att.* 3.8.3, *Sest.* 67–68; Dio 38.30.2–3). Gabinius, whose loyalty to Pompey was deeper than that inspired by Clodius's actions for his provincial command, began to counter Clodius's street gangs with a group of his own in violent clashes (Dio 38.30.2–3; Cic. *Pis.* 27–28). Pompey even sought to invalidate Clodius's tribunate (Cic. *Sest.* 67–68, *Dom.* 40).

Clodius mounted a strong counterattack. First, he advocated repealing the legislation of Caesar's consulship (Cic. *Dom.* 40, *Har. Resp.* 48–49).[49] This move was an attempt to drive a wedge between Pompey and the *optimates,* many of whom would have favored such action with its obvious danger to Pompey as well as to Caesar. It was also designed to neutralize

46. Cf. Gelzer, *Caesar,* pp. 112–13.
47. T. R. S. Broughton, *The Magistrates of the Roman Republic* 2 (New York, 1953), p. 193.
48. For Clodius's interests in the East, see E. Rawson, "The Eastern Clientelae of Clodius and the Claudii," *Historia* 22 (1973): 235–38.
49. Marsh argues that, as before, the reference to Caesar's laws was only to the *leges Juliae,* whose repeal would have hurt mostly Pompey, since Crassus's friends among the *Equites* would have received their profits from the revision of the Asian tax contract and Vatinius sponsored the legislation benefiting Caesar. For Crassus's position, see n. 10 above. As for Caesar, Marsh's argument breaks down in view of the attacks on Vatinius and the Senate's offer to repass all the laws of Caesar's consulship with proper observances of religious law if Caesar would make cause with the senatorial leadership (Cf. Cic. *Prov. Cons.* 46, *Vat.* 33; Suet. *Iul.* 23, *Nero* 2.2; Schol. Bob. *ad Sest.* 40, *ad Vat.* 15, 35, 38: 130, 146, 150–51 St).

Caesar or even force him to put pressure on Pompey to desist from his attacks on Clodius.[50]

In both respects it produced results. Despite the *optimates'* assurances that no danger would come to him if he cooperated with them in voiding Clodius's tribunate, Caesar refused (Cic. *Prov. Cons.* 46, *Sest.* 71, *Att.* 3.18.1). It was safer to side with Clodius. After all, Clodius and his friends could nullify any optimate safeguards through legislation passed by the *Concilium Plebis*. In reaction, moreover, important *optimates* like Hortensius and Bibulus now began to cooperate with Clodius in the hope of breaking both Pompey and Caesar once and for all (Cic. *Har. Resp.* 50, *Q. Fr.* 2.2.2–3).[51] Finally, Clodius terrorized Pompey by staging an assassination attempt. One of Clodius's servants was "discovered" stealing towards Pompey with knife in hand on 11 August. From that time until the end of Clodius's tribunate, Pompey shut himself up at home. Even there he was hounded by one of Clodius's agents (Cic. *Pis.* 28; Ascon. *Mil.* 37, 46–47 C/40 St).

Despite Clodius's efforts to undo the results of his own earlier actions, however, Crassus had reason to be optimistic. As he probably foresaw, Clodius's attacks only made Pompey long for Cicero's return even more. The prospects seemed good. The elections for 57 had gone well from Cicero's point of view. P. Cornelius Lentulus Spinther was a good friend of Pompey and worked hard for Cicero's recall. Metellus Nepos, though a cousin or step brother of Clodius and a harsh critic of Cicero in 62, was eventually persuaded to follow Lentulus's

50. Pocock argued that Clodius was making this attack as an agent of Caesar in order to embroil Pompey with the *optimates:* "Publius Clodius," *CQ* 18 (1924): 59–64, and "A Note on the Policy of P. Clodius," *CQ* 19 (1925): 182–84. It is better, however, to see Clodius trying to put pressure on both Pompey and Caesar: cf. P. Grimal, *Études de chronologie ciceronienne* (*annés 58 et 57 av. J.-C.*) (Paris, 1967), pp. 113–19.

51. Cf. Chr. Meier, *Res Publica Amissa* (Wiesbaden, 1966), p. 286. One can imagine their elation at Clodius's hostility toward Caesar and Pompey now, in contrast with his obstruction of attempts by Domitius and Memmius to overturn Caesarian legislation earlier in 58 (cf. citations in n. 49 above). The attack by one L. Antistius on Caesar's quaestor, which Suetonius reports for 58 (*Iul.* 23.1), seems actually to belong to 56: see E. Badian, "Two Roman Non-Entities," *Classical Quarterly* 19 N.S. (1969): 198–204; "The Attempt to Try Caesar," *Polis and Imperium, Studies in Honor of Edward Togo Salmon*, ed. J.A.S. Evans (Toronto, 1974), pp. 145–66.

lead.[52] On 1 January 57, Lentulus made a motion in the Senate that Cicero be recalled, and even Clodius's brother, the praetor Appius Claudius Pulcher, did not oppose it (Cic. *Sest.* 72–74, *Red. Sen.* 5, *Pis.* 34–35).[53]

Clodius, however, attempted to block the measure through two friendly tribunes and hired gangs of street fighters (ibid.; Dio 39.6–8.2; Plut. *Cic.* 33.1–3), but to no avail. Clodius and his gangs were successfully met by those of Pompey's man, T. Annius Milo, and by P. Sestius, whom Crassus may have secretly supported.[54] Finally, on 4 August, the Centuriate Assembly passed the bill for Cicero's return, and on 4 September Cicero arrived home in glory (Cic. *Dom.* 90, *Att.* 4.1.4–5).[55] There, as he entered the Porta Capena, one of the first to greet him was Marcus Crassus (Plut. *Cic.* 33.5).

After Cicero's return, there was a great effort to increase Pompey's power. Within limits, Crassus favored this movement because its effect would have been to damage Pompey's relations with Caesar. Cicero took the lead. On 7 September, Cicero proposed in the Senate that Pompey be granted an extraordinary commission to ensure the grain supply for Rome in the face of an acute shortage that then existed (Cic. *Att.* 14.1.6). On the next day the consuls, Lentulus and Nepos, presented a specific legislative proposal giving Pompey fifteen *legati*, with Cicero as the first, and giving him management of all grain supplies in the Mediterranean world for five years (ibid., 1.7). A tribune in the employ of Pompey, however, made a more far-reaching proposal that would have given Pompey unlimited access to public funds, a fleet, an army, and an *imperium* greater than that of provincial governors.

Pompey's old optimate enemies vehemently opposed this tribunician proposal (ibid.). No doubt, Crassus joined them.[56]

52. Broughton, *MRR* 2, pp. 199–200.

53. Crassus may have had some influence with both Nepos and Appius, but more likely, in view of the favorable attitude that many of Cicero's friends showed to Clodius because of his attacks on Pompey, they themselves thought it politic to remain as neutral as possible at this point.

54. Crassus defended Sestius in 56 when the latter was prosecuted for his activity during 57 (Schol. Bob. *ad Sest. argumentum*, 125 St).

55. Concerning the unique use of the *Comitia Centuriata*, see L. R. Taylor, *Roman Voting Assemblies* (Ann Arbor, 1966), pp. 103–4.

56. Crassus had found it discreet to remain absent from the Senate on the 7th of September, as did many other *consulares*; on the 8th, however, all the *consulares* were present (Cic. *Att.* 4.1.6–7).

The dangers in this measure were simply too great, for it seemed, at least in part, to be an attempt to give Pompey control of Egypt.[57] Crassus was not, however, opposed to Cicero's original idea or the consuls' motion, which subsequently passed. He wanted to give Pompey some rope, but not too much—just enough to hang himself. On the one hand, he wanted Cicero to think that he was strong enough politically to lead Pompey into a grand coalition with the *optimates*. On the other, he needed to keep enough pressure on Pompey so that the latter would have to make concessions to them that would be serious enough to jeopardize his relations with Caesar.

Accordingly, Crassus probably manifested support for Cicero by voting in his favor when the *pontifices* were asked to rule if Clodius had acted correctly in demolishing Cicero's house on the Palatine and consecrating it for a religious shrine (Cic. *Att.* 4.2.2, *Har. Resp.* 12).[58] At the same time, he obliquely opposed Pompey on the question of restoring Ptolemy Auletes to the throne of Egypt. In the summer of 57, Auletes arrived at Rome and worked with Pompey to effect his return (Dio 39.14.3). This effort was contrary to the wishes of the consul Lentulus Spinther, who had already proposed that the king be restored by the governor of Cilicia, a position that he himself would occupy (Cic. *Fam.* 1.1.3; Dio 39.12.3). Pompey hoped to receive this commission with all of its potential for power himself (Cic. *Fam.* 1.2.1, 4.1.7, 3–4, *Q. Fr.* 2.2.3, 4.5; Plut. *Pomp.* 49.6; Dio 39.16.1).

Therefore, in order to gain the favor of his old opponents in the Senate, Pompey had the tribune Rutilius Lupus propose to reconsider the Campanian land bill of Caesar (Cic. *Q. Fr.* 2.1.1).[59] Clearly, this proposal was an exploratory step on

---

57. Stockton, *Cicero*, p. 195, n. 4. There were, however, practical administrative considerations, too: J.P.V.D. Balsdon, "Roman History, 58–56 B.C.," *Journal of Roman Studies* 47 (1957): 17. See also, I. Shatzman, "The Egyptian Question in Roman Politics (59–54 B.C.)," *Latomus* 30 (1971): 363–69.

58. For arguments that Crassus was a pontiff, see Chapter Eight, p. 204, n. 38.

59. For Lupus and Pompey, see M. Cary, "*Asinus Germanus*," *Classical Quarterly* 17 (1923): 103–7. T. N. Mitchell did not consider Pompey's designs on Egypt when he denied that Pompey had little reason to be unhappy with his situation at this time: "Cicero before Luca," *Transactions and Proceedings of the American Philological Association* 100 (1969): 305, n. 5.

Pompey's part. It served his purpose very well. The Campanian land bill had originally aroused heated opposition from the *optimates* in the Senate and would be a good piece of bait in fishing for their friendship (cf. Cic. *Att.* 2.16). The senators heard the proposal in silence, and Lentulus Marcellinus, consul designate for 56, expressed the *optimates'* feelings when he said that their silence indicated neither approval nor disapproval, but, rather, that they did not wish to discuss the matter in the absence of Pompey himself (Cic. *Q. Fr.* 2.1.1). They were not sure if Pompey was serious or merely setting a trap for them, and they did not soften their opposition to his desires.

Neither Crassus nor Clodius wanted to see Pompey gain control of Egypt. They sought to ensure that the *optimates* remained adamant on this point. At the beginning of January, the tribune C. Cato, friend of Crassus and Clodius, took advantage of a portentious lightning bolt to produce a Sybilline verse that forbade using an army to restore Auletes (Cic. *Fam.* 1.1.3, 4.2, 7.4; Dio 39.15.1–3).[60] Cicero, who was working to get the commission for Lentulus Spinther, had no doubt that the oracle was conveniently forged (*Fam.* 1.4.2, 7.4).[61] Nevertheless, a majority of senators seized upon it and voted not to authorize use of an army to restore Auletes.[62] In this way, they hoped to hamstring Pompey effectively even if he were to receive the commission to undertake Auletes's restoration.

Indeed, it did seem that Pompey may have been too strong to be blocked completely. By 13 January, Cicero was becoming pessimistic (*Fam.* 1.1.3). Crassus, therefore, sought to restrict Pompey even further, should he succeed in obtaining the task in question. Shortly before 13 January, Crassus proposed that Auletes be restored by a commission of three chosen from those currently holding *imperium* (ibid.). Thus, Pompey was

60. Deknatel views Crassus's opposition to the use of an army as a move against Lentulus and, hence, Cicero. He was in no way hostile on their account, however. The real reason was his opposition to Pompey.

61. L. R. Taylor suggested that this use of the oracle may reflect Crassus's position as a priest, perhaps one of the *quindecemviri sacris faciundis: Party Politics in the Age of Caesar* (Berkeley and Los Angeles, 1949), p. 215, n. 48. If he were a pontiff, as I have argued it is even more likely: see Chapter Eight, p. 204, n. 38.

62. The *optimates* Hortensius and Lucullus would have ignored this difficulty for Lentulus's sake if they could have (Cic. *Fam.* 1.1.3).

not excluded, since he held *imperium* by virtue of his grain commission. In no way was this motion made to please Pompey, however.[63] Rather, it was to handicap him with two colleagues (ibid.). Certainly, the prospect of having Pompey away from Rome without an army and with two, perhaps less-than-devoted colleagues to see that he did not acquire one would have been very pleasing to Crassus.[64]

Crassus's motion received little support, however. Instead, most of the leading senators favored the subsequent motion of Bibulus, who proposed that a commission of three be chosen from those not holding *imperium* (ibid.). This motion suited Crassus at least as well as his own, since it would have excluded Pompey entirely. Therefore, Crassus did not object and apparently withdrew his motion in cooperation with Bibulus when the Senate met on 13 January.[65]

Nevertheless, procedural wrangles between the *optimates* and Pompey's supporters blocked further action at this meeting and the following one on 15 January (Cic. *Fam.* 1.2.1–3, 4.1–2, *Q. Fr.* 2.2.3). The issue continued to be hotly debated as Pompey and his followers exerted pressure through parliamentary maneuvers, lobbying, and outright bribery to have the task of restoration removed from Lentulus and given to himself (Cic. *Q. Fr.* 2.2.3). Pompey, however, feigned a denial that he was interested and pretended to favor Lentulus (cf. Cic. *Fam.* 1.2.3, *Q. Fr.* 2.2.3).

The hearing of deputations having been postponed until 13 February, the struggle continued in the Senate (Cic. *Q. Fr.* 2.3.1). Sometime between 3 and 6 February, C. Cato promulgated a law to deny Lentulus the right to conduct Auletes's restoration (ibid.). At first glance, this move would seem to favor Pompey. More likely, it was an attempt by Crassus, Clodius, and men such as Curio and Bibulus to make way for Bibulus's proposal concerning a commission of three. That they and C. Cato were working against Pompey at that time can be seen in the events surrounding the trial of Pompey's friend Milo on 6 February.

On the day of the trial, Clodius and his partisans verbally

63. *Contra* Gruen, "P. Clodius," *Phoenix* 20 (1966): 129, n. 49.
64. Garzetti, "Crasso," *Athenaeum* 22 (1944): 17–18.
65. Cf. Stockton, *Cicero*, p. 201, n. 14.

assailed Pompey when he finished speaking on Milo's behalf. When Clodius asked who was responsible for the grain shortage, his men answered "Pompey"; when he demanded who wanted to restore Auletes, they replied "Pompey"; but when he questioned who the People wanted to go to Egypt, they shouted "Crassus" (Cic. *Q. Fr.* 2.3.2).[66] The mention of Crassus was probably intended to frighten Pompey more than anything. It is doubtful that, under the conditions proposed, Crassus actually would have been interested even in being a member of Bibulus's commission. It is possible, of course, that he was, since he had a long-standing interest in Egypt and later acquired a great Eastern command. Conceivably, with optimate cooperation in obtaining friendly colleagues, he could have reaped great political and pecuniary profit from the restoration of Auletes. At this point, however, he probably was content with blocking Pompey.

After a riot completely broke up the proceedings of Milo's trial, a meeting of the Senate was summoned. Bibulus, Curio, Favonius, and the younger Servilius attacked Pompey, while Clodius obtained postponement of the trial until 17 February, which would give him more time to work for Milo's condemnation (ibid.). Pompey defended himself at a meeting in the temple of Apollo on the 7th and again on the 8th. At the latter meeting, C. Cato issued a stinging rebuke to him and humiliated him by accusing him of betraying Cicero in the matter of Cicero's exile. Pompey made a vehement reply and accused Crassus of plotting against him. In the end, a motion of censure was carried. Pompey was utterly crushed. He confided to Cicero that Crassus, Clodius, C. Cato, Curio, and Bibulus were all working against him (*Q. Fr.* 3.3–4). He was right.

Having successfully helped to block Pompey's hope of re-

66. Crassus was present at the trial, as Cicero says, with no friendly disposition towards Milo: *Is aderat tum, Miloni animo non amico.* Some have taken this sentence to mean that Crassus actually appeared on Milo's side at the trial, but with hostile intent: e.g., Meier, *RPA,* p. 20 and D. R. Shackleton Bailey, *Cicero* (London, 1971), p. 80. Depending on how one punctuates it, the sentence can be taken in this way. It seems more logical, however, to place a comma before *Miloni,* not after it, so that Cicero is saying that Crassus attended the trial but not to show support in any way for Milo.

storing Auletes, Crassus thereby forced Pompey to work closely with Cicero on Lentulus's behalf. Pompey feared that otherwise someone hostile to him would be given the task (ibid.). Legislative action was completely stalled, however, since the consul Marcellinus, who supported Lentulus, had cancelled all comitial days so that C. Cato's bill to deny Lentulus the task could not be acted upon (Cic. *Fam.* 1.1.2, 21, *Q. Fr.* 2.4.4.–5).[67] Therefore, while other matters came to occupy the minds of key figures at Rome, that is basically the way matters stayed regarding Auletes until Pompey obtained the consulship in 55, and it became possible for his friend A. Gabinius finally to restore the king in that year (Cic. *Att.* 4.10.1, *Rab. Post.* 19–21, *Pis.* 48–50).

It was Caesar who set political activity on its new course. As a result of his successes in Gaul, he had become the darling of the Roman populace. Pompey grew more and more jealous and increasingly sought to curb his growing popularity and prestige (Dio 39.25.1–4). The tribune Antistius Vetus, who had already supported Pompey against Clodius at the beginning of his tribunate in December (Cic. *Q. Fr.* 2.1.3), sought to remove Caesar from his command by prosecuting him for the acts committed during his consulship (Suet. *Iul.* 23).[68] Caesar put pressure on the tribunes to rule that he could not be prosecuted, because he was absent on public service (ibid.).[69] Whatever he said had great effect, for he received

67. Meier sees Crassus in league with Marcellinus: *RPA*, p. 286. The references that he cites give nothing concrete to back up this interpretation. It is possible, of course, that Crassus did encourage his action. Indeed, one of the purposes of Cato's bill was to get the opponents of Pompey and the supporters of Lentulus, who were not necessarily the same, to join forces in blocking Pompey. Marcellinus was no friend of Lentulus, but he disliked Pompey even more (Cic. *Fam.* 1.1.2, *Q. Fr.* 2.4.5).

68. There would have been little threat to Roman security in Gaul if Caesar had been removed. The campaigning season was over, and Caesar was in winter quarters in Cisalpine Gaul. E. Badian has convincingly argued that this attack of Antistius should be dated to early 56 and not to 58: "Two Roman Non-Entities," *Classical Quarterly* 19 (1969): 200–204. Although he would link Antistius primarily with the *optimates*, it seems better to link him with Pompey. Pompey had ties with the Antistii through his first wife, and Dio says specifically that Pompey tried at this point to undo all that Caesar had done (39.25.3).

69. From his winter quarters in Cisalpine Gaul, Caesar had no trouble maintaining contact with people at Rome: cf. the trip of Appius Claudius Pulcher (Cic. *Q. Fr.* 2.4.6).

no trouble from tribunes for the rest of the year.[70] When extravagant honors (*monstra*, as Cicero calls them) were proposed for Caesar in keeping with growing public adulation (Dio 39.25.1–2), not a tribune was found to veto them. It was only the obstructionist tactics of the consul Marcellinus that prevented action (Cic. *Q. Fr.* 2.4.5).

At this point, Crassus sought to encourage Cicero to believe that he and Pompey had the strength to oppose Caesar successfully. On 11 March, Crassus helped Hortensius, Pompey, C. Licinius Macer Calvus, and Cicero defend P. Sestius. As tribune in 57, Sestius had worked on Cicero's behalf (Cic. *Fam.* 1.9.7, *Sest.* 48; Schol. Bob. *Sest.* 125 St). During the course of his speech for Sestius, Cicero outlined his ideal of a government based on enlightened conservatism and the co-operation of the senatorial aristocracy of Rome with the propertied classes of Italy (*Sest.* 96–103). Furthermore, he cautioned his audience on the dangers of following a path designed to earn the title "Friend of the People" (*popularis*). Specifically, he cited the examples of C. Alfius Flavus and P. Vatinius, who had been tribunes loyal to Caesar in 59, but had enjoyed no further political advancement since then (ibid., 104–14).

Against Vatinius in particular, the major sponsor of Caesar's legislation during 59, Cicero launched a vicious attack, which he published separately as the *in Vatinium*. He declared every act of Vatinius either morally reprehensible or illegal (*Vat.* 5, 13, 15–32, cf. *Fam.* 1.9.7). Thus, though he diplomatically claimed to separate Caesar from any share of the blame for Vatinius's illegalities and held out the possibility of reconciliation with the Senate (*Vat.* 13, 15, 22), Cicero systematically attacked the foundations of Caesar's power. This fact can in no way be disguised.[71] Indeed, this attack was but a prelude to a formal prosecution by C. Licinius Macer Calvus, which Cicero hoped would formalize these charges and hence high-

70. In view of his tremendous popularity, it is conceivable that he threatened to use his influence with the voters to have any unfriendly tribune deposed by an act of the People. Of course, massive bribery helped, too (Plut. *Pomp.* 51.2).

71. U. Albini argued that Cicero sincerely meant no attack on Caesar's position: "L'orazio contro Vatinio," *La Parola del Passato* 14 (1959): 172. Despite Cicero's obviously self-serving denial, an attack on Vatinius's acts as tribune was *ipso facto* an attack on Caesar, and Cicero and others well knew it.

light the illegality of Caesar's position by virtue of the in-
validity of the laws upon which it rested (ibid., 10, *Q. Fr.*
2.4.1). The favor that greeted Cicero and his co-pleaders is
indicated by the unanimous acquittal of Sestius.

On 3 and 4 April, Crassus helped Cicero defend another
man, M. Caelius Rufus (Cic. *Cael.* 23, *Q. Fr.* 2.3.4). How
much political significance one should assign to Crassus's role
here is difficult to assess. In part, at least, he was acting out of
a personal obligation to Caelius. Caelius had been placed under
the care of both Crassus and Cicero when he was preparing
for a public career (Cic. *Cael.* 10, 72). On the other hand,
Caelius's case provided an admirable opportunity for Crassus
to encourage Cicero's belief that his preexilic political strength
was returning and to embolden Pompey.[72]

First of all, Caelius was being prosecuted through the
machinations of Cicero's tormenters, P. Clodius and that
man's sister, Clodia, the infamous mistress of Catullus and
then of Caelius himself (ibid., 1, 17–18, 29–38, 47–53, etc.;
Q. Fr. 2.13.2). For Crassus, openly siding with Cicero in this
case probably seemed more advantageous now than not offending Clodius. Secondly, Caelius was friendly with Pompey. It
was charged that he took part in the armed attack on the
deputation sent by the enemies of Ptolemy Auletes and in
the subsequent murder of their leader, Dio (Cic. *Cael.* 23).
If these charges had any basis for belief, it was in some connection between Caelius and Ptolemy's patron at Rome,
Pompey. Earlier, for example, in 59, Caelius had prosecuted
C. Antonius, whom Pompey had threatened to have prosecuted
when he returned from the East (Cic. *Cael.* 74, *Att.* 1.12.1).[73]

Although not specifically stated in any source, the trial must

72. No doubt Crassus took great delight in denouncing the acts of
Pompey's friend, King Ptolemy (Cic. *Cael.* 18). He could have taken the
opportunity to attack Pompey directly as well: cf. Gelzer, *Cicero*, p. 166).
Nevertheless, the friendly attitude that Cicero shows toward Crassus
throughout would suggest that he did not; *contra* E. Ciaceri, *Cicerone e i
suoi Tempi* 2 (Milan, Genoa, Rome, Naples, 1941), p. 91.

73. According to Dio (38.10.4), Cicero claimed that Caesar had been
the instigator of this prosecution. No doubt, Caesar approved and probably even encouraged this move. Still, Cicero may have been seeking to
disguise Pompey's role in this case by emphasizing Caesar's. Caelius's part
in the prosecution also may have been urged by Crassus. Cf. E. S. Gruen,
"The Trial of C. Antonius," *Latomus* 32 (1973): 301–10.

have been another elating victory for Cicero.[74] Crassus's plan
of encouraging Cicero and Pompey to challenge Caesar
proceeded apace. On the next day, 5 April, Cicero committed
himself to an attack on Caesar's position with the tacit approval of Pompey.[75] It was then that the question of reconsider-
ing the Campanian Land Law, already introduced by Pompey's
tribune Lupus at the end of December, came up for debate.
After heated discussion, Cicero, apparently believing that the
law could be terminated, called for action to be taken at a
meeting of the Senate on 15 May, when advance notice would
bring a full house (*Fam.* 1.9.8). Writing to Lentulus Spinther
a little less than two years later, Cicero claimed that by this
move he had rushed into the very citadel of the opposition
(ibid.).[76] Unfortunately for Cicero, the outcome of events
would be very different from what he expected, but Crassus
would profit a great deal.

The second half of 59 and all of 58 and 57 had been hectic
for Crassus as he sought to reestablish his position vis à vis his
erstwhile partners, Pompey and Caesar. These years clearly
reveal his deftness in political maneuvering. His goal was to
drive a wedge between them and then play one off against
the other in bargaining for an arrangement more favorable to
himself. Often he received considerable help in this enterprise
from P. Clodius, not that Clodius was Crassus's tool. Rather,
he worked with Crassus because he shared a common dislike of
the dominant position gained by Pompey and Caesar. On the
other hand, Crassus and Clodius sometimes worked at cross-
purposes to each other when their interests were different.

In the elections of 59, they shared the same interests.

74. Caelius continued to be present at Rome after the trial (Cic.
Q. Fr. 2.13.2); cf. Ciaceri, *Cicerone* 2, p. 96; Gruen, *LGRR*, p. 308.
Therefore, his acquittal seems assured.

75. Cf. Cic. *Fam.* 1.9.8–9, *Q. Fr.* 2.5.1–4. It is usually thought that
Pompey was merely dissembling his true feelings, as he did so often, since
he later bluntly reprimanded Cicero through the latter's brother, Quintus.
It must be remembered, however, that Luca intervened and that Pompey
had changed course as a result. At the time, he really does seem to have
approved of Cicero's actions, as will be seen. Nor was he cynically using
Cicero and the attacks on Caesar as a means of putting pressure on the
latter to win concessions, as some have urged: e.g., Syme, *RR*, p. 37, n. 3;
Stockton, *Cicero*, pp. 208–11. For a good discussion, see E. S. Gruen,
"Pompey, the Roman Aristocracy, and the Conference of Luca," *Historia*
18 (1969): 91.

76. For the validity of this claim, see the Appendix to this chapter.

Clodius campaigned as Caesar's enemy. It looked as if everything was working to Crassus's advantage. Popular hostility to Pompey and Caesar became increasingly vocal, as witnessed by the *Equites*' applause for Curio and the public's approval of Bibulus's edicts. Pompey even sought close ties with Caesar's optimate enemies.

Unfortunately for Crassus, the *optimates* rejected Pompey's overtures. In August 59, therefore, Pompey arranged with Vettius for an apparent assassination attempt upon himself, in order to shift public sympathy in his favor. Despite premature revelation of the "plot" and Vettius's clumsy attempt to repair the damage, Caesar stepped in and saved the situation by coaching Vettius before his mysterious death. Therefore, the plan worked, Pompey's popularity was largely restored, and the consular candidates backed by him and Caesar won.

Crassus countered by supporting C. Cato's prosecution of Pompey's man, Gabinius. When Pompey blocked this action, Crassus sought to reestablish rapport with Caesar. Caesar responded favorably, since he was about to leave for his provincial governorship and hoped that Crassus would be useful to him at Rome while he was away.

Crassus also sought the friendship of Cicero. He did not cooperate with Clodius in the attacks that drove Cicero into exile. Rather, he supported Cicero. Despite Cicero's own fevered misperceptions, this support can be seen through the actions of Crassus's son Publius and the visits of his friend Arrius and a freedman to Cicero in exile. At Rome, Crassus himself cooperated with Atticus, who was working for the orator's recall.

By aiding Cicero's return, Crassus hoped that Pompey could then be joined with the optimate leadership of the Senate. That would open up a breach between Pompey and Caesar. Therefore, Crassus played a double game by encouraging Clodius's attacks on Pompey, in order to make the latter's position more intolerable and rapprochement with Cicero and the *optimates* more desirable. When Clodius realized what was happening, he tried to counteract it, but he failed, and Cicero returned in September 57.

Now, Crassus had to tread a narrow path. On the one hand, he supported moves by Cicero and others to increase Pompey's power. On the other hand, he opposed the proposal of a tribune friendly to Pompey that Pompey restore Ptolemy Auletes to the throne of Egypt. That would have made Pompey too strong. While Crassus and Clodius successfully opposed this measure, Pompey was forced to make more overtures to Caesar's optimate enemies in the hope of gaining their support. Crassus's attempt to drive a wedge between Pompey and Caesar was beginning to work.

Crassus did all that he could to take advantage of the situation. With the dramatic growth of Caesar's power and popularity as a result of the war in Gaul, Pompey was anxious to maintain a dominant position at Rome. He needed the help of the *optimates,* who distrusted him. Therefore, Crassus supported Cicero, as in the trials of Sestius and Caelius, and thereby encouraged Cicero to believe that he was in a position to unite Pompey with the *optimates* against Caesar. At the end of December 57, Cicero thought that his dream would be realized as he promoted the proposal of Pompey's man Lupus to repeal Caesar's Campanian Land Law. Unwittingly, Cicero had played right into Crassus's hands, as Crassus sought a way to cut Pompey and Caesar down to size and force them into a better bargain with him.

Appendix IX

Cicero and the Debate over the Campanian Land Law

Concerning the debate over Caesar's Campanian Land Law in 56, attempts have been made to deny that Cicero really was doing what he later claimed he did when he wrote to Lentulus Spinther (*Fam.* 1.9.8), or that the issue of the *lex Campana* was in any way an attack on Caesar.[1] Mitchell sees no connection between Lupus's raising of the question in December and the appearance of debate on 5 April. He argues rather that it "arose spontaneously and was inspired by the mood and pressures of the moment than that it represented a prearranged and carefully calculated political maneuver."[2] The gap between December and April is really no problem. Five April was probably the first real opportunity to debate the question in the light of the time spent on the issue of Auletes's restoration, the hearing of embassies, and the normal interruptions of the calendar. Lupus had not really wanted a debate at first. He spun out his remarks until late and did not ask for a vote (*Q. Fr.* 2.1.1). He was testing the Senate's reaction, and knew that it would take time to convince many important senators that he was serious.

Balsdon argued that when Cicero wrote to Quintus a few days later, his complete silence on any role played in the debate of 5 April shows that Cicero, with an eye to history, later gave a false account of his actions. But, the *Acta Diurna*, published minutes of senatorial meetings instituted by one of Caesar's laws, would have revealed him as a liar[3] and, as Dorey said, the recantation about which Cicero wrote to Atticus in May 56 clearly implies that "his recent conduct had constituted a dangerous attack on the Triumvirs and tends to support

1. J. P. V. D. Balsdon, "Roman History 58–56 B.C.: Three Ciceronian Problems," *Journal of Roman Studies* 47 (1957): 15–20; T. N. Mitchell, "Cicero before Luca," *Transactions and Proceedings of the American Philological Association* 100 (1969): 295–320.
2. Mitchell, ibid., p. 305.
3. Cf. D. Stockton, "Cicero and the *Ager Campanus*," *Transactions and Proceedings of the American Philological Association* 93 (1962): 472–73.

Cicero's claims to have threatened Caesar's Lex Campana."[4]
Furthermore, although the *lex Campana* by itself was not one
of Caesar's central concerns, one must remember that L.
Domitius Ahenobarbus was announcing his candidacy for the
consulship with a promise to remove Caesar from his command
(Suet. *Iul.* 24.1). Accordingly, termination of the *lex Campana*
must be viewed as an important test case with serious implications for all that Caesar had accomplished in the past few years.

Dorey also argued that Cicero would not have wanted
Quintus to know exactly what he was doing because Quintus
had personally pledged that Cicero would do nothing to harm
the "Triumvirs" in return for their support for Cicero's recall.[5]
That seems unlikely, however. Quintus made the pledge to
Pompey, not to the "Triumvirs" (Cic. *Fam.* 1.9.9–10), and he
was now serving on Pompey's staff in Sardinia to deal with the
grain supply.[6] There would be no need to conceal from
Quintus Cicero's role in an action that one of Pompey's other
friends had already proposed. Indeed, Quintus probably would
have learned about it from other correspondents anyway.[7]

Therefore, it is puzzling that the letter in question (*Q. Fr.*
2.5) does not contain more information on Cicero's role in the
debate of 5 April. Perhaps the text of this letter was altered
after Pompey's displeasure became known, in order to protect
Quintus from being compromised by what his brother had
been doing. The transition between sections one and two seems
very abrupt, and it is interesting that the letter which Cicero
wrote to Quintus either late on 4 April or very early on 5 April
and in which, among the *cetera de re publica privataque*, he
might have given information on plans for the upcoming meeting of the Senate is lost (cf. *Q. Fr.* 2.5.1).

Fortunately, the lack of information in *Q. Fr.* 2.5 is not
decisive. Most discussions of the problem have overlooked the
next letter to Quintus,[8] which corroborates Cicero's claim to
have played a central role in a move to terminate the operation
of the *lex Campana*. In this letter, Cicero expressed agreement

4. T. A. Dorey, "Cicero and the Lex Campana," *Classical Review* 9
(1959): 13.
5. Ibid.; cf. D. R. Shackleton Bailey, *Cicero* (London, 1971), p. 81.
6. Cf. T. R. S. Broughton, *The Magistrates of the Roman Republic* 2
(New York, 1952), pp. 205, 213.
7. Stockton, "Cicero and the *Ager Campanus*," TAPA 93 (1962): 476–
77; Mitchell, "Cicero before Luca," TAPA 100 (1969): 307.
8. Number 8 in the MSS but following 5 in the rearrangement of
Mommsen.

with Quintus that everything should be kept for personal conversation, but he goes on to say:

> *What had been stated would be done on the Ides of May and the day following has not been done. In this affair, I have gotten soaked.[9] But I have said more than I intended. Wait till we're face to face. (Q. Fr. 2.8.2)*

Clearly, Cicero had been involved in something very important concerning the *lex Campana* that was offensive to the reconciled "Triumvirs" at Luca; whereupon, he was pressured to refrain from his contemplated action, and he absented himself from the meeting on 15 May (ibid., 8.1, *Fam.* 1.9.9–10). Without his presence, the movement to challenge Caesar in the Senate collapsed.

9. *In hac causa mihi aqua haeret*. It is common to explain the metaphor of the water in this sentence as an allusion to running water meeting an obstacle or the water in a water clock running out on a speaker: see Lewis and Short, *A Latin Dictionary*, "haereo" I, b. Hence, translators render it in some way to indicate that Cicero had been prevented from talking on the subject as he wanted to: e.g., Tyrrell and Purser, *The Correspondence of M. Tullius Cicero* 2 (Dublin and London, 1906), p. 84, "I am in a fix"; W. G. Williams, *Cicero, Letters to His Friends* 3 LCL (Cambridge, Mass., and London, 1929), p. 509, "In this business I am at a deadlock"; D. Stockton, *Cicero: A Political Biography* (London, 1971), p. 208, "I am up against a brick wall"; Shackleton Bailey, *Cicero*, p. 83, "On this matter, I am muzzled."

There really seems to be little basis for this interpretation. The phrase *haeret in salubra* (Cic. *Fin.* 5.84) cited by Lewis and Short is no parallel at all. The simple literal translation, "In this affair water clings to me," makes very good sense and might best be rendered in a free translation as "In this matter, I cannot escape blame." As when a person is caught unprepared in a rainstorm or has carelessly stepped into a puddle of water, his bad luck or carelessness is obvious and undeniable, so Cicero could not deny that he had miscalculated and damaged himself politically. More than that he could not say under the circumstances.

X

From Luca to Carrhae

Cicero's attack on the *lex Campana* and Pompey's approval, as evidenced by Lupus's earlier action and the present lack of Pompeian interference, was just what Crassus needed. Now he had a chance to enhance his position vis à vis his two erstwhile partners. He immediately departed Rome and met Caesar in Ravenna, about 13 April, to accuse Pompey and Cicero of planning Caesar's downfall.[1] Appius Claudius Pulcher had already preceded him there and had probably laid the groundwork for Crassus's accusations (Cic. *Q. Fr.* 2.4.6; Plut. *Caes.* 21),[2] as proof of which Crassus would now adduce Cicero's motion on the *lex Campana* (Cic. *Fam.* 1.9.9).

Crassus had Pompey and Caesar where he wanted them, and he planned to exploit his advantage. His proposal to Caesar would be simple and obvious. He would cooperate with Caesar to restrain Pompey and Pompey's friends, if Caesar would be willing to help him get what he wanted. Together they could then bring Pompey back into line with a new triple alliance. Otherwise, he would continue to support the growing effort

1. This trip is usually dated to some time in March: cf. M. Gelzer, *RE* 13.1 (1926), 316, s.v. "Licinius" (68); A. Garzetti, "M. Licinio Crasso," *Athenaem* 22 (1944): 20; W. E. Heitland, *The Roman Republic* 3 (Cambridge, 1909), p. 182; T. Rice Holmes, *The Roman Republic* 2 (Oxford, 1923), pp. 73–74. A March date is highly unlikely, however. He probably left Rome on 6 April. Crassus was in Rome at the trial of Sestius on 11 March and on 3 April at the trial of Caelius. With a ten percent allowance for variations of terrain not apparent on a map, Ravenna is about 245 miles from Rome by the most direct road. With much hard travelling and a couple of days to confer with Caesar, Crassus could have made the round trip between 11 March and 3 April, but, there was no compelling reason for him to have subjected himself to such a rigorous schedule at that time. On 6 April, the day after the senatorial meeting on the *lex Campana*, there was. The political situation was just right, and Pompey was preparing to leave Rome, so that Crassus had to move fast. A quick pace of thirty to thirty-five miles a day would have brought him to Ravenna on 12 or 13 April.

2. Cf. M. Cary, *CAH* 9 (1932), p. 534.

to take away Caesar's command. It was an offer that Caesar could not refuse. Accordingly, word was sent to Pompey that they wished to meet with him at Luca in northeastern Etruria (Plut. *Crass.* 14.5, *Pomp.* 51.3, *Caes.* 21.3; Suet. *Iul.* 24; App. BC 2.3.17).[3]

It is often suggested that before he left Rome, Pompey had already intended to meet with Caesar.[4] He did not give Cicero any indication that he so intended (*Q. Fr.* 2.5.5), nor would one expect him to if he were trying to deceive Cicero. Yet, it might seem suspicious that Pompey was thinking of going so far as Pisa, about 200 miles north of Rome by the best roads, to take a ship to Sardinia, which is south of the latitude of Rome.[5] Cicero, however, reveals no surprise in his account of Pompey's intentions when he mentions them to Quintus (ibid.). Probably the reason was connected with Pompey's supervision of the grain supply. The unidentifiable Labro and the port of Pisa probably were both cities from which grain, still an important crop in northern Italy, was shipped to Rome.[6] Therefore, it is possible that before he left Rome, Pompey was planning to meet Caesar and Crassus at Luca under the guise of a perfectly reasonable trip connected with his duties as grain commissioner.

On the other hand, it seems more likely that Pompey had no prior intention of going to Luca and that he was summoned there after he had left Rome. Pompey departed on 11 April (ibid.). Only after Crassus had conferred with Caesar, on or about 13 April, would there have been a need for a meeting such as the one at Luca. Since Pompey's itinerary had been no secret, Crassus and Caesar could have sent couriers to intercept Pompey (already on his way north) and so requested him to meet with them at Luca, just a short distance from

3. Suetonius (*Iul.* 24) says that Caesar summoned the meeting because he was concerned about the threats of L. Domitius Ahenobarbus, who was campaigning for the consulship. By themselves, however, these threats would have been meaningless if other factors had not been involved.

4. E.g., W. Drumann, *Geschichte Roms* 4, ed. 2, P. Groebe (Berlin and Leipzig, 1908), p. 520; Cary, *CAH* 9 (1932), p. 534; D. Stockton, *Cicero: A Political Biography* (London, 1971), pp. 308–11; D. R. Shackleton Bailey, *Cicero* (London, 1971), p. 82.

5. As Holmes also noted: *RR* 2, p. 73. Heitland erroneously relates that Pompey sailed to Luca from Sardinia: *RR* 3, p. 183.

6. Holmes identifies Labro with Leghorn (Livorno): ibid.

Pisa and about 150 miles from Ravenna by main roads, or less, if more direct, secondary roads were available. Hence, if Crassus and Caesar left Ravenna on 14 or 15 April, they could have met with Pompey as early as 19 April, about a week after he had left Rome.[7]

At Luca, Crassus and Caesar must have made it clear that they would oppose Pompey unless he acceded to their demand for a renewal of the alliance of 59 and an equal role for Crassus this time. They both could have threatened to make common cause with Pompey's optimate enemies, who then would have been in a position to satisfy their ever-present resentment of him. On the other hand, in return for his cooperation, they must have been prepared to give him what he wanted from the *optimates*—a large military command of his own. The three agreed, therefore, that Crassus and Pompey were to be elected consuls for 55, with proconsular commands of five years to follow. Caesar, to keep things equal, was to receive a five-year extension of his command and send troops to Rome to guarantee his colleagues' election (Vell. Pat. 2.46.1; Plut. *Crass.* 14.5–6, *Pomp.* 51.4, *Caes.* 21.3; Suet. *Iul.* 24; App. *BC* 2.3.17).[8]

Crassus had scored a great political victory. He had gone to Ravenna with no official position at all to support the role he wished to play. He left Luca with the promise of a second consulship, hope of a great proconsular command, and assurances that the power of the others could be no greater.[9]

After the meeting, Caesar returned to Gaul, and Pompey went on to Sardinia, whence he informed Cicero that further attacks on Caesar were forbidden (*Fam.* 1.9.9–10). Crassus re-

7. For a sensible discussion of the importance of the conference, see C. Luibheid, "The Luca Conference," *Classical Philology* 65 (1970): 88–94, *contra* J. F. Lazenby, "The Conference of Luca and the Gallic War," *Latomus* 18 (1959): 67–76.

8. For a discussion about how the details of equal importance and duration of commands were arranged, see M. Gelzer, *Caesar, Politician and Statesman*, trans. P. Needham (Cambridge, Mass., 1968), p. 122.

9. It is customary to view the conference as a victory for either Caesar or Pompey. For the former, see Cary, *CAH* 9 (1932), pp. 534–35; Gelzer, *Caesar*, p. 123. For the latter, see R. Syme, *The Roman Revolution* (Oxford, 1939), p. 37; Stockton, *Cicero*, pp. 208–9. Only Chr. Meier seems to give adequate emphasis to the position of Crassus. He even points out that as governor of Syria, Crassus would be able to block Pompey's access to valuable eastern clients: *Res Publica Amissa* (Wiesbaden, 1966), p. 287.

turned to Rome to make preparations for putting the new agreement into effect. First, he probably helped persuade Clodius that he should no longer attack Pompey (cf. Dio 39.29.1–3). Indeed, with Crassus, Caesar, and Pompey presenting a united front against him, Clodius would have been foolish to continue. Already the gangs of Milo had blunted his power. The visible sign of his cooperation with the renewed coalition was his public declaration of reconciliation with Pompey (Cic. *Har. Resp.* 51–52).[10]

Second, Crassus kept an eye on Cicero, who, after having written his "Palinode" to Caesar (*Att.* 4.5.1–3), gave public expression of his new stance towards the latter. When it was proposed in the Senate that Caesar be removed from the commands of both Gauls, Cicero argued for his right to remain in control of these key provinces (*Prov. Cons.*, passim).[11] Later, after Pompey had returned from Sardinia, Crassus joined him and Cicero in defending that astute, useful friend of Pompey and Caesar, Lucius Cornelius Balbus (Cic. *Balb.* 2, 17, 50). Surely, if there had been any previous doubts about the relationship of the "Triumvirs" after Luca, it was now clear that they had agreed to cooperate closely.[12] What their political plans were remained to be seen.

Despite the presence of any others at Luca, the decisions reached at the private meetings of the "Triumvirs" were not general knowledge.[13] Nevertheless, rumor had it that Crassus

10. For the date of the *Har. Resp.*, see E. Ciaceri, *Cicerone e i suoi Tempi* 2 (Milan, Genoa, Rome, Naples, 1941), p. 74, and J. O. Lenaghan, *A Commentary on Cicero's De Haruspicum Responso* (The Hague and Paris, 1969), pp. 22–28.

11. The "Palinode" was a letter to Caesar, and the date of the *de Provinciis Consularibus* was probably in early June. For a complete discussion of these points, see Holmes, *RR* 2, pp. 292–99.

12. M. Gelzer, *RE* 13.1, 317, s.v. "Licinius" (68).

13. The report in Plutarch (*Pomp.* 51) and Appian (*BC* 2.3.17) that there were 200 senators and 120 lictors at Luca, along with the "Triumvirs," appears to be highly exaggerated, particularly as regards the number of senators. It is clear from Cicero (*Fam.* 1.9, *Q. Fr.* 2.5.5) that there existed no prior knowledge at Rome of any conference to be held. If 200 senators had known about any impending conference, certainly Cicero would have learned about it, too. No doubt, there were a number of lictors at Luca who were serving on the staffs of the conferees. Quite likely some senators were also present, just as App. Claudius Pulcher had been present at Ravenna. On the whole, however, the figures supplied by Plutarch and Appian are best regarded as exaggerations. Nevertheless, R. Seager's objection ["Review of Balsdon, *Julius Caesar and Rome*,"

and Pompey planned to stand for the consulship of 55 (Plut. *Crass.* 15.3, *Pomp.* 51.5–6; Dio 39.30.1–2). Although the sources are rather muddled, it seems that the two were afraid to stand for election at the normal time of the *comitia consularia* in July. Cato and his optimate friends were becoming increasingly tough, and Caesar's soldiers would be away on summer campaigns, unavailable for helping voters to make the right choice at election time.

For the moment, then, Crassus and Pompey allowed events to proceed normally. They even appeared to back other candidates, while friends kept their own names before the public as possible choices (Dio 39.27.2–3). When asked by the consul Marcellinus if they really were seeking the consulship, Pompey gave a typically evasive reply, but added that if he should stand, it would be with a view to the good citizens, not the bad (Plut. *Crass.* 15.2–3, *Pomp.* 51.4–5; Dio 39.30. 1–2). Crassus, the true politician, simply said that he would do what was best for the state (ibid.).

Once the legal date for proclaiming one's candidacy had passed, however, they openly campaigned (ibid.). By waiting till this time, they raised a legal issue that could be used to postpone the elections to a more favorable time. Accordingly, Crassus's friend C. Cato, now a tribune, proposed that elections be postponed till the beginning of the next year, when they would be conducted by an *interrex*. In this way, Crassus and Pompey could duly declare their candidacy by the requisite number of days before the elections (Dio 39.27.3). More importantly, it would be January, and Caesar could send down troops from winter quarters to aid Crassus and Pompey against any opposition.

The actions of Crassus and his electoral partner stirred up a great deal of commotion. When partisans of Crassus and Pompey sought to intimidate their opponents, the Senate voted to adopt the garb of mourning as a sign of national

Journal of Roman Studies 58 (1968): 260] that the "triumvirs'" decisions could not have been kept secret if 200 senators had been present can be met if, as Plutarch asserts, the three men made their decisions in private and told no one the truth, [*Pomp.* 51.3].) Nor can even a small number of senators be specifically identified as present at Luca, despite the recent attempt by L. Hayne: "Who went to Luca?" *Classical Philology* 69 (1974): 217–20. The evidence is simply too scanty or ambiguous.

calamity and in the hope of stirring up public indignation against them (Plut. *Crass.* 15.4; Liv. *Per.* 105).[14] Crassus's friend C. Cato sought to block the motion, even to the extent of summoning a mob into the Senate house. Other tribunes negated his efforts. When he also opposed a motion of the senators not to attend the current public games, the consul Marcellinus led the senators, dressed in mourning, to the Forum, where he presented their case directly to the people (Dio 39.28.1–5).

Encouraged by public reaction to their stance, Marcellinus and his optimate friends prepared to take strong measures against Crassus and Pompey. The latters' ally, Clodius, sought to stir up public opposition to this action and very nearly met his end at the hands of angry senators and *Equites* before he was rescued by an enraged crowd that had answered his calls for help (ibid., 29.1–3). In the end, however, it was the personal appearance of Pompey that prevented the Senate from adopting strong measures against himself and Crassus (ibid., 30.1).

For the rest of the year, the Senate ceased to function. Some senators, as the only way of protest left to them, and others, out of fear, avoided senatorial meetings, so that a quorum was always lacking. Many continued to wear mourning attire and avoided all public games and religious festivals (ibid., 30.4). Thus the year dragged on at an impasse until the beginning of 55, when an *interrex* was appointed and elections were finally held (ibid., 31.1).

Even at this point, however, Crassus and his colleague did not have smooth sailing. The most intransigent of the optimate leaders, Marcus Cato, kept up serious opposition. When all other candidates had backed down in the face of Crassus and his partner, Cato bolstered the resolve of their most dangerous rival, L. Domitius Ahenobarbus, his brother-in-law, and persuaded him to continue his campaign (Plut. *Cat. Min.* 41.2–3, *Crass.* 15.2–3). Now the strategy of postponing the elections until Caesar could send some troops to support his allies paid off. Crassus's son Publius had arrived in Rome with a detachment of men just prior to the electoral assembly (Cic. *Q. Fr.*

14. For the political significance and goals of putting on mourning, see A. W. Lintott, *Violence in Republican Rome* (Oxford, 1968), pp. 16–21.

2.9[7].2; Dio 39.31.2). On election eve, Domitius and his friends set off for the Campus Martius before dawn. No doubt, they anticipated an attempt to block his appearance at the polling, and on the way they were met by an armed band. Domitius's torchbearer perished in the ensuing fray, and Cato received a wound. Domitius retreated to his house, where he remained shut up to leave the field to Crassus and Pompey (Plut. *Crass.* 15.4–5, *Comp. Nic. Crass.* 2.1, *Pomp.* 52.1–2, *Cat. Min.* 41.4–5; App. *BC* 2.3.17). Thus, early in 55, Crassus secured his goal of a second consulship and entered office with his colleague of 70, Pompey.[15]

Once in office, Crassus proceeded with Pompey to guarantee their powers and to obtain legislation aimed at fulfilling the agreements that they and Caesar had worked out at Luca. As a contemporary letter of Cicero confirms, there was no question of their getting what they wanted. They were in complete control of the political situation (*Q. Fr.* 2.9[7].3). Cicero himself had learned his lesson and bit the bullet. The optimate opposition was bitter but, at this point, impotent in the face of men who had unrivaled military power and cynically manipulated the constitution to benefit themselves (*Fam.* 1.8).

Now that Crassus and Pompey had gained the consulship, the next battles would be fought at the elections for the other curule magistracies, which had been delayed along with that for the consulship. Therefore, Crassus and Pompey immediately launched a legislative program designed to discourage opposition to their favored candidates. At a meeting of the Senate on 11 February, with little advance notice, Pompey's friend Afranius proposed a motion relating to electoral bribery (Cic. *Q. Fr.* 2.9[7].3). Apparently the motion was to increase the penalties for that offense (Dio 39.37.1).[16] The purpose was to

15. It is clear that they had entered office before February 11 (Cic. *Q. Fr.* 2.9[7].3).

16. Cf. E. Meyer, *Caesars Monarchie und das Principat des Pompeius,* ed. 2 (Stuttgart and Berlin, 1919), p. 155, n. 1. Dio (39.37.1) does not mention any proposal relating to bribery until after a number of other events, including the elections. Nevertheless, the words καὶ μετὰ τοῦτο, which introduce the relevant part of the sentence, need not indicate a strict temporal sequence here, but, rather, a distinction in importance: Dio had discussed what he considered the consuls' major activities, and now he was giving brief mention to lesser items to complete the narrative. Plutarch (*Cat. Min.* 42.1–2) correctly saw the motive behind Afranius's

discourage opposition candidates, who were liable to prosecution if they lost. Of course, candidates favored by Crassus and Pompey need not have worried. They probably had enough resources at their disposal to outbribe most competitors. Once elected, they would enter office immediately and thereby obtain magisterial immunity from prosecution. Still, with this bill, Crassus and his colleague could have hoped to lessen the cost of bribery by eliminating many opponents before the elections.

M. Cato, as spokesman for the *optimates* and candidate for the praetorship, tried to foil the consuls' designs. He agreed to the increased penalties for electoral bribery, but sought to attach a rider that would have made newly elected praetors private citizens for sixty days (Cic. *Q. Fr.* 2.9[7].3). This rider, therefore, would have made the victorious candidates in the praetorian contest just as liable to prosecution as the losers. Crassus and his colleague, however, inveighed against the rider and easily brought about its defeat (ibid.).

Crassus's next move was to propose, again jointly with Pompey, a law against *luxuria*, excessive personal expenditure (Dio 39.37.2). Dio points out the obvious irony of this action, and it has been suggested that they were prompted by Caesar, who enacted such a law as dictator.[17] Others have simply passed over it in silence.[18] It is important, however, because it

---

proposal, but seems to have misconstrued its nature. He says that the proposal was that the praetors enter upon their offices immediately after their election so that they might be free from prosecution for the bribery that Crassus and Pompey would employ on their behalf. Others seem to have accepted Plutarch: e.g., R. Y. Tyrrell and L. C. Purser, *The Correspondence of M. Tullius Cicero* 2 (Dublin and London, 1906), pp. 95–96; Gelzer, *RE* 13.1 (1926), 318.48–56, s.v. "Licinius" (68). If that were the case, however, Cato and his friends simply would have opposed the proposal outright, instead of attaching the rider described below. Indeed, such a proposal as Plutarch describes would have been superfluous. Since the year had already begun, the newly elected magistrates would have entered office immediately, without the interval that usually occurred after elections normally held in the previous calendar year. For the prosecution of magistrates-elect, see D. R. Shackleton Bailey, "The Prosecution of Magistrates-Elect," *Phoenix* 24 (1970): 162–65; E. Weinrib, "The Prosecution of Magistrates-Designate," *Phoenix* 25 (1971): 145–50.

17. Chr. Deknatel, *De Vita M. Licinii Crassi* (Diss., Leyden, 1901), p. 105.

18. E.g., Holmes, *RR* 2, pp. 88, 145–47; Gelzer, *RE* 13.1 (1926), 319–20, s.v. "Licinius" (68); Garzetti, "Crasso," *Athenaeum* 22 (1944): 28–29.

fits into a concerted legislative effort on the part of Crassus and Pompey to undercut the power of the optimate *nobiles* who opposed them, an effort that need not have been suggested by Caesar, despite similar action on his part later.

By ostentatious display of wealth, political figures at Rome advertised themselves and won over the electorate. The erection of public works, the presentation of great games, and distribution of food at their own expense were only slightly more subtle forms of bribery by wealthy office seekers than the wholesale purchases of votes, which commonly occurred. Simply the private display of wealth might earn one supporters who hoped for future benefits.

The *optimates* brought out Hortensius, their wealthiest and most accomplished orator, to oppose it. He expounded upon the inconsistency of Crassus's support for such a law. More skillfully, he played up the benefits that people received from traditional aristocratic expenditure, in much the same way that Cicero had convinced voters not to give up the easy, exciting way of life in the city for the land allotments proposed by Rullus in 63. No doubt remembering that earlier event, Crassus agreed to a withdrawal of the bill (Dio 39.37.3–4) and concentrated on less popular evils. While Pompey brought in a bill to lessen the possibility of bribery in jury trials, Crassus carried a law to prevent the use of *sodalicia,* clubs organized within the tribes, to facilitate violence and bribery in elections (Cic. *Phil.* 1.20, *Pis.* 94, *Planc.* 36–40, 49, *Fam.* 8.2.1; Ascon. *Pis.* 17 C/21 St; Schol. Bob. *Planc.* 152 St).

A year earlier, on 10 February, at a meeting just after Clodius's disruption of Milo's trial, the Senate had passed a decree commanding the dissolution of these clubs and requesting passage of a law making their members subject to the punishment established for *vis* (Cic. *Q. Fr.* 2.3.5). No mention that the requested law was passed is to be found, and any attempt at passage was probably abandoned under the pressure of events and triumviral opposition.[19]

This situation raises the question of Crassus's motive in ob-

19. J. Linderski, "Ciceros Rede *Pro Caelio* und die Ambitus—und Vereingesetzgebung der ausgehenden Republik," *Hermes* 89 (1961): 106–19; E. S. Gruen, *The Last Generation of the Roman Republic* (Berkeley and Los Angeles, 1974), pp. 228–30.

taining passage of his similar law only a year later. It has been maintained that the action of 10 February 56 concerned only the urban tribes, since they were controlled by clubs that Clodius and his cohorts had organized, and that Crassus's law was aimed at the *optimates*, who similarly controlled the rural tribes and thereby wielded great power in the electoral assemblies.[20] This distinction seems unwarranted, however. If the letter of the decree of 56 had concerned only the urban tribes, both the decree, which Cicero quotes, and Cicero himself would have given some indication. Nevertheless, the spirit of that decree probably was aimed at the urban tribes, where Clodius was influential. With their family connections in the great majority of tribes, from all of whom juries were empaneled, the *optimates* could have protected their friends from harm in court, despite any ban on the abuse of clubs.[21]

Crassus's law, however, severely limited the opportunity for the *optimates* to protect any of their friends who might be prosecuted. It provided that the prosecutor name four tribes to provide jurors. The accused could challenge only one, and the jury would be drawn from the remaining three (Cic. *Planc.* 38; Schol. Bob. *ad Planc. argumentum,* 36: 152 and 160 St). Obviously, the prosecutor would choose tribes whose members were as sympathetic to his cause as possible, so that the defendant would face a jury stacked against him from the start.[22]

Crassus's law was damaging to the *optimates,* but it also would have reinforced any previous senatorial decree aimed at Clodius. Although that was probably not the primary object of the law, it would not have been overlooked or thought unfortunate. Both Crassus and his colleague must have vividly

---

20. F. de Robertis, *Il diritto associativo romano dai collegi della repubblica alle corporazioni del basso impero* (Bari, 1938), pp. 110ff.; L. R. Taylor, *Party Politics in the Age of Caesar* (Berkeley and Los Angeles, 1949), p. 210, n. 101 and *The Voting Districts of the Roman Republic* (Rome, 1960), p. 122.

21. Linderski, "Ciceros Rede," *Hermes* 89 (1961): 106–19.

22. Cicero's assertion that the spirit of the law intended that the prosecutor nominate those tribes with whom the defendant was familiar and whom he had allegedly bribed is pure, rhetorical nonsense (*Planc.* 39–44). It would have vitiated the law completely, since either favoritism or unwillingness to admit that they had been bribed would have procured verdicts of acquittal in most cases. Cicero was engaging in mere casuistry to shame Plancius's enemies on the jury that he faced under this law.

remembered the trouble that Clodius had caused in 58. Despite his recent cooperativeness, they were anxious to see this volatile force constrained, lest he once more upset their designs for reasons of his own. Immediately after their election, they had supported a move to grant him a *legatio libera* to the citizens of Byzantium or to Brogitarus, son-in-law of the Galatian king, Deiotarus. In each case, he had considerable sums of money to collect (Cic. *Q. Fr.* 2.9[7].2). Now, having removed him from the scene temporarily, Crassus was quite happy to undercut the organizational basis of Clodius's power in the urban tribes by his law against the abuse of *sodalicia.*

As the trial of Crassus's friend Plancius in 54 demonstrates, the legislation that Crassus and his colleague sponsored potentially cut more than one way. Nevertheless, their first concern was to guarantee the success of their electoral candidates in 55 so that they could manipulate the government for their own ends during their consulship. They had the resources to circumvent their own electoral "reforms." Once elected, their men would enjoy immunity from prosecution for violating the laws that they had obtained to discourage others, and they could proceed unhindered. Moreover, after they had obtained their goals and their friends, having finished their terms of office, were liable to prosecution, they could still count upon using their immense resources to obtain acquittal. Indeed, of their six adherents known to have been prosecuted in 54, C. Cato, Sufenas, Vatinius, and Drusus Claudianus were acquitted, while Messius and Plancius may have been.[23] Therefore, without eliminating themselves, Crassus and his partners were trying to raise the stakes of the old political game beyond the reach of most traditional players.[24]

Cato, nevertheless, was undeterred in his candidacy for the praetorship, and with good reason. The *optimates* were beginning to make their strength felt. On the day of the elections, Cato was doing so well in the polling that Pompey, an augur,

23. Gruen, *LGRR*, pp. 321–22.

24. Gruen interprets the legislation of Crassus and his colleague as a statesmanlike program designed for "the strengthening of Republican institutions" (ibid., p. 233). What he fails to point out, however, is that the political motive of this strengthening was to help them acquire an inordinate amount of power, which was incompatible with the spirit of Republicanism.

had the proceedings nullified by declaring that he had heard thunder, a bad omen (Plut. *Pomp.* 52.2, *Cat. Min.* 42.3). Subsequently, Crassus and Pompey redoubled their campaign of bribery on behalf of their own candidates and forcefully barred Cato's supporters from the second balloting. As a result, Cato lost, and their own candidates were successful.[25]

At this turn of events, one of the two tribunes friendly to Cato summoned a *contio*, and Cato vehemently attacked the actions of Crassus and Pompey before a crowd of sympathetic citizens. Heartened by this harangue, many of them sought to block Crassus's and Pompey's nominees at the elections for the curule aediles. The fighting of rival blocs was intense. Supposedly, Pompey himself was so splattered with blood that when Julia, his pregnant wife, saw his bloodstained clothes, as some servants were exchanging them for fresh ones, she fainted and had a miscarriage (Plut. *Pomp.* 52.3; Dio 39.32.2). Nevertheless, Crassus and his colleague seem to have prevailed. Two men linked to them were elected curule aediles for 55. One was Cn. Plancius, whose father was a publican with ties to Crassus (Cic. *Planc.* 32), and the other was A. Plotius, who, as a tribune of 56, had supported Pompey's bid to restore Auletes (Dio 39.16.2).[26]

After gaining control of most important magistrates, Crassus and Pompey returned to legislation. First, they needed a law that would designate the consular provinces that they desired in accordance with the agreements made at Luca. Although the *lex Sempronia de provinciis consularibus* required the Sen-

25. All of the known or possible praetors for 55 have links with the "Triumvirs." Dio implies that all of the praetors had been backed by Pompey and Crassus (39.32.2–3). T. Annius Milo had raised gangs of streetfighters for Pompey to oppose those of Clodius. P. Plautius Hypsaeus had been Pompey's proquaestor from 65 to 61. The mysterious Gutta, if that is his name, later seems to have enjoyed Pompey's support as a candidate for the consulship of 52 (Cic. *Q. Fr.* 3.8.6). Q. Caecilius Metellus Pius Scipio Nasica was linked to Crassus through the marriage of his daughter to Publius Crassus. Finally, M. Nonius Sufenas (the Nonius "Struma" of Catullus 52) was a notorious supporter of the "Triumvirs." For the addition of Nonius to the list of praetors for 55, see L. R. Taylor, "Magistrates of 55 B.C. in Cicero's *Pro Plancio* and Catullus 52," *Athenaeum* 42 (1964): 18–21.

26. T. R. S. Broughton, *The Magistrates of the Roman Republic* 2 (New York, 1952), p. 216, has listed L. Aemilius Paullus and Nonius Struma as the curule aediles for 55. Taylor, however, has successfully argued for Cn. Plancius and A. Plotius: "Magistrates of 55 B.C.," *Athenaeum* 42 (1964): 12–28.

ate to meet before the consular elections each year to assign provinces to the consuls who would be elected for the following year, the Senate had not done so in 56. When it finally did take up this matter, Cicero had stoutly defended the right of Caesar to retain his provinces and had recommended P. Servilius Vatia's proposal that Macedonia and Syria be designated as the new consular provinces (*Prov. Cons.* 1–39).[27] If a clear decision was reached, one of the provinces finally assigned probably was Syria, which Crassus wanted (Cic. *Pis.* 88). The other may have been Macedonia, as Cicero advocated, or one of the two Spains, both of which Pompey wanted.[28]

Even if both Spains, as well as Syria, had been designated, the Senate's action would have been defective from Crassus's and Pompey's points of view, because they would have been liable to recall from their provinces after only one year. Therefore, Crassus and Pompey enlisted the services of the tribune C. Trebonius to obtain passage of a law similar to the earlier *lex Vatinia* enjoyed by Caesar. The *lex Trebonia* superceded any previous senatorial action and designated Syria and the two Spains as the provinces to be taken up by the consuls of 55 for a period of five years. They were also to have the right to make war or peace as they saw fit (Plut. *Crass.* 13.5, *Pomp.* 52.3, *Cat. Min.* 43.1; Dio 39.33.1–2).

The sources of information on the *lex Trebonia* are very conflicting. Velleius Paterculus has Pompey propose the law and does not even mention the assignment of a province to him, only Syria to Crassus (2.46.2). In two places, Plutarch claims that the *lex Trebonia* included Africa with the Spains (*Pomp.* 52.3, *Cat. Min.* 43.1), while Livy (*Per.* 105) and Appian (*BC* 2.3.18) are found to agree with him. It is clear, however, that both Cyrenaica and Africa Proconsularis had their own gover-

27. This was the meeting at which Cicero delivered his *de Provinciis Consularibus*, probably in late June or early July, not long before the normal time for the consular elections in July.

28. Holmes believed that the Senate had not assigned any provinces to the consuls of 55: RR 2, p. 87. That seems unlikely, however, in view of the debate revealed by Cicero's *de Provinciis Consularibus* and the confirmation that one of the steps advocated therein was taken—namely, the immediate reassignment of Macedonia, which was governed by Caesar's father-in-law, Piso, to another proconsul (Cic. *Pis.* 88–89). Nevertheless, absolute certainty that the Senate did reach a decision on the consular provinces is not possible: Heitland, RR 3, p. 188.

nors within the quinquennium decreed for Pompey's command of the two Spains (Caes. *BC* 1.31; Cic. *Fam.* 8.8.8). Therefore, Pompey can have been assigned no provincial governorship in Africa. Perhaps the law did, however, give him some rights or responsibilities concerning the client kingdoms of Numidia and Mauretania.[29]

Similarly, Dio (39.33.2) and Appian (*BC* 2.3.18) say that Trebonius included the "neighboring lands" with Syria. In one place, Plutarch says specifically that Egypt was included in the command with Syria (*Cat. Min.* 43.1), and both Plutarch (*Pomp.* 52.3) and Livy (*Per.* 105) say that the law charged Crassus with the expedition against the Parthians. No doubt, the *lex Trebonia* did give Crassus the right to wage war in lands bordering Syria as he saw fit, but it is very probable that Plutarch, or his source for *Pompey* 52.3, erroneously specified Egypt in recollection of Crassus's earlier designs on that kingdom. That the law specified an expedition against the Parthians is unlikely. The more general provision concerning his ability to make war would have been more desirable.[30] In specifically mentioning the Parthian War, Livy and Plutarch were probably stating what in fact came about as a result of the law.

The sources also disagree about the provisions for an extension of Caesar's command in Gaul. All, except Dio (39.36.2), claim that Caesar received an extension of a quinquennium for his command.[31] Velleius Paterculus, alone and in clear error, says that Pompey had proposed the additional time for Caesar and had at the same time asked for the granting of Syria to Crassus (2.46.2). Plutarch (*Cat. Min.* 43, *Pomp.* 52.3) and Dio (39.36.2) make it clear that there were two laws, one designating the new consular provinces and one giving more time to Caesar.[32] They disagree, however, as to

---

29. Cf. Heitland, ibid., p. 225, n. 3, and J. Cobban, *Senate and Provinces 78–49 B.C.* (Cambridge, 1935), p. 96.

30. Cf. Cobban, ibid.

31. For a discussion of exactly what is meant by a *quinquennium*, see H. Gesche, "Die quinquennale Dauer und der Endtermin der gallischen Imperien Caesars," *Chiron* 3 (1973): 179–220.

32. Plutarch *Crass.* 15.5 seems to be a shortened version of his other two remarks and need not be taken as assuming only one law, while Livy (*Per.* 105) makes no mention of Caesar's command at all, and Suetonius (*Iul.* 24.1) mentions nothing about the provinces. Appian (*BC* 2.3.18) presents his version in such a way that one cannot determine if he had one law or two in mind.

who proposed the law in favor of Caesar. Plutarch (*Pomp.* 52.3) says that it was again Trebonius, but Dio (39.36.2) claims that Crassus and Pompey proposed the law themselves. On this point, Dio is correct (Hirt. *BGall.* 8.53.1).[33]

As for the reason Crassus joined with Pompey to gain an extension of Caesar's command, Dio is wide of the mark.[34] Following the view that Crassus had united with Pompey against Caesar and failing to mention anything about Luca, Dio sees Crassus and Pompey obtaining commands as great as Caesar's behind his back, whereupon his supporters became very hostile to them (39.33.3). Accordingly, in order to pacify these opponents, Crassus and Pompey are shown promising to obtain an extension of Caesar's term if the law for their commands is allowed to pass (ibid.). This interpretation seems very doubtful. Pompey and Crassus had already agreed at Luca to support the extension of Caesar's command in return for approval of their own requests for great provinical commands (Suet. *Iul.* 24.1; Plut. *Pomp.* 52.3).

Opposition to the *lex Trebonia* was particularly fierce. Cato, supported by Favonius and two tribunes, P. Aquillius Gallus and C. Ateius Capito, was the mainstay of the optimate resistance. Crassus found that he would not get his way easily, despite the full backing of Pompey and Caesar. At the assembly called by Trebonius, Favonius and Cato tried to filibuster the bill giving Crassus and Pompey their provincial commands. Favonius consumed the full hour granted him, but Cato, after exhausting his generous allotment of two hours, continued to hold forth (Dio 39.34.2–3).

Dio claims that Cato's strategy was to raise sympathy for himself by making Trebonius forcibly remove him from the rostra (ibid., 3–4). If so, Cato received his wish, and after he was ejected, he fought his way back to prove his point (ibid.)—several times, according to Plutarch (*Cat. Min.* 43.3). Finally, in exasperation, Trebonius ordered him carried off to jail. This action suited Cato perfectly. Now, people began a great demonstration in his favor. Trebonius, or perhaps Crassus and

33. Cf. Groebe, in Drumann, *Geschichte* 3, p. 254, n. 3, 4, p. 524, n. 4; Garzetti, "Crasso," *Athenaeum* 22 (1944): 28; J. Carcopino in G. Bloch and J. Carcopino, *Histoire romaine* 2 (Paris, 1929), pp. 743–44; Cobban, *Senate and Provinces*, p. 95.

34. Cf. Gelzer, *Caesar*, p. 128, n. 2.

Pompey themselves, saw the danger, and he quickly rescinded his order (ibid.; Dio 39.34.4). Further action was halted, however, by darkness.

Aquillius Gallus, afraid that Crassus's and Pompey's men would try to keep him out of the Forum on the following day, spent the night in the Senate house. When he awoke the next morning, he found himself shut in like a prisoner by the armed men whom Publius Crassus had brought from Caesar for just such contingencies (Dio 39.35.3–4; Plut. *Cat. Min.* 43.4). Others sought to deny Cato, Favonius, Ateius, and their friends entrance to the Forum. When Ateius and Cato tried to dissolve the assembly by announcing an unfavorable omen of thunder, major violence ensued. Crassus, whose patience with the tactics of obstruction had been exhausted, took a lively part in the melee, and sent a senator, Lucius Annalis, fleeing from the Forum with a bloodied face (Dio 39.35.5; Plut. *Cat. Min.* 43.4, *Comp. Nic. et Crass.* 2.2).[35] Nor were the rest any match for Crassus's armed supporters. Aquillius Gallus and others were wounded, and at least four men perished (ibid.). Thus, the way was finally cleared for a vote, and the law that Crassus wanted concerning the consular provinces for 54 was passed (ibid.).

Next, before the assembly could disperse, Crassus and Pompey suddenly proposed and obtained passage of the law guaranteeing tenure of Caesar's provinces for the same length of time as theirs (Dio 39.36.1–2). There was a very good reason for not having this provision a part of Trebonius's original bill. Crassus and his colleagues calculated that many might be willing to accept great commands for him and Pompey if they were thought to last longer than Caesar's. For, in this way, Caesar eventually would be placed at a great disadvantage in power, which might be useful to his opponents. Therefore, if both measures had been combined as one, Crassus and his colleagues might have met even more vigorous and concerted opposition than Cato otherwise was able to arouse.[36]

---

35. Plutarch (*Comp. Nic. et Crass.* 2.2) calls him L. Annalius, but Annalis seems preferable (cf. Cic. *Fam.* 8.8.5).

36. Plutarch (*Cat. Min.* 43.5–6) has Cato issue a prophetic warning at the time Caesar's command was voted on. Supposedly, Cato said that

Along with his attempts to secure his position through legislation and elections in 55, Crassus also sought favor with Cicero, whose influence and oratory could be of great use. In February, circumstances were propitious. Cicero was anxious to set up some dedication in honor of his brother, Quintus, probably for the latter's services as governor of Asia (61–58 B.C.). On Pompey's advice, Cicero went to Crassus, who received him graciously. Crassus told him that there would be no problem so long as he did not oppose Clodius's *legatio libera*. The prospect of having the hated Pulcher removed from Rome delighted Cicero, and he left Crassus's house in high spirits (Cic. *Q. Fr.* 2.9[7].2, cf. *Fam.* 1.9.20). This détente between Crassus and Cicero did not last very long, however. It was destroyed over the issue of Aulus Gabinius, Pompey's friend and governor of Syria.

At first, it looked as if Crassus and Cicero would be on the same side. Cicero had a grudge against Gabinius, who, as consul in 58, had done nothing to help him, but had favored Clodius, his enemy. Then the *publicani*, whom Cicero favored as part of his policy of *concordia*, had lodged complaints about Gabinius's administration of Syria. In 56, therefore, Cicero had taken the opportunity to denounce him during the debate over the consular provinces (*Prov. Cons.* 9–17). Now, in 55, Crassus also had begun to attack Gabinius (Cic. *Fam.* 1.9.20).

No doubt, he, too, was concerned about the complaints of the *publicani*, among whom he had many friends. Yet, there may have been concomitantly a more personal motivation for Crassus's attack. Recently, after receiving a huge bribe, Gabinius had illegally restored Ptolemy Auletes to the throne of Egypt, an assignment for which Crassus himself may have been hoping (Cic. *Att.* 4.10.1; Dio 39.56.3–58.3). Even worse, before he had been diverted to Egypt, Gabinius had set out on a Parthian expedition, which Crassus clearly desired for himself (Strabo 12.3.34, 17.1.11; Joseph. *AJ* 14.98, 102, *BJ* 1.175–76; Iustin. 42.4.1–2; App. *Syr.* 8.51).

Nevertheless, within a few days, when Cicero was denounc-

Pompey was creating for himself a burden that was greater than he would be able to bear and that would bring misfortune on Rome. This prophecy is probably the product of the hagiographic tradition that enveloped the memory of Cato after his death.

ing Gabinius's illegal military adventures, Crassus reversed himself and suddenly appeared in defense of Gabinius. Cicero might have tolerated this *volte face* by itself, but when Crassus personally abused him and called him "exile" in the process, Cicero could not contain his rancor. He lashed out in a scathing denunciation of Crassus (Cic. *Fam.* 1.9.20; Dio 39.60.1).[37]

The reason for Crassus's change of attitude toward Gabinius is not difficult to understand. Malicious propaganda asserted that Gabinius had sent him a large bribe (Dio 39.60.1), but such an explanation is crude and unnecessary. Gabinius already was one of Pompey's closest friends, and in 54, Pompey went to great lengths to protect him from punishment for his actions (Dio 39.60.1–63.5). No doubt, a heart-to-heart talk with Pompey sufficed to account for Crassus's change of mind here in 55. Together they worked out arrangements for satisfying the needs of Crassus's friends, the *publicani*, and Crassus was obliged to cooperate (Cic. *Att.* 4.11.1).[38]

Gabinius apparently was not appeased. Before Crassus set out for Syria, he sent ahead a legate to receive the province from Gabinius and prepare the way for his own assumption of the governorship. Gabinius, however, refused Crassus the courtesy of complying with his wishes and did not budge until he appeared in person (Dio 39.60.4).

Ironically, Cicero's breach with Crassus could not be tolerated by the other two "Triumvirs." It immediately had raised the hopes of their opponents and, if left unmended, might have led to a rallying of forces against them. Caesar issued a stern rebuke to Cicero, and Pompey urgently counselled reconciliation (Cic. *Fam.* 1.9.20). Cicero did not need to learn a bitter lesson twice. He followed their wishes.

The stage was set shortly before Crassus departed for his province. Cicero and Crassus broke bread together and toasted

---

37. Some have incorrectly dated this episode to 56; e.g., Drumann, *Geschichte* 4, pp. 102–3, and Vonder Mühl, *RE* 7.1 (1912), 428, s.v. "Gabinius" (11). For the correct date, cf. Meyer, *Caesars Monarchie*, pp. 168–69; Gelzer, *RE* 13.1 (1926), 320, s.v. "Licinius" (68).

38. Cf. Gelzer, ibid., 319. He dates the meeting between Pompey and Crassus concerning the tax-farmers to 28 April. D. R. Shackleton Bailey, however, dates Cicero's letter that tells of the expected meeting to 26 June: *Cicero's Letters to Atticus* 2 (Cambridge, 1965), p. 102. This date seems preferable in light of the mention of gladiatorial games soon to be held at Rome (probably a reference to the *Ludi Apollinares* held from 5 to 13 July).

each other in friendship at the house of Cicero's son-in-law (ibid.; Plut. *Cic.* 26.1). To be sure, this act was more political than personal. In a letter to Atticus, Cicero revealed that his personal feelings towards Crassus had hardly changed: when he heard of the difficulties that Crassus had experienced upon leaving Rome, he remarked, *O hominem nequam!* (*Att.* 4.13.2). Later, he treated his meeting with Crassus as a bit of a joke when he was approached about also being reconciled with Vatinius (Plut. *Cic.* 26.1).

Crassus received what he wanted, nevertheless—Cicero's political support. The consuls-elect for 54 were Domitius Ahenobarbus, Crassus's bitter opponent in the previous elections, and Appius Claudius Pulcher, whose brother, P. Clodius, now had no reason to favor Crassus. Immediately upon entering office, these new consuls made proposals that would have seriously curtailed Crassus's designs for a great war against Parthia. Cicero leapt to Crassus's defense in the Senate and helped to defeat their purpose (Cic. *Fam.* 1.9.20, 5.8.1). His own letter describing the event to Crassus overflows with eloquent protestations of his loyalty and good will (*Fam.* 5.8.1–5). It ends with a verbal avalanche that must have left Crassus breathless:

> Quam ob rem velim ita et ipse ad me scribas de omnibus mini-
> mis, maximis mediocribusque rebus ut ad hominem amicissi-
> mum et tuis praecipias ut opera, consilio, auctoritate, gratia
> mea sic utantur in omnibus publicis, privatis, forensibus,
> domesticis tuis, amicorum, hospitum, clientium tuorum
> negotiis, ut, quoad eius fieri possit, praesentiae tuae desiderium
> meo labore minuatur. (Fam. 5.8.5)

Thus Cicero faithfully protected Crassus's political flanks while he pursued the elusive Parthian Chimaera.

Although there had been no specific mention or sanction of a war against Parthia in the *lex Trebonia*, it was common knowledge that Crassus was busily planning this expedition during his year of office (Plut. *Crass.* 16.3). By the time Crassus had met with Caesar and Pompey at Luca, Parthia had already attracted Roman attention. During the Mithridatic war, Phraates III, king of Parthia, had allied himself with Pompey against king Tigranes of Armenia in return for a promise of certain territories controlled by Tigranes. The Armenian king surrendered to become Pompey's friend, however, and Pompey then sent his lieutenant Afranius to expel Phraates from the promised territories. Phraates protested, and Pompey thought of going to war with him, but decided that it would be too difficult, so that relations between Rome and Parthia were at a standoff (Dio 37.5.1–7.5). When Crassus met with Pompey and Caesar at Luca, however, civil discord in Parthia presented an opportunity for Roman intervention.

Some time around 57, Phraates' sons, Orodes (Hyrodes) and Mithridates, murdered their father, and the elder brother became King Orodes II. Mithridates quickly revolted and overthrew his brother. He ruled for a short time, until Orodes regained the throne with the help of a talented general, Surenas. In 56, Mithridates sought refuge with Gabinius in Syria and asked for Roman aid against Orodes. Gabinius was already in the process of complying, when his attention was diverted by the restoration of Ptolemy Auletes (App. *Syr.* 8.51).

It was natural for Crassus to want Syria so that he could take advantage of the Parthian situation for himself. The great military commands, first of Pompey and now of Caesar, clearly demonstrated that if he were going to compete successfully for the status of the greatest man at Rome, he, too, would have to have one.[39] It was not petty jealousy of Caesar, mere avarice, or the simple desire for military glory that compelled Crassus to seek a war with Parthia, as the ancient authors might lead one to believe (Vell. Pat. 2.46.2; Plut. *Crass.* 14.4; App. *BC* 2.3.18; Dio 40.12.1). Rather, it was the same thing that had motivated the rest of his career, the desire for unparalleled *dignitas* and *auctoritas* among the ruling elite.

It is in this context that the other motives adduced must be viewed. Caesar's success in Gaul aroused jealousy because it was making him one of the greatest rivals for that position in the state to which Crassus aspired. Glory in battle was important, too, because military laurels captured the public imagination and gave one great political influence with the populace, as both Caesar and Pompey had demonstrated.[40]

39. Drumann, *Geschichte* 4, p. 105; cf. Syme, *RR*, p. 38.
40. Drumann stressed Crassus's need of a triumph to balance the military glory of Pompey and Caesar: *Geschichte*, 4, p. 105; cf. Garzetti, "Crasso," *Athenaeum* 22 (1944): 33.

Nor were thoughts of money absent from Crassus's mind as he contemplated the conquest of the Parthian realm. Great military commands procured the commander not only glory and loyal troops or veterans useful in the political wars of the Forum, but also the money to finance them.

Increasingly, Crassus was finding himself at a financial disadvantage, despite his former dominance in that sphere. Pompey, by virtue of the immense sums procured in the war against Mithridates, was now richer than Crassus was.[41] With these resources, Pompey was building a great stone theater (the first in Rome) as a daily, visible reminder of his greatness, and he was preparing celebrations that would make an indelible impression on the minds of the populace (Plut. *Pomp.* 40.5, 52.4; Dio 39.38.1–6, 40.50.2; Tac. *Ann.* 14.20). Of course, the influence of Pompey's money had already been demonstrated at the polls. Soon, moreover, Caesar, "the greatest brigand of them all," [42] would be able to duplicate Pompey's financial power with the loot from battered Gaul.[43] Clearly, therefore, Crassus had to find a comparable source of revenue for himself if he were to remain competitive with his two colleagues.

For their own reasons, they were willing to support him. In 55, Caesar wrote from Gaul in express approval of Crassus's plan to seek war with Parthia (Plut. *Crass.* 16.3). Later, he even sent Crassus a detachment of 1,000 picked Gallic cavalrymen under the command of Publius Crassus, who had been serving with him in Gaul (ibid., 17.4). Caesar hoped that Crassus, with a great victory and a strong army in the East, would be a useful ally as a check on Pompey, should the need arise. Crassus would be in a perfect position to tamper with Pompey's friends and clients and thereby undercut his power. On the other hand, given his long history of rivalry with Pompey, the chances were slight that Crassus would combine with Pompey against Caesar once he had attained his goals as a commander.[44]

Even if Caesar considered that Crassus might suffer defeat,

41. E. Badian, *Roman Imperialism in the Late Republic* (Ithaca, N. Y., 1968), p. 89.
42. Ibid., p. 82.
43. Ibid., pp. 89–90.
44. Cf. Gelzer, *RE* 13.1 (1926), 320, s.v. "Licinius" (68).

he still could have calculated his own advantage. Unsettled conditions that could have resulted in the region might have denied Pompey the enjoyment of his eastern base of support as effectively as a victorious Crassus. Moreover, a defeat would have given Caesar useful information on the Parthians and an excuse for another great command to be taken up when his current one ran out.

Pompey was probably even more cynical in agreeing to support Crassus's aspirations. He knew better than anyone at Rome the difficulties presented by a full-scale war with Parthia. Such a war would take a long time, time that Crassus would have to be away from Rome. Crassus was also over sixty years old and might not live very long to enjoy the fruits of victory, if he were able to gain one. Moreover, despite any hopes that Caesar or Crassus might have of subverting his eastern support, Pompey probably calculated that he held the trump cards. If Crassus were to succeed, he needed the support and cooperation of client kings and princes loyal to Pompey. Pompey would be at Rome, where he could hope to procure favors to ensure that these clients would remain loyal and would deny their services to Crassus if Crassus misbehaved. Therefore, Pompey was not at all reluctant to assist Crassus's departure from Rome in the face of considerable opposition (Plut. *Crass.* 16.3–6).

Crassus also had support from some of the *optimates*. His basic temperament was more conservative than Caesar's and, except for his election to the consulship in 55, his political career had not done such violence to the established norms as Pompey's had. Nor had he neglected to cultivate the *optimates* when he could. At times, he had cooperated with them against Pompey, and he had married his son Marcus into the family of Q. Caecilius Metellus Creticus.[45]

To those *optimates* who were not so inflexible as Cato, Crassus now appeared to offer them an opportunity for breaking up the coalition that had challenged their control of Rome and, thereby, for ridding themselves of at least Pompey and Caesar. Crassus's old rivalry with Pompey was well known and still smoldered beneath the surface of unity. Considering that

45. Cf. Chapter Eight, p. 203, n. 35.

Caesar had given his daughter to Pompey in marriage and that they had both abandoned him in 59, Crassus could not entirely trust Caesar either. Finally, Crassus was the oldest of the triumvirs, eager to achieve preeminence at Rome before it was too late. He would have been willing to make use of any opportunity to gain an advantage over his two younger associates.

Therefore, now that they had failed to block Crassus's command, a number of *optimates* reasoned that, by offering to ally themselves with Crassus, they could use his army and resources when he returned from the east to checkmate the power of Pompey and Caesar. It was a time-honored solution to get rid of powerful enemies. They had used Sulla to get rid of Marius, his former commander, and Pompey to get rid of M. Aemilius Lepidus, his one-time friend. Now Crassus could help rid them of his partners, Pompey and Caesar. Crassus himself could be dealt with later if necessary, but time and temperament were on their side. With Pompey and Caesar out of the way and the optimate oligarchy in firm control once more, an elderly Crassus would have been satisfied to enjoy in peace the honors of victory.

It is impossible to say who made the first move, Crassus or his potential optimate allies. It is possible, however, to see that they were courting each other before Crassus left Rome in 55. First of all, it is in this year that Crassus's son Publius married Cornelia, the young daughter of Q. Caecilius Metellus Pius Scipio. Her father had been a Cornelius Scipio by birth and had been adopted through testamentary provisions by Q. Metellus Pius, one of the foremost *optimates* of his day.[46] It was also in this year that Publius replaced the recently deceased L. Licinius Lucullus, another leading optimate, in the college of Augurs.[47] Although it is possible that Publius was nominated under the influence of Pompey, who was an augur

46. Cf. F. Münzer, *RE* 13.1 (1926), 292–93, s.v. "Licinius" (63). Since her father was not consul until 52, she would have been born probably in the late 70s and would have been sixteen or seventeen years old when Publius came back to Rome in 55, after three years in Gaul.

47. G. J. Szemler, *The Priests of the Roman Republic* (*Collection Latomus*) 127 [Brussels 1972], p. 152, no. 9. Lucullus died between mid-December 57 and 13 January 56: see W. H. Bennett, "The Date of the Death of Lucullus," *Classical Review* 22 (1972): 314.

at the time,[48] his marriage to Cornelia indicates that his election also may have been pleasing to a number of *optimates*. Finally, even Cicero may have seen an advantage in promoting Crassus's cause.[49] That may explain the vigor with which he worked on his behalf in 54.

With others, however, Crassus fared less well. The people of Italy were angered over the levying of troops for a war that they viewed as unjust, illegal, and designed solely for Crassus's personal profit and aggrandizement (Dio 39.39.1–2; Plut. *Crass.* 16.3; App. *BC* 2.3.18). The uncompromising Cato and his followers sought to take advantage of Crassus's growing unpopularity. Some of the tribunes sought to block the raising of troops and instituted suits against the legates of both Pompey and Crassus. The latter sought to gain sympathy for their cause by the traditional ploy of adopting mourning dress. This action produced no favorable results, however, and Crassus, who had more to lose than Pompey, threatened the hostile tribunes with arms (Dio 39.39.2–5).

This threat cowed most of them; but one, Ateius Capito, Cato's friend, continued unabated. During Crassus's preparations for leaving Rome, Ateius announced dire portents and omens concerning his plans. Public criticism mounted, and Crassus was so concerned that he summoned the assistance of Pompey to escort him through the hostile crowds on the day of departure. Pompey effectively prevented any popular demonstrations, but Ateius tried to place Crassus under arrest. The other tribunes objected, however, and he had to release him. Ateius then tried one last maneuver. He met Crassus at the gate and reissued his ominous warnings. This time, they were sanctioned by the most terrible spirits that a Roman could summon. In effect, he placed Crassus under a dire curse when Crassus predictably ignored him and marched off to Parthia (Cic. *Div.* 1.29–30; Plut. *Crass.* 16.5–6; Dio 39.39.5–7; App. *BC* 2.3.18).[50]

48. Szemler, *Priests of the Roman Republic*, p. 151, no. 35.
49. For Publius's friendship with Cicero, see Cicero, *Q. Fr.* 2.9(7).2, *Fam.* 5.8.2–4, 13.16.1; Plut. *Cic.* 33.5.
50. This traditional account of Crassus's departure has been challenged: see A. D. Simpson, "The Departure of Crassus for Parthia," *Transactions and Proceedings of the American Philological Association* 49 (1938):

The past two years had seen the fruition of Crassus's efforts to restore himself to a position of equality with Pompey and Caesar, one from which he could hope to outstrip them. To recapitulate, in 56, when Cicero, with Pompey's tacit approval, began an attack on Caesar's Campanian Land Law, Crassus went to Ravenna and obtained Caesar's support in dealing with Pompey. At Luca, Pompey agreed to a renewed, more equitable coalition among the three of them. Crassus emerged with the prospect of a consulship with Pompey for 55 and then the governorship of Syria, which implied a great command against the Parthians, in 54.

Optimate opposition to the rumored candidacy of Crassus and Pompey was strong. By waiting until after the legal deadline for declaring their candidacy, they obtained an advantageous postponement of the elections with the help of Crassus's friend C. Cato, one of the tribunes. Most of the optimate leaders abandoned the Forum and Senate in frustration, but the indomitable Marcus Cato kept up a strong attack and persuaded L. Domitius Ahenobarbus to continue his campaign for the consulship. Only an armed band kept Domitius from the electoral assembly, which, after an *interregnum*, bestowed the consulship on Crassus and Pompey in early 55.

After their election, they obtained passage of several laws that would curb the power that their optimate opponents

---

532–41. She argues that the story of Ateius's attempt to arrest Crassus and of his appearance at the gate are unhistorical embellishments: Cicero does not mention these incidents (*Att.* 4.13.2; *Div.* 1.29–30), and they seem to be derived from a confusion with events surrounding the defeat of P. Licinius Crassus Mucianus in Asia and the actions of the tribune Atinius against the censor Metellus in the years 131 and 130, respectively (Liv. *Per.* 59), as well as with ritual curses mentioned by Cicero in his *de Domo Sua*, 123–25. This collocation of facts that she has produced is interesting but not convincing. That Cicero did not go into detail in his letter to Atticus is understandable. He had not been at Rome when Crassus departed and had only secondhand reports (*aiunt*). The passage in the *de Divinatione* could refer to both times when Ateius is said to have warned Crassus of the unfavorable omens, for there is no specific mention of time and place. The sources used by Plutarch and Dio could have been embellished for propagandistic reasons by enemies of the "Triumvirs," but basically the story of Ateius's attempt to arrest Crassus and his dramatic appearance at the gate is consistent with Cicero's reference to Crassus's undignified departure and his need of Pompey to calm the crowd that Ateius would have been doing everything in his power to prejudice and incite against Crassus.

could employ through bribery and *sodalicia*. Next, against M. Cato's continued opposition, Crassus and Pompey obtained the election of other magistrates favorable to them. Then, through the legislative action of the tribune C. Trebonius, they obtained the future governorships of Syria and the two Spains for five years, Syria being reserved for Crassus and the Spains for Pompey. Finally, they themselves gained passage of a law to extend Caesar's command for another *quinquennium*.

Thus far, Crassus had acted to assure himself of a great military command against the Parthians. He needed it to obtain political and financial resources at least equal to the amounts that Pompey had already acquired in the East and that Caesar was amassing in Gaul. Now he began to prepare for his return from Parthia. Having failed to defeat him, some *optimates* began to find him compatible. By combining with him, they might be able to use him against Pompey and Caesar, whom they feared more. Accordingly, Crassus's son Publius married the daughter of Metellus Scipio and replaced the deceased L. Lucullus in the prestigeous college of augurs. By 54, even Cicero may have seen positive advantages in helping Crassus. It was mainly the impolitic Cato and his uncompromising friends who kept up the attack as Crassus set out for Syria and the Parthian War.

At no time had Crassus's prospects for becoming the "First Citizen" of Rome seemed brighter. Since 70, he had tenaciously and skillfully pursued this goal in rivalry first with Pompey and now with both Pompey and Caesar. A victory against the Parthians promised to give him the strength to overcome them, especially if he could return as the champion of their optimate enemies. Then he could hope to spend his final years basking in the glory of unrivaled prestige at Rome.

That was not to be, however. A year and a half later, Crassus, his son Publius, and the overwhelming bulk of his great army lay dead in the sands of Parthia—not so much victims of the Parthian archers and executioners as of the vested interests and unbridled ambitions that were destroying the fabric of the Roman Republic. Not long afterwards, when Julius Caesar and Pompey had helped advance the process of destruction to the point of crisis, the censor Appius Claudius Pulcher reprimanded Ateius Capito for the curses that he had brought down upon the departed general (Cic. *Div.* 1.29–30). Crassus and his legions were sorely needed now to shore up the tottering edifice that he himself had helped to undermine in his struggle for the honor of being "First Citizen."

XI

Conclusion

Earlier in his career, Crassus had acquitted himself well on the field of battle under Sulla and in the war against the dangerous Spartacus. Now, advancing age and his haste to outrun his younger competitors caused him to make a number of serious military blunders during the campaign against the even more dangerous Parthians (Plut. *Crass.* 17–31; Dio 40.12–27). It is neither necessary nor particularly illuminating to treat his actions in detail here. Suffice it to say that they were fatal to him. Accordingly, they removed from the Roman political scene a very powerful and influential figure. In the 70s, 60s, and early 50s B.C., he had played a complex, often puzzling role in the events that ultimately led to the dissolution of the Roman Republic.

In an attempt to put his career during this period in perspective, Syme once said, "One of these days the unpretentious truth may emerge—Crassus was a conservative politician." [1] That is an oversimplification, but there is no doubt that Crassus's basic temperment was more compatible with the optimate nobles than with others. The career of his father on the side of the *optimates* and the deaths of his father and brother at the hands of Marian forces are bound to have affected him. In exile, his first instinct was to join men like Metellus Pius and Sulla, when Sulla's return from the East made it possible to revive the optimate cause (Plut. *Crass.* 6.1–3). It was only when he could not find the hoped-for support of his ambitions from these men or felt suddenly

1. R. Syme, "Review of Gelzer," *Journal of Roman Studies* 34 (1944): 96; cf. F. E. Adcock, *Marcus Crassus, Millionaire* (Cambridge, 1966), p. 13.

threatened by his rivals that he turned towards less conservative methods.[2]

His reluctance to commit himself to a really *popularis* career and his desire to secure the cooperation of the *optimates* whenever he could naturally led to some erratic behavior. Plutarch says:

> Making many changes in his political course, he was neither a firm friend nor an unrelenting foe, but according to his interest, he quickly abandoned good will or wrath, so that very often without space of time he appeared both the promoter and the opponent of the same men or proposals. (Crass. 7.8)

As a result, Crassus has been severely censured by both ancient and modern commentators. Plutarch reports that many criticized him for bad faith (*Comp. Nic. and Crass.* 2.1). Drumann echoed Cicero (*Off.* 1.109) when he said that Crassus scrupled at nothing to gain his ends.[3]

It is incorrect, however, to view Crassus as an unprincipled scoundrel. Gelzer, the great German historian of Rome and biographer of Crassus as well as of Cicero, Pompey, and Caesar, was wrong when he claimed that Crassus was even prepared to proceed to revolution against the regime that he had helped establish, in order to gain his political goals.[4] His communication to Cicero of evidence against Catiline made it clear that Crassus was not prepared to travel the revolutionary route (Plut. *Crass.* 13.4, *Cic.* 15.1–2; Dio 37.31.1).[5] Instead, Dio was more accurate when he characterized Crassus's course as usually a middle one (Dio 39.30.2).[6]

2. Cf. A. Garzetti, "M. Licinio Crasso," *Athenaeum* 19 (1941): 19.
3. W. Drumann, *Geschichte Roms* 4, ed. 2, P. Groebe (Berlin and Leipzig, 1908), p. 126.
4. M. Gelzer, *RE* 13.1 (1926), 299.58–62, s.v. "Licinius" (68).
5. Cf. Chapter Six above.
6. Cf. Plut. *Crass.* 7–8; Ps. Sall. *in Cic.* 3; Adcock, *Crassus*, pp. 10–13. Garzetti claimed that Sallust places Crassus at the head of a *factio media:* "Sallustio nelle Storie (*Hist.* 3.48.8 M) pone Crasso a capo di una *factio media*" ("Crasso," *Athenaeum* 19 [1941]: 20). This assertion seems to rest on a misinterpretation of Gelzer, *RE* 13.1 (1926), 302.22–23, s.v. "Licinius" (68). The passage from Sallust makes no such claim. Indeed, Sallust's words *ex media factione* are in reference to C. Aurelius Cotta and do not mean "from a middle faction," but rather "from the middle of the faction" in reference to the whole nobility: cf. M. I. Henderson, "Review of Scullard," *Journal of Roman Studies* 42 (1952): 115.

Conclusion

Crassus often tended toward the *via media*.[7] Much of his background and training naturally predisposed him to a course of moderation in most things.[8] Plutarch rightly stressed the influence of the simplicity practiced in his father's household (*Crass.* 1.1). Crassus continued to live modestly for a man of his means after he had acquired immense wealth. He did not throw it away on lavish villas and luxurious living. Plutarch quotes him as saying that those with a mania for houses were ruined by themselves, not their enemies (ibid. 2.5). Indeed, there is no record that he had the numerous ostentatious country villas and seaside retreats for which his contemporaries, even a man of comparatively modest wealth like Cicero, were known.[9] Likewise, his table, though made available to many, was graced more by good company than expensive cuisine (ibid., 3.1).

In his personal life, too, Crassus showed moderation, which was scandalously lacking in a day famous for the frequency of divorce, amorous intrigue, and promiscuity among the nobility. The one scandal concerning his relations with another woman was more the stuff of malicious gossip than of truth.[10] He is almost unique among his peers in having remained married to the same woman till the end of his life. Unlike Caesar, who speciously argued that his wife must be above suspicion in order to free himself for a more opportune match

7. Gelzer, as has become clear, was unfair when he said that Crassus pursued a moderate course because of laziness, uncertainty of which side would win, and a reluctance to jeopardize his wealth: *RE* 13.1 (1926), 302.15–31, s.v. "Licinius" (68).

8. Cf. Plut. *Crass.* 1.1; Vell. Pat. 2.46.2.

9. Cf. J. D'Arms, *Romans on the Bay of Naples* (Cambridge, Mass., 1970) and T. P. Wiseman, *New Men in the Roman Senate 139 B.C.–A.D. 14* (Oxford, 1971), Appendix III, pp. 191–96. His large landholdings were purely for investment (Plut. *Crass.* 2.5). No doubt, the two properties specifically mentioned by Plutarch were in this category (ibid., 6.5, 7). He did, apparently, acquire one suburban villa at a low price, but at the cost of no little malicious gossip, from his relative Licinia, a Vestal Virgin (ibid. 1.2). Nor, apparently, did he keep eels: A. M. Ward "Crassus' Slippery Eel," *Classical Review* 24 (1974): 185–86.

10. See the previous note. For the evidence that this "scandal" was used for political purposes by Crassus's enemies, see Chapter Three, pp. 74–75. That he reportedly enjoyed the company of two female slaves during his exile would hardly have offended Roman moral standards (Plut. *Crass.* 5.2–4). At one point, Cicero even referred to *M. Crassi castissima domo* (*Cael.* 9).

(Plut. *Caes.* 10.6), Crassus remained faithful to Tertulla when she became the subject of evil rumors.[11]

Crassus's predilection for moderation shows up even in his taste in philosophy. Whereas most of his contemporaries followed either Stoicism or Epicureanism, Crassus preferred Aristotle, the most profound exponent of the golden mean (μὴ λίαν) in personal and political life among all ancient philosophers.[12] Indeed, one of his permanent companions was a certain expounder of Aristotelian doctrine by the name of Alexander (Plut. *Crass.* 3.3).[13] How seriously Crassus applied Aristotle's philosophy can be questioned.[14] It would be far-fetched, for example, to suggest that Crassus failed to exact interest on personal loans because of Aristotle's strictures against usury.[15] The point is that for some reason, Crassus, in the Roman noble's usual practice of acquiring a gentlemanly knowledge of philosophy, found Aristotle most congenial, and Aristotle's love of the mean seems compatible with the marked tendency toward moderation observed in Crassus.[16]

11. Suetonius includes Tertulla in a list of prominent wives reportedly seduced by Caesar (*Iul.* 50.1). Rumors of such a liaison were probably circulated by Caesar's political foes in attempts to break up cooperation between him and Crassus. According to another rumor, recorded by Plutarch, one of Crassus's sons so closely resembled a certain man by the name of Axius that Axius was reputed to have been the real father (*Cic.* 25.4). When once asked about a well-received speech that this son had made, Cicero replied with a punning Greek phrase, Ἄξιος Κράσσου, which could mean "worthy of Crassus" or "Axius, son of Crassus" (ibid.). If such a rumor did exist in Crassus's lifetime, it probably was more readily believable because of friendship between Axius and Crassus. This Axius was probably Q. Axius of Reate (cf. Wiseman, *New Men*, p. 216 [61]). His family apparently had interests in banking, which probably would have brought them into contact with Crassus (cf. ibid. [62]). In this case, then, Axius may well have been one of Crassus's clients from the local Italian aristocracy.

12. Cf. Aristotle's *Nicomachean Ethics* and *Politics*.

13. B. Perrin suggests that this man was Alexander Polyhistor, whom a certain Cornelius Lentulus had brought back from Asia Minor and freed: *Plutarch's Lives* 3, LCL (Cambridge, Mass., and London, 1916), p. 321, n. 1. Garzetti does likewise: "Crasso," *Athenaeum* 19 (1941): 13, n. 1. This identification does not seem very sound. Alexander Polyhistor was primarily a Stoic, and Plutarch's description of Crassus's Peripatetic companion does not fit the picture of Polyhistor's prolific achievements: cf. V. Schwartz, *RE* 1.1 (1894), 1449–52, s.v. "Alexandros" (88).

14. Cf. Garzetti, "Crasso," *Athenaeum* 19 (1941): 13.

15. For Crassus's interest-free loans, see Plut. *Crass.* 3.1; for Aristotle's strictures on interest, see Aristotle, *Politics* 1.10, 1258b.

16. That is not to say that Crassus was always a paragon of moderation and self-restraint. He could lose his temper as well as anyone. Recall, in

In one area alone could Crassus actually be called im-
moderate: this area was ambition, not avarice. What many
have seen as avarice and unbounded greed in Crassus is really
a function of his supreme ambition to be the most important
man at Rome, the *princeps civitatis,* so to speak. Money was
primarily a political weapon. Cicero, in a candid moment,
analysed Crassus well in this respect (*Off.* 1.25).[17] As the only
surviving member of a tightly knit noble family and the son
of a man who had reached the censorship and celebrated a
triumph, Crassus was duty-bound to strive to match these
achievements and preserve the glory of his name. Another
potent goad was the thought of relative upstarts like Pompey
and Caesar gaining the honors that in more stable times he
could have looked forward to obtaining almost as a foregone
conclusion at birth.[18]

Accordingly, Crassus found himself in rivalry first with Pompey, then with both Pompey and Caesar, who had fewer
family laurels to support them. At times, Crassus found that
Pompey or Caesar had stolen a march on him and that he
had to outmaneuver them (Vell. Pat. 2.44.2; Dio 37.56.4).
Often, therefore, he reversed his course and started off on
another tack, as the previous chapters have shown. These
shifts may seem mercurial and inconsistent, even impossible,

55, for example, that when L. Annalis was speaking against Crassus, Crassus
punched him in the face and sent him bleeding from the Forum (cf.
Chapter Ten, p. 277, n. 35).

17. Cf. Vell. Pat. 2.30.5, 44.2, 46.2; Dio 37.56.4; H. Frisch, "The First
Catilinarian Conspiracy: A Study in Historical Conjecture," *Classica et
Mediaevalia* 9 (1947): 29–30; and T. J. Cadoux, "Marcus Crassus: A
Revaluation," *Greece and Rome* 2nd ser. 3 (1956): 155.

18. An attitude that was common among the nobility, according to
Cicero's bitter comment (*Verr.* 2.5.180). Pompey's father had only recently raised his branch of the Pompeii to the ranks of the nobility, and
Julius Caesar's direct ancestors had not distinguished themselves for some
time, despite their patrician origin. I would disagree with Chr. Deknatel,
however, who believed that Crassus was incited more by hatred and
jealousy than by ambition and, but for Pompey first and then Caesar,
would have conducted his life in silence and leisure: *De Vita M. Licinii
Crassi* (Diss., Leyden, 1901), p. 19. The traditions and honor of his
family would have led him to seek an important political career without
the added goads of Pompey and Caesar. F. B. Marsh held that Crassus
was simply a man who loved power for its own sake; *A History of the
Roman World 146–30 B.C.,* ed. 3, H. H. Scullard (London, 1963), p. 180.
No doubt, as a Roman noble, Crassus had a certain innate love of power
and its exercise, but, again, one cannot overlook the weight of family tradition and honor that impelled him.

but they are not, when viewed in the light of his consistent goal of countering his rivals at every opportunity. They reveal his great flexibility and skill in political maneuvering.

This flexibility and Crassus's natural bent towards moderation in most things are reflected in his willingness to compromise in order to advance his aims (Plut. *Crass.* 7.8). He compromised with his greatest rival, Pompey, in 71 and gained the consulship.[19] He compromised with Pompey again at the end of 60 or in early 59 and initially reaped the benefit of mutual cooperation in gaining political favors.[20] He compromised with Pompey and Caesar in 56 and received his second consulship as well as command of Syria and the Parthian War,[21] and before he left Rome in 55, he made peace with Cicero, despite Cicero's longstanding hostility. At the same time, he seems to have reached an understanding with some of his optimate opponents in the Senate in order to promote his interests against Pompey and Caesar when he should return.[22]

Because of these shifts, many have seen a fatal lack of judgment and decisiveness in Crassus.[23] On the contrary, his willingness to compromise was an asset. Had he returned successfully from Parthia, he probably would have supported the optimate leaders of the Senate. His conservative background and tendency toward moderation and compromise would have prevented him from establishing the kind of personal absolutism that Caesar later sought. He would have been more attractive to those who relied upon Pompey against Caesar in 49 only because there was no alternative.

If Pompey had been more flexible and willing to compromise with Caesar in 49, he might have rescued his cause.[24] If Caesar had been more willing to compromise between Republicanism and absolutism in his reordering of the Roman government, he would have been the first Roman *Princeps*, not the last Roman dictator. It is a mark of Crassus's ability and

19. See above, Chapter Five.
20. See above, Chapter Seven.
21. See above, Chapter Nine.
22. See above, Chapter Ten.
23. E.g., Garzetti, "Crasso," *Athenaeum* 19 (1941): 18, 20, 37; 22 (1944): 23; Gelzer, RE 13.1 (1926), 312, 320, s.v. "Licinius" (68); Ch. Meier, *Res Publica Amissa* (Wiesbaden, 1966), p. 274.
24. Cf. M. Gelzer, *Caesar, Politician and Statesman*, trans. P. Needham (Cambridge, Mass., 1968), pp. 198–99.

the worth of his policy that he went so far and survived so long in the Roman political arena.[25] Unfortunately, in the competition for prestige and honor with his fellow aristocrats, Crassus himself helped to aggravate the social, economic, and political problems destroying the very Republic that gave their lives meaning.

25. Crassus's only real failing as a contestant in this arena was that he was not as great a general as Caesar. But, Caesar did not have to meet the test of Parthian tactics, and no one knows what special case Cassius was pleading, upon whose memoirs most accounts of Crassus's Parthian campaign in great part depend. For a sensible appraisal of Crassus's generalship, see Adcock, *Crassus*, pp. 8–9. For the importance of Cassius's account in the sources, see K. Regling, *De Belli Parthici Crassiani Fontibus* (Diss., Berlin, 1899).

Bibliography

Adcock, F. E. *Marcus Crassus, Millionaire, Cambridge*, 1966.

Afzelius, A. "Das Ackerverteilungsgesetz des P. Servilius Rullus." *Classica et Mediaevalia* 3 (1940): 214–35.

Albini, U. "L'orazio contro Vatinio." *La Parola del Passato* 14 (1959): 172–84.

Allen, W., Jr. "The Vettius Affair Once More." *Transactions and Proceedings of the American Philological Association* 81 (1950): 153–63.

———. "Cicero's Provincial Governorship in 63 B.C." *Transactions and Proceedings of the American Philological Association* 83 (1952): 233–41.

Astin, A. E. *The Lex Annalis before Sulla* (*Collection Latomus* 32). Brussels, 1958.

———. *Scipio Aemilianus*. Oxford, 1967.

———. *Politics and Policies in the Roman Republic: An Inaugural Lecture delivered before the Queen's University of Belfast on 1 May 1968*. Belfast, 1968.

Babcock, C. L. "The Early Career of Fulvia." *American Journal of Philology* 86 (1965): 1–32.

Babelon, E. *Monnaies de la République romaine* 2. Paris, 1886.

Badian, E. "The Date of Pompey's First Triumph." *Hermes* 83 (1955): 107–18.

———. "Caepio and Norbanus." *Historia* 6 (1957): 318–46.

———. *Foreign Clientelae* (264–70 B.C.). Oxford, 1958.

———. "From the Gracchi to Sulla (1940–1959)." *Historia* 11 (1962): 197–245.

———. "Waiting for Sulla." *Journal of Roman Studies* 52 (1962): 47–61.

———. *Studies in Greek and Roman History*. Oxford, 1964.

———. "M. Calpurnius M. F. Piso Frugi." *Acta of the Fifth Epigraphic Congress* (1967): 209–14.

———. *Roman Imperialism in the Late Republic*. Ithaca, N. Y., 1968.

———. "Two Roman Non-Entities." *Classical Quarterly* 19 N.S. (1969): 198–204.

Bibliography

———. "Additional Notes on Roman Magistrates." *Athenaeum* 48 (1970): 3–14.

———. "Lucius Sulla, The Deadly Reformer." *Seventh Todd Memorial Lecture.* Sydney, 1970.

———. "The Family and Early Career of T. Quinctius Flamininus." *Journal of Roman Studies* 61 (1971): 102–11.

———. *Publicans and Sinners.* Ithaca, N. Y., 1972.

———. "Tiberius Gracchus and the Roman Revolution." *Aufstieg und Niedergang der Römischen Welt,* vol. 1, pp. 668–731. Berlin and New York, 1972.

———. "Marius' Villas: The Testimony of the Slave and the Knave." *Journal of Roman Studies* 63 (1973): 121–32.

———. "The Attempt to Try Caesar." In *Polis and Imperium. Studies in Honor of Edward Togo Salmon.* Edited by J. A. S. Evans, pp. 145–66. Toronto, 1974.

Balsdon, J. P. V. D. "*Roman History* 58–56 B.C.: Three Ciceronian Problems." *Journal of Roman Studies* 47 (1957): 15–20.

———. "Roman History, 65–50 B.C.: Five Problems." *Journal of Roman Studies* 52 (1962): 134–41.

———. "Fabula Clodiana." *Historia* 15 (1966): 65–73.

Bardon, H. *Catulli Carmina.* Brussels, 1970.

Bauman, R. A. *The Crimen Maiestatis in the Roman Republic and Augustan Principate.* Johannesburg, 1967.

Bennett, W. H. "The Death of Sertorius and the Coin." *Historia* 10 (1961): 459–72.

———. "The Date of the Death of Lucullus." *Classical Review* 22 (1972): 314.

Bloch, G. *La république romaine: les conflits politiques et socieux.* Paris, 1919.

Bloch, G., and Carcopino, J. *Histoire romaine,* vol. 2. Paris, 1929.

Bonghi, R. *Spartaco, Atti Della Reale Accademia di Science Morali e Politiche di Napoli* 16. Naples, 1881.

Boren, H. C. "The Urban Side of the Gracchan Economic Crisis," *American Historical Review* 63 (1957/8): 890–902.

———. "Cicero's *Concordia* in Historical Perspective." *Studies in Memory of Wallace Everett Caldwell: The James Sprunt Studies in History and Political Science* 46 (1964): 51–62.

Brisson, J.-P. *Spartacus.* Paris, 1959.

Broughton, T. R. S. *The Magistrates of the Roman Republic.* 2 vols. New York, 1951–52.

———. *Supplement to the Magistrates of the Roman Republic.* New York, 1960.

Bruns, C. G. *Fontes iuris romani antiqui.* 7th ed. Edited by O. Gradenwitz. Tübingen, 1909.

Brunt, P. A. "Cicero: *Ad Atticum,* 2.24." *Classical Quarterly* 3 N.S. (1953): 62–64.

————. "Three Passages from Asconius." *Classical Review* 71 (1957): 193–95.

————. "'Amicitia' in the Late Roman Republic." *Proceedings of the Cambridge Philological Society* 11 N.S. (1965): 1–20.

Buck, C. D. *A Comparitive Grammar of Greek and Latin.* Chicago, 1933.

Burn, A. R. "A Metellus in Two Passages of Dio (CR lxii, p. 59)." *Classical Review* 63 (1949): 52–53.

Cadoux, T. J. "Marcus Crassus: A Revaluation." *Greece and Rome* 2nd series. 3 (1956): 153–61.

Caldwell, W. E. "An Estimate of Pompey." *Studies presented to David Moore Robinson*, pp. 954–61. St. Louis, 1953.

Carcopino, J. *Sylla ou la monarchie manquée.* 3rd ed. Paris, 1931.

Carney, T. F. *A Biography of C. Marius. Proceedings of the African Classical Association* Supplement 1. 1962.

————. "Prosopography: Payoffs and Pitfalls." *Phoenix* 27 (1973): 156–79.

Cary, M. "*Asinus Germanus.*" *Classical Quarterly* 17 (1923): 103–7.

Checkland, S. G. *The Mines of Tharsis.* London, 1967.

Ciaceri, E. *Cicerone e i suoi Tempi.* 2 vols. Milan, Genoa, Rome, Naples, 1939–41.

Cichorius C. *Römische Studien.* Leipzig and Berlin, 1922.

Cobban, J. *Senate and Provinces 78–49 B.C.* Cambridge, 1935.

Constans, L. A. *Cicéron: Correspondance*, vol. 1. Paris, 1934.

Cowles, F. H. *Gaius Verres, an Historical Study.* Ithaca, N. Y., 1917.

Crook, J. A. "A Metellus in Two Passages of Dio." *Classical Review* 62 (1948): 59–61.

D'Arms, J. H. *Romans on the Bay of Naples.* Cambridge, Mass., 1970.

Davison, J. A. "Cicero and the lex Gabinia." *Classical Review* 44 (1930): 224–25.

Dederich, A. *Sex. Iulii Frontini Strategematicon Libri Quattuor.* Lipsiae, 1855.

Degrassi, A. *Inscriptiones Italiae*, vol. 13.1. Rome, 1949.

Deknatel, Chr. *De Vita M. Licinii Crassi.* Diss., Leyden, 1901.

De Robertis, F. M. *Il diritto associativo romano dai collegi della repubblica alle corporazioni del basso impero.* Bari, 1938.

Dessau, H. *Inscriptiones Latinae Selectae.* 3 vols. Berlin, 1892–96.

Dittenberger, W. *Sylloge Inscriptionum Graecarum.* 3rd ed. 2 vols. Leipzig, 1903–5.

Dorey, T. A. "Cicero and the Lex Campana." *Classical Review* 9 (1959): 13.

————. "A Note on the Pro Roscio Amerino." *Ciceroniana* 2 (1960): 147–48.

————, ed. *Cicero*. New York, 1965.

Douglas, A. E. *Brutus*. Oxford, 1966.

Drumann, W. *Geschichte Roms*. 2nd ed., P. Groebe. 6 vols. Berlin and Leipzig, 1899–1929.

Duggan, A. *Julius Caesar*. New York, 1955.

Dumézil, G. *La religion romaine archaique*. Paris, 1966.

Earl, D. C. *Tiberius Gracchus: A Study in Politics* (*Collection Latomus* 66). Brussels, 1963.

Ferrero, G. *The Life of Caesar*. Translated by A. E. Zimmern. New York, 1962.

Frank, T. "Cicero and the Novi Poetae." *American Journal of Philology* 40 (1919): 396–415.

————. *Economic Survey of the Roman Empire*, vol. 1. Baltimore, 1933.

Frisch, H. "The First Catilinarian Conspiracy: A Study in Historical Conjecture." *Classica et Mediaevalia* 9 (1948): 10–36.

Fulford-Jones, P. W. "Calvus ex Nanneianis." *Classical Quarterly* 21 N.S. (1971): 183–85.

Gabba, E. "Le origini delle guerra sociale e la vita politica romana dopo l' 89 a. C." *Athenaeum* 32 (1954): 41–114, 293–345.

————. "Il ceto equestre e il senato di Sulla." *Athenaeum* 34 (1956): 124–38.

————. *Appiani Bellorum Civilium Lib. I*. Florence, 1962.

Gardner, R. "The Early Career of L. Cornelius Balbus." *Cicero, The Speeches pro Caelio, de Provinciis Consularibus, pro Balbo*, pp. 613–16. Cambridge, Mass., and London, 1958.

Garzetti, A. "M. Licinio Crasso." *Athenaeum* 19 (1941): 1–37.

————. "M. Licinio Crasso." *Athenaeum* 20 (1942): 12–40.

————. "M. Licinio Crasso." *Athenaeum* 22 (1944): 1–61.

Gelzer, M. "Die Lex Vatinia de imperio Caesaris." *Hermes* 63 (1928): 113–37.

————. Review of J. Carcopino, *Sylla ou la monarchie manquée*. *Gnomon* 8 (1932): 607.

————. *Pompeius*. 2nd ed. Munich, 1959.

————. *Kleine Schriften*. 2 vols. Wiesbaden, 1962.

————. *Caesar, Politician and Statesman*. Translated by P. Needham. Cambridge, Mass., 1968.

————. *The Roman Nobility*. Translated by R. Seager. Oxford, 1969.

————. *Cicero. Ein biographischer Versuch*. Wiesbaden, 1969.

Gesche, H. "Die quinquennale Dauer und der Endtermin der gallischen Imperien Caesars." *Chiron* 3 (1973): 179–220.

Grant, M. *Julius Caesar*. London, 1969.

Grieco, E. *Buccino* (*antica Volcei*). Salerno, 1959.

Griffin, M. "The Tribune C. Cornelius." *Journal of Roman Studies* 63 (1973): 196–203.

Grimal, P. *Études de chronologie cicéronienne (anneés 58 et 57 av. J.-C.)*. Paris, 1967.

Gruen, E. S. "P. Clodius: Instrument or Independent Agent?" *Phoenix* 20 (1966): 120–30.

———. "Pompey and the Pisones." *California Studies in Classical Antiquity* 1 (1968): 155–70.

———. *Roman Politics and the Criminal Courts, 149–78 B.C.* Cambridge, Mass., 1968.

———. "Notes on the 'First Catilinarian Conspiracy.'" *Classical Philology* 64 (1969): 20–24.

———. "Pompey, The Roman Aristocracy, and the Conference of Luca." *Historia* 18 (1969): 71–108.

———. "Veteres Hostes, Novi Amici." *Phoenix* 24 (1970): 237–43.

———. "Pompey, Metellus Pius, and the Trials of 70–69 B.C.: The Perils of Schematism." *American Journal of Philology* 92 (1971): 1–16.

———. "The Trial of C. Antonius." *Latomus* 32 (1973): 301–10.

———. *The Last Generation of the Roman Republic*. Berkeley and Los Angeles, 1974.

Hamilton, C. D. "The Tresviri Monetales and the Republican Cursus Honorum." *Transactions and Proceedings of the American Philological Association* 100 (1969): 181–91.

Hardy, E. G. "The Policy of the Rullan Proposal in 63 B.C." *Journal of Philology* 32 (1912–13): 228–60.

———. "The Table of Heraclea and the Lex Julia Municipalis." *Journal of Roman Studies* 4 (1914): 77–82.

———. "The Transpadane Question and the Alien Act of 65 or 64 B.C." *Journal of Roman Studies* 6 (1916): 63–82.

———. "The Catilinarian Conspiracy in Its Context, A Restudy of the Evidence." *Journal of Roman Studies* 7 (1917): 153–228.

Harris, W. V. *Rome in Etruria and Umbria*. Oxford, 1971.

Hathorn, R. Y. "Calvum ex Nanneianis." *Classical Journal* 50 (1954): 33–34.

Hawthorn, J. R. "The Senate after Sulla." *Greece and Rome* 9 (1962): 53–60.

Hayne, L. "Who Went to Luca?" *Classical Philology* 69 (1974): 217–20.

———. "The Politics of M'. Glabrio, Cos. 67." *Classical Philology* 69 (1974): 280–82.

Heaton, J. W. "Mob Violence in the Late Roman Republic." *University of Illinois Studies in the Social Sciences* 23.4. Urbana, Ill., 1939.

Heinze, R. "Ciceros politische Anfänge." *Abhandlungen der*

Bibliography

Akademie der Wissenschaft zu Leipzig, Philologische-historische Klasse 27 (1909): 945–1010.

———. "Ciceros Rede Pro Caelio." Hermes 60 (1925): 193–258.

———. Vom Geist des Römertums. Leipzig and Berlin, 1938.

Heitland, W. E. The Roman Republic, vol. 3. Cambridge, 1909.

Hellogouarc'h, J. Le vocabulaire Latin des relations et des partis politiques sous la république romaine. Paris, 1963.

Henderson, M. I. Review of Scullard, Roman Politics, 220–150 B.C. Journal of Roman Studies 42 (1952): 114–16.

———."The Establishment of the 'equester ordo.'" Journal of Roman Studies 53 (1963): 61–72.

Hill, H. "Sulla's Military Oligarchy." Proceedings of the Classical Association (1931): 63–65.

———. "Sulla's New Senators in 81 B.C." Classical Quarterly 26 (1932): 170–77.

———. The Roman Middle Class in the Republican Period. Oxford, 1952.

Holmes, T. Rice. The Roman Republic, vols. 1 and 2. Oxford, 1923.

How, W. W. Cicero, Select Letters, vol. 2. Oxford, 1926.

Jameson, S. "Pompey's Imperium in 67: Some Constitutional Fictions." Historia 19 (1970): 539–60.

Jashemski, W. F. The Origins and History of the Proconsular and the Propraetorian Imperium to 27 B.C. Chicago, 1950.

John, C. "Der Tag der erste Rede Ciceros gegen Catilina." Philologus 46 (1888): 650–65.

———. "Die Entstehungsgeschichte der catilinarischen Verschwörung." Jahbücher für Classische Philologie, Supplementband 8 (1876): 703–819.

Jones, A. H. M. The Criminal Courts of the Late Roman Republic and Principate. Oxford, 1972.

Laffi, U. "Il Mito di Silla," Athenaeum 55 (1967): 177–213.

Lange, D. "Two Financial Maneuvers of Cicero." Classical World 65 (1972): 152–55.

Last, H. Review of Bloch and Carcopino, Journal of Roman Studies 34 (1944): 116–21.

Lazenby, J. F. "The Conference of Luca and the Gallic War." Latomus 18 (1959): 67–76.

Lenaghan, J. O. A Commentary on Cicero's DE HAURUSPICUM RESPONSO. The Hague and Paris, 1969.

Lewis, R. G. "Appian B.C. I, 49, 214 δεκατεύοντες: Rome's New Tribes 90–87 B.C." Athenaeum 46 (1968): 272–91.

Linderski, J. "Ciceros Rede Pro Caelio und die Ambitus- und Vereinsgesetzgebung der ausgehenden Republik," Hermes 89 (1969): 106–19.

————. "Constitutional Aspects of the Consular Elections in 59 B.C." *Historia* 14 (1965): 423–33.

————. "Were Pompey and Crassus Elected in Absence to Their First Consulship?" *Mélanges offerts à K. Michalowski*, pp. 523–26. Warsaw, 1966.

————. "Two Quaestorships." *Classical Philology* 70 (1975): 35–38.

Lintott, A. W. "P. Clodius Pulcher—Felix Catilina?" *Greece and Rome* 14 (1967): 157–69.

————. *Violence in Republican Rome*. Oxford, 1968.

Luibheid, C. "The Luca Conference." *Classical Philology* 65 (1970): 88–94.

McDermott, W. C. "*Vettius ille, ille noster index*." *Transactions and Proceedings of the American Philological Association* 80 (1949): 351–67.

————. "*In Caelianam*." *Athenaeum* 48 (1970): 408–9.

————. "*De Lucceiis*." *Hermes* 97 (1969): 233–46.

————. "The Sisters of P. Clodius." *Phoenix* 24 (1970): 39–47.

————. "Q. Cicero." *Historia* 20 (1971): 702–17.

————. "Curio *Pater* and Cicero." *American Journal of Philology* 93 (1972): 381–411.

————. "Cicero: The Human Side." *Classical Bulletin* 49 (1972): 17–25.

————. "Cicero's Publication of his Consular Orations." *Philologus* 116 (1972): 277–84.

————. "LEX POMPEIA DE TRIBUNICIA POTESTATE (70 B.C.)." *Classical Philology* 72 (1977): 49–51.

McDonald, W. "The Tribunate of Cornelius." *Classical Quarterly* 23 (1929): 196–208.

Marrou, H. I. *A History of Education in Antiquity*. Translated by G. Lamb. New York, 1964.

Marsh, F. B. "The Policy of P. Clodius from 58–56 B.C." *Classical Quarterly* 21 (1927): 30–36.

————. *A History of the Roman World from 146 to 30 B.C.* 3rd ed., H. H. Scullard. London, 1963.

Marshall, B. A. "Crassus and the Command against Spartacus." *Athenaeum* 51 (1973): 109–21.

————. "Crassus' Ovation in 71 B.C." *Historia* 21 (1972): 669–73.

————. "Crassus and the Cognomen Dives." *Historia* 22 (1973): 459–67.

————. "Pompeius' Temple of Hercules." *Antichthon* 8 (1974): 80–84.

————. "Cicero and Sallust on Crassus and Catiline." *Latomus* 33 (1974): 804–13.

————. "Q Cicero, Hortensius and the Lex Aurelia." *Rheinisches Museum für Philologie* 118 (1975): 136–52.

Bibliography

Marshall, B. A. and R. J. Baker. "The Aspirations of Q. Arrius." *Historia* 24 (1975): 220–31.

Mattingly, H. "The Denarius of Sufenas and the *Ludi Victoriae.*" *Numismatic Chronicle* 16 (1956): 189–203.

Maurenbrecher, B. C. *Sallusti Crispi Historiarum Reliquiae.* Leipzig, 1891.

Meier, Chr. "Zur Chronologie und Politik in Caesars ersten Konsulat." *Historia* 10 (1961): 68–98.

——. "Pompeius' Rückher aus dem Mithridatischen Kriege und die Catilinarischen Verschwörung." *Athenaeum* 40 (1962): 103–25.

——. *Res Publica Amissa.* Wiesbaden, 1966.

——. "Die loca intercessionis bei Rogationen. Zugleich ein Beitrag zum Problem der Bedingungen der tribunischen Intercession." *Museum Helveticum* 25 (1968): 86–100.

Mello, M. "Sallustio e le elezioni consolari del 66." *La Parola del Passato* 18 (1963): 47–54.

Mess, A. Von. *Caesar, Sein Leben, Seine Zeit und Seine Politik.* 3rd ed. Leipzig, 1913.

Meyer, E. *Caesars Monarchie und das Principat des Pompeius.* 2nd ed. Stuttgart and Berlin, 1919.

Mitchell, T. N. "Cicero before Luca." *Transactions and Proceedings of the American Philological Association* 100 (1969): 295–320.

——. "Veteres Hostes, Novi Amici (Cic. *Fam.* V.7,1)." *Historia* 24 (1975): 618–22.

Mommsen, Th. *Geschichte des römischen Münzwesens.* Berlin, 1860.

——. *Römische Staatsrecht.* 3 vols. Leipzig, 1887.

——. *The History of Rome.* vols. 4 and 5. Translated by W. P. Dickson, New York, 1895.

Münzer, F. "Der erste Gegner des Spartacus." *Philologus* 55 (1896): 387–89.

Nicolet, C. "*Consul Togatus:* Remarques sur le vocabulaire politique de Cicéron et de Tite-Live." *Revue des études latines* 38 (1960): 236–63.

——. *L'Ordre équestre à l'Epoque Républicaine.* Paris, 1966.

Oost, S. I. "Cato Uticensis and the Annexation of Cyprus." *Classical Philology* 50 (1955): 98–112.

——. "The Date of the *Lex Julia de Repetundis.*" *American Journal of Philology* 77 (1956): 19–28.

Ooteghem, J. Van. *Lucius Licinius Lucullus.* Namur, 1959.

Panebianco, V. "A proposito della capitale della confederazione lucana." *Rassegna Storica Salernitata* 6 (1945): 109–23.

Pareti, L. *La Congiura di Catilina.* Catania, 1934.

——. *Storia di Roma* 3. Turin, 1953.

Parrish, E. J. "Crassus' New Friends and Pompey's Return." *Phoenix* 27 (1973): 357–80.

———. "M. Crassus Pontifex: By Whose Patronage?" *Latomus* (forthcoming).

Perrin, B. *Plutarch's Lives,* vol. 3. LCL. Cambridge, Mass., and London, 1916.

Peter, H. W. *Historicorum Romanorum Reliquiae.* 2 vols. 1914–16. Reprint. Stuttgart, 1967.

Phillips, E. J. "Cicero and the Prosecution of Manilius." *Latomus* 29 (1970): 595–607.

———. "Asconius' *Magni Homines.*" *Rheinisches Museum für Philologie* 116 (1973): 353–57.

Piganiol, A. "Un Épisode inconnu de la vie de Pompée." *Studi in onore di Aristide Calderini e Roberto Paribeni,* vol. 1. Milan, 1956.

Pocock, L. G. "Publius Clodius and the Acts of Caesar." *Classical Quarterly* 18 (1924): 59–65.

———. "A Note on the Policy of P. Clodius." *Classical Quarterly* 19 (1925): 182–84.

———. "*Pompeiusve Parem.*" *Classical Philology* 22 (1927): 301–6.

Puccioni, I. (J.). *Orationum deperditarum fragmenta.* Milan, 1963.

Purser, L. C. M. *Tulli Ciceronis Epistulae,* vol. 2.1. Oxford, 1903.

Rackham, H. *Cicero, De Oratore Book III, De Fato, Paradoxa Stoicorum, Partitiones Oratoriae.* Cambridge, Mass., and London, 1942.

Ranieri, L. *Basilicata.* Turin, 1961.

Rathke, G. *De Romanis Bellis Servilibus.* Diss., Berlin, 1904.

Rawson, B. "Pompey and Hercules." *Antichthon* 4 (1970): 30–37.

———. "*De lege agraria* 2.49." *Classical Philology* 66 (1971): 26–29.

Rawson, E. "The Eastern Clientelae of Clodius and the Claudii." *Historia* 22 (1973): 219–39.

Regling, K. *De Belli Parthici Crassiani Fontibus.* Diss., Berlin, 1899.

Reid, J. S. "On Att. I," 87–109; "On Att. II," 354–92. *Hermathena* 13 (1905).

Reynolds, J. "Cyrenaica, Pompey, and Cn. Cornelius Lentulus Marcellinus." *Journal of Roman Studies* 52 (1962): 97–103.

Rotondi, G. *Leges Publicae Populi Romani.* Milan, 1912.

Rowland, R. J., Jr. "Crassus, Clodius, and Cicero in the Year 59 B.C." *Historia* 15 (1966): 217–23.

Rubinsohn, Z. "A Note on Plutarch *Crassus* X.1." *Historia* 19 (1970): 624–27.

Sage, E. T. "Cicero and the Agrarian Proposals of 63." *Classical Journal* 6 (1920/21): 230–36.

Salmon, E. T. "Catiline, Crassus, and Caesar." *American Journal of Philology* 56 (1935): 302–16.

Sanders, H. A. "The So-Called First Triumvirate." *Memoirs of the American Academy in Rome* 10 (1932): 55–68.

Schoell, F. *Orationum deperditarum fragmenta.* Leipzig, 1917.

Schulten, A. "Ein römisches lager aus dem sertorianishen Kriege." *Jahrbuch des Kaiserlich deutschen archäologischen Instituts* 33 (1918): 75–106.

Schulze, W. *Zur Geschichte lateinischer Eigennamen.* Reprint of 1904 ed. Berlin, Zurich, Dublin, 1966.

Scullard, H. H. *From the Gracchi to Nero,* 2nd ed. London, 1963.

Seager, R. "The First Catilinarian Conspiracy." *Historia* 13 (1964): 338–47.

———. "Clodius, Pompeius, and the Exile of Cicero." *Latomus* 24 (1965): 519–31.

———. Review of Balsdon, *Julius Caesar and Rome. Journal of Roman Studies* 58 (1968): 259–60.

———, ed. *The Crisis of the Roman Republic.* Cambridge, 1969.

———. "The Tribunate of Cornelius. Some Ramifications." *Hommages à Marcel Renard,* vol. 2 (*Collection Latomus* 101). Edited by J. Bibauw, pp. 680–86. Brussels, 1969.

———. "*Factio*: Some Observations." *Journal of Roman Studies* 62 (1972): 53–58.

———. "*Iusta Catilinae.*" *Historia* 22 (1973): 240–48.

Shackleton Bailey, D. R. "The Roman Nobility in the Second Civil War." *Classical Quarterly* 10 (1960): 253–67.

———. *Cicero's Letters to Atticus.* 6 vols. Cambridge, 1965–68.

———. "The Prosecution of Roman Magistrates-elect." *Phoenix* 24 (1970): 162–65.

———. *Cicero.* London, 1971.

Shatzman, I. "The Egyptian Question in Roman Politics (59–54 B.C.)." *Latomus* 30 (1971): 363–69.

———. "Four Notes on Roman Magistrates." *Athenaeum* 46 (1968): 345–54.

Sherwin-White, A. N. "Violence in Roman Politics." *Journal of Roman Studies* 46 (1956): 1–9.

Simpson, A. D. "The Departure of Crassus for Parthia." *Transactions and Proceedings of the American Philological Association* 49 (1938): 532–41.

Smith, R. E. "*The Lex Plotia Agraria* and Pompey's Spanish Veterans." *Classical Quarterly* 7 (1957): 82–85.

———. *Service in the Post-Marian Roman Army.* Manchester, 1958.

———. *Cicero the Statesman.* Cambridge, 1966.

Stangl, T. *Ciceronis Orationum Scholiastae.* Vienna, 1912.

Stanton, G. R., and Marshall, B. A. "The Coalition between

Pompeius and Crassus, 60–59 B.C." *Historia* 24 (1975): 205–19.

Stevens, C. E. "The 'Plotting' of B.C. 66/65." *Latomus* 22 (1963): 397–435.

Stockton, D. "Cicero and the *Ager Campanus.*" *Transactions and Proceedings of the American Philological Association* 93 (1962): 471–89.

———. *Cicero: A Political Biography*. London, 1971.

Strasburger, H. *Concordia Ordinum*. Diss., Borna and Leipzig, 1930.

———. *Caesars Eintritt in die Geschichte*. Munich, 1938.

Sumner, G. V. "Manius or Mamercus?" *Journal of Roman Studies* 54 (1964): 41–48.

———. "The Consular Elections of 66 B.C." *Phoenix* 19 (1965): 226–31.

———. "Cicero, Pompeius, and Rullus." *Transactions and Proceedings of the American Philological Association* 97 (1966): 569–82.

———. *The Orators in Cicero's* BRUTUS: *Prosopography and Chronology*. *Phoenix*, Supplement 11. 1973.

Sydenham, E. A. *The Roman Republican Coinage*. Revised ed. London, 1952.

Syme, R. "The Allegiance of Labienus," *Journal of Roman Studies* 28 (1938): 113–21.

———. "Caesar, the Senate, and Italy." *Papers of the British School at Rome* 14 (1938): 1–31.

———. *The Roman Revolution*. Oxford, 1939.

———. Review of Gelzer, *Caesar*. *Journal of Roman Studies* 34 (1944): 92–103.

———. Review of A. E. Gordon, *Potitius Valerius Messalla Consul Suffect 29 B.C. Journal of Roman Studies* 45 (1955): 155–60.

———. Review of Broughton, *Magistrates of the Roman Republic. Classical Philology* 50 (1955): 127–38.

———. "Missing Senators." *Historia* 4 (1955): 52–71.

———. "Imperator Caesar: A Study in Nomenclature." *Historia* 7 (1958): 172–88.

———. "Piso Frugi and Crassus Frugi." *Journal of Roman Studies* 50 (1960): 12–20.

———. *Sallust*. Berkeley and Los Angeles, 1964.

Szemler, G. J. *The Priests of the Roman Republic* (*Collection Latomus* 127). Brussels, 1972.

Taylor, L. R. "Caesar's Early Career." *Classical Philology* 36 (1941): 113–32.

———. "The Election of the Pontifex Maximus in the Late Republic." *Classical Philology* 37 (1942): 421–24.

———. "Caesar and the Roman Nobility." *Transactions and Pro-*

ceedings of the American Philological Association 73 (1942): 1–24.

———. "Caesar's Colleagues in the Pontifical College." *American Journal of Philology* 63 (1942): 385–412.

———. *Party Politics in the Age of Caesar*. Berkeley and Los Angeles, 1949.

———. "The Date and Meaning of the Vettius Affair." *Historia* 1 (1950): 45–51.

———. "On the Chronology of Caesar's First Consulship." *American Journal of Philology* 72 (1951): 254–68.

———. "On the date of *Ad Atticum* 2.24." *Classical Quarterly* 4 (1954): 187–88.

———. "The Rise of Julius Caesar." *Greece and Rome* 4 (1957): 10–18.

———. *The Voting Districts of the Roman Republic*. Rome, 1960.

———. "Magistrates of 55 B.C. in Cicero's *Pro Plancio* and Catullus 52." *Athenaeum* 42 (1964): 12–28.

———. *Roman Voting Assemblies*. Ann Arbor, 1966.

———. "The Dating of Major Legislation and Elections in Caesar's First Consulship." *Historia* 17 (1968): 173–93.

Taylor, L. R., and Broughton, T.R.S. "The Order of Consuls' Names in Official Republican Lists." *Historia* 17 (1968): 166–72.

Thompson, L. A. "Cicero the Politician." *Studies in Cicero*. Edited by J. Ferguson et al., pp. 37–79. Rome, 1962.

Trencsényi-Waldapfel, I. "Calvus ex Nanneianis." *Athenaeum* 43 (1965): 42–51.

Twyman, B. L. "The Metelli, Pompeius and Prosopography." *Aufstieg und Niedergang der Römishen Welt* 1.1, pp. 839–62. Berlin, New York, 1972.

Tyrrell, R. Y., and Purser, L. C. *The Correspondence of M. Tullius Cicero*. 6 vols. Dublin and London, 1904–33.

Tyrrell, W. B. "Labienus' Departure from Caesar in January 49 B.C." *Historia* 21 (1972): 424–40.

———. "The Trial of C. Rabirius in 63 B.C." *Latomus* 32 (1973): 285–300.

Walter, G. *Caesar*. Translated by E. Craufurd. New York, 1952.

Ward, A. M. "Cicero's Support of Pompey in the Trials of M. Fonteius and P. Oppius." *Latomus* 27 (1968): 802–9.

———. "Cicero's Support of the *Lex Gabinia*." *Classical World* 63 (1969): 8–10.

———. "Cicero and Pompey in 75 and 70 B.C." *Latomus* 29 (1970): 58–71.

———. "The Early Relationships between Cicero and Pompey until 80 B.C." *Phoenix* 24 (1970): 119–29.

————. "Politics in the Trials of Manilius and Cornelius." *Transactions and Proceedings of the American Philological Association* 101 (1970): 545–56.

————. "Cicero's Fight against Crassus and Caesar in 65 and 63 B.C." *Historia* 21 (1972): 244–58.

————. "Caesar and the Pirates." *Classical Philology* 70 (1975): 267–68.

————. "Crassus' Slippery Eel." *Classical Review* 24 (1974): 185–186.

————. "Caesar and the Pirates II: The Elusive M. Iunius Iuncus and the Year 75/4." *American Journal of Ancient History* (forthcoming).

Ward, C. O. *The Ancient Lowly*, vol. 1. Washington, D. C., 1889.

Warren, L. B. "Roman Triumphs and Etruscan Kings: The Changing Face of the Roman Triumph." *Journal of Roman Studies* 60 (1970): 49–66.

Waters, K. H. "Cicero, Sallust, and Catiline." *Historia* 19 (1970): 195–215.

Watson, G. R. *The Roman Soldier*. London, 1969.

Weinrib, E. "The Prosecution of Magistrates-Designate." *Phoenix* 25 (1971): 145–50.

Williams, W. G. *Cicero, Letters to his Friends*, vol. 3. Cambridge, Mass., and London, 1929.

Wiseman, T. P. "Prosopographical Notes." Appendix Two of M. H. Crawford, "The Coinage of the Age of Sulla." *Numismatic Chronicle* 4 (1964): 156–58.

————. "Lucius Memmius and his Family." *Classical Quarterly* 17 (1967): 164–67.

————. "Two Friends of Clodius in Cicero's Letters." *Classical Quarterly* 18 (1968): 297–302.

————. "The Census in the First Century B.C." *Journal of Roman Studies* 59 (1969): 59–75.

————. "The Definition of 'eques Romanus' in the Late Roman Republic and Early Empire." *Historia* 19 (1970): 67–83.

————. "Celer and Nepos." *Classical Quarterly* 21 (1971): 180–82.

————. *New Men in the Roman Senate 139 B.C.–A.D. 14.* Oxford, 1971.

Index

A

Acilius Glabrio, M.' (cos. 67), 27
Aelia (wife of Sulla), 123n
Aemilia (step-daughter of Sulla), 11, 27
Aemilius Lepidus, M. (cos. 78): and Pompey, 11n, 21, 239, 284; and Catulus, 15–16; political allegiance, 21; and Sullan proscription, 71n48; and Caesar, 110; and *optimates*, 284; mentioned, 37
Aemilius Lepidus, M.' (cos. 66), 28, 142n49
Aemilius Lepidus Livianus, Mam. cos. 77): political allegiance, 21–22; witness against Cornelius, 22, 141–42; and Curio *pater*, 23; and Caesar, 110, 111
[Aemilius Lepidus], Mam. (son of Mam. Aemilius Lepidus Livianus), 22
Aemilius Lepidus Paullus, L. (cos. 50): accused by Vettius, 236, 239, 240; aedileship, 237n26
Aemilius Scaurus, M. (cos. 115), 20n, 27
Aenus. *See* Ainos
Aesis River, 63n
Afranius, L. (cos. 60): adherent of Pompey, 33, 210, 281; provincial command, 223; proposes bribery law, 268
Ainos, 195
Alba Longa, 170
Alfius Flavus, C. (pr. 54), 254
Alexander (Peripatetic philosopher), 292
Alexander Polyhistor, 292n13
Alexandria, 134, 135
Alexas of Heraclea, 81

Allobroges, 178, 184, 188–89, 223, 224
Amisus, 195
Ampius Balbus, T. (pr. 59), 155–56, 162, 195
Annalis, L. (senator), 227, 292n16
Annalius, L. *See* L. Annalis
Annius Milo, T. (pr. 55): and Pompey, 11n, 273n; opposes Clodius, 248, 265; trial, 251–52, 270
Antemnae, 64
Antistia (Pompey's first wife), 122
Antistius (aed. or *iudex quaestionis* 86), 122
Antistius, L., 247n
Antistius, Vetus (tr. 56), 253
Antistius Vetus, C. (pr. 70), 122
Antonius, M. (cos. 99), 31
Antonius, M. (cos. 44, 34), 81n, 134, 155n
Antonius Creticus, M. (pr. 74), 13n, 30, 110
Antonius Hibrida, C. (cos. 63): political allegiance, 31; relations with Crassus and Caesar, 31, 110, 145–51 passim, 172–73, 255n; *praefectus equitum* 155n; and Catiline, 172–73, 176; provincial governorship, 176; and *lex Tullia de ambitu*, 176–77; and Cicero, 176–77, 187, 202; and L. Tarquinius, 180n; trial in 59, 218n, 219, 255
Appuleius Saturninus, L. (tr. 103, 100), 51, 165
Aquillius Gallus, P. (tr. 55), 276, 277
Aquilonia, 93
Archias (poet), 130n10
Ariminum, 63
Aristotle, 292

Index

Index

Index

cultivates *optimates*, 283–85, 287; death, 287, 289

Licinius Crassus, M. (quaest. 54): younger son of Crassus, 55–57; married Caecilia, 112n, 203, 225, 283; not *contubernalis* of Flaccus, 193n; question of pontificate, 204n

Licinius Crassus, M. (cos. 30), 203n

Licinius Crassus, M. (cos. A.D. 14), 203n

Licinius Crassus (Agelastus), M. (pr. ca. 126), 50

Licinius Crassus, P. (cos. 171), 49–50

Licinius Crassus, P. (cos. 97), 47, 50–53, 74

Licinius Crassus, P. (eldest brother of Crassus), 48, 53, 55, 56

Licinius Crassus, P. (leg. 54): elder son of Crassus, 55–56; quaestorship, 56n; supports Cicero, 243–44, 257; serves with Caesar, 243; bring troops from Gaul to Rome, 267; marries Cornelia, 273n, 284–85, 287; shuts in Aquillius Gallus, 277; augurate, 204, 284–85, 287; accompanies Parthian expedition, 282, 287; death, 287

Licinius Crassus Dives, P. (pr. 57), 47, 244n42

Licinius Crassus Dives Mucianus, P. (cos. 131), 47, 286n

Licinius Lucullus, L. (cos. 151), 58

Licinius Lucullus, L. (cos. 74): optimate leader, 10, 15, 23; and Cethegus, 13n; helped by Catulus, 16; and C. Scribonius Curio, 21n3; and son of Mam. Aemilius Lepidus, 22; and Hortensius, 26; and C. Calpurnius Piso, 27; and M.' Acilius Glabrio, 27; and Cicero, 31; and Murena, 32, 170, 171; opposes Pompey, 37, 45, 204; triumph delayed, 159; and Clodius, 205, 206, 207; opposes Caesar's land bill, 281; accused by Vettius, 237, 241; death, 284

Licinius Lucullus, M. *See* Terentius Varro Lucullus, M.

Licinius Macer, C. (pr. ca. 68), 15, 16, 18, 38, 116, 117

Licinius Macer Calvus, C. (poet and orator), 150, 227–29, 254

Licinius Murena, L. (pr. ca. 88), 32

Licinius Murena, L. (cos. 62), 32, 79, 170, 171, 174, 178, 186–88, 191

Licinius Nerva, A. (pr. 166), 58

Licinius Nerva, C. (pr. 167), 58

Licinius Sacerdos, C. (pr. 75), 31

Livius Drusus, M. (cos. 112), 7n

Livius Drusus, M. (tr. 91), 7, 8

Livius Drusus Claudianus, M. (defendant on *praevaricatio* charge), 272

Livorno. *See* Leghorn

Lollius Palicanus, M. (pr. ca. 69), 27, 43, 106

Luca, 261, 263, 264, 276, 281, 286

Lucceius, L. (pr. 67), 144n55, 213, 215n

Lucilius, C. (poet), 50

Lucretius Ofella, Q. (prefect 82), 63n20, 155n

Lucullus. *See* Licinius Lucullus, L.

Ludi Apollinares, 225

Ludi Romani, 83n

Ludi Victoriae Sullanae, 56n

Lurco (M. Aufidius?) (tr. 61), 210

Lutatia (wife of Hortensius), 26

Lutatius Catulus, Q. (cos. 78): optimate leader, 10, 15–16; and jury reform, 18; censorship, 19, 120, 128–29; and M. Aemilius Lepidus, 21; and Hortensius, 26; and prosecution of Opimius, 26; opposes Pompey, 35, 36, 45, 113; and restoration of tribunician powers, 41; and Crassus, 120, 128–29; and Catiline, 139–40; witness against C. Cornelius, 141; and election for P.M., 169–70; implicates Caesar with Catiline, 180, 189; and rebuilding of Capitoline temple, 197; death, 214; mentioned, 30

M

Malaca, 60–61, 67

Manilius, C. (tr. 66), 115–16, 136–41, 145, 175, 178

Manilius Crispus (identity uncertain), 139n38

Manlius, C. (Catilinarian), 173, 178, 181, 185, 186, 187

Manlius, L. (pr. ca. 79), 35n3

Manlius Torquatus, L. (cos. 65), 30, 141n, 143–44, 145, 149

Index

Satrius, M. (adherent of Pompey), 76n

Scilla. *See* Scyllaeum

Scolacium, 90n

Scribonius Curio, C. (cos. 76), 21n3, 22–23, 26, 236, 240

Scribonius Curio, C. (tr. 50), 231, 234n12, 235, 236, 237, 238, 239, 240, 242, 252, 257

Scyllaeum, 89

Seleucia Pieria, 198n

Sempronius Gracchus, C. (tr. 123, 122), 6, 108

Sempronius Gracchus, Ti. (tr. 133), 6, 22, 113, 153n68

Sena Gallia, 63n

Septimius, C. (secretary to Bibulus), 236

Sergius Catilina, L. (pr. 68): and P. Cornelius Lentulus Sura, 25; consular campaign of 64, 135–36, 144, 151; relations with Crassus and Caesar, 136–52 passim, 171–78; and trial of Manilius, 139–41, 178; and Pompey, 143; prosecuted *de repetundis*, 143–44, 147–48; prosecuted *de sicariis*, 144n55, 172; and fictional first conspiracy, 145–51; consular campaign of 63, 171–78; conspiracy, 178–92 passim; and Vettius, 238–39; mentioned, 30, 170

Sergius Orata, C. (defended by L. Crassus), 73

Sertorius, Q. (pr. 83), 12, 14, 35–40 passim, 59, 60, 85, 111, 122

Servilia (step-sister of M. Cato), 170, 171, 238, 241

Servilia (wife of Lucullus), 171

Servilius (*praef. classis*, 65), 154–55

Servilius Caepio (leg. or pref. 67), 154–55

Servilius Caepio Brutus, Q. *See* Junius Brutus (Caepio), M.

Servilius Glaucia, C. (pr. 100), 51

Servilius Globulus, P. (pr. 64), 142n50

Servilius Rullus, P. (tr. 63), 152–61, 201, 270

Servilius Vatia Isauricus, P. (cos. 79), 20, 110, 111, 169–70, 274

Servilius Vatia Isauricus, P. (cos. 48), 154–55, 252

Sestius, P. (pr. ca. 54), 70, 202n33, 248, 258

Siler River, 93, 94, 96n37

Sicinius, Cn. (tr. 76), 17, 65n30, 77–78

Sicinius, Q. (*iii vir mon.* 49), 78n69

Slavery, 84–85

Social War, 8, 53

Sodalicia, 270–72, 287

Spartacus, 12, 24, 64, 82, 83–98 passim

Spoletium, 62–63

Squillace. *See* Scolacium

Sthenius of Himera (client of Pompey), 43

Sulpicius Galba, P. (pr. ca. 66), 31

Sulpicius Rufus, Ser. (cos. 51), 32, 170, 174, 187

T

Tanager River, 93n30, 94n31

Tarquinius, L. (informer), 78, 178–80, 189

Tarquitius, L. (identity uncertain), 179n

Tempsa, 89n

Terentia (wife of Cicero), 245

Terentius Varro, M. (pr. uncertain date), 217n65

Terentius Varro Lucullus, M. (cos. 73), 23, 94, 141

Tertulla (wife of Crassus), 48, 55, 81, 292

Thurii, 90n

Tigranes (King of Armenia), 233, 246, 280–81

Tigranes (son of preceding), 246

Transpadanes, 122–23, 128–29, 131–32, 145n, 164

Trebellius, L. (tr. 67), 113

Trebonius, C. (tr. 55), 274–77, 287

Tremellius Scrofa, Cn. (pr. ca. 58), 80, 94, 95

Tribunes of the plebs: as political weapon, 7; privileges and powers, 7–8; regain right to higher magistracies, 16–17; regain full powers, 19, 23, 25–26, 41, 77–78, 80, 100, 103, 116

Tribuni Aerarii, 106n

"Triumvirate": beginning, 196–97, 214–17, 226; deterioration after April 59, 220–25; Crassus seeks more equitable arrangement, 231–58; popular discontent with, 234–35, 257; renewed at Luca, 263–65, 286

Tuder, 62, 67

Index

Tullius Cicero, M. (cos. 63): misrepresentation in orations, 17; view of Crassus, 68; background and ideals, 117–18, 254

—— Early Career: relation to *optimates*, 30–31, 45, 138; supported by L. Domitius Ahenobarbus, 31; and Pompey, 31, 45, 118–19, 132, 137–38, 141–44, 151; prosecutes Verres, 43–45, 107, 118; defends Roscius Amerinus, 66–67; supports *lex Manilia*, 116–19; and Crassus, 116, 119, 129, 132, 136, 143–151 passim; and trial of Licinius Macer, 116–17; defends P. Oppius, 118; elected aedile, 118; defends M. Fonteius, 118; and *lex Gabinia*, 119; elected praetor, 119; opposes annexation of Egypt, 129, 132; fabricates "First Catilinarian Conspiracy," 136, 145–51; and Manilius's trial, 137–41; defends C. Cornelius, 143–53; declines to defend Catiline, 143–44; opposes election of Catiline and Antonius, 145–51; elected consul, 151

—— Years 63–59: defends P. Sulla, 29, 33; and M. Valerius Messala, 32–33, 77; supports Ser. Sulpicius Rufus, 32, 170; change after 63, 126, 200; and Pompey, 126, 173–74, 197, 200–201, 210; and Crassus, 152–61, 164–66, 173–78, 181–84, 188, 191, 198n, 200–201, 202, 211, 216, 219, 225; opposes Rullan proposal, 152–61, 270; defends C. Calpurnius Piso, 164; defends C. Rabirius, 164–66; and Caesar, 164–66, 180, 189, 190–91, 200–201, 215–16, 218n, 219, 234; opposes Catiline's election in 63, 173–78; *lex Tullia de ambitu*, 174–76; and C. Antonius, 176–77, 202, 219; rearrangement of provincial commands, 176; suppression of Catilinarian Conspiracy, 179–82, 184, 189; and Tarquinius, 179–80; defends Murena, 188, 191; *supplicatio* for, 189; consulship praised, 202, 225; buys expensive house, 198n, 202, 225; and Clodius, 207–8, 216, 219; and *Equites*, 210n, 211; supports tax farmers, 211; dis-

enchantment with Cato, 216; implicated by Vettius, 237, 241

—— Years 58–53: exile, 243–45; and Clodius, 243–44, 249; and Crassus, 243–45, 248, 249, 253, 254, 255, 257–58, 262, 265, 278–80, 294; and Caesar, 243, 254–55, 256, 258, 259–61, 262, 264–65, 274, 279, 286; recall, 245–48; and Lentulus Spinther, 247–48, 253; and Metellus Nepos, 247; and Pompey, 247, 248, 252, 253, 255, 256, 257, 258, 259–61, 262, 264, 265, 279; defends Sestius, 254, 258; attacks Vatinius, 254–55; defends Caelius, 255–56, 258; attacks Campanian Land Law, 256–62, 286; "palinode," 165; speech on consular provinces, 265, 274; defends Cornelius Balbus, 265; attacks Gabinius, 278–79; capitulates to "Triumvirs," 279

Tullius Cicero, Q. (pr. 62), 190, 211n, 244, 259–62, 263, 278

V

Valeria (wife of Sulla), 32
Valerius Flaccus (pr. 63), 166n105, 193n
Valerius Messala Niger (cos. 61), 32–33, 48, 202n32, 206
Vargunteius, L. (sen. 63), 81
Vatinius, P. (cos. 47), 159–60, 221n, 233, 237, 241, 246n, 254, 280
Veii, 63n
Venuleia. *See* Vinuleia
Verres, C. (pr. 74): and Scribonius Curio, 23; and Cassius Longinus, 24; and consuls of 72, 25; and Hortensius, 26, 76; and M.' Acilius Glabrio, 27; and the Caecilii Metelli, 42, 44; trial, 42–45, 118, 204; military activities, 89n19; and Myron's Hercules, 102n13
Vettius, L. (informer), 47, 180, 236–42, 257
Vettius Picens (identity uncertain), 238
Via Appia, 94, 97n43, 121
Via Cassia, 63n
Via Flaminia, 63n
Via Latina, 97n43
Via Popilia, 92, 93